European Bloc Imperialism

Studies in Critical Social Sciences

Series Editor
David Fasenfest
Wayne State University

The titles published in this series are listed at brill.nl / scss.

European Bloc Imperialism

Dennis C. Canterbury

Haymarket Books
Chicago, IL

First published in 2010 by Brill Academic Publishers, The Netherlands

Published in paperback in 2012 by
Haymarket Books
P.O. Box 180165
Chicago, IL 60618
773-583-7884
www.haymarketbooks.org

ISBN: 978-1-60846-204-9

Trade distribution:
In the US, Consortium Book Sales, www.cbsd.com
In Canada, Publishers Group Canada, www.pgcbooks.ca
In the UK, Turnaround Publisher Services, www.turnaround-psl.com
In Australia, Palgrave Macmillan, www.palgravemacmillan.com.au
In all other countries, Publishers Group Worldwide, www.pgw.com

Cover design by Ragina Johnson.

This book was published with the generous support of Lannan Foundation and the Wallace Global Fund.

Printed in the United States.

10 9 8 7 6 5 4 3 2 1

Library of Congress Cataloging-in-Publication data is available.

CONTENTS

ACKNOWLEDGEMENTS

The idea for this book evolved out an original concern for the economic and political independence of the Caribbean in the light of the declaration by the US neoconservatives that the 21st century was the "new American century." I was concern to find out about the prospects for the Caribbean under the doctrine of the "new American century." With the help of Carmen Cid, Dean of the School of Arts and Sciences, Eastern Connecticut State University, I undertook a one-month fieldwork visit in Trinidad and Tobago, Barbados and Jamaica in August 2006. While there I interviewed many people mainly in the non-governmental sector, including trade unions, the University of the West Indies, including the Sir Arthur Lewis Institute for Social and Economic Research (SALISES), the Caribbean Community (Caricom), the Association of Caribbean States (ACS), the Caribbean Regional Negotiating Machinery (CRNM), the Caribbean Development Bank (CDB), and the Caribbean Food and Nutrition Institute (CFNI). The goal was to obtain a sense of regional thinking on the "new American century" doctrine, and to find out about ideas on regional development alternatives.

The Caribbean Forum (CARIFORUM) was identified as a creature of the European Union, and as a survival institution for the Caribbean. The Economic Partnership Agreement (EPA) was branded as a post-World Trade Organization agreement, and just a footnote in the wider European imperialism. The European Union's (EU) assistance on governance was seen to be forcing the Caribbean to put policy into action. The critical tradition in Caribbean was perceived to be at a low.

I wrote a book manuscript entitled "The Caribbean in the 'New American Century,'" in which there is a small section on the EPA. Events, including the retreat of the US neoconservatives whose ideas turned out to be highly unpopular globally, took their course over that manuscript. Subsequently, with the assistance of Dean Cid, I presented a paper on the EPA at the Canadian Association for the Study of International Development conference at the University of British Colombia, in Vancouver, Canada in 2008. While discussing the outline for the paper with James Petras, he suggested that I expanded it into a book.

James Russell, Connecticut State University (CSU) Professor and a colleague in the Department of Sociology, Anthropology and Social Work, at Eastern Connecticut State University, Henry Veltmeyer of Universidad Autónoma de Zacatecas, Mexico, and St. Mary's University, Canada, and James Petras, patiently listened to my ramblings as I tried to clarify ideas for the book. Petras commented on three of the chapters, and Russell suggested that Brill might have an interest in the publishing the manuscript and he put me in contact with Ricardo Dello Buono. Clive Thomas, Distinguished Professor and Director of the Institute of Development Studies, University of Guyana helped me to clarify my ideas on the CRNM's critique of its critics.

The technical assistance from Kevin Gill, Coordinator of Web Communications, Center for Instructional Technology, Eastern Connecticut State University was crucial to the completion of this book, as well as the ECSU Library Inter-Library Loan arrangement.

Bonsu Osei in the Department of Mathematics and Computer Science at Eastern Connecticut State University introduced me to Jeff Onyame the Senior Assistant Registrar (Academic) at the University of Cape Coast, which opened the door for me to conduct research at the Institute for Development Studies, and Department of Sociology and Anthropology at the University of Cape Coast, in Ghana. Steve Kendie, Victor Mensah, Francis Enu-Kwesi, Kodjo Ekumah, and Patrick Agbesinyale, of the IDS, and Mansah Prah, Dominick Agyeman, and Nancy Lundgren of the Department of Sociology and Anthropology, gave me a hearty welcome and appropriate socialization while I was a Visiting Professor there. Steve Kendie the then Director of the IDS deserves special thanks for graciously giving me the opportunity, to participate in the research work of the institute, and to observe at first-hand the results of imperialism in Elmina, the first European settlement in West Africa.

David Fasenfest, Ricardo Dello Buono, Marjolein Schaake and the editorial team at Brill were of tremendous assistance in bringing the book to fruition. Finally, my wife Sandra Jennifer patiently endured my schedule, and kept me going.

Thanks to all those mentioned by name above and those unmentioned for their help in making the book a reality.

The views espoused in the book and the mistakes herein are entirely my own and should not in anyway be ascribed to any of the persons or institutions named above.

Cover Photograph

This is a photograph taken by the author of what was formerly Fort São Jorge da Mina now called Elmina, the first-ever European settlement in West Africa, established by a 600-strong medieval Portuguese expedition, for the purpose of trade in gold, five hundred and twenty-seven years ago in 1482. The local Africans called the area where Elmina stands, Amankwakurom or Amankwa. Elmina became the flagship fort for the Portuguese in West Africa until the Dutch captured it in 1637. The Dutch held Elmina for 237 years until they sold it to the British in 1872 that held it for 85 years until Ghana became an independent country, in 1957. The poverty stricken Elmina is a testament to the outcome of imperialist trade between Africa and Europe. By contrast, Lisbon, Amsterdam and London look in no way as poor as Elmina although the town was in existence and actively traded with the Portuguese, Dutch and English for hundreds of years. The proposition is that the Economic Partnership Agreement will not change for the better the living conditions in Elmina or indeed for the African Caribbean and Pacific Group of countries. The EPAs will continue to reproduce poverty in the ACP countries, and may even make the social and economic conditions in these states become worse than they are today.

CHAPTER ONE

OUTLINE OF EUROPEAN BLOC IMPERIALISM

Introduction

The dramatic collapse of Eastern European communism that signaled the end of the cold war at the close of the twentieth century left only one super-"hyper"-power standing – the United States of America. Immediately, thereafter, it became clear to rich and poor nations alike that the ulterior motive of the US, in its struggle against the former Soviet Union, was its sole military and economic domination of the globe in the furtherance of US-style capitalism. The US intended to dominate the globe through what became known as "US-led globalization," which Petras and Veltmeyer (2001) characterize as "imperialism in the twenty-first century."[1] This book is organized within the general theoretical framework that US-led globalization in imperialism. Its uniqueness, nonetheless, is that it seeks to establish the thesis about EU bloc imperialism a phenomenon that was hitherto overlooked in the current literature, which attempt to provide an understanding of the *modus operandi* of present-day capitalism, under the rubric of new imperialisms in the twenty-first century.

Problematic and Method

The problematic of this book concerns the development options for the Caribbean entrapped by two imperialisms – US-led globalization and European bloc imperialism, the foundation of both of which is neoliberalism. It brings a new perspective to the issues of Caribbean development compared with the views found in the dominant literature on the region on the economic partnership agreement, US-led globalization, the model of economic development with unlimited

[1] Petras, James and Henry Veltmeyer. 2001. *Globalization Unmasked: Imperialism in the 21st Century*. London: Zed Books.

supplies of labor,[2] cultural pluralism,[3] plantation dependence,[4] Creole society,[5] and dual society.[6] It challenges this literature and the current discourse on globalization as it relates to the Caribbean that is taking place on the terms of US-led globalization and the economic partnership agreement. In the main the discussion on globalization is merely reactive to the agendas set by US-led globalization and European Union (EU).

[2] Lewis, W. Arthur. 1954. Economic Development with Unlimited Supplies of Labor. *The Manchester School.* (22) 2: 139–91. See also Lewis, W. Arthur. 1950. The Industrialization of the British West Indies. *Caribbean Economic Review.* 2: 1–39.

[3] For detailed discussions on pluralist societies see Furnivall, John Sydenham. 1939. *Netherlands India A Study of Plural Economy.* London: Cambridge University Press; Furnivall, John Sydenham. 1948. *Colonial Policy and Practice: A Comparative Study of Burma and Netherlands India.* London: Cambridge University Press; Smith, Michael Garfield. 1965. *The Plural Society in the British West Indies.* Los Angeles: University of California Press; Despres, Leo. 1967. *Cultural Pluralism and Nationalist Politics in British Guiana.* Chicago: Rand Mc Nally and Company; and Mars, Perry. 1989. "Competing Theories and Third World Political Practice", in Michael T. Martin and Terry R. Kandal eds., *Studies of Development and Change in the Modern World.* Oxford. Oxford University Press, pp. 373–398. The pluralist debate has taken different forms and includes the discussion on deliberative democracy. The discussion on deliberative democracy focuses on the inclusion of multiple elements—individuals, groups and interests—in the decision-making process. A social order is plural—characterized by difference—represented by class, gender, race and other social categories. For a democracy to function properly, therefore, these differences or plurality of interests represented by race, class, gender and other social groups must be involved and reflected at all levels of decision-making in the country. See for example the articles in Benhabib, Seyla, ed. 1996. *Democracy and Difference: Contesting the Boundaries of the Political.* New Jersey: Princeton University Press; Elster, Jon, ed. 1998. *Deliberative Democracy.* New York: Cambridge University Press; Bohman, James and Rehg, William, eds. 1997. *Deliberative Democracy: Essays on Reason and Politics.* Cambridge: Massachusetts Institute of Technology Press; and Koh, Harold Hongju and Slye, Ronald, eds. 1999. *Deliberative Democracy and Human Rights.* New Haven: Yale University Press.

[4] Weber, Max. 1961. *General Economic History.* Translated, F. H. Knight. New York: Collier; and Weber, Max. 1978. *Economy and Society: An Outline of Interpretative Sociology,* Vol. 2., Guenther Roth and Claus Wittich, eds. Berkeley: University of California Press; Wolf, Eric and Mintz, Sydney. 1957. Haciendas and Plantations in Middle America and the Antilles. *Social and Economic Studies* (6) 3: 380–412. Beckford, George. 1984. *Persistent Poverty.* London: Zed Press; and Beckford, George. 1971. Plantation Society. *Savacou* 5: 5: 7–22; Best, Lloyd. 1968. Outline of a Model of Pure Plantation Economy. *Social and Economic Studies* (17) 3: 283–326; Brown, Adlith and Havelock Brewester. 1974. A Review of the Study of Economics in the English-Speaking Caribbean. *Social and Economic Studies.* (23) 1: 48–68.

[5] Brathwaite, Edward. 1971. *The Development of Creole Society in Jamaica: 1770–1820.* Oxford: Oxford University Press; Smith, Raymond. 1962. *British Guiana.* London: Oxford University Press; and Goveia, Elsa. 1965. *Slave Society in the British Leeward Islands to the End of the 19th Century.* New Haven: Yale University Press.

[6] Curtin, Philip. 1970. *Two-Jamaicas: The Role of Ideas in a Tropical Colony, 1830–1865.* New York: Athenum.

The Caribbean intellectual tradition characterized by the works of scholars such as C. L. R. James, Walter A. Rodney, and Clive Y. Thomas, among others seems more appropriate for the analysis of Caribbean development issues in the current period and contexts of US-led globalization and economic partnership agreements.[7] This tradition is distinguished primarily by its application of Marx's historical method to explain social, political, and economic conditions in the Caribbean as distinct from the Marxist ideological sloganeering associated with some sections of the Caribbean Left.[8] In this connection the exploration of European bloc imperialism as a contribution to the debate on development must begin with an investigation of the concrete political economy situation faced by the Caribbean region at the time that it commenced negotiating the economic partnership agreement.

There is need to have an understanding on the prevailing political economy circumstances in the Caribbean that led-up to and during the EPA negotiations. How did they impact on the negotiators from both sides of the Atlantic bearing in mind that the US was bullying both the EU and the Caribbean? The wider issue nonetheless, which is the primary concern of this book that explores the phenomena described as European bloc imperialism, concerns the possibilities for the economic partnership agreement to bring about socio-economic transformation in the Africa, Caribbean and Pacific (ACP) group of states couched as sustainable development and good governance.

Despite the many experiments these countries have had with development their economies are characterized by a basic reality. Production for market exchange has generated economic surpluses that accumulate in the hands of a few while the vast majority of working people are excluded from the wealth they produce. Simultaneously, political

---

[7] For recent reviews of the Caribbean intellectual tradition see Bogues, Anthony. 1998. Investigating the Radical Caribbean Intellectual Tradition. *Small Axe*. 4: 29–45; and Henry, Paget. 1998. Philosophy and the Caribbean Intellectual Tradition. *Small Axe*. 4: 3–28. See also Lewis, Rupert. 1998. *Walter Rodney's Intellectual and Political Thought*. Detroit: Wayne State University Press; and Benn, Denis. 1987. *The Growth and Development of Political Ideas in the Caribbean, 1994–1983*. Kingston, Jamaica: Institute of Social and Economic Research, University of the West Indies.

[8] Reference is made here to Marxist-Leninist political groups—the Workers Party of Jamaica headed by Trevor Munroe and the People's Progressive Party headed by the late Dr. Cheddi Jagan—in the Caribbean during the 1970s that blindly followed a doctrinaire Soviet line. For a discussion on these types of groups see Mars, Perry. 1998. *Ideology and Change: The Transformation of the Caribbean Left*. Detroit: Wayne State University Press.

power is concentrated in the hands of the few who accumulate the most wealth. However, we must not lose sight of the phenomenon in the ACP countries in which the political elites, who do not own personal wealth, use the state apparatus to accumulate wealth, as a characteristic feature of their rule. The concentration of accumulated capital and political power in the hands of the same few individuals perpetuates economic and social inequalities, and systems of laws, violence, and military apparatuses designed to facilitate the suppression of the majority by the few.

From the perspective of the ACP countries, therefore, sustainable development must mean the transformation of those characteristics of their economies and societies. All sober and right-minded policymakers, academics, workers, etc., in the ACP states must be concerned to know about the possibilities of the economic partnership agreement to transform those characteristic features of their political economy. The position is taken in this book that the EPAs will perpetuate rather than transform the class divisions and the power relations based on the concentration of accumulated wealth and political power in the hands of the few in the ACP countries, and in the developed states.

European Trade and Theories of Imperialism

European Trade

It is an undeniable historical fact that centuries of European trade arrangements with its former colonies that now comprise the ACP regions have had a debilitating effect on those countries.[9] Reinert (2007) noted that President Roosevelt pointed to this fact in a conversation with Winston Churchill around the time of the Second World War. President Roosevelt observed that the "trade agreements" of the British Empire are the cause that "the people of India and Africa," and "of the colonial Near East and Far East, are still as backward as they are" (Reinert 2007: 168–69). Undoubtedly, the economic partnership agreements are the latest in a litany of such trade policies that Europe has foisted on the peoples in the ACP regions. The historical evidence on trade relations between Europe and its former colonies suggests that there will be no major transformative change for the better that

[9] Reinert, Erik S. 2007. *How Rich Countries Got Rich and Why Poor Countries Stay Poor*. London: Constable and Robinson.

will occur in the ACP states from the EPAs with the EU. The EPAs will reinforce the status quo of the ACP states as suppliers of raw materials and Europe as supplier of manufactured goods. Essentially, this means the continued impoverishment of the ACP countries and enrichment of Europe.

The EPA is founded on the classical political economy theory that all countries could become wealthy no matter what they produce so long as they engage in free trade. This comparative advantage approach nonetheless has historically benefited only the industrialized countries.[10] Also, it does not take into consideration the political and social dimensions of the effect of free trade. The ruling elites who embrace the EPAs do not fully appreciate its political and social consequences. The EPA will perpetuate the lack of true political independence or what is termed "flag independence" in the ACP countries increasing their socio-economic and political dependence on Europe. Furthermore, it will not transform the political power relations decidedly in the favor of working people in the ACP states, but will perpetuate the class divide over politics in these countries. It is not only that the EPAs lack a social component also they will perpetuate social backwardness in the ACP countries by their failure to address the inequalities that would derive from their implementation, and lead to "Welfare Colonialism" programs such as the Millennium Development Goals.[11]

Theories of Imperialism

The debate on imperialism has gained fresh momentum since the use of the term "globalization" as a neoliberal prescription for the poor countries to attain development, and as a description of the process by which they implemented the neoliberal medicine.[12] The current wave of theorizing about the "new imperialism" seeks to explain the present phase of capitalism characterized by US-led neoliberal globalization. Some of these works seek to expand on Marxist theories

---

[10] Reinert, Erik S. 2007. *How Rich Countries Got Rich and Why Poor Countries Stay Poor*. London: Constable and Robinson.

[11] Reinert, Erik S. 2005. Development and Social Goals: Balancing Aid and Development to Prevent 'Welfare Colonialism'. *Post-Autistic Economics Review*, (30) 21: 1.

[12] Petras, James and Henry Veltmeyer. 2001. *Globalization Unmasked: Imperialism in the 21st Century*. London: Zed Press.

of imperialism[13] and are distinguished inter alia by themes such as globalization as imperialism,[14] empire without imperialism,[15] empire with imperialism,[16] and empire and imperialism,[17] while others merely broach the subject from a neoliberal perspective categorizing US-led neoliberal globalization as "benevolent imperialism"[18] or "reluctant imperialists."[19] Petras and Veltmeyer's[20] thesis that globalization is a synonym for imperialism is established within the Marxist framework. Imperialism is analyzed within this framework in terms of "the historical development of the capitalist mode of production," characterized by central tendencies such as "the internationalization of production, and the interpenetration of private capital and the nation-state."[21]

Hardt and Negri (2001) advanced a theory on imperialism that is stripped of any factual basis and utility for analysis of present-day world capitalism. This is the conclusion gleaned from the refutation of their thesis about imperialism without empire or the imperialism of autonomous markets and multinational corporations that do not have a national basis for their existence, undertaken by Petras and Veltmeyer (2005) and Boron (2005). As did Panitch,[22] Petras and Veltmeyer (2005) and Boron (2005) supplied the evidence that demonstrated the centrality of the imperial state in the current form of global capitalism.

---

[13] Nabudere, D. Wadada. 1983. *The Political Economy of Imperialism: Its Theoretical and Polemical Treatment from Mercantilism to Multilateral Imperialism*. London: Zed Press; Brewer, Anthony. 1990. *Marxist Theories of Imperialism: A Critical Survey* (Second Edition). London: Routledge.

[14] Petras, James and Henry Veltmeyer. 2001. *Globalization Unmasked: Imperialism in the 21st Century*. London: Zed Press.

[15] Hardt, Michael and Antonio Negri. 2001. *Empire*. Cambridge: Harvard University Press.

[16] Petras, James and Henry Veltmeyer, with Luciano Vasapollo and Mauro Casadio. 2005. *Empire with Imperialism: The Globalizing Dynamics of Neoliberal Capitalism*. London: Zed Press.

[17] Boron, Atilio A. 2005. *Empire and Imperialism: A Critical Reading of Michael Hardt and Antonio Negri*. London: Zed Press; Foster, John Bellamy. 2001. Imperialism and 'Empire.' Monthly Review. (53) 7: 1–9.

[18] Jacobs, Didier. 2007. *Global Democracy: The Struggle for Political and Civil Rights in the 21st Century*. Nashville: Vanderbilt University Press; Mead, Walter Russell. 2007. *God and Gold: Britain, America, and the Making of the Modern World*. New York: Knopf.

[19] Mallaby, Sebastian. 2002. The Reluctant Imperialist: Terrorism, Failed States, and the Case for Empire Building. *Foreign Affairs* (81) 2: 2–7.

[20] Petras, James and Henry Veltmeyer. 2001. *Globalization Unmasked: Imperialism in the 21st Century*. London: Zed Press.

[21] Callinicos, Alex. 2005. Imperialism and Global Political Economy. *International Socialism: A Quarterly Journal of Socialist Theory*. Issue 108. October 17.

[22] Panich, Leo. 2000. The New Imperial State. *New Left Review*. 2: 5–20.

The debates on the new imperialism nonetheless seem to have two discernable foci – US imperialism,[23] and the relationship between imperialism (capitalism in its expansionary mode), the state (the coercive apparatus of the nation-state), and the nation-state (a geographic area).[24] They seek to explain the process by which surplus capital accumulated in a nation-state expands to other nation-states under the protection of the state of the capital exporting nation-state, and in collusion with the ruling elites and state in the capital receiving nation-state.

The consolidation of the powerful EU economic bloc as part of the "global Europe" vision and its relationship with the former colonies that comprise the ACP states however call for analysis that considers an imperialist bloc characterized by leading nation-states that act in consort with regards to the expansion of European capital and the reconstitution of European mercantilist trade relations. The EU occupies a unique status as a global entity as evidenced by the fact for example that it sat along with other nation-states, including those from Europe, at the table of the recently concluded G-20 Summit on the global financial crisis and restructuring of the global financial system. No other regional bloc in the globe occupies such a position.

Ten Theses on the Characteristic Features of European Bloc Imperialism

European bloc imperialism at the turn of the twentieth century has certain distinguishing characteristics. First, it is a product of US-led neoliberal globalization, i.e., US imperialism in the twenty-first century. Europe ceded its world leadership to the US and the former Soviet Union at the end of World War II. Almost immediately however, Europe began to take steps to prevent future wars on the continent that would eventually lead to the emergence of the EU, simultaneously that the US and former Soviet Union engaged in a cold war, which ended with the collapse of Eastern European communism from 1989. The US became the sole global hegemon as the former Soviet Union dissolved, but Europe began to rise again this time as an imperialist bloc.

[23] See for example, Panitch, Leo and Sam Gindin. 2004. *Global Capitalism and American Empire.* London: Merlin Press.

[24] Kiely, Ray 2006. United States Hegemony and Globalization: What Role for Theories of Imperialism. *Cambridge Review of International Affairs*, (19) 2: 205–221.

Second, European bloc imperialism operates on the basis of free trade in the ACP regions but protectionism in Europe. It promotes free trade in commodities that the European nations produce in mature industries, while protecting its vulnerable industries and sectors. For example, the EU protects its susceptible farmers[25] while insisting that the ACP regions open their agricultural sectors to free trade.[26]

Third, European bloc imperialism is more of a geographically concentrated type of imperialism in that the European states in the EU are exercising their imperialist designs as an economic geographic region. The European idea of "global Europe" is intended to present common European economic policies towards the rest of the globe. European Trade Commissioner Peter Mandelson describes "global Europe" in terms of trade policies that would "open markets and create new opportunities for trade and ensure European companies are able to compete fairly in those markets."[27] The concern of "global Europe" is how European trade policy can contribute to creating growth and jobs in Europe.[28] This is vintage imperialism by a bloc of countries rather than by a single country. European bloc imperialism however is driven by key European nation-states such as the United Kingdom, France, and Germany. Capital is not accumulated evenly across the geographic region, but the EU has built-in mechanisms to redistribute the spoils of imperialism to the poorer areas within the union under its "economic and social cohesion" program to "accelerate economic growth in the less wealthy member states."[29]

Fourth, European bloc imperialism ties the ACP states to Europe as a power bloc rather than to individual European countries. This takes place through the EPAs that are trade arrangements that indefinitely

[25] Petras, James. 2003. *The New Development Politics: The Age of Empire Building and New Social Movements*. Aldershot: Ashgate, p. 28.

[26] Atkins, Vincent J. 2002. The US Farm Bill of 2002: Implications for Caricom's Agricultural Export Trade. Caribbean Regional Negotiating Machinery, Staff Papers; Rozo, Carlos A. 2001. Protectionism in the European Union: Implications for Latin America. *Intereconomics* (36) 3: 141–152

[27] Mandelson, Peter. 2006. Global Europe Competing in the World. *Trade Issues*. http://ec.europa.eu/trade/issues/sectoral/competitiveness/global_europe_en.htm; Mandelson, Peter. 2006. Remarks to the Global Europe Conference. Brussels, November 13.

[28] Commission of the European Communities. 2006. Global Europe: Competing in the World, A Contribution to the EU's Growth and Jobs Strategy. Brussels

[29] Commission of the European Communities (2007). *Growing Regions Growing Europe: Fourth Report on Economic and Social Cohesion*. Luxembourg: Office for Official Publications of the European Communities.

bind the ACP trade to the EU in a new type of mercantilism. Rather than restricting the trade of the colonies as in the old days to a single European "mother country," the new mercantilism seeks to confine trade in the ACP regions to the EU as a whole.

Fifth, divide-and-rule tactics, and coercion[30] are integral components of European bloc imperialism. It divided the formerly united ACP states into smaller regions for the purpose of negotiating EPAs. Furthermore, the EPAs threaten to break-up economic integration efforts among ACP states and sow seeds of discord among them. Examples of this are the Caribbean Community (Caricom), the Caribbean Single Market Economy (CSME), the South African Development Community (SADC), and the Economic Commission of West Africa (ECOWAS). The EPAs call into question the future of the ACP group that would seem to have no usefulness once the agreements are entered into. The European Center for Development Policy Management (ECDPM) suggests that the ACP could continue to act collectively in other forums a such as the WTO,[31] which in effect is an admission that the ACP will have no future role in negotiating trade arrangements with Europe, the purpose for which the organization was established.

Sixth, unlike its predecessors, however, European bloc imperialism does not have a "civilizing mission" in the ACP regions, but one of "trade liberalization," "sustainable development," and "good governance" the pretexts by which it protects and creates markets and secures raw materials for European multinational corporations. It advocates sustainable development and good governance as code phases that are the new imperialist ideals through which it protects and creates markets and secures raw materials.

Seventh, it perpetuates the traditional international division of labor that would maintain the economic status quo of the global capitalist system. The ACP regions will continue to produce raw materials, consume finished products produced by the EU multinational corporations, and be plagued by food and financial crises. European bloc imperialism nonetheless must now take into consideration the

---

[30] Hurt, Stephen R. 2003. Co-operation and Coercion? The Cotonou Agreement between the European Union and ACP States and the End of the Lomé Convention. *Third World Quarterly*, (24) 1: 161–176.

[31] Bilal, Sanoussi and Aurélie Walker. 2008. Economic Partnership Agreements and the Future of the ACP Group. Maastricht, The Netherlands. European Center for Development Policy Management, September 22.

pushback by the emerging market economies such as South Africa and India in the ACP regions. The EU is doing so at several levels for example it regards South Africa, as a stumbling bloc in the way of the implementation of the EPA in the Southern African region, while India came in for blame along with Brazil for the collapse of the Doha Round negotiations of the WTO in July 2008. Also the central argument of the "global Europe" strategy inter alia is in regards to increasing Europe's "presence in the fast-expanding, highly populated markets of the emerging economies."[32]

Eight, European bloc imperialism promotes the subsidization of the EU by the ACP regions through migration to the EU of the professionals such as nurses, teachers, doctors, etc., trained at the expense of taxpayers in the ACP regions.[33] The UNDP reported for example that migration among tertiary-educated persons to the rich countries was close to "25% in the island LDCs, West Africa and East Africa."[34]

Ninth, European bloc imperialism struggles not only to incorporate non-capitalist environments into the capitalist system, as did the old imperialism,[35] but also to shore-up capitalist environments created and left behind by colonialism and the old imperialism, in what is now the ACP region. There is hardly any territory left for European bloc imperialism to conquer, thus it represents a reinvention of imperialist relations based on EPAs. Thus, the "global Europe" strategy "identifies geographical priorities for a new generation of bilateral trade agreements," as Mandelson pointed out. In his view, the "global Europe" strategy is not "narrow-minded mercantilism" implying it is open-minded mercantilism "creating free trade around the world as an essential condition for global growth." Furthermore he sees the strategy as "an economic necessity for Europe and for Europeans business" (Mandelson 2006).

Tenth, European bloc imperialism is an extension of the old imperialism in which according to Hilferding (1981), "the development towards finance capital" enhances "the importance of the size of the

---

[32] Mandelson, Peter. 2006. Remarks to the Global Europe Conference. Brussels, November 13.

[33] Hosein, Roger and Clive Thomas. 2007. CSME and the Intra Regional Migration of Nurses: Some Proposed Opportunities. *Global Social Policy* (7) 3: 316–338.

[34] United Nations Conference on Trade and Development. 2007. Least Developed Countries Report 2007. United Nations: New York and Geneva.

[35] Luxemburg, Rosa. 1968. *The Accumulation of Capital*. New York: Monthly Review, p. 446.

economic territory" and as economic power centralizes it "confronts the state as a cohesive body."[36] Finance capital in the current period of global capitalism also concentrates the powers of the state of several nation-states in a specific geographic region, the EU, bringing them to act in unison in their economic interests. While a distinguishing feature of the old imperialism was its concentration of finance capital in a single nation-state that confronted the state, European bloc imperialism witnesses the concentration of finance capital across a geographic region bringing several nation-states together in a political union that exercises concentrated state power in the interest of capital accumulation in that geographic regions. Capital is not accumulated evenly across the geographic region, but European bloc imperialism has built-in mechanisms to redistribute the spoils of imperialism to the poorer areas within the union. Although European bloc imperialism represents imperialism of a geographic region it is founded on the nation-state and the exercise of state power by capitalist class interest.

Structure of Arguments

The book is presented in thirteen chapters beginning with a descriptive analysis of the neoliberal hemispheric settings that prevailed in which the Caribbean was embroiled as it encountered European bloc imperialism, in Chapter 2. The transition from colonialism to "new American century doctrine," authoritarianism in the service of imperialism, and the US neoconservative terrorist threat to democracy in Latin America and the Caribbean, are its foci. It proposes that the most dominant factor that shaped the hemispheric political economy settings at the time was the US neoconservative declaration of the twenty-first century as "the New American Century" and the accompanying measures and activities implemented by the US to achieve that objective.

These measures included the US-EU deal over their trade conflict that eventually sped-up the advent of European bloc imperialism through the EU's economic partnership agreements (EPA) with the ACP regions. European bloc imperialism divided the ACP group of countries into different regions for the purposes of negotiating separate EPAs. The ACP Caribbean region is called the Caribbean Forum

[36] Hilferding, Rudolf. 1981. *Finance Capital: A Study of the Latest Phase of Capitalist Development*. London: Routledge & Kegan Paul, p. 311.

(CARIFORUM). Arguably, the hemispheric political economy of the neoconservative new American century doctrine bear responsibility for pushing the Caribbean towards European bloc imperialism as a counterbalancing force against US-led globalization.

Chapter 3 critically analyzes the anatomy of two imperialisms – US-led globalization and European bloc imperialism, which focus inter alia on their similarities, differences and *modus operandi*. Specifically, it focuses on structural adjustment and economic partnership agreements, the "Global Europe" doctrine, and the idea of "Global Europe" versus US-led globalization. Much is written about US-led globalization but there is scarcely any analysis of European bloc imperialism, which is manifested through EU-EPAs, of which the CARIFORUM-EU EPA is the most comprehensive. The EPAs is the conduit of EU bloc imperialism to secure and maintain raw materials, etc. for the EU transnational corporations.

Chapter 4 examines the rise of European and ACP blocs, and US hegemony engaging in a theoretical discussion on regional blocs and alternative regional unions, the coming to fruition of the EU and the ACP group of states, and US hegemony over the EU with respect to the power struggle to force open the EU markets to bananas from the US multinationals. It shows how US-led globalization paved the way for the emergence of EU bloc imperialism, demonstrating the manner in which the US exercised its hegemony over the EU, and how US banana multinationals forced-opened the EU banana market to bananas produced in Latin America.

Chapter 5 traces the origins of European bloc imperialism in the current period of US-led neoliberal globalization. It focuses on the hitherto unexplored dimension of imperialism termed "bloc imperialism" associated with US-led neoliberal globalization to liberalize the trade relations between Europe and the ACP Group of States. It takes the position that the actions taken by the US banana multinationals and ruling elites to force open the EU banana market to bananas grown in Latin America, "dollar bananas," played a significant role in the emergence of European bloc imperialism through the implementation of EU-ACP EPAs. It highlights the process by which the trade war between the EU and the US over bananas eventually led to the liberalization of the Lomé Conventions via the Cotonou Agreement and the eventual completion of the EPAs, the process by which the Europe asserts itself as a bloc imperialist power under the doctrinal rubric of "global Europe." Specifically, it analyses the European bloc imperialist backlash to the banana trade war, the CARIFORUM-EU EPA, the European bloc imperialist stranglehold on the ACP countries, and the pushback against the EPA.

Chapter 6 is an exposition on the theoretical foundations of European bloc imperialism. It examines the theoretical lineage of the EPAs, the neoliberal foundation of the EPAs, neoliberalism in the Caribbean, the prospects of the CARIFORUM-EU EPA, and the weaknesses of neoliberal theory. It takes the position that the EPAs will not bear much fruit for the ACP group of states, because the EPAs will not transform the power configurations between the EU and the ACP states. It argues that the European imperialist powers have historically implemented policies in the Caribbean with the view to develop the region but these always benefit Europe and not the region.

Chapter 7 engages in a critical analysis of the CARIFORUM-EU EPA and development theory. The EPA is not seen as a development plan but it is allegedly founded on governance and sustainable development. The EPA is marketed as a trade arrangement based on good governance and sustainable development, which the ACP countries must sign on to if they are to experience development at this particular historical juncture of global capitalism. Conversely, if the ACP countries do not sign the EPAs they will be left behind in terms of their economic development. Because of this the EPA could be classified under the general rubric of development theory, which has thus far failed the Caribbean by keeping the region locked-in to global economic arrangements from which it receives very little benefits. If previous trade arrangements that the Caribbean entered into had lived up to their promise and loft ideals then the region would have been in a much better position that it is in today.

Specifically, it focuses on the false origins of development theory, and prevailing ideas on Caribbean development including regional integration and trade arrangements, and foreign direct investment. Also, it examines the issue of the deepening of Euro-American domination of the region through current trade arrangements, and critically analyses the CARIFORUM-EU EPA as a development strategy. Finally, it discusses alternative development visions to the CARIFORUM-EU EPA, focusing on "another development" outlined for the region, method for conceptualizing alternative development, and outlines some tentative ideas on development alternatives to the EU EPA.

Attention is turned in Chapter 8 to the critics of the CARIFORUM-EU EPA. There is a discussion on the definitions of civil society and the roles ascribed to it by European bloc imperialism. The conclusion is drawn that because of their funding sources many Caribbean civil society agencies are mere mouthpieces of European bloc imperialism. These agencies fit squarely within the civil society model defined by EU bloc imperialism. They claim to be involved in the democratization of Caribbean society, and have formulated reformist critiques of the CARIFORUM-EU EPA, rather than taking steps to stop it. Thus, the critiques made by the Caribbean Banana Exporters Association, the Federation of Independent Trade Unions and NGOs, the Group of Concerned Caribbean Citizens, and the business community, are discussed. Also, there is a discussion of some critical and supportive views that emanate from the Caribbean public sector, and prominent Caribbean academics. Finally, a critique is undertaken of the reformist critics of the CARIFORUM-EU EPA.

The central argument is that the critics of the CARIFORUM-EU EPA merely want to reform it, but not to overthrow it. The critics of the CARIFORUM-EU EPA are therefore prepared to enter into a trade deal with European bloc imperialism, while trying to squeeze something positive from it for the region. Thus, in reality, the critics and the proponents of the CARIFORUM-EU EPA are basically on the same side in that they support the neoliberal "free trade" model as the principal engine of growth and development in the Caribbean.

The dispute really concerns the manner in which the region pursues "free trade," and not whether "free trade" exists or not, or is good or bad for the CARIFORUM countries at this stage of their capitalist development. The debate between the critics and proponents of the CARIFORUM-EU EPA is not about alternative development models to replace the neoliberal "free trade" approach that is the backbone of the EPA. There is hardly or no comparative analysis between the Bolivarian Alternative for Latin America (ALBA) and the CARIFORUM-EU EPA as alternative instruments for the sustainable development of the Caribbean.

Chapter 9 demonstrates how the Caribbean negotiators of the EPA identified with the neoliberal ideology of European bloc imperialism, and as a consequence had no problem with advancing the bloc imperialist interests of the EU. It focuses on the Caribbean Regional Negotiating Machinery (CRNM), its strategy against its critics, its denial that the EU pressurized it to sign the EPA, and its defense of the EPA. Also, discussion is undertaken on what the CRNM describes as its "facts" versus the "fiction" of the opponents of the EPA, and presents different positions taken by supporters of the EPA. Also, there is a discussion on the CRNM's approach to the EPA negotiations.

Caribbean neo-colonials collaborated with their colonial masters to gain political power at the time of political independence. Then, they proceeded to govern in the interest of the former colonial masters. European bloc imperialism also needs the collaboration of the domestic ruling elites in order to be fully effective in ACP countries. The negotiators of the EPAs, by cooperating with European bloc imperialism, are playing a major role in the transfer of power obtained by the neo-colonial elites back to Europe. The key argument is that the EPA negotiators wrested power from the neocolonial state elites in the Caribbean, and handed it back to the EU bloc imperialist through the supra-national governance structure of the EPA in which the EU has a decisive role and over which it exercises considerable economic and political leverage. They are depleting the independent states of power rather than enhancing their power. They are taking power out of the hands of the neo-colonial economic and political elites in the ACP regions, and transferring it back to Europe, as a bloc, and in this sense are worse than the neo-colonials. This phenomenon where local elites are negotiating with Europe to transfer power from the neo-colonials back to Europe is yet to be labeled and properly analyzed and theorized in politics. This highlights the class dimension of the EPA negotiations process.

Chapter 10 broaches the subject of the EPA and the food and fuel crises in the Caribbean exploring the link between them. Specifically, it discusses the central issues and neoliberal views in Caribbean agriculture, the food security crisis in the Caribbean, agricultural trade concerns of small states, and policies to reverse the food security crisis. The fuel crisis and the rescue role performed by Petrocaribe are also discussed. The position is taken that the failure of the agricultural policies in the region is the leading cause of the food crisis, coupled with the implementation of structural adjustment. The region has failed to adequately engage in land reform, to diversify its agricultural sector, and has gone too far in implementing marketization policies in agriculture.

The neoliberal view is that the Caribbean nationalist agricultural policies are the cause of the crisis in agriculture, because they protect the region's agricultural sector from global competition. This is the basic argument in favor of free trade in agriculture, which has proved to be a myth because of the protective agricultural policies employed by EU bloc imperialist countries, and the US.

Chapter 11 establishes connections between the global financial and economic crises, and the EU EPAs. It discusses the idea that state protection exists for the rich capitalist countries, while the ACP states are forced to engage in free market policies. An analysis is undertaken on the emergence of the financial crisis, its manifestation in Europe, and EU state interventionist solutions. This is followed by a discussion on worker-layoffs and social unrest that have resulted from the financial crisis. Analyses are also undertaken of, the false debate between the efficient market and inefficient state, and the state interventionist prescriptions by the G-20 and the IMF.

The problem is that the EU engages in state protectionist measures to resolve the global financial and economic crises while its EPA is founded on market liberalization measures. As the global financial crisis epitomizes the collapse of neoliberal free market policies and the state is the preferred agency to save the capitalist system, theoretical debate rages on the virtues of the state versus the market in economic development. The position is taken that this debate is a major distraction because the real issue is not whether the state or the market must lead development, but which class controls the state, and in whose interest the state operates. The collapse of the financial markets has led to a sort of left triumphalism similar to right triumphalism after the collapse of the former Soviet Union. This is a false and dangerous position to adopt because it elevates the capitalist state to position as savior of the world, the very state that needs to be overthrown.

The focus shifts in Chapter 12 to the Caribbean in the global financial and economic crises. It assesses the impact of the crises on the Caribbean, examines the fraud perpetuated by Stanford Financial Group, and analyses the collapse of the CL Financial Group and its bailout by the Trinidad and Tobago government. It descriptively analyses the policy options for the Caribbean presented by regional experts, and proposes some alternative actions that the region could engage in. Specifically, it discusses the link between the crises and the CARIFORUM-EU EPA in terms of policies being pursues by EU bloc imperialism and those foisted on the Caribbean. It argues that the Caribbean is currently experiencing the twin threat respectively, from the CARIFORUM-EU EPA, and the global financial and economic crises.

Finally, Chapter 13 broaches two pet areas of European bloc imperialism – governance and sustainable development, demonstrating how they are mere ploys to facilitate the smooth operations of European bloc imperialism in the ACP countries. Its basic arguments are first that the European bloc imperialist goal of "good governance" in the ACP countries is really to institutionalize a political framework that would provide the political protection for the smooth and uninterrupted transfer of wealth from the ACP regions to Europe. Second, the EU bloc imperialist goal of "sustainable development" is to secure and maintain the supply of raw materials to Europe, and open-up markets in the ACP regions for EU corporations to operate freely to sell their products.

CHAPTER TWO

HEMISPHERIC SETTINGS FOR EUROPEAN BLOC IMPERIALISM

Introduction

The Caribbean encountered European bloc imperialism around the time when the US neoconservatives declared the twenty-first century as "the new American century." In order to realize their goal, the US neoconservatives set out to subjugate the ACP countries and the EU to their brand of neoliberal economic and political measures. Perched at the forefront of US-led globalization the neoconservatives promoted US-styled liberal democracy as a necessary condition for the economic development of the ACP countries. However, the primary objective of democracy promotion by the US is the maintenance of the American way of life. If all countries have similar US-styled democratic systems, the US will have greater leverage to control them for the prime purpose of stripping them of their economic resources so that the US citizens could maintain their luxurious lifestyles of high mass consumption. Democracy promotion nonetheless, undermines genuine democracy in the developing states and has resulted in a variety of new authoritarianisms at the global and domestic levels. The recent record of US democracy promotion in the Caribbean, Latin America, the Middle East, Eastern Europe and Africa provides the evidence in support of the proposition concerning the rise of authoritarian regimes disguised as liberal democracies (Canterbury 2005; Ottaway 2003).

The purpose of this chapter is to provide the reader with an overview of the neoconservative settings in the Caribbean and Latin American region, in which the Caribbean was subsumed as it entered into EPA negotiations with the EU. An important deduction from the exploration of these settings is that the Caribbean is caught in the middle of two competing imperialisms that pull and push it in different directions. The Caribbean could transform this dilemma into an advantage by looking elsewhere, namely towards the emerging economies amongst the developing nations, and to regional unions such as the ALBA and Petrocaribe, for alternative visions of development to those proffered by European bloc imperialism and US-led globalization.

To achieve its purpose, the chapter is divided into four parts beginning with a discussion on the transition from European colonialism to the "new American century doctrine." The focus here is on the dynamics of the transition from colonies to independent states in the Caribbean, the passage of hegemonic power from the UK to the US, cold war politics, the Caribbean under the US sphere of influence, and an outline of the new American century doctrine. This is done to provide a brief background to the arrival of the Caribbean in the twenty-first century.

Second, it examines some key dimensions of the political dynamics and militarization in the region focusing on the defeatist view about the powerlessness of poor states, the rebellious tradition of Caribbean peoples, the transition of the Caribbean from the US' back yard to its front door, and US democracy machinations and military threat to the region. Third, there is an analysis of the manner in which the US neoconservatives used authoritarian tactics to terrorize and subjugate the Caribbean and Latin American countries, in the furtherance of the US' imperialist objectives. The discussion here centers on politics in the Caribbean, the neoconservative idea about the "survival of liberty" in the US, the process by which democracy was subverted in Haiti, and the bullying of the Caricom countries by the US to change their position on the overthrow of President Jean-Bertrand Aristide. The final section presents a critical analysis of the US neoconservative terrorist threat to democracy in Latin America focusing on the overthrow and reinstatement of President Hugo Chávez in Venezuela, and further challenges to democracy in the Caribbean and Latin America, as posed by these same forces.

Transition from Colonialism to New American Century Doctrine

The Transition from Colonies to Independent States

The Caribbean countries began the twentieth century as European colonies and ended it as politically independent states under US domination.[1] Their transition from colonies to independent states in the

[1] This refers to the English-speaking Caribbean. These states gained their political independence in the 1960s and 1970s. Currently, however, there are only a few

latter half of the twentieth century coincided with unprecedented economic prosperity in the US, the establishment of US global dominance as leader of the capitalist world, and US engagement of the former Soviet Union in the cold war. Under those conditions, a dark shadow was cast over the Caribbean, as it transmuted from British colonies to politically independent states. Thus, as the Caribbean states became politically independent, they emerged as new types of colonies directly under the US sphere of influence, subjected more so to US than British imperialism. Currently, in the first decade of the twenty-first century, British imperialism is now subsumed under European bloc imperialism that is making a stake to rest back from the US, control over the Caribbean.

Britain, for economic reasons associated with its reconstruction embarked on a strategy to first grant internal self-government to the colonies, before they were upgraded to fully politically independent states. This process commenced with the institution of universal adult suffrage that was first introduced in the Caribbean in Jamaica in 1944. In Africa, Kwame Nkrumah emerged from the prison cell in which the British had incarcerated him, to become leader of an independent Ghana in 1957. With each colony receiving the free vote the next step in the British plan for the Caribbean was to federate the region in a single political unit and then to grant it political independence, within the British Commonwealth. The collapse of the top-down British-sponsored federation movement in 1962 led to the alternative, which was to grant the Caribbean colonies political independence as separate countries.

The Passage of Hegemonic Power from the UK to the US

The achievement of political independence in the Caribbean must therefore be examined from the vantage points of two sets of influencing factors. These are first the global economic and political conditions completely out of the hands of the Caribbean peoples, and second domestic factors within the region. Looming large externally were the end of World War II, US pressure on the European imperial powers to give up their colonial possessions, the US' perception of the military, political, and economic challenges posed by the former Soviet Union,

English-speaking Caribbean countries, Montserrat, and Turks and Caicos Islands that remain as British colonies.

and the actual mechanisms of the transfer of imperial domination of the region from British to US imperialism.

In terms of the external factors, the British came around to the US position on political independence to the colonies evidenced in the *The Atlantic Charter* signed by Winston Churchill and Franklyn Roosevelt. The US' position was that the colonies should be granted political independence, and allowed to participate freely in world trade. The political independence of the European colonies would give the US military, economic, and political leverage over them, in the light of the collapse of the British Empire. US imperial domination would be complete and more effective in a community of independent states in which it is the strongest economically and militarily. The US understood the British position however that the colonies would get their freedom only after Britain had fleeced them sufficiently to aid in its post-War reconstruction, in combination with the Marshall Plan.

At the internal level the most important factors were the general conditions of underdevelopment that spurred the nationalist movement, the awakened consciousness of Caribbean peoples due to foreign travel, the expansion of the education system, and Marxism that provided an alternative view to the capitalist system.

Cold War Politics

The cold war constrained the Caribbean countries' abilities to pursue an independent path of political and economic development thereby creating major problems for the advancement of region. The Caribbean countries whose political leadership chose to align themselves with the former Soviet Union and Cuba set the stage for the classic cold war politics of subversion in the region. Guyana, Jamaica, and Grenada were engulfed in the cauldron of cold war politics. British military forces invaded Guyana in 1953, and 1962, setbacks from which the country is yet to recover. Guyana now ranks as one of the poorest countries in the hemisphere next to Haiti.

The US military invaded Grenada in 1979 during the Regan era that signaled the rise of the neoconservative movement. Also, US backed political violence destabilized the Manley government in Jamaica that brought about its downfall during the early 1980s.

The Caribbean in the US Sphere of Influence

Under the US sphere of influence, Caribbean states pursued political and economic agendas supported by the US. Political and economic nationalism in the region however interfered with the transition from British to US imperial dominance, and the operationalization of the US sphere of influence in the area. Nationalism took three basic forms – a radical form that wanted to push the imperialist forces completely out of the region, another type that encouraged imperialist penetration but wanted a greater role for locals in the economy, and a pseudo-socialist state capitalist type (Kwayana 1972; Thomas 1983).

The historical evidence shows however that the US achieved its political and economic objectives in the Caribbean through hard-nosed diplomacy, sanctions, and military invasion. Possible fear of US power, the promotion of personal ambitions, or winning curry favor with the US has also pushed some regional politicians to willingly become US lackeys in the region, and espoused and implement pro-US anti-communist policies.

The New American Century Doctrine

While the cold war dominated Caribbean-US relations in the latter half of the twentieth century, the US began the twenty-first century as the sole imperialist "*hyper power*" in a post-cold war globe. The US neoconservatives envisioned US military and economic domination of the entire globe throughout the twenty-first century,[2] through doctrines such as "pre-emptive strike,"[3] "globalization," "war on terror,"[4] and "democracy promotion."[5] The US' position is currently under challenge from European bloc imperialism, China, and other emerging economies such as Brazil, India and South Africa, when they act in unison. The US' unprecedented hegemonic position in the globe in the immediate post-cold war period has caused its neoconservative ideologues to declare the twenty-first century, as the "new American century."

---

[2] See The Project for the New American Century. 2000. *Rebuilding America's Defenses: Strategy, Forces and Resources For a New Century*, A Report of The Project for the New American Century. Washington, DC. Kagan, Robert and William Kristol ed. 2000. *Present Dangers: Crisis and Opportunity in American Foreign and Defense Policy*. San Francisco, California: Encounter Books.

[3] The National Security Council. 2002. The National Security Strategy of the United States of America, 2002. Washington.

[4] The National Security Council. 2002. The National Security Strategy of the United States of America, 2002. Washington.

[5] Carothers, Thomas. 2002. Democracy Promotion: A Key Focus in a New World Order. *Issues of Democracy* (5)1: 23–28; Dobriansky, Paula J. 2005. Strategies on Democracy Promotion: Remarks to the Hudson Institute. Washington, DC.

The neoconservative so-called "non-profit educational organization" labeled "The Project for the New American Century" has dedicated itself to the propositions "that American leadership is good both for America and the world; that such leadership requires military strength, diplomatic energy and commitment to moral principle; and that too few political leaders today are making the case for global leadership."[6] The key individuals in the "The Project for the New American Century," occupied senior policy positions in the Bush administration, where they had the opportunity to implement their sinister plans of the neoconservatives' "Mein Kempt" for global dominance.

The "founding Statement of Principles" of The Project for the New American Century states as follows:

> As the 20th century draws to a close, the United States stands as the world's most preeminent power. Having led the West to victory in the Cold War, America faces an opportunity and a challenge: Does the United States have the vision to build upon the achievement of past decades? Does the United States have the resolve to shape a new century favorable to American principles and interests? [What we require is] a military that is strong and ready to meet both present and future challenges; a foreign policy that boldly and purposefully promotes American principles abroad; and a national leadership that accepts the United States' global responsibility....The history of the past century should have taught us that it is important to shape circumstances before crises emerge, and to meet threats before they become dire. The history of the past century should have taught us to embrace the cause of American leadership (The Project for the New American Century 2000: i).

In the light of these founding principles the question faced by the ACP countries is: what is the role of the developing states in the "new American century?" Could the Caribbean states ever achieve political and economic independence under the doctrine of the "new American century," or are they condemned eternally to be the obedient servants of the US, empire? What are the prospects for Caribbean economic development in the "new American century"? In what ways

[6] The Project for the New American Century. 2000. *Rebuilding America's Defenses: Strategy, Forces and Resources For a New Century*, A Report of The Project for the New American Century. Washington, DC. See also, Kagan, Robert. 2003. *Of Paradise and Power: America and Europe in the New World Order*. New York: Knopf; Kristol, William and Christopher DeMuth. 1995. *The Neoconservative Imagination: Essays in Honor of Irving Kristol*. Waschington DC: AEI Press. Kagan, Robert and William Kristol ed. 2000. *Present Dangers: Crisis and Opportunity in American Foreign and Defense Policy*. San Francisco, California: Encounter Books.

could the Caribbean states resist the domination of their Cyclops neighbor to the north? These were some of the questions pertinent to Caribbean political and economic development at the time of the intervention of European bloc imperialism through EPA negotiations in the region.

Political Dynamics and Militarization

Consideration is given in this section to the views on the powerlessness of poor states, the rebellious tradition of the Caribbean, the change in the region's status, from being in the back- to the front-yard of the US imperialism, and US democracy machinations and military threat to the region.

The Powerlessness of Poor States?

The hemispheric political economy conditions as the Caribbean encountered European bloc imperialism involved the debate on the new imperialism associated with the neoconservative doctrine of the "new American century," which raises a major problem for economic and political development in the region. The predicament for the region is that both the right and left seem to have a common position in this debate on the all-powerfulness of the US military and economy and the powerlessness of the poor states. The US neoconservatives that hankered after US global dominance have hedged their bets on the US military and economic strengths.[7] However, the critics that systematically expose the new imperialism, US hegemony, and the grand design for the new American century also convey the impression that the US' military and economic strength is unstoppable in the current period.[8]

This line of reasoning renders the developing countries helpless when they are up against the military and economic might of the US.

[7] The Project for the New American Century. 2000. *Rebuilding America's Defenses: Strategy, Forces and Resources For a New Century*, A Report of The Project for the New American Century. Washington, DC. See also, Kagan, Robert. 2003. *Of Paradise and Power: America and Europe in the New World Order*. New York: Knopf; Kristol, William and Christopher DeMuth. 1995. *The Neoconservative Imagination: Essays in Honor of Irving Kristol*. Waschington DC: AEI Press. Kagan, Robert and William Kristol ed. 2000. *Present Dangers: Crisis and Opportunity in American Foreign and Defense Policy*. San Francisco, California: Encounter Books.

[8] See for example Chomsky, Noam. 2003. *Hegemony, or Survival: America's Quest for Global Dominance*. New York: Henry Holt and Company.

It follows, therefore, that the US could do whatever it wants without reprisals because there is no other competitive power that could match that of the US'. While the boastful neoconservatives convey the view that the US could do as it pleases in a global community of states, and that any resistance to it would be crushed, the Left seems to have bought into the neoconservative propaganda about the helplessness of the poor states. The real meaning of this is that the US will not allow the poor countries to experiment with alternative approaches in organizing their economic and political systems. This spells major problems for alternative development agendas in the developing states.

Caribbean Tradition of Rebellion

The Caribbean region however has had a strong tradition of rebellion against political and economic repression of imperialist powers dating back to its earliest opposition to European imperialism. The aborigines in the region were conquered only because in their brave resistance to European feudal, mercantilist and capitalist occupation, they were outmatched in weaponry. The Caribbean was thereafter incorporated into the global capitalist system as a colonial slave mode of production or slavery-*cum*-capitalist social formation to produce commodities for exchange in capitalist world markets.

But, the colonial slave mode of production was also a hotbed of resistance in the form of slave revolts, riots, and sabotage. The successful Haitian revolution of 1798 struck a major blow against the global capitalist system at that time. Furthermore, a major slave revolt in Guyana in 1763 brought limited liberation to the slaves in the county of Berbice, until it was defeated due to infighting among the revolutionaries. In Jamaica the Maroons[9] fought against the Spaniards for their freedom. The British were forced to sign a treaty with the Maroons of Jamaica in 1739 that recognized them as a free people, granted them 1,500 acres of land, and allowed them to administer their own laws. These are examples of successful struggle by ordinary people in the

---

[9] The Maroon is a slave that successfully ran away from slavery to lead an independent life in the new lands the Africans were taken to such as Suriname, Guyana, and Jamaica. While the Maroons in Guyana were unsuccessful in their attempts to establish separate and independent communities, those in Suriname and Jamaica were. The word Maroon comes from the Spanish word "cimmarron" meaning "wild" or "untamed."

Caribbean against global powers for independence from political and economic bondage.

Resistance against global capitalism was also a hallmark of Caribbean society in the post-slavery period. Working peoples' struggles to participate in the national and local political and economic decision-making processes, to organize labor, and to improve their social welfare, were the main arenas of resistance against global capitalist repression in the post-slavery period.

Working people in the Caribbean registered the first blows against the repressive global capitalist system for their freedom and democracy. These blows took the form of revolts, revolutions, strikes, mass demonstrations, and nationalist struggles. Political independence in the Caribbean states in the post-World War II period was the direct product of nationalist, anti-imperialist, and in cases anti-capitalist, working class struggle. The struggle for freedom and democracy in the Caribbean in the new American century is therefore against a global capitalist system presided over by the two imperialisms – US globalization and European bloc imperialism. What should be the nature and form of the struggle for freedom and democracy in the Caribbean in the historical period characterized by the "new American century" and European bloc imperialism? This question is yet to be answered.

The Caribbean: From US Back Yard to Its Front Door

Historically, the US authorities considered the Caribbean to be in the US' "backyard," but nowadays the region is seen to be "at" the US' front door.[10] During the Cold War, the US "defended" the Caribbean from communism, while in the period of neoconservative dominance the Caribbean is forced to join the US "war on terror" that catapulted the region from the US' backyard to its front door. The Caribbean is no longer a buffer zone against communism, its new role in the age of US empire building is to help to protect and defend the US against "terrorism." The Caribbean must therefore be in a state of permanent "war on terror," fighting to defend the US in the same way that it defended the British empire, in the first and second world wars.

---

[10] Former President Bill Clinton in a speech he delivered on globalization at Yale University, referred to the Caribbean as being in the U.S. "backyard," but he quickly corrected himself by using instead the term "front door." See Clinton, Bill. 2001. Remarks as Delivered by Former President Clinton at the Yale University Tercentennial. Cross Campus, Yale University.

The greatest challenge Caribbean countries face is that of pursuing their national socio-economic, political, and military interests, as front door occupants of the US Empire, while the region has signed an EPA with European bloc imperialism. Caribbean politicians, policy makers, and scholars have seen this challenge in a different way namely in terms of "contending with destiny" under US-led globalization. It would seem that they are merely trying to contend with the destiny of the region in the twenty-first century as humble servants of the US Empire or European bloc imperialism.[11]

Undoubtedly, an analysis of recent economic, political, and military developments in the Caribbean unmasks the *modus operandi* of US imperialism in the region. Through its domination of the international financial institutions, it implements neoliberal economic policies on the Caribbean. These measures give US corporations, full protection in Caribbean markets, and the freedom of entry and exit. But as discussed later, European bloc imperialism promises to crowd-out the US from Caribbean trade. The US-led globalization measures foster unfair trade practices, and promote the neoliberal restructuring of regional trade blocs such as the Caribbean Community and the Association of Caribbean States.

The Free Trade Area of the Americas (FTAA) dominated by the US, but now on the backburner, is proposed as a viable alternative framework for hemispheric trade. The Bolivarian Alternative for the Americas (ALBA) and Petrocaribe, however, definitely represent the better direction in which the Caribbean should go concerning hemispheric trade. Furthermore, money laundering in offshore banking institutions that hide the corrupt, dirty transactions of the rich and powerful in the US has become a major new activity in the Caribbean. Meanwhile, Caribbean scholars are merely debating ways in which regional economies must be repositioned to curry favor with US imperialism in order for them to develop (Bernal 2000). In the new "American century," however, any repositioning of the Caribbean is merely to facilitate the efficient rape of the region by the US transnational corporations.

---

[11] See Benn, Denis and Kenneth Hall, eds. 2000. *Contending with Destiny: The Caribbean in the 21st Century*. Kingston: Ian Randle. No article in this major text that sets the policy tone for the Caribbean's response to U.S., empire offers any radical option. The prescriptions are well within the expectations of the neoconservatives that head-up the American empire.

US Democracy Machinations and Militarization Threat

The biggest contradiction that Caribbean scholars must be well aware of but turn a blind eye to is the US' democracy machinations that promote authoritarianism. The promotion of democracy was the grand political design by the US neoconservatives for the US' front door occupants. But, the US is notorious for its abuse of democracy. In the course of furthering its imperialist interests during the cold war the US has destabilized and overthrew democratically elected governments in the Caribbean and Latin America, including in Guyana, Jamaica, Guatemala, and Chile. In the post-cold war period, the US continues to subvert democracy evidenced by its role in the overthrow of democratically elected governments in Haiti and Venezuela. Despite its treacherous behavior, the promotion of democracy is a cornerstone of the political agenda of US imperialism in the Caribbean. However, democratization rapidly became the new authoritarianism in the Caribbean and Latin America,[12] as regional elites explore mechanisms for "good governance" for the region, an integral component of democratization.

The devolution of military duties and operations is a major feature of US imperialism in the Caribbean that poses a threat to the region. The US engages in joint-military exercises with regional military personnel. The overall strategy however is the Caribbeanization of domestic, political, and military conflicts in the region. The devolution of military operations is done through peacekeeping forces drawn from regional military forces, and outsourcing. The US military provides the high command, overall strategy, training, equipment, and minimal personnel on the ground. The exception to these is outright military invasion by the US as in the cases of Grenada and Panama. Future devolution of military operations will involve joint regional forces to invading a recalcitrant country, to protect the US' interests, paraded as the interests of the Caribbean.

Authoritarianism in the Service of Imperialism

The analysis of authoritarianism in the service of imperialism is undertaken to highlight some of the pertinent political economy issues that

[12] See Canterbury, Dennis C. 2005. *Neoliberal Democratization and New Authoritarianism*. Aldershot, Hampshire: Ashgate.

provided the background and faced by the Caribbean as the region negotiated the CARIFORUM-EU EPA. The focus here is on politics in the Caribbean, the US neoconservative notion about "the survival of liberty" in the US, the subversion of democracy in Haiti, and the Caricom's shifting stance on Haiti. The analysis provides some more details on the workings of US authoritarianism in the Western Hemisphere. This analysis is continued in the next section that focuses on the US neoconservative terrorist threat to democracy in Latin America.

Politics in the Caribbean

Here we explore the challenges posed for politics in the Caribbean by the new American century doctrine, as the region embraces notions about "good governance" promoted by both US-led globalization and European bloc imperialism. Caribbean politics is the contest between different social classes to control the state in the different countries in the region, and to dominate regional economic, political, and social institutions. It originated in the globalization of capitalism that commenced in the region in the post-1492 period, and has been going on since that time. But, as the capitalist system of commodity production for market exchange spread from Europe to the Caribbean it brought with it different forms of authoritarian political arrangements. Politics originated in the region therefore in an authoritarian setting representing the absence of any class contest by the local people to determine which class controls the state. The system of sporadic and absolute rule that was put in place in the region had its origins in Europe. Indeed, the first contests for state power in the Caribbean were among the Europeans who settled in the area. These were essentially contests by people of similar class background, although the society became stratified in a typical European fashion between the rich and poor.

Mass politics emerged in the region in the context of the abolition of slavery when in theory large numbers of working people became free to take part in politics. They had to develop their class-consciousness, form political and civic organizations, produce political leaders, and learn how to conduct class struggle for state power. There were considerable legal constraints on mass participation in politics however until the post-World War II period when universal adult suffrage was granted to the British colonies in region. Thus, real mass politics came to the Caribbean when the working class people were allowed to caste their votes for the first time to elect political representatives of their choice. Only then, did politics really become a contest between different classes in the region to exercise control over the powers of the state. Nevertheless, the authoritarian dynamics of the state in the Caribbean, developed as a part of the imperative by the global capitalists to extract the region's wealth, persisted into the period of mass politics.

This is the main reason why the theoretical framework formulated by Mars (1998) to explain left politics in the Caribbean is problematic. Mars (1998) correctly argues however that the interplay of local and global factors had a role in the derivation of the class and social positions of the Caribbean left and by extension left politics. He noted that political movements in the Caribbean are derived from the middle classes located in an intermediary position between the international capitalist classes and the masses and subordinate classes of the domestic population (Mars 1998: 11). Mars (1998) stops short at saying that his framework appears to resemble that of Modern World System, Dependency, and Hegemonic Stability theories, but rather speaks to the hierarchical and unequal relationship between international and national capitalist structures.

What is missing in Mars' (1998) analysis is the authoritarian dynamic of the Caribbean state that impacts directly on left and right politics. This dynamic involves the centripetal external and internal class forces that exert tremendous pressure on the Caribbean state to move to the center of the economic and political demands of dominant imperialist powers. The Caribbean state is the actual product of the spread and sustenance of capitalism in the region. The continued participation of the region in the global capitalist system that created it to serve the economic interests of Europe is a prime stimulant of authoritarian politics in the area, which dovetails with the personal ambitions of particular individuals who become dictators.

While authoritarian dynamics is ever present, the degree to which they take hold in politics is determined by a variety of domestic and external factors, including personal political ambitions of politicians, race, and political expediency on the part of the global capitalists. Politics serve the interests of the local ruling elite, who must as a condition of their rule and support by the global capitalists, uphold the economic and political platform of the dominant imperialist power of the day. The workers are yet to put politics to work in their self-interest, as they tend to join forces with other class forces, in specific contests with the state, which then push them aside in the end. This is not an uncommon historical feature, as Marx (1969) analyzed it in his famous essay on Class Struggles in France.[13] However, Mars (1998) formulates a theoretical framework that operates as though politics in the Caribbean is purely a contest between the domestic left and right.

Apart from Cuba, the left was never really in power in the Caribbean except briefly in Guyana in 1953 under the original PPP, and Grenada, under the New Jewel Movement (NJM). British military forces invaded Guyana and overthrew the democratically elected left government that held power for 133 days. The stated objective of the British imperialist in Guyana in 1953 was to prevent a communist take-over of the country. US military forces invaded Grenada under the dubious pretext of wanting to protect US medical students on the island after the Grenadian military seized power from the popular Maurice Bishop and established a Ruling Military Council (RMC).

The short-lived experiences of those two left experiments demonstrated however that the state in the Caribbean guarantees the reproduction of the conditions and social relations of capitalism, and to protect the unequal distribution of property engendered by that system. Thus, in the contest for state power in the Caribbean, it is always those classes that align themselves with global capital that come out victorious. In turn, these classes operate the state machinery to carry out their traditional functions to further the combined interests of domestic and global capital.

"The Survival of Liberty" in the US

The external dimension of the authoritarian dynamic in Caribbean politics could be gleaned from the neoconservative notions about "the survival of liberty" in the US. In his second term inaugural speech in January 2005, President Bush outlined the essence of the external threat the US posed to the Caribbean with respect to the deepening authoritarian dynamic in the region through military invasion, destabilization, coups, and the entire arsenal of American interventionist tactics. President Bush said, "The survival of liberty in our land increasingly depends on the success of liberty in other lands." The US therefore linked its own freedom with the freedom of the Caribbean and other countries around the globe, defined on US terms.

[13] Marx, Karl. 1969. Class Struggles in France, 1848–1850, in *Selected Works*, Volume 1, Progress Publishers, Moscow.

The neoconservatives therefore extended their doctrine of "preemptive strike" in which the US militarily could attack weaker states that it claims are a threat to US national security. The list of transgressions for which the US reserved the right of preemptive military attack against another country include a military threat, a country's attempt to acquire weapons of mass destruction, what the US conceives as crimes against humanity, or the lack of "liberty" in a country. The US asserted the right, to intervene in any Caribbean country including militarily in the name of "freedom" and "democracy." The neoconservatives therefore assumed for the US the responsibility to "democratize" the entire globe by any means necessary.

The neoconservative idea about the "survival of liberty" represented the new global authoritarianism in the post-cold war period. Caribbean countries are not given a choice to experiment with democracy as the US did after its War of Independence with Britain. The US has established its own version of democracy based on something called the "Electoral College," which is not founded on the principle of majority rule, as is under British democracy. The US therefore rejected British democracy and formulated its own that suits its unique demographic and geographic conditions. In the view of the "founding fathers" of the US, the idea of the "Electoral College" is to counteract the "tyranny of the majority" by giving smaller states what is considered to be a fair say in the election of the US president. Neoconservative US-styled democracy became the new global tyranny that placed the Caribbean countries in a box with no room for political maneuver. Caribbean politics had to be conducted within the framework of the "survival of liberty."

The new global authoritarianism however only succeeded in reproducing authoritarian states in the countries that were "democratized," rather than creating genuine democratic states. The new global authoritarianism that is simultaneously the new imperialism was designed to maintain US control over the economic resources of the countries that are "democratized." This control is maintained by force or violence usually through economic and political destabilization, military occupation, or lackey domestic governments. Economic and political destabilization takes the form of debilitating sanctions against recalcitrant countries, and/or the US fermentation of social unrest in them. US military occupation takes the following principal forms – its military may occupy a country all by itself, lead a military coalition with subservient states to occupy another country, lead a UN peacekeeping occupying force, or the US may subcontract out military occupation to a regional coalition headed by a sub-imperialist power, or mercenaries. The best-case scenario for US occupation is through a lackey government "democratically" elected that represses any opposition to the status quo, namely US control over the country's domestic economic resources and political system.

The case of Iraq, where the government of Sadam Hussein was destabilized and overthrown and the US established a governing authority, represents all of these examples of how the US exercises control over "democratized" states. The Paul Bremer-led Coalition Provisional Authority (CPA) that governed Iraq imposed structural adjustment on the country to facilitate the rape of its economy by US corporations. Among other things, the CPA promoted

> the widespread privatization of public enterprises, which – combined with allowing for 100% foreign ownership of Iraqi companies – renders key sectors of the Iraqi economy prime targets of burgeoning American corporations. It imposed a 15% flat tax, which primarily benefits the wealthy and places a disproportionate burden on the poor. It virtually eliminated import tariffs, resulting in a flood of foreign goods into the country; since smaller Iraqi companies – weakened by over a dozen years of sanctions – are unable to compete, hundreds of factories have recently shut down, adding to already-severe unemployment. It permitted 100% repatriation of profits, which severely limits reinvestment in the Iraqi economy. It lowered the minimum wage, increasing already widespread poverty, and it leased on contracts for as long as 40 years, making it impossible for even a truly sovereign government to legally make alternative arrangements.[14]

The products of the global new authoritarianism are themselves authoritarian, since these so-called democratic countries must engage in political repression to maintain US domination. The new global authoritarianism under the new American century doctrine was therefore characterized by the deepening of state sponsored terrorist violence, and violation of civil, economic, and political rights in the global capitalist economic system.

This is quite the opposite of what the American revolutionaries fought for against the British imperialists. In an Op/Ed on anti-imperialism (The Nation, February 20, 2005) John Nichols observed that the American revolutionaries fought to establish a democracy that would replace the divine right of kings with the consent of the

[14] Zunes, Stephen. 2009. The U.S. Invasion of Iraq: The Military Side of Globalization? *Globalizations* (6) 1: 99–105.

governed. According to Nichols (2005) George Washington the commander of the revolutionary forces in particular was unrepentantly anti-imperialist, and anti-empire. Nichols (2005) argues that Washington's position was that the US would pay with a portion of its independence if it became involved in projects of hostility instigated by pride, ambition, and other sinister and pernicious motives. Washington's principle that America's independence would be jeopardized if the US engaged in hostility against other nations is quite different to the neoconservative dogma that the survival of liberty in the US depends on the success of freedom in other countries. The neoconservative dogma is not only a recipe for US military intervention, empire building, imperialism, and absolute rule, but also stimuli of ingenuous responses by the oppressed people in the countries that the US seeks to incorporate into its empire.

According to David Corn in an article entitled "Bush Gives the UN the Finger" (The Nation March 8, 2005a) the neoconservatives treated the global community of nation-states with the highest level of contempt. The nomination of John Bolton as US ambassador to the UN was a clear indication of their disrespect for the global community. Corn observed in his work entitled "John Bolton: Ally of Drugrunners," which links Bolton to the US Central Intelligence Agency (CIA) drugrunners (The Nation, March 30, 2005b) that Bolton was not only a known critic of the UN, but disregarded its functions as stated in its charter. Bolton is on record as saying that the UN "is valuable only when it directly serves the United States" (Carter 2005: 98). Furthermore, he has a record of undermining efforts at US arms control, a major area of operation of the UN (Carter 2005: 98). Bolton's record as under secretary of state for arms control in President Bush's first term was so poor that fifty-nine former US diplomats on both side of the isle wrote to the Senate Foreign Relations Committee in protest of his nomination as ambassador to the UN and blocked his appointment to the position (Carter 2005: 98).

Bolton falsely accused Cuba of developing biological weapons, and without proof claimed that Syria posed a serious weapon of mass destruction threat to the US (Carter 2005: 98). Furthermore, Bolton was in a scandal involving his acceptance of money from a political fund in Taiwan while being a strong advocate for Taiwan in US congressional testimony. Bolton hid the fact that he received the money to write policy papers for the Taiwanese organization involved. Questions were raised about him breaking US laws because he failed to register as a foreign agent. In addition, David Corn pointed out that Bolton was involved in the cover-up of the contra drug- and gun-running activities conducted by the US CIA during the Regan-Bush I administration.

The US did not emerge overnight as the new global authoritarian this process began in the decades after 1945, when the US pressured the Europeans to break-up the colonial system at the end of World War II. The collapse of colonialism was hailed as an end to imperialism as a historical phenomenon. Harry Magdoff[15] forewarned however that a new imperialism under US leadership emerged when the colonial system collapsed (Magdoff 2003). According to Magdoff (2003) the new imperialism was not defined in terms of the ownership of colonies, but in the context of the domination of the global capitalist market by the US. Magdoff (2003) argues that the new imperialism generates inequality, repression, militarism, and plays a critical role in the development of US capitalism.

The Subversion of Democracy in Haiti

The overthrow of the democratically elected President Jean-Bertrand Aristide of Haiti is further evidence of the challenge to democracy posed by the US threat to the Caribbean, under the Bush administration. In an article on the coup in Haiti that overthrew the Aristide administration (Counterpunch, March 5/6, 2005) Tom Reeves observed that consumers of the US and Canadian media would believe that Aristide was a vicious corrupt dictator, who violated human rights and had lost his popularity. Reeves (2005) noted that the people of the US and Canada would never know from media coverage that Aristide was removed at gunpoint. The US and France disagreed over the invasion and occupation of Iraq by the US led so-called "coalition of the willing," but they were certainly on the same page with regards to the destabilization of Haiti and the overthrow of President Aristide. The US and France, colluded to block international economic assistance to Haiti, demanding that President Aristide repaid the debt to foreign banks and countries incurred by past Haitian dictators. The poverty-stricken Haiti was unable to repay the unjust debt and so the US and France, claiming that they were promoting democracy, resorted to

[15] Magdoff, Harry. 2003. *Imperialism Without Colonies*. New York: Monthly Review Press.

funding antigovernment organizations to destabilize the democratically elected government in the country.[16]

Peter Hallward noted in his article in guardian.co.uk (March 2, 2004) that Aristide was regarded as a threat to the US and France and that was why those two countries overthrew his government. Hallward pointed out however that Aristide's US/France backed opponents refused to compromise and demanded that he be removed from office. Knowing that they could not defeat the popular president at the polls, the opposition boycotted the national election in 2000, leaving Aristide to win 92% of the votes. France and the US then declared that the electoral process in Haiti was flawed. The US and France then collaborated on blocking all direct aid to Haiti, while simultaneously financing the Haitian opposition. This was the cause of the chaos that created the pretext for military intervention by US and French forces and to overthrow Aristide. The *coup de grace* was carried out by a small group of ex-Army and paramilitaries stationed in and supplied from the Dominican Republic.[17]

The International Republican Institute (IRI) assumed for itself the mission of building democracy and therefore had a major role in the overthrow of President Aristide. The IRI is regarded as an organization that "serves only as a screen for its energetic and unscrupulous promotion of an ultraconservative Republican foreign policy agenda."[18] It is supposed to be a research institution but is really as a "cloak-and-dagger operation." There is evidence that the IRI was allied with the extreme antidemocratic forces in Haiti and contributed towards inciting the coup, while asserting that it was involved in "party building," and "educational seminars" in the country (Leight 2004).

The IRI received $1.2 million from the National Endowment for Democracy (NED) for its operations in Haiti. The IRI openly funded, equipped, and lobbied for the conservative and White House-backed opposition parties, the Democratic Convergence and Group 184 in Haiti. Together, these two groups provided the most vocal and hostile opposition to President Aristide. The Group 184 comprised the major

[16] McCollester, Charles. 2004. Haiti Matters! *Monthly Review* (56) 4: 26–46; Chossudovsky, Michel. 2004. The Destabilization of Haiti. www.globalresearch.ca

[17] McCollester, Charles. 2004. Haiti Matters! *Monthly Review* (56) 4: 26–46; Chossudovsky, Michel. 2004. The Destabilization of Haiti. www.globalresearch.ca

[18] Leight, Jessica. 2004. The International Republican Institute: Promulgating Democracy of Another Variety. Washington. Council On Hemispheric Affairs, Memorandum to the Press 04.40, July 15.

businesses, church, and professional figures in Haiti. These organizations stubbornly refused a compromise with Aristide even after he made major concessions to them. The so-called "non-violent" opposition endorsed the former military and paramilitary leaders who swept through the country.

Also, the IRI and the NED funded two anti-Aristide conservative trade unions, the Federation of Trade Union Workers and the General Organization of Haitian Workers, to scuttle the radicalism of Haiti's left leaning trade union movement, which was regarded as a threat to the US and local business interests. The NED also funded the Haitian Center for Human Rights (CHADEL), led by Jean-Jacques Honorat, a former prime minister in the Haitian military junta a brutally repressive government that beat, and murdered thousands of political dissidents between 1991 and 1994.

The IRI also received funding from the US Agency for International Development (USAID). John Bolton described the USAID as "a subsidiary of the CIA which serves to promote political and economic desiderata of the federal government through its financial assistance programs abroad."[19] Otto Reich directed the USAID Latin American division between 1981 and 1983, and almost a decade later became the US special envoy to the Western hemisphere. USAID funded the Haitian International Institute for Research and Development (IHRED), which was close to the military government under the post-Duvalier dictator General Henry Namphy, who ruled Haiti briefly in 1988. The IHRED participated in the formation of the Group of 10 an organization of anti-communist Haitian political leaders led by Mark Bazin. The former World Bank official and technocratic Bazin received US backing as the conservative, pro-business candidate in the presidential election in 1990. However, Aristide, the former priest won that election overwhelmingly.

The USAID received the authorization from the US Congress to spend $24.5 million in a four-year Democracy Enhancement Project in Haiti beginning in 1991. The goal of that project was to "strengthen legislative and other constitutional structures ... local governments [and] independent organizations" in Haiti. But America Watch the human rights group maintained that the real purpose of the

[19] Leight, Jessica. 2004. The International Republican Institute: Promulgating Democracy of Another Variety. Washington. Council On Hemispheric Affairs, Memorandum to the Press 04.40, July 15.

Democracy Enhancement Project was to bolster conservative organizations to "act as an institutional check on Aristide" (Leight 2004). The project was suspended after the military coup in Haiti in 1991, but it was reactivated in important ways such as through support for conservative trade unions throughout the tenure of the coup government. The organizations supported by the NED and USAID were spared of any form of repression by the military government because they were regarded as non-threatening. However, the military brutally crushed the radical or autonomous civil society agencies.[20]

The Clinton Administration had a role in the Aristide's return from exile to Haiti in 1994, accompanied by 20,000 US troops. Fresh parliamentary and presidential elections were held in 1995, but while the Clinton Administration hailed the process as "highly successful," the IRI questioned the reliability of the procedures, and the trustworthiness of the results, claiming that the election was an "organizational catastrophe." Republican Florida representative Porter Gross, leader of an IRI delegation to Haiti condemned the elections in public statements claiming that the elected parliament did not "have sufficient credibility as an independent, separate branch of government for the customary checks and balances role" but that it would "be just an Aristide rubber stamp" (Leight 2004). The IRI's real grievance however was that the wrong man had won the election, which the USAID funded to the tune of $11 million. The IRI's Republican patrons and corporate donors saw little or no prospects for themselves in an Aristide victory.[21]

---

[20] Leight, Jessica. 2004. The International Republican Institute: Promulgating Democracy of Another Variety. Washington. Council On Hemispheric Affairs, Memorandum to the Press 04.40, July 15.

[21] In 2004 the IRI board was chaired by Senator John McCain of Arizona, and comprised republicans Senator Chuck Hagel of Nebraska, Representative David Dreier of California, Representative Jim Kolbe of Arizona, N.Y. Republican James A. Garner, the first African-American mayor on Long Island and president of the U.S. Conference of Mayors, Frank J. Fahrenkopf, Jr, a former chairman of the Republican Party, Michael Grebe, a former General Counsel to the Republican National Committee, Brent Scowcroft, National Security Adviser to the first President Bush, Lawrence Eagleburger, Secretary of State under President George H.W. Bush, Dr. Jeane Kirkpatrick, Ambassador to the U.N. under the Reagan administration and member of the American Enterprise Institute a conservative think tank, Alison Fortier, a director of Lockheed Martin Missile Defense Programs, and J. William Middledorf II, former Secretary of the Navy and ambassador to the Organization of American States under the Reagan administration. The corporate sector was also represented, with Ford, AOL Time Warner, Chevron, and Texaco among the multinational corporations with officials that served or were serving on the IRI board. See Hamburger, Sarah. 2008.

The presidential election held in December 1995 to elect Aristide's successor was also a source of conflict between the Clinton administration and the IRI. The IRI opposed the election results claiming that there was a low voter turnout, which was evidence that the Haitians were dissatisfied and had a low level of democratic awareness. The real grouse of the IRI was that René Preval won the election. He was a member of the Lavalas party, and a strong supporter of Aristide. The Preval government and Lavalas legislators accused the IRI of challenging Haiti's sovereignty by its support for former members of the dissolved military and opposition groups in the country. The IRI shut its Port-au-Prince office in 1999, and began to run its Haitian operations from the Dominican Republic (Leight 2004).

The IRI used its strategy of information technology to help to launch the coup against Aristide in 2002. Claiming that its program in Haiti was to help to develop information technology in the country, the IRI launched a website www.haitigetinvolved.org that cannot now be located on which so-called "timely and accurate data and analyses" on Haiti were posted. The website had chat rooms and mailing lists, and claimed to be promoting efforts to include the Haitian Diaspora into the political process in the island. But the vast majority of Haitians did not have access to electricity and potable water, much less to the Internet, only a privileged few (Leight 2004).

The IRI used the Dominican Republic as a base to organize conferences attended by up to 600 Haitian opposition political leaders. It is not co-incidental therefore that after the neoconservatives seized power in the US presidential elections in 2000, the Dominican Republic was used as the launching pad for the rebellion in February 2002, and the overthrow of Aristide. The US' reward to these cutthroat Haitian politicians and business people was the execution of an economic boycott of Haiti that disrupted Aristide's program of social justice in aid of his poor urban and rural supporters, undermining his public support. The US demanded that Aristide reached an agreement with the opposition Group of 184 before it sends an international force to Haiti to protect the government. The Group of 184 however would accept no

A Hidden Agenda: John McCain and the IRI. Washington. Council on Hemispheric Affairs, June 25; Kozloff, Nikolas. 2008. John McCain: Mr. Big Stick in Latin America. *CounterPunch*, February 19; Leight, Jessica. 2004. The International Republican Institute: Promulgating Democracy of Another Variety. Washington. Council On Hemispheric Affairs, Memorandum to the Press 04.40, July 15.

compromise with Aristide short of his resignation. Indeed, the US led international force arrived in Haiti only after Aristide was overthrown in the thirty-third coup in that country (Leight 2004).

US Forced Caribbean Community to Back Off from Its Principled Stand on Haiti

The overthrow of the democratically elected Aristide government demonstrated in clear terms the influence that the US exerts over the Caribbean countries. In the period right before and after the coup, the Caricom leaders adopted a progressive stance on Haiti, a fellow Caricom member. Caricom advocated very publicly for the maintenance of democracy and the sovereign rights of Haiti. It refused to recognize the junta government led by interim Prime Minister Gerard Latortue that was formed on February 29, 2004, to replace the Aristide government. But following a visit to Haiti by a five-member Caricom foreign minister delegation, led by Barbadian Dame Billie Miller it was recommended that the regional governments return to "full engagement" with the illegal Latortue junta. By reversing their stance, the Caricom leaders chose to ignore the ruthless hounding of the Aristide's political party, and virtual slaughter of persons that supported him.

The Caricom countries were forced to drop their advocacy in the United Nations (UN) and the Organization of American States (OAS), for democracy to prevail in Haiti, and for a UN investigation of the coup. The US and France opposed the investigation, but on the persistence of the Caricom, the OAS passed a resolution, which recognized that "an unconstitutional alteration of the constitutional regime" had taken place in Haiti "that seriously impairs the democratic order in a member state."[22]

Although Caricom promotes regional unity, its members placed their self-interest and political expediency over continuing support for the maintenance of democracy in Haiti. This was the dilemma of Caribbean countries in the light of the new American century doctrine. But the Caricom countries themselves do not have a history of democracy, but one of authoritarianism. Patrick Manning, Prime

[22] Kramer, Kirstin. 2004. Caricom's Action on Haiti: Honor for a Few, Shame for Most. Washington. Council On Hemispheric Affairs, Memorandum to the Press 04.50, August 12, 2004.

Minster of Trinidad observed about the Haitian affair, "What has happened in the past we consider very unfortunate, we don't like it at all. However, we think the time has come to move on" (Kramer 2004).

It is no surprise that Owen Arthur, Prime Minister of Barbados, remained silent on the issue. Barbados played a significant role in facilitating the US invasion of Grenada in 1983. Tom Adams then Prime Minister shut down the Grandly Adams Airport in Barbados to prevent US medical students from leaving Grenada for his Island thus facilitating Washington's excuse to invade Grenada to free the students.

US Neoconservative Terrorist Threat to Democracy in Latin America

The US neoconservative terrorist threat to democracy was not only limited to the Caribbean but was ever present in Latin America. This threat was gravest to countries like Venezuela, Cuba, Guatemala, Columbia, EL Salvador, Nicaragua and Bolivia, among others. The US terrorist activities in these countries deflated any attempt at democracy building in them. This section provides a descriptive analysis of US terrorist activities in those Latin American countries.

The Overthrow and Reinstatement of Hugo Chávez in Venezuela

The threat that US neoconservative new American century doctrine posed to democracy in the Caribbean is further borne out by US subversive activities in Latin America. First, we examine the temporary overthrow of the democratically elected President Hugo Chávez in Venezuela, two days after which he was reinstated by the courageous struggle of ordinary Venezuelans. Petras (2002) observed that Washington was pursuing in Venezuela "a combined civil political-economic destabilization strategy planned to culminate in a military coup,"[23] thereby predicting the coup. The overthrow of Chávez must be understood in the context of the US military-political offensive worldwide that is manifested in Latin America in specific ways. Not only did the US propped up putrefying client regimes, it also destabilized independent countries, pressurized the center-left to move to

[23] Petras, James. 2002. US Offensive in Latin America: Coups, Retreats, and Radicalization. *Monthly Review* (54) 1: 15–32.

the right, and destroyed or isolated budding popular movements that challenge the US Empire and its clients.[24]

President Chávez was ousted from power in a military coup in April 2002. The International Republican Institute, and US State Department and embassy in Venezuela were implicated in conspiring with the Venezuelan military personnel to plan the coup.[25] Otto Reich, described as "the Bush administration's chief dirty-tricks operator for the western hemisphere," met with Pedro Carmona the head coup plotter, and his co-conspirators. Roger Noriega, the then Assistant Secretary of State for Inter-American Affairs, hastily recognized the government formed after the coup (Leight 2004).

There is an abundance of evidence that since 1998 the IRI had been funding so-called "civil society" groups that opposed Chávez. The IRI started to produce newspapers, television, and radio campaigns with anti-Chávez organizations in 1998. The IRI funded visits by anti-Chávez politicians, union leaders, and "civil society" leaders to Washington to meet with US officials. Only a month before the coup there was such a meeting in Washington, amidst widespread rumors that a military uprising was eminent.[26]

The NED, which is the main source of funds of the IRI, simultaneously launched its own initiative in support of anti-Chávez organizations. The NED grants, laundered through the IRI, played a significant role in the anti-Chávez destabilization campaign leading up to the coup. The Confederation of Venezuelan Workers (CTV), a grouping of Chávez arch rivals with historical links to corrupt political parties, he renounced after he won the elections, was a major recipient of such generous NED laundered grants (Leight 2004).

Leonardo Carvajal leader of the Assembly of Educators, which was one of the first groups to organize anti-Chávez demonstrations that led up to the coup, was also a beneficiary of the NED financial support. Carvajal became the education minister in the two-day Carmona coup government. Furthermore, the NED gave financial support to Prodel

---

[24] Petras, James. 2002. US Offensive in Latin America: Coups, Retreats, and Radicalization. *Monthly Review* (54) 1: 15–32.

[25] Leight, Jessica. 2004. The International Republican Institute: Promulgating Democracy of Another Variety. Washington. Council On Hemispheric Affairs, Memorandum to the Press 04.40, July 15.

[26] Leight, Jessica. 2004. The International Republican Institute: Promulgating Democracy of Another Variety. Washington. Council On Hemispheric Affairs, Memorandum to the Press 04.40, July 15.

a group led by prominent Chávez opponent Ignacio Betancourt, a former secretary to the former dictator Carlos Pérez Jiménez, who was directly involved in plotting to overthrow Chávez. The NED directly funded Súmate, an organization devoted to mounting a signature-gathering campaign to present a petition that demanded Chávez's recall.

The NED increased its funding to the IRI programs in Venezuela from $50,000 in 2000 to $399,998 in 2001. This money was used by the IRI to organize "subterfuge 'party building' activities." These activities included a workshop series attended only by opposition candidates, and the funding of Primero Justicia a "vehemently anti-Chávez organization directly linked to the coup." Indeed, "Leopoldo López and Leopoldo Martinez, who was named finance minister in the short-lived coup government," were leaders of Primero Justicia who "signed the Carmona decree during the brief coup that dissolved several of Venezuela's basic democratic institutions," along with "the heads of a number of other NED-funded organizations" (Leight 2004; Hamburger 2008a).[27]

George A. Folsom the neoconservative ideologue and president of the IRI jubilantly welcomed the overthrow of Chávez, declaring that "the Venezuelan people rose up to defend democracy in their country…[and] were provoked into action as a result of systematic repression by the Government of Hugo Chávez." Folsom claimed that the coup's restoration of "genuine democracy" to Venezuela was due to "the bravery of civil society leaders – members of the media, the Church, the nation's educators and school administrators, political party leaders, labor unions and the business sector – who have put their very lives on the line" (Leight 2004; Clement 2005).

The IRI created and partnered the ephemeral Federación Participación Juvenal (FPJ, the Youth Participation Foundation) in Venezuela, about which "a large number of Venezuelan politicians and civil society leaders declared that they had never heard of" (Leight 2004). The IRI, which claimed that the FPJ was in existence in 1998, was forced to concede that it was extant.

The Bush administration kept up the pressure on Chávez after his restoration to power by mass revolt two days after the coup. The US urged Venezuela's neighbors to isolate Chávez, and to voice their

[27] See also Golinger, Eva. 2006. *The Chavez Code: Cracking US Intervention in Venezuela*. Northampton: Olive Branch Press, for more on US intervention in Venezuela to overthrow President Chavez.

concerns regarding press freedom, human rights, and judicial independence in Venezuela. Among Chávez's crimes in the eyes of the Bush administration were his association with leftist groups abroad and Columbian guerrillas, the cancellation of a 35-year military cooperation agreement with the US, and the ordering of four American military instructors out of the country for fomenting unrest.

Reportedly, Venezuela has canceled dozens of routine exchange programs with the United States. The US was displeased with Venezuela's energy ties with China and Iran not only because the US imports 15 percent of its oil from Venezuela but also because Chávez claimed that Iran had the right to pursue atomic energy. In addition, the US believed that Chávez created a popular militia that was projected to reach two million in numbers, and had plans to buy 100,000 AK-47 assault rifles from Russia and fighter jets from Brazil.[28]

The US neoconservatives renewed their efforts to destabilize Chávez in the light of the fact that he was expected to receive another six-year term in the 2006 Venezuelan elections. The Bush administration established a multi-agency taskforce to shape the new confrontational hardline approach towards Venezuela. This meant that the US would strengthen its support for anti-Chávez groups. However, the US did not have influence over Venezuela, which was lush with money due to the high oil prices and did not need loans or aid that the US could use as leverage.[29]

The US did not find willing allies in its policy to isolate Chávez in Latin America, save for the pro-Washington Uribe government in Columbia. Indeed, left-leaning leaders in Ecuador, Brazil, Venezuela, Uruguay, Bolivia and Argentina governed two-thirds of the South American continent. The US neoconservatives had the temerity however to criticize this so-called "pink tide" or "pink revolution" for corrupting democracy in Latin America.[30]

Further Challenges to Democracy in Latin America and the Caricom

The US neoconservatives continued to talk about democratization in the Caribbean and Latin America while their policies restricted

---

[28] Forero, Juan. US Considering Toughening Stance Towards Venezuela. *New York Times International*, April 26, 2005.

[29] Forero, Juan. US Considering Toughening Stance Towards Venezuela. *New York Times International*, April 26, 2005.

[30] USATODAY. 2005. In South America, Democracy Stumbles in Second Act. Op/ED USATODAY.COM Monday April 25.

democracy in the region.[31] The US State Department for example disgracefully clamped down on the freedom of speech and movement of people, by restricting US citizens from traveling to Cuba and blocking Cuban academics from attending conferences in the US. The State Department vetoed visas to sixty-seven Cuban academics, who were going to attend the Latin American Studies Association International Congress in Las Vegas, in 2004.[32] The US authorities resorted to the Immigration and Naturalization Act that "suspend entry…to officials and employees of the Cuban government and members of the Communist Party," to restrict entry for the first time to an entire contingent of Cuban scholars traveling to the US.

The denial of visas to the Cuban scholars was a classic demonstration of the link between US domestic politics and its foreign policy. The strong anti-Castro swing voters in Florida and the American-Venezuelan community in the US were appeased by the neoconservative decision to restrict the freedom of movement of the Cuban academics. The neoconservatives derived the political benefits of their sinister act at the expense of the Cuban scholars when they won Florida in the election in November 2004. Neoconservative ideologues including Roger Noriega, then Assistant Secretary for the Bureau of Western Hemisphere Affairs; John Bolton, then Under-Secretary of State for Non-Proliferation; and Otto Reich, from whom Noriega took over, were all behind the move.[33] The democratic rights of the Cuban scholars were restricted in order to satisfy the political self-interest of the US neoconservatives.

For nearly 45 years US policy was obsessed with isolating Castro by starving the Cuban people through an economic blockade. A similar policy was applied in Iraq, namely the sanctions that did more harm to the Iraqi people than to Sadam Hussein. US isolationist policies against Cuba resurged under the neoconservatives.

---

[31] Petras, James. 2002. US Offensive in Latin America: Coups, Retreats, and Radicalization. *Monthly Review* (54) 1: 15–32.

[32] Gonzalez, Gabriel Espinosa. 2004. Disgracefully, For All of Its Talk about Democratization, the State Department's Ideologues Clamp Down on Open Dialogue. Washington. Council On Hemispheric Affairs, Memorandum to the Press 04.69, October 7.

[33] Gonzalez, Gabriel Espinosa. 2004. Disgracefully, For All of Its Talk about Democratization, the State Department's Ideologues Clamp Down on Open Dialogue. Washington. Council On Hemispheric Affairs, Memorandum to the Press 04.69, October 7.

In Guatemala, Colombia, and El Salvador the US neoconservatives adopted a different strategy to subvert the democratic processes in those countries. Democracy was more apparent than real in these countries, where free elections and political rallies, were accompanied by US supported intimidation and murders.[34] The neoconservatives claimed that there were no overtly authoritarian or military government in Latin America, except Cuba, although US Secretary of State Condoleezza Rice labeled Venezuela as a "negative force" in Latin America. The Guatemalans voted against Efraín Ríos Montt in the presidential election in 2003, in a season of assassinations of political candidates, journalists, and human rights activists. The defeat of Efraín Ríos Montt, Guatemala's murderous military dictator in the early 1980s, was a victory however slender, against undemocratic practices such as "corruption, cronyism, and the sale of justice."[35]

Argentina, Mexico, and Chile took steps to prosecute the official perpetrators of past politically motivated assassinations in these countries. Argentina implemented measures to prosecute retired military personnel involved in political murders and the disappearances of tens of thousands of individuals between 1976 and 1983. A Supreme Court ruled in Mexico that there was no statute of limitation on political disappearances, and President Vicente Fox's opened up the archives of Mexico's secret police. These two developments cleared the way for "investigations into the murders and disappearances of hundreds of leftist dissidents in the country in the 1960s and 70s." General Augusto Pinochet and some of his henchmen were investigated in Chile, and were to stand trial for the crimes committed against the Chilean and other peoples in the 1970s and 1980s.[36]

Despite these developments, politics in the Latin American countries remain bedeviled by political intimidation and murders. In theory, democratic institutions are mushrooming in the region, but the ruling elites are quite comfortable with turning to political repression

---

[34] Green, W. John. 2004. Violence Remains a Viable Option Throughout "Democratic" Latin America. Washington. Council On Hemispheric Affairs, Memorandum to the Press 04.15, March 29, 2004.

[35] Green, W. John. 2004. Violence Remains a Viable Option Throughout "Democratic" Latin America. Washington. Council On Hemispheric Affairs, Memorandum to the Press 04.15, March 29, 2004.

[36] Green, W. John. 2004. Violence Remains a Viable Option Throughout "Democratic" Latin America. Washington. Council On Hemispheric Affairs, Memorandum to the Press 04.15, March 29, 2004.

including assassinations as a political tool directed at reformist and ordinary citizens, to protect their privileged positions. The ruling elites have no qualms about threatening and intimidating "populist movements, politicians, labor activists, journalists, intellectuals, church people, or human rights advocates."[37]

El Salvador dissidents, including ethnic minorities and reformist political parties were overtly abused as a part of the daily conduct of the government.[38] The murder of in excess of 80,000 left dissidents in El Salvador between 1978 and 1991 is crying out for justice. Many of the persons responsible for those systematic killings remained in high positions in public offices, the military and state bureaucracy.

The Guatemalan experience was equally disturbing in terms of the demonstration by former members of the military and paramilitary of their impunity regarding their political crimes. These groups that engaged in murders and other crimes were called the "hidden powers" in Guatemala that worked in conjunction with the state institutions or in parallel but autonomous paths.

A similar type of organization called the "phantom squad" that engaged in extrajudicial murders operated in Guyana. While in Brazil, the police carried out routine "social cleansing" that is the murdering of drug addicts and street children. The "attacks against human rights activists, labor organizers, journalists, indigenous leaders, and forensic scientists engaged in excavating the sites of earlier massacres" in Guatemala continued unabated throughout 2002 and 2003 (Green 2004). The arsenal of the Guatemalan elites included intimidation and death threats, kidnapping, murder, and disappearances.

These tactics are habitually chronic in Colombia that has a long history of politically motivated murders. Columbia's savage repression of the Unión Patriótica, the political wing of the Revolutionary Armed Forces of Colombia (FARC) dates back to the 1980s. The right wing Autodefensas Unidas de Colombia (AUC), led by Carlos Castaño allied with paramilitary bands to carry out some of the most gruesome murders in the countryside of anyone suspected of being remotely sympathetic to the leftist guerrillas in Colombia. In many districts in

---

[37] Green, W. John. 2004. Violence Remains a Viable Option Throughout "Democratic" Latin America. Washington. Council On Hemispheric Affairs, Memorandum to the Press 04.15, March 29, 2004.

[38] Green, W. John. 2004. Violence Remains a Viable Option Throughout "Democratic" Latin America. Washington. Council On Hemispheric Affairs, Memorandum to the Press 04.15, March 29, 2004.

Colombia, the political opposition had ceased to operate out of fear of the rightist paramilitary vigilante bands. Their activities had dampened governmental structures at all levels including the local level where right-wing elements govern municipalities, the national congress, and the presidency. Colombian President Uribe's decision to grant amnesty to the *paras* that were willing to demobilize begged the question of his complicity with the right-wing vigilante groups.

The US State Department in its report entitled *Patterns of Global Terrorism, 2003*, described the FARC established in 1964, as "Latin America's oldest, largest, most capable, and best-equipped insurgency of Marxist origin."[39] The State Department described the FARC's activities as including "Bombings, murder, mortar attacks, narco-trafficking, kidnapping, extortion, hijacking, as well as guerrilla and conventional military action against Colombian political, military, and economic targets."[40] The State Department claimed that the FARC received medical care and political consultation from Cuba. Three members of the Irish Republican Army were arrested for allegedly providing advanced explosive training to the FARC. The State Department classified the FARC as a terrorist organization, so Washington ignored the repression and murder of its leaders, supporters, and sympathizers by the right-wing vigilante groups.

The neoconservatives were not only supportive of political repression and the suppression of democracy in Latin America. Their policies include unilateral intervention in Caribbean and Latin American countries. In three recent cases, Nicaragua, Bolivia, and El Salvador, the US State Department directly intervened in national elections. In each country, the US threatened publicly that there would be economic and political retaliation if leftist candidates Washington did not support succeeded in winning power in free, democratic elections.[41]

Rose Likins, the former US Ambassador to El Salvador threatened that US companies could pull out their investments in the country if the Frente Farabundo Martí para la Liberación Nacional (Farabundo Marti National Liberation Front – FMLN), a former leftist guerrilla

[39] US Department of State. 2004. *Patterns of Global Terrorism, 2003*. Washington.

[40] US Department of State. 2004. *Patterns of Global Terrorism, 2003*. Washington.

[41] Strunk, Chris. 2003. The Bush Administration's Policy of Unilateral Interventions in Latin America. Washington. Council On Hemispheric Affairs, Memorandum to the Press 03.36, June 25, 2003.

group that held the largest bloc of delegates in the country's parliament, won the presidential election in 2004. Likins stated that the election of an FMLN president in El Salvador would damage the country's relations with Washington because of the FMLN's opposition to US interests in the Central American region.

The FMLN opposed the US dominated Central American Free Trade Agreement (CAFTA), which won for the party broad public support, much to the irritation of Washington. The FMLN also rejected dollarization implemented as a dual currency alongside the El Salvadoran colón in 2001, and opposed the privatization of health care. The FMLN popular stance on CAFTA, dollarization, and privatization of health care, caused the party to win 31 seats in the 84 seats National Assembly, while the right wing National Republican Alliance (ARENA) founded by the late death squad leader Roberto D'Aubuisson, and controlling the presidency for the last 15 years won 27, in the legislative and municipal elections in March 2003. ARENA was still able to maintain control of the National Assembly by forming an alliance with the conservative National Conciliation Party (PCN).

The US backed ARENA candidate Elias Antonio "Tony" Saca who succeeded President Francisco Flores Perez as leader of the ARENA won the election over the FMLN's *commandante* Schafik Handal, both of whom could trace their roots to the Palestinian population in Bethlehem in the West Bank. ARENA resorted to a campaign of fear about what might happen if an FMLN leader was elected president.[42] Both Perez and Saca resorted to driving fear in the minds of the Salvadoran population about the so-called dangers of electing an FMLN president.

They terrorized the Salvadoran people by arguing that an FMLN presidency would place the country at "immense risk," and jeopardize and put an end to the protected migration enjoyed by Salvadoran immigrants in the US, and could lead to their possible deportation. The Salvadoran economy depends heavily on foreign investment, and billions of dollars in remittances from Salvadoran immigrants living in the US. Perez argued that an FMLN presidency would put an end to foreign investment in El Salvador, and clamed that he had met with foreign investors who had begun to rethink their investment plans towards the country.

---

[42] Rubin, Joe. 2004. El Salvador: Pay Back. *Frontline*, October 12.

Right-wing propaganda and the attacks on the FMLN became more severe after the so-called "orthodox" gained control of the organization in a leadership struggle. Five moderates in the National Assembly left the party in 2001, and Facundo Guardado, former FMLN presidential candidate was expelled for his support of the dollarization policy championed by ARENA.

US intervened in the democratic process by influencing the outcome of Salvadorian election. The US sought to punish the FMLN because it espoused a Marxist ideology, and waged armed guerilla war against America from 1980 to 1992. Over 70,000 people were murdered in that war mostly at the hands of US-backed security forces and right-wing death squads. Recently the "Salvadoran option" meaning the use of death-squads to murder innocent people that supported or sympathized with guerillas was suggested for Iraq.[43] The Salvadoran regime under President Saca maintained troops in Iraq in support of the US occupation of that country. The neoconservatives got Saca elected, and he paid them back by supporting the US occupation of Iraq.

The US used its "war on terrorism" and "war on drugs" as justification to bully and to interfere in the democratic processes in the Caribbean and Latin American countries. Like it did to the FARC, the US tried publicly to connect the FMLN to terrorism by evoking the activities of the organization during the Salvadorian civil war in the 1980s. The US insinuated that the FMLN was not committed to fighting terrorism and organized crime, and questioned the organization's positions on democracy and the free market. The US criticized the FLMN for its support of liberation movements, and pledged solidarity to Cuba, Vietnam, and China. The US used these so-called intransigencies on the part of the FMLN as a pretext to intervene in the democratic process in El Salvador.

The US had its way until the municipal and legislative elections in El Salvador in January 2009. At those elections

> Salvadorans went to the polls to elect mayors and council members for the country's 262 municipalities as well as 84 deputies for the National Assembly—the unicameral legislature. After a tense day of voting, the FMLN declared itself the "leading political force" in the country after winning the most seats in the National Assembly...result indicate the FMLN has increased its number of deputies by four or five, while

[43] Fuller, Max. 2005. Death-squad Style Massacres For Iraq, "The Salvador Option" Becomes Reality. Montreal. Center for Research on Globalization, June 2.

> ARENA's share of the 84-member legislature has either stayed the same or been slightly reduced. The FMLN will have 37 or 38 seats, while ARENA will have 33 or 34.[44]

Also, Mauricio Funes the FMLN candidate defeated Rodrigo Ávila the ARENA candidate 1,354,000 to 1,284,588 votes, or by 51.32% to 48.68%, to win the Salvadoran presidential elections in March 2009.

The US had employed similar tactics to subvert the democratic process in the Nicaraguan presidential election in November 2001. Daniel Ortega the leader of the Frente Sandinista por Liberación Nacional (FSLN), a guerilla organization that fought against the US-backed Somoza dictatorship, was opposed by the State Department as a presidential candidate in Nicaragua. The US vilified the Sandinistas as having ties to terrorism, and accused the organization of being in close contact with Iraq, Libya, and the FARC guerillas in Colombia. The US argued that Ortega would undermine its global "war on terrorism," despite the fact that Ortega converted to the Christian faith and is now a supporter of the free market ideology. The US believed that Ortega would work with Fidel Castro and Hugo Chávez to support and give resources to terrorist in the Caribbean and Latin American region.

Bolivia was also drawn into the loop by the US State Department as a country in which it must intervene in the democratic process. The US employed similar tactics in the Bolivian presidential election in 2002, as it did in El Salvador and Nicaragua. The political practice of the US neoconservatives is to prevent anyone who opposes Washington's policies, from taking political power in democratic elections. That is indeed the very essence of the new global authoritarianism in the new American century.

Evo Morales, the leader of the "cocaleros," a group of coca farmers that opposed US-backed policies of forced coca eradication in Bolivia as a part of the "war on drugs" in Latin America, fell victim to the new global authoritarianism. Morales' transgression was not only his opposition to forced coca eradication, but also his threat to halt payments on Bolivia's foreign debt, and to nationalize foreign-owned industries. The political propaganda against Morales was quite familiar. His opponents warned that if Morales was elected in defiance of Washington,

---

[44] Committee in Solidarity with the People of El Salvador (CISPES), North American Congress on Latin America (NECLA), Upside Down World. 2009. The 2009 El Salvador Elections: Between Crisis and Change. A Joint Report, January.

aid to the country could be withdrawn. The people responded by voting Morales into office with even more votes than it was estimated he would receive. The US engaged in what Golinger (2007) termed "the silent subversion" of Bolivia.[45]

As opposition leader, Morales successfully led the "cocaleros" and working people in street actions against US supported Bolivian government programs. As many as 1,500 trucks with rotting cargoes were stranded on main roads as working people resorted to blocking roads in a spate of social unrest to force the Caros Mesa government to increase taxes levied on foreign energy companies from 15% to 50% of their sales. "Plans to export the country's gas sparked a wave of deadly protests in October 2003 and resulted in President Mesa's predecessor being forced from office" (Gotkine 2005). President Mesa resigned amidst the protests but the Bolivian Congress did not accept his resignation, which under the constitution meant that he had to remain as President. Mesa decided to call an early election. Meanwhile, Morales called off the social unrest and ended the blockades after the Bolivian Congress decided to raise taxes on profits from gas sales from 18% to 32%, in March 2005.[46]

The Caricom countries experienced US neoconservative bullying that directly threatened their sovereignty and democracy in 2003. President Bush's envoy to the Western Hemisphere Mr. Otto Reich bullied Caricom leaders to silence their public opposition to the US invasion and occupation of Iraq. At a conference in Barbados on April 2, 2003, Reich expressed the US' displeasure with Caricom leaders who made statements opposing the US' decision to invade Iraq without UN approval. Reich threatened the Caribbean Community to "study very carefully not only what it says, but the consequences of what it says."[47] He warned the Caricom leaders that opposition to US policies in Iraq was equivalent to undermining the US' "war on terrorism." This was a

---

[45] Golinger. Eva. 2007. USAID in Bolivia and Venezuela: The Silent Subversion. Vnezuelananalysis.com, September 12.

[46] For more on US-Bolivia relations see Gamarra, Eduardo A. 2007. Bolivia on the Brink. Washington. Council on Foreign Relations. CRS No. 24, February; Mathis. William. 2009. US-Bolivian Relations: Halting an Avalanche. Washington. Council On Hemispheric Affairs, June 15; Joseph, Anita. Direct Intervention: A Call for Bush and Bolivia's Morales to Take a Leap of Faith and Change Presidential Issues into Personal Ones. Washington. Council On Hemispheric Affairs, June 8.

[47] Strunk, Chris. 2003. The Bush Administration's Policy of Unilateral Interventions in Latin America. Washington. Council On Hemispheric Affairs, Memorandum to the Press, 03.36, June 25.

very serious threat to the Caricom because of the neoconservative doctrine that countries that are not supportive of the US are against it, and therefore subject to the wide array of US terrorist tactics as those used in Latin America including military invasion and occupation. Reich's scare tactics against the Caricom leaders was an attempt to stifle the freedom of speech in the region, a vital component of the expression of liberal democracy.

Under the "new American century" doctrine the Caribbean had to brace itself for brazen US military interventions in the region, such as political destabilization, as we saw in Venezuela in 2002, support for domestic insurgents, as in the coup against President Aristide in Haiti, direct military intervention as in the case of Grenada, economic sanctions, etc., against governments that step out of line with US policies. This was indeed the new imperialism, US-led globalization, at its zenith. Democracy was not the real issue, because democratically elected governments were overthrown. Democracy did not matter in the Western Hemisphere, what did was the US national interest as determined by the US neoconservatives.

Conclusion

The Caribbean region began its negotiations of the EPA at a time when the US neoconservative doctrine of the "new American century" was on the rise. This doctrine set the economic and political parameters for the negotiations – market liberalization and US-styled liberal democratization that is political arrangements that supported the maintenance of the American way of life. The US went to great lengths to reign-in the economic and political systems in the Caribbean and Latin America in order to sustain its lifestyle. It engaged in the destabilization and overthrow of democratically elected governments and the establishment of puppet regimes. It subverted the electoral processes in several countries in order to influence the outcome of national and presidential elections. It promulgated the dangerous doctrine that the freedom of the US depends on the freedom of other states, and that countries are either for or against the US.

The transition to the "new American century" doctrine was made possible by the passage of hegemonic power from the UK to the US after World War II that brought the newly independent states in the Caribbean within the US sphere of influence, and the US' victory in the cold war. The Caribbean needs to dig deep, drawing on its rebellious tradition that helped to defeat European colonialism, in order to provide an adequate response to US-led globalization and European bloc imperialism. In order to do this there is need for a clear exposition on what is European bloc imperialism.

CHAPTER THREE

THE ANATOMY OF TWO IMPERIALIST REGIMES

Introduction

This chapter engages in a comparative discussion of US-led globalization and European bloc imperialism. Its purpose is the highlight the similarities and differences of these two modern forms of imperialism in terms of their *modus operandi.* European bloc imperialism was spawned during the decade of US triumphalism that followed the collapse of the former Soviet Union, within the bowels of US-led globalization, among the US' closest allies during the cold war. The US cannot dominate the global all by itself, it has rivals including the European Union, Brazil, Russia, India and China (BRIC), and to a lesser extent the alternatives being experimented with in Latin America. However, US-led globalization, and European bloc imperialism are currently two major forms of co-existing imperialisms in competition for global dominance in the twenty-first century. The former is imperialism of a single country, while the latter is imperialism of a bloc of countries. Historically, Europe has known imperialisms of single countries but never before did Europe operate as an imperialist bloc.

The practice of US-led globalization is well documented in the literature on new forms of imperialisms in the current period, but there is scarcely much written about its major competitor EU bloc imperialism the subject matter of this book. EU bloc imperialism has been off of the radar of the modern debate on imperialisms due largely to the fact that it is a fairly recent phenomenon. It is being manifested through the current negotiations of economic partnership agreements (EPAs) between the European Union and the Africa, Caribbean and Pacific group of countries. The CARIFORUM-EU EPA, the first comprehensive EPA to result from those negotiations is the evidence of the practice of European bloc imperialism.

The principal goal of European bloc imperialism is economic to secure and maintain the supply of raw materials and tropical products from the ACP countries and to acquire and preserve markets in these states for the manufactured goods produced by European transnational companies and sellers of European services. Second, in order to achieve its economic objectives the political mission of European bloc imperialism is to exercise control over the governments and political systems in the ACP countries, through what is known as "good governance." The theory and practice of "good governance" has replaced military conquest and occupation as the legitimate use of force and power by European bloc imperialism to corner markets and raw materials, and to protect them.

Hitherto, military conquest and occupation for economic gain were the main ingredients in the imperialist arrangements by European powers. The US still exercises the military option such as in the case of Iraq, but the enlightened globe frowns on such action. The preferred method of imperialism in the twenty-first century is the enforcement of "good governance" in the countries that provide the raw materials and markets. A third ambition of European bloc imperialism is to restore Europe as a global actor *albeit* as a bloc, and not necessarily as individual countries, with the political, economic and military credentials to face-off with the US or any emerging power, for global dominance. These goals are being achieved through the "global Europe"[1] (Piening 1997: 14) doctrine and the economic partnership agreements.

The EPAs economic and political objectives of free trade and good governance, however, will merely deepen capitalist relations in the ACP countries to the advantage of European bloc imperialism. Analyzed in the context of Prebisch (2008) free trade and good governance or economic and political liberalism do not work in the case of peripheral capitalism. They promote the "concentration of economic power and distributional inequity. And the concentration of economic power brings in its train that of the political power of the advantaged strata" (Prebisch 2008: 32).

The conundrum is that the US in its quest for global dominance under the disguise of neoliberal globalization has helped Europe to further its imperialist goals by strengthening the EU in its position to force the EPAs on the ACP countries, and in the promotion of the principles of "global Europe."[2] When the contents of the first

---

[1] Piening, Christopher. 1997. *Global Europe: The European Union in World Affairs.* Boulder Colorado: Lynne Rienner.

[2] See a similar view in Sbragia, Alberta M., Mark A. Nordenberg, and Jean Monnet. 2008. The European Union and Trade Agreements: Development and Competition in

comprehensive EPA was revealed, it seems that only then that the US came to the full realization of the true implications of its globalization agenda in Europe – the restoration of Europe as its major competitor in the Caribbean and other ACP regions. Thus, the US former trade representative urged the Caribbean countries not to sign the EPA with the EU because it would jeopardize the existing trade agreements (the Caribbean Basin Initiative) between the US and the Caribbean and make it difficult for the US and the Caribbean to enter into future trade deals.

European bloc imperialism emerged in the specific contexts of US imperialism, disguised as globalization, in which the US badgered the EU to liberalize its trade relations, in particular the Lomé Conventions[3] and the EU Banana Regime. However, the EU and the ACP countries separately and collectively resisted US pressure to liberalize their trade agreements. However, the EU caved-in to US pressure and sacrificed the ACP countries at the altar of US-led market liberalization that threatened to bring socio-economic and political mayhem to the ACP states because of the economic loses they will suffer from trade liberalization.

The EU began to liberalize its trade relations with the ACP countries in stages starting with the introduction of the Cotonou Partnership Agreement (CAP) a partial trade liberalization deal. The economic partnership agreement is to follow on the CPA, but with the goal of achieving full trade liberalization between the EU and ACP regions in specific time periods. It is quite clear from the CARIFORUM-EU EPA however, that the EPA goes beyond trade liberalization, and ties the region as a whole into a mercantilist trade arrangement with Europe as an imperialist bloc.

The signature policies of US-led globalization and EU bloc imperialism are structural adjustment and economic partnership agreement, respectively. Caribbean countries are currently co-existing with these two sets of policies that are pulling them in two different directions – towards US-led globalization and EU bloc imperialism.

---

a Post-WTO/Post-NAFTA World. Prepared for delivery at the conference "Europe and the Management of Globalization" Park City, Utah, May 24.

[3] On the origins, history and evolution of the Lomé Conventions see Brown, William. 2002. The European Union and Africa: The Restructuring of North-South Relations. New York: IB Tauris and Co. Ltd.

Structural Adjustment and Economic Partnership Agreement

The objectives of structural adjustment programs and economic partnership agreements reveal the similarities and differences of the imperialist agendas of US-led globalization and European bloc imperialism, respectively. The economic partnership agreements foisted on the ACP countries by the European Union is the means by which the imperialisms of the former European powers are reconstituted into a single imperialism of Europe as a bloc. Structural adjustment however is the handmaiden of US-led globalization as imperialism. The ACP countries, nonetheless, are being forced to transition from structural adjustment programs (SAPs) implemented through neoliberal economic recovery programs (ERPs), to economic partnership agreements. The ACP states are being kicked around by the dominant imperialisms. As one imperialism declines or gains strength vis-à-vis the other, the economic development programs in the ACP countries change accordingly to satisfy the new masters. Many of these countries are now faced with the untenable situation of trying to implement structural adjustment and economic partnership agreements, simultaneously.

Meanwhile, as the ACP countries liberalize their economies in keeping with structural adjustment and/or economic partnership agreements, the US is at the tail end of its globalization experiment. The current financial and economic crises have forced both the US and European bloc imperialist to concede the failures of economic liberalization and to openly promote the very state-interventionist policies that structural adjustment and economic partnership agreements required the ACP countries to dismantle. This vacillation by the two leading imperialist powers with respect to the role of the state in economic development has placed the ACP countries in a state of confusion. As the ACP countries liberalize their economies at the dictates of the US-led globalization and EU-led EPAs, the US and the EU are currently engaged in state-interventionist measures to protect their economies from the global financial and economic crises caused by economic liberalization. The above scenario is the problematic for the ACP countries as they engage European bloc imperialism to assert their political and economic independence.

Objectives of Two Imperialist Regimes – SAPs and EPAs

Economic recovery programs represent the specific measures to achieve the broader goals of structural adjustment. The objective of

SAPs is the same for all countries – economic liberalization, although the ERPs contain country-specific measures by economic sectors. The randomly selected SAP/ERP of Guyana, a Caribbean country on the South American continent, stipulates that its broad goals were to bring about the recovery of the country's economy, and to lay the foundation for its self-sustained growth and development. To improve economic incentives the ERP put into operation exchange rate and domestic pricing policies, exchange and trade restrictions, and measures to enhance the role of the private sector and to promote competition. It targeted for reform the agriculture, forestry, fishery, mining and manufacturing sectors. It sought to reform the central government and public enterprises through fiscal policy and public sector measures, and instituted a public sector investment program (PSIP) to rehabilitate the basic infrastructure with the aim to increase exports and private investment.

Its monetary measures enabled the Central Bank to pursue a credit policy consistent with inflation and balance of payments targets, while its incomes policy retrained wages with the aim to increase employment, protect the external competitiveness of firms, and reduce inflation. The goal was to keep wage increases below the rate of inflation. Finally, its Social Impact Amelioration Program (SIMAP) to help the poor "cushion" the social impact of the policy measures sought to increase pensions, implement school feeding and food for work programs, and put into practice vocational training for young school leavers, unemployed, unskilled and semi-skilled young people (Government of Guyana 1989).

The framers of the ERP envisaged that the multilateral financial institutions – the IMF, the World Bank and the Caribbean Development Bank (CDB); friendly traditional and non-traditional bilateral donor countries; the private sector; and the sale of Guyanese products and exports would finance the program (Government of Guyana 1989). These measures were basically the essence of all SAPs/ERPs implemented in the ACP countries.

The Guyana-ERP has failed to achieve its stated objectives, as the country remains worse-off than it was when the program was first started. Guyana and its Caribbean neighbors that constitute the Caribbean Forum (CARIFORUM), an ACP-EPA region in the Western Hemisphere, have now signed on to the CARIFORUM-EU EPA with the aim to achieve self-sustained growth through sustainable development and good governance.

The EU-EPA is not created for a specific country but for a group of countries or ACP-EPA regions formulated by the EU. Each region has specific issues that the EPA will address but there are overall objectives and principles that are common to all EPAs. The Cotonou Partnership Agreement (CPA) provides the basic objectives and principles of the EPAs, whose overall objectives are the sustainable development of ACP countries, their smooth and gradual integration into the global economy, and the eradication of poverty. The specific objectives of EPAs are the promotion of sustained growth, an increase in the production and supply capacity of the ACP countries, the fostering of the structural transformation of the ACP economies and their diversification, and support for regional integration.

According to the Africa Caribbean and Pacific Group of Countries and European Commission (2003), there are four main principles that underpin the EPAs concerning, the instruments for development, regional integration, the preservation of the acquis, World Trade Organization (WTO) compatibility, and special and differential treatment. The EPAs are considered as development instruments and not ends in themselves that will contribute to the fostering of the smooth and gradual integration of the ACP countries into the global economy, taking into consideration their political choices and development priorities, while promoting their sustainable development and being a factor in the eradication of poverty.[4]

The Africa Caribbean and Pacific Group of Countries and European Commission (2003) posit that as development instruments the EPAs will seek to do certain specific things to directly contribute to the development of the ACP states. These specifics are the enlargement of the markets of the ACP states, and improving the predictability and transparency of their regulatory framework for trade in order to create the conditions for increased investment and the mobilization of private sector initiatives to enhance their supply capacity.[5] It is stated further that the achievement of these specifics would require the EPAs to take into account the particular economic, social, environmental and structural constraints of the ACP countries and regions concerned, and their capacity to adapt their economies to the EPA process.

[4] Africa Caribbean and Pacific Group of Countries and European Commission. 2003. ACP-EC Negotiations Joint Report on the All-ACP – EC Phase of EPA Negotiations. Brussels: ACP/00/118/03 Rev. 1

[5] Africa Caribbean and Pacific Group of Countries and European Commission. 2003. ACP-EC Negotiations Joint Report on the All-ACP – EC Phase of EPA Negotiations. Brussels: ACP/00/118/03 Rev. 1

Furthermore, the view is that the EPAs must also take into account the development policy objectives of the ACP countries and regions, and must be economically and socially sustainable.[6]

The Africa Caribbean and Pacific Group of Countries and European Commission (2003) argue that the regional integration principle means that the EPAs must support regional integration initiatives existing within the ACP and not undermine them. The view is that the EPAs will need to be based on the integration objectives of the regions concerned, and should also contribute to reinforcing regional integration, particularly by contributing to the harmonization of rules, regionally. In this context it is believed that the EPAs' first emphasis should be to consolidate ACP markets, before fostering trade integration with the EC.

This view is farcical however considering the fact that the EU gave an ultimatum to the ACP countries to sign the EPAs by December 2007 or face the penalty of increased tariffs on their exports to the European market. There was no emphasis on consolidating ACP markets before fostering trade integration with the EC, when the EU issued that threat to the ACP countries.

The principle concerning the preservation of acquis means that the EPAs will maintain and improve the current level of preferential market access into the EC for ACP exports. It requires the EPAs to review commodity protocols, in terms of the new trading arrangements, particularly concerning their compatibility with WTO rules, in order to safeguard the benefits derived from current acquis, bearing in mind the special legal status of the Sugar Protocol. Also, the EC will access the situation of non-ACP countries that are not in a position to enter into EPAs, to determine alternative possibilities to provide these countries with a new framework for trade that is equivalent to their existing situation and in conformity with WTO rules.

The WTO compatibility principle means that EPAs must be compatible with prevailing WTO rules, taking into consideration their evolutionary nature, and in particular the context of the Doha Development Agenda. The view is that the ACP countries and the EU must co-operate closely in the context of the WTO to defend the

[6] Africa Caribbean and Pacific Group of Countries and European Commission. 2003. ACP-EC Negotiations Joint Report on the All-ACP – EC Phase of EPA Negotiations. Brussels: ACP/00/118/03 Rev. 1

arrangements reached. Concerning the final principle, the idea is that special and differential treatment should be provided to all ACP States, and in particular to LDCs and vulnerable small, landlocked and island countries.[7]

The ERP and EPA: Imperialist Economic Regimes

The ERPs and EPAs are imperialist regimes because they both have the same effect on the ACP countries, as did European imperialism in the nineteenth century. They secure cheap raw materials in the ACP countries, and create and maintain markets in them for US and European products. The ERPs have resulted in a net transfer of wealth from ACP countries to the US and Europe via the activities of US and European owned multinational corporations in the developing countries.[8] A comparative analysis of the structural adjustment programs and the economic partnership agreements is undertaken in an attempt to elucidate the *modus operandi* of the two leading imperialisms in the ACP countries.

The first point is that the ERP sets out to stimulate economic recovery that would be the foundation for self-sustained growth and development. Its basic goal is economic recovery followed by self-sustained growth and development. In other words, growth and development are not possible without economic recovery. Thus, the economic recovery program is not truly a development program; it is merely a pre-condition for development. In this sense it represents a version of Rostow's (1960) pre-conditions for the take-off into self-sustained growth. Whereas Rostow's (1960) pre-conditions for the "take-off" involves the translation of the insights of modern science into new production methods in industry and agriculture, the economic recovery program is a formulation of policy instruments to contract the public sector's role in the economy, while simultaneously expanding that of the private sector. Measures to reduce production costs to the private sector are critical to this process.

[7] Africa Caribbean and Pacific Group of Countries and European Commission. 2003. ACP-EC Negotiations Joint Report on the All-ACP – EC Phase of EPA Negotiations. Brussels: ACP/00/118/03 Rev. 1.

[8] See Petras, James and Henry Veltmeyer. 2001. *Globalization Unmasked: Imperialism in the 21st Century*. London: Zed Books; and Petras, James and Henry Veltmeyer. 2007. *Multinationals on Trial: Foreign Investment Maters. Aldershot, Hampshire*: Ashgate, on the economic power of multinational corporations and their activities in the developing countries.

On the other hand, the EPAs want generally to bring about the "sustainable development" of the ACP countries, integrate them into the global economy, and eradicate poverty. Specifically, the EPA wishes to cause sustained growth in the ACP countries, expanded output and supply, structurally transform their economies, bring about their economic diversification, and buttress regional integration. Although the EPAs set these general and specific development goals, it claims that it is merely a development instrument to further the achievement of those development objectives and that it is not an end in itself. Like the ERP therefore, the EPA is merely a pre-condition for take-off into sustainable development.

Thus, both US-led globalization as imperialism and EU bloc imperialism promote economic programs in ACP countries and regions they exploit that promise to assist these states to take-off into self-sustained growth and sustainable development. There is an abundance of evidence, which establishes however that after decades of experimentation with US-led globalization the ERPs have failed to achieve their stated objective of self-sustained growth in the ACP countries. It is too early nonetheless to make a definite pronouncement on the performance of the EPA vis-à-vis its stated objective of sustainable development. But, the historical evidence is there to substantiate the argument from the perspective of the ACP countries that hardly anything good will, come of the EPAs judging from the previous economic relations between Europe and the ACP countries. It is an established fact that trade and investment agreements between the rich and poor countries undermine the development of the latter states.[9]

The second point concerns the origins of the two imperialist programs at different historical junctures. The ERP emerged in the historical contexts of the debt crisis and the neoliberal counter-revolution against Keynesianism, socialism, Marxism and special theories of development adumbrated by the so-called pioneers of development, for the developing countries. The ERP represents an ideological pushback against the segmentation of economics into economic development theory characterized by principles and laws good only for the developing countries, and economic theories for the developed countries. The perpetrators of the ideological pushback argue that there is

[9] Jones, Emily. 2007. Signing Away The Future: How Trade and Investment Agreements between Rich and Poor Countries Undermine Development. Oxford: Oxfam Briefing Paper No. 101, March 2007.

only a single economics with universal market laws applicable to all countries regardless of their conditions of development.[10]

Also, the ERP represents an ideological repulsion of state-involvement in the economy, the trademark of Keynesianism, development theory, socialism and Marxism proffered as the solution to the problems of economic development in the poor countries. Those who engaged in the campaign against development theory advocated for the free market approach. They became known as neoliberals or neoconservatives, and their outlook, theories, policies, and programs as neoliberalism or neoconservatism. The ERP is therefore a neoliberal economic reform program, which means basically the extrication of the state as an economic actor, the deregulation of its control over the economy, and its replacement with the private sector and market forces as the main stimuli of economic growth and development. Neoliberalism was emboldened by the end of the cold war, the collapse of Eastern European communism, and the seizure of power in the US by the neoconservatives in 2000.

The ERP emerged within the neoliberal framework championing its trade liberalization agenda. However, the circumstances surrounding the emergence of the EPA were different. The EU maintained preferential trade arrangements with the ACP countries, which were objected to by the US transnational corporations. The US then used as many of the political and economic weapons in its arsenal to force the EU to liberalize those trade arrangements, the end result of which is the EPA, which now threatens to restrict US trade with the ACP regions. The EPA promotes free trade but primarily between the EU and the ACP regions, hence its mercantilist undertone.

The US used the WTO and international financial institutions (IFIs) such as the World Bank and the IMF to implement its globalization objectives, which these latter agencies designed for individual ACP countries. EU bloc imperialism designs and implements economic partnership agreements on its own without using the IFIs and the

---

[10] See for example Lal, Deepak. 1983. *The Poverty of 'Development Economics'*. London: The Institute of Economic Affairs, Hobart Paperback 16; Bauer, Peter Thomas. 1976. *Dissent on Development Revised Edition*. Cambridge, Massachusetts: Harvard University Press; Bauer, Peter Thomas. 1984. *Reality and Rhetoric: Studies in the Economics of Development*. Cambridge, Massachusetts: Harvard University Press; Hirschman, Albert O. 1984. *Getting Ahead Collectively: Grassroots Experiences in Latin America*. Oxford: Pergamon Press; World Bank Group. 1997. World Development Report 1997. Oxford: Oxford University Press.

WTO as its foot soldiers, although it has recourse to these global institutions. EU bloc imperialism is creating new local institutional structures to govern the implementation of the economic partnership agreements. EU bloc imperialism utilizes the very ACP regions on which it forces EPAs, to police themselves through these local institutions with the EU keeping an overall watchful eye. US-led globalization used the IFIs to police the SAPs in the ACP countries.

The SAPs are drawn-up on a country-by-country basis, but its fundamentals remained basically the same, conformation to the neoliberal free trade ideology. EU bloc imperialism however does not necessarily operate on a country-by-country basis its economic partnership agreements are drawn-up on a regional level. EU bloc imperialism formulates EPAs for entire ACP regions it created, but the fundamentals of the EPAs are the same, conforming to the European free trade ideology, regardless of region. However, due to regional opposition to EPAs European bloc imperialism at times enters into interim economic partnership agreements with individual countries.

The EPAs tie the ACP countries indefinitely to mercantilist trade arrangements with the EU giving rise to the phenomenon described by the title of this book – EU bloc imperialism. US-led globalization boxed-in the ACP countries to US-style free trade in which the US multinational corporations are the winners, implicitly binding the ACP countries to trade with the US multinationals. The EPAs explicitly tie-in the ACP countries to trade with the EU, which makes it difficult for other countries to trade with the ACP regions. Finally, the political goal of SAPs is neoliberal democratization in the ACP states as a political conditionality for financial support. The EPAs emphasizes good governance as a condition for participation.

Third, EU bloc imperialism and US-led globalization have a number of other similarities, which are identified as follows. They are premised on the identical theoretical view that no matter what commodity a country produces, it will develop so long as it finds its niche in which to specialize and engages in free trade. They are both economic liberalization programs – structural adjustment (SAPs) under US-led globalization and economic partnership agreement (EPAs) under European bloc imperialism. Both SAPs and EPAs promote democratization and 'good governance' as necessary conditions for their success. They are both externally determined by powerful imperialist forces and foisted on the poor countries. They are both class projects that require the collaboration between the states and the ruling elites in the rich and poor countries. Finally, the sundry population in countries where they are implemented greets them both with opposition, and the ruling elites are prepared to use state violence to snuff-out the resistance.

Fourth, the primary differences between EU bloc imperialism and US-led globalization are as follows. The latter is led by a single imperialist nation-state, the US, while an imperialist bloc, the EU, leads the former. The institutional mechanisms used to push through SAPs and EPAs are different although there is some overlap in terms of the role of global institutions such as the WTO. US-led globalization uses the international financial institutions, namely the World Bank and the International Monetary Fund (IMF) to push SAPs on the poor countries. The EPA is not dependent on those institutions instead it relies on EU agencies, and organizations it creates and has a role in the recipient regions of EPAs. Thus, while the poor countries under structural adjustment have to be on the look out for the IMF and World Bank, those in the EPA regions are under EU control. The EPAs represent a kind of neocolonial control in that local institutions with recourse to the EU have oversight over them – the EPA contractual obligations of the poor countries, but not those of the EU. The EU therefore has the EPA regions policing themselves on behalf of the EU.

The global Europe doctrine that is put into practice through the EPAs provides the general framework in which the EU is prepared to engage the ACP and other countries, for the purposes of achieving its imperialist objectives.

The "Global Europe" Doctrine

The Commission of the European Communities (EC) formulated the "global Europe" doctrine, which provides the rationale for European bloc imperialism. In essence "global Europe" is a strategy for Europe's domination of the globe. Europe will achieve this goal by maintaining its competitiveness in global markets, creating the opportunities for European companies to operate freely abroad through targeting the regulatory frameworks in other countries, and by building strong European companies through creating a more business-friendly environment in Europe (Seattle Brussels Network 2006). This strategy is the foundation of European bloc imperialism. The EU-EPAs target the overall regulatory environment in the ACP regions, to set them to benefit EU companies, and to generate more wealth and increase employment in Europe.

The "global Europe" strategy is intended to serve European corporations operating both worldwide and in the EU. Moving beyond the World Trade Organization (WTO), the "global Europe" trade policy provides the broad outline of the EU's framework for bilateral free trade agreements with major emerging economies in order to secure new and profitable markets for EU companies.[11] This framework advocates stronger intellectual property rights and reduced non-tariff barriers in its trading partners and for business friendly reforms in Europe and abroad. The EU is pursuing "an aggressive 'external competitiveness' strategy" to ensure that competitive European companies with the support of appropriate EU policies will be able to gain access to and operate securely in world markets.

Furthermore, according to the Seattle to Brussels Network (2006) the EU is taking a more "activist" stance in dealing with its trade partners. It initiates bilateral trade agreements, and forces prior consultation with businesses in the design of new regulations. It promotes private access to dispute settlement for EU companies, restricts access to government procurement contracts in the EU for countries that do not reciprocate, and encourages full parity in bilateral negotiations. The "global Europe" strategy seeks to expunge all barriers to trade, which obstruct the activities of EU companies and to ensure that the EU's agenda at home and abroad make certain that all regulations only have minimal distortion of trade.

The most important strategy employed by European bloc imperialism is the breaking down of the regulatory environment in other countries. This gives the EU greater leverage in its external relations with the ACP countries. Sanitary and Phytosanitary (SPS) Measures and the Agreement on Technical Barriers to Trade (TBT) agreements, regulations on services, public procurement, intellectual property rights (IPR), investment, and competition policy regimes of third countries are all part of the EU's arsenal to break down the regulation environment in the ACP countries to give European corporations the upperhand in trade with these former colonies. The "global Europe" strategy

[11] European Commission Directorate-General for Trade. 2006. Global Europe: Competing in the World. Brussels: Ref. 318/06. Commission of the European Communities. 2006. *Annex to the* Communication from the Commission to the Council, the European Parliament, the European Economic and Social Committee and the Committee for the Regions, Global Europe: Competing in the World, A Contribution to the EU's Growth and Jobs Strategy. Brussels.

is founded on more competition, flexibility, and deregulation, and the dismantling of the European social model.[12]

The European bloc imperialist "global Europe" approach is fostering a new generation of bilateral agreements. The EU identifies a number of criteria as the bases to select target countries for bilateral agreements. The most important criteria are

> market potential (the size of the market and its growth and profit prospects), the level of protection against EU export interests, and the number of bilateral agreements countries already have with other trading partners (establishing privileged relations which shut out the EU and establishing a common regulatory regime that is not compatible with that of the EU). These steps are followed by: access to resources; the balance between offensive and defensive interests; and the effect on the multilateral system (Seattle to Brussels Network 2006: 174–175).[13]

On the bases of these criteria the EC has identified the ASEAN group, South Korea and Mercosur (Argentina, Brazil, Paraguay, Uruguay, Venezuela), along with India, Russia and the Gulf Cooperation Council as its priority targets for bilateral agreements. The EU has patched its differences with Mercosur over agriculture, industrial goods, investment and services, and resumed FTA negotiations with that Latin American trade area suspended since 2005. Also, the EU is seeking economic partnership agreements with India. However, the EU regards China at one and the same time as a threat, an opportunity and a prospective global partner.[14]

The EU's new bilateral trade agreements with these countries and areas will secure market access for European companies for basically all trade in goods and services, and seeks full parity with what other

[12] Seattle to Brussels Network. 2006. The New 'Global Europe' Strategy of the EU: Serving Corporations Worldwide and at Home. In *Budgeting for the Future: Building another Europe European Economic Policies from a Civil Society Perspective*, edited by Maisano, Teresa and Tommaso Rondinella 173–179. Amsterdam, The Netherlands: Transnational Institute.

[13] Seattle to Brussels Network. 2006. The New 'Global Europe' Strategy of the EU: Serving Corporations Worldwide and at Home. In *Budgeting for the Future: Building another Europe European Economic Policies from a Civil Society Perspective*, edited by Maisano, Teresa and Tommaso Rondinella 173–179. Amsterdam, The Netherlands: Transnational Institute.

[14] Seattle to Brussels Network. 2006. The New 'Global Europe' Strategy of the EU: Serving Corporations Worldwide and at Home. In *Budgeting for the Future: Building another Europe European Economic Policies from a Civil Society Perspective*, edited by Maisano, Teresa and Tommaso Rondinella 173–179. Amsterdam, The Netherlands: Transnational Institute.

countries have obtained in their bilateral agreements with other trade partners. Besides this, the EU's new bilateral agreements tackle non-trade barriers and seek to bring about the convergence of regulatory frameworks. In addition to focusing on matters concerning sanitary and phytosanitary measures, technical barriers to trade, and intellectual property rights, the new bilateral agreements seek to expand new frontiers by recognizing trade barriers in certain measures, and how they are introduced, especially if this is done without prior consultation with the EU. Thus, if a country wants to change its business and trade rules it must do so in consultation with the EU. The EU therefore insists on discipline, dispute avoidance mechanisms, early warning procedures, exchange of information and the possibility to comment on the formation of trade rules of its partners, stronger monitoring, and enforcement in its new bilateral agreements.

The new bilateral agreements also forces countries to negotiate procurement agreements by threatening to reduce their access to European markets if they do not have reciprocal open public procurement markets. Furthermore, the EU's verification mechanism ensures that its trading partners share the same level of ambition before they commence trade negotiations. This is to avoid the risk of stalled negotiations due to a mismatch of expectations.

Global Europe Versus US-Led Globalization

Global Europe is a European bloc imperialist world order that challenges a US-led globalization world order. Hettne (2003: 11–12) summarizes the differences between these two imperialist world orders, termed the "European model world order" and "Pax Americana," identified in the recent debates on regional blocs and globalization. According to Hettne (2003) there are three principal differences between the two models. The first is that the EU embraces the sanctity of international institutions, and enthusiastically supports inter-regionalism, but that the US does not share a similar position. The US prefers to engage in bilateralism in its external relations. For example, NAFTA is the result of the US wanting to complement its bilateral trade agreement with Canada through a similar agreement with Mexico. The EU prefers long-term "multidimensional, horizontal, institutional arrangements, whereas the USA prefers more temporary 'coalitions of the willing' under its own leadership and established for specific purposes" (Hettne 2003: 11).

The second major difference concerns the contrasting political culture characterized by the "US religious approach to foreign policy," and the "rationalist and secular" style employed by the EU. "Thus the USA tends to see political conflict as a struggle between good and evil, or God and the Devil. Europe has a tradition of making a political analysis of conflict, pragmatically looking for compromises" (Hettne 2003: 12).

Third, they have contrasting ideas in political philosophy in which the "Europeans (from Venus) prefer to live in the ideal world of 'permanent peace' of Immanuel Kant, which is the natural choice of the weak, whereas the Americans (from Mars) live in the real world of Thomas Hobbes" (Hettne 203: 12). Hettne (2003) pointed out however that realism "as is made clear from the skepticism shown by the Kissinger-Brzezinski realist school in international analysis, is not the same as trigger-happiness. On the contrary, realism implies a realistic assessment of what can be achieved by war, in comparison with the costs and consequences of war" (Hettne 2003: 12). While Europe lacked a single authoritative voice on its foreign policy doctrine of inter-regionalism, the US has such a person in its President, like George Bush who authoritatively presided over his doctrine of pre-emptive warfare.

CHAPTER FOUR

THE RISE OF EUROPEAN AND ACP BLOCS AND US HEGEMONY

Introduction

The main purpose of this chapter is to present the case in support of the proposition that US-led globalization paved the way for the emergence of EU bloc imperialism. It is divided into three parts, which first engages in a discussion of some relevant theoretical issues concerning regional blocs, second, assesses the rise of the European and ACP blocs, and third, analyses the exercise of US hegemony over the European Union. The theoretical discussion summarizes key issues in the debate on the rise of regional blocs in the current period of the globalization of the capitalist system of production and market exchange. Also, it provides a critique of these theories and advances the idea about alternative regional blocs as their counterpoint.

Second, it focuses on the coming to fruition of the EU, followed by a discussion on the emergence of the ACP Group of States. Third, it analyses the manner in which the US exercised its hegemony over the EU. The focus here is two-fold; first it scrutinizes the power-struggle between the US and the EU over the EU banana regime. Second, it dissects the class nature of the US-EU power struggle by providing evidence of the command that the owners of the US banana multinational corporations exert over US trade policy. Also, it details the manner in which the US banana multinationals forced-opened the EU banana market to bananas produced in Latin America. The main questions are: Why did the EU and ACP Group of States emerged as blocs? How did the US-led globalization prepared the ground for the emergence of its rival, EU bloc imperialism?

It takes the position that the actions taken by US banana multinationals and ruling elites to force open the European Union's banana market to bananas grown in Latin America, "dollar bananas," played a significant role in the emergence of European bloc imperialism. Because of these actions, the EU was forced to liberalize the Lomé Conventions, and the economic partnership agreement the conduit of EU bloc imperialism, is the end produce of that process.

Some Theoretical Considerations

Regional Blocs

The literature on regional blocs or regionalism in the current debate on globalization has never come to terms with the phenomenon of a hegemonic country paving the way for a regional bloc to become a bloc imperialist entity. In that literature regionalism and not globalization, is regarded as the fitting way to describe the changing activities of the state and corporate structures, globally. Regionalism is seen to be either compatible with neoliberal globalization or in competition with it. Europe, the Americas and East Asia are regarded as the major regional blocs characterized by the European Union, the North American Free Trade Agreement (NAFTA) and the proposed Free Trade Area of the Americas (FTAA), and the Association of South East Asian Nations (ASEAN) plus three China, Japan and South Korea. Contemporary capitalism is described as regional rather than global due primarily to the "strong regional biases to trade and investment flows as well as on the regional supranational political structures, which have been put in place" (Bowles 2008: 27).

According to Bowes (2008), there is considerable difference in the way regionalism at varying stages of development is occurring around the world meaning that it is not a homogenous phenomenon and that it may or may not be accompanied by neoliberalism. While each region has its own political dynamic, regionalism has a variety of purposes, and there is no common agreement about its relationship with globalization, since regional blocs are regarded as either "stumbling blocs" or "building blocs" for the global economy (Bowles p. 29). The "stumbling bloc" view is that the EU or the NAFTA for example, could lead to a return to the insularity of the imperialist trading blocs of the 1930s, while the "building bloc" perspective is that regionalism promotes greater "openness" and global integration. In this latter case regions are central to the dynamics of neoliberal globalization, hence regionalism is a neoliberal phenomenon.

Langenhove and Costea (2005) identified three generations of regionalism the first focusing on trade and economic integration, the second referred to as "new regionalism" that broadened integration to internal policies and regulations, and the third that emphasizes the role of regions as global actors. In their view the third generation of regionalism could lead to a new regional world order that is best described as neo-Westphalian and not post-Westphalian. This means that regionalism does not transcend the nation-state idea but extends it to the regional level. The third generation of regionalism in their view could lead to a rethinking of multilateralism along the lines of "multiregionalism" as suggested by Hettne (2003).

Alternative Regional Unions

The problem with the three regionalisms theory summarized above is that it reinforces the status quo of global domination of the weak by the strong. It merely envisions the transmutation of the nation-states into regions that maintain the international division of labor in which the poor regions will continue as the suppliers of raw materials and the rich regions as the producers of finished products, and all of the dynamics associated with that international political economy reality. The poor countries need to form alternative regional unions such as the Bolivarian Alternative for the Americas (ALBA) and Petrocaribe in which Latin American and Caribbean countries come together to pursue their socio-economic development. These regional unions challenge development theorists and practitioners to find alternatives to development theory that focus primarily on progress in the capitalist nation-state.

The theoretical differences between the three regionalisms theory and alternative regional unions such as the ALBA and Petrocaribe are as follows. First, the idea of regions as global actors suggests regions that portray characteristics as a single nation-state – single economy, currency, parliament, flag, military apparatus, judicial system, free movement of people and free trade in goods and services, common foreign policy, single constitution, etc. The alternative regional unions such as the ALBA and Petrocaribe do not have to take on the formalities of nation-states, their members may just have a commitment to help each other and proceed to do so on the basis of mutual respect. It is a deliberately political process in which member-states seek to redistribute wealth and political power to counteract US-led globalization and European bloc imperialism.

Second, the nation-state and regions must accumulate wealth to develop, but they are faced with the same problem concerning the distribution of wealth and political power among the economic classes within them. The main goal of alternative regional unions such as the ALBA and Petrocaribe is to redistribute the wealth accumulated in the region and to reverse the imbalance in the political power structure bringing working people into the decision-making processes. Thus, the distribution problem in these alternative regional unions is tackled head on in the sense that the redistribution of wealth and power is their very foundation. The alternative regional union comes into existence for the explicit purpose to redistribute wealth so its institutional structures and instruments are explicitly geared towards that goal.

The sharing of the wealth among nation-states within the alternative regional union is therefore a different proposition to that found in international development theory. The latter seeks to redistribute wealth among capitalist nations in order to develop the poorer countries within the capitalist system. However, whereas the world capitalist system is characterized by competitive realist states, the nation-states in the alternative regional union such as the ALBA and Petrocaribe do not operate on that basis of competition against each other.

Third, powerful capitalist nation-states form regional blocs with a view to further their imperialist ambitions to domination as collectives rather than as individual nation-states. This is a situation of imperialist domination by regional blocs as against the imperialist domination by a single nation-state. The regional bloc reinforces the domination by powerful nation-states of weaker ones. This regional bloc phenomenon is described as bloc imperialism. In this situation, imperialism is manifested in the foisting of socio-economic programs spearheaded by powerful regional blocs on the rest of the world. The best examples of these socio-economic programs are structural adjustment spearheaded by US-led globalization and the economic partnership agreements lead by the EU. Alternative regional unions such as the ALBA nonetheless are anti-imperialist by their very nature. They are founded on the need to find alternatives to neoliberal globalization and European bloc imperialism.

Fourth, the alternative regional unions raise the possibility for the dismantling of nation-states. This should not be confused with the false idea peddled in neoliberal theory that states are losing their sovereignty to the transnational corporations (TNCs) and international financial institutions (IFIs). The rich states control the transnational corporations and international financial institutions, as well as regional blocs such as the EU and the NAFTA. The transnational corporations and financial agencies have a national basis, they operate in nation-states and fall under the domination of the ruling classes in nation-states – thus the nation-state is not disappearing but is strengthening under neoliberalism (Petras and Veltmeyer 2001).

Also, the dismantling of the nation-state through alternative regional unions is not to be understood in the same sense as the environmentalist argument about post-development. Post-development which seeks a form of development outside of the realm of the nation-state does not tell us much about the alternative social organization that it seeks. The alternative regional unions however raise the possibility for their member-states to disregard amongst themselves their national borders, a key ingredient for the existence of nation-states.

Furthermore, the transformation of the nation-state is not a theory of economic integration in the sense proposed by neoclassical theorists as beneficial to economies. Whereas neoclassical theory is about deepening capitalist economic integration, which concentrates wealth and political power in the hands of the few, the alternative regional union seeks to redistribute wealth and power in the favor of working people. But, although national-borders may disappear amongst its member-states the alternative regional unions will have to maintain a sense of self-defense in a realist international political economy.

The alternative regional union refers to the conscious and systematic creation of alternative forms of socio-economic and political spaces that do not correspond to actually existing nation-states, for the purposes of transforming the lives of the people in it and based on a non-capitalist approach to capital accumulation and redistribution of wealth and political power. Eventually, the countries within these spaces would have no need for individual political borders, although they may initially maintain their nation-state identity.

The EU Comes to Fruition[1]

World War II dismantled individual European colonial empires, and catapulted the US and the former USSR to the leadership of the so-called capitalist "free world" and socialist/communist world, respectively. These two worlds became known as the Western and Eastern blocs ideologically distinguished and each with its own political and economic organizations. Within this post-World War II scenario Europe began to take action to form itself into a European bloc.

Winston Churchill called for the building of a United States of Europe in 1946, but the first pan-European organization was the

[1] Dent, Christopher M. 1997. *The European Economy: The Global Context*. London: Routledge.

Council of Europe launched in 1949. The French government then proposed that Europe formed the European Coal and Steel Community (ECSC),[2] to integrate its coal and steel industries. Thereafter, there was a steady push towards the establishment of what became known as the European Union.

The Treaty of Rome in 1957 created the European Economic Community (EEC) and the European Atomic Energy Community (EURATOM), and the Merger Treaty of 1967 brought together the three separate communities – ECSC, EEC and EURATOM, into a single body the European Communities (EC).[3] Thereafter, the EC expanded to incorporate more European states, and since the 1990s a number of former Eastern bloc countries have become its members. The EC had expanded to 25 member-states, with a population of 456 million on 4104 thousand km, in 2004. The EU was established by the Treaty of Maastricht in 1992 and came into effect in 1993 alongside the EC. There is a European Parliament elected by universal suffrage, a European Flag, a European currency the Euro, a European Central Bank, and moves towards a common European foreign policy in what is now knows as "global Europe." The stated reasons for the initial actions that led to the emergence of the EU had to do with the curtailment of Germany, the maintenance of peace in Europe, and the control of coal and steel the then main elements war weaponry.

The unification of Europe however constitutes more of a challenge to US global hegemony and the restoration of Europe as a global imperialist force not as single states but as a bloc. The EU has even incorporated states that were in the former Eastern European bloc. Europe is therefore leading the way in the dismantling of individual nation-states in favor of a larger bloc that would become something other than a nation-state. An entity that behaves like, and with all of the trappings of a nation-state but which is not in itself, a nation-state. Presently, we call it a bloc because its composition is that of nation-states. However it will no longer be a bloc after the complete political and economic unification of Europe – it will become something yet unnamed in political economy theory. We are witnessing in Europe the transition

[2] The ECSC was created by France, Italy, Belgium, Netherlands, Luxembourg, and West Germany in 1952 and made possible by the Treaty of Paris in 1951.

[3] Europa. The History of the European Union, http://europa.eu/abc/history/1945-959/index_en.htm

from nation-states to a yet undetermined form of social, political and economic organization.

The ACP Group of States

World War II broke-up European colonialist empires, which brought into existence a number of newly independent nation-states in Africa, Asia and the Caribbean in search of economic, social and political development. Development became a national goal and subject for study in the newly independent nation-states modeled on the cold war ideological framework of socialism/communism or capitalism that ended in the 1990s. The newly independent nation-states began to forge their unity at the Africa-Asia Bandung Conference in 1955, an important signpost in the development of the non-aligned movement (NAM). The principal aims of the Bandung Conference were to promote Africa-Asia economic and cultural cooperation and to oppose colonialism and neocolonialism by the US, the USSR, or any other imperialist nation.

Participating countries at the Bandung Conference indicated their intentions not to become involved in the cold war and declared their objectives to promote world peace and cooperation based on five basic principles. These principles were mutual respect for each other's territorial integrity and sovereignty; mutual non-aggression; mutual non-interference in domestic affairs; equality and mutual benefit; and peaceful co-existence.[4] These very principles became the basis for the NAM that held its first official heads of state summit in Belgrade, Yugoslavia in September 1961.

The Havana Declaration of the NAM in 1979[5] stated that the organization's purpose is to ensure the national independence, sovereignty, territorial integrity and security of non-aligned countries in their struggle against imperialism, colonialism, neo-colonialism, racism, Zionism, and all forms of foreign aggression, occupation, domination, interference or hegemony as well as against great power and bloc politics. The non-aligned states represent nearly two-thirds of the

---

[4] Köchler, Hans, ed., 1982. *The Principles of Non-alignment VII*. Vienna and London: International Progress Organization and Third World Centre.

[5] Final Declaration of the Conference of Heads of State or Government of Non-Aligned Countries 3–9 September 1979, Havana, Cuba.

United Nations' members and comprise 55 percent of the world population, predominantly in developing countries.

In their development quest during the 1970s, the non-aligned states put forward several proposals through the United Nations Conference on Trade and Development (UNCTAD) for the establishment of a new international economic order (NIEO) to counter the international division of labor that kept them at the bottom of the development ladder. The UN General Assembly adopted the Declaration for the Establishment of a New International Economic Order in 1974. The NIEO pursued an agenda that promoted talks – known as the North-South Dialogue, between the rich and poor countries to restructure the world-economy such that the non-aligned states would have greater participation and derive more benefits from their involvement in the international capitalist system. These countries sought to promote their economic development interests by seeking inter alia the implementation of international measures to improve their terms of trade, increase the development assistance they received, and reduce tariffs by the developed countries. In essence, the NIEO sought to revise the international economic system to bring more support to the developing states, by replacing the Bretton Woods' system that essentially benefits the US and European states that created and continue to dominate it.

The main tenets of the NIEO included the right of poor countries to regulate and control the activities of multinational corporations operating within their territory. In addition, the poor countries demanded that they be freed to nationalize or expropriate foreign-owned companies, and asserted their right to form associations of primary commodities producers similar to the Organization of Petroleum Exporting Countries (OPEC). In recognition of this right, the NIEO required all other states to refrain from any punitive economic, military, or political measures to curb its implementation. The NIEO also sought to promote a stable and equitable international trade system, based on remunerative prices for raw materials, and generalized tariff preferences that were non-reciprocal and non-discriminatory. It also favored technology transfer to the poor countries and the provision by the rich states of economic and technical assistance to the poor countries without any strings attached.[6]

---

[6] Hudson, Michael. 2005. *Global Fracture: The New International Economic Order*, 2nd edition. London: Pluto Press.

Two years after the Belgrade Conference, the Association of African and Malagasy States (AAMS) and the European Economic Community (EEC) entered into the Yaoundé[7] Convention 1 in 1963, and a subsequent one Yaoundé 2, in 1969, which ended in 1975. The Yaoundé Conventions created the avenue for cooperation between the signatory countries – Germany, Belgium, France, Italy, Luxembourg and Holland with their Overseas Countries and Territories (OCTs), i.e. essentially the West and Central African countries with ties to France. It allowed the African and Malagasy States members to export their manufactured goods duty free into the EEC but with much less preference for exports of agricultural products that had the potential to undermine the Common Agricultural Policy (CAP) of high food prices that protected EEC farmers. In return, for EEC preferential treatment for their limited industrial exports the AASM countries would accept comparable exports from EEC countries.

The accession of Britain to the EEC in 1973 gave the UK's numerous Commonwealth territories greater access to the Yaoundé Conventions. It paved the way for the extension of the Europe-Africa cooperation to the Commonwealth countries, whether African, Caribbean, or Pacific. This expansion transformed the economic relationship between Europe and the ACP countries as the Lomé Conventions replaced the Yaoundé Conventions in 1975. Lomé I, however, while including Britain's African territories in preferential arrangements with the EEC, excluded Asian countries such as India, Pakistan, Malaysia, Singapore, Hong Kong, and Indonesia. Lomé I covered 46 African, Caribbean and Pacific countries and nine EEC states, but by 1995, there were 70 ACP countries and 15 EC states.

The ACP Group of states was created by the Georgetown Agreement in 1975, the Group's fundamental charter, which was signed at the time that Lomé I came into force, laying down the rules for cooperation between the countries of the three continents, the main link being shared aid from the European Community.[8] The ACP Group consists of 79 Member-States – 48 countries from Sub-Saharan Africa, 16 from the Caribbean and 15 from the Pacific, all of whom excepting Cuba are signatories to the Cotonou Agreement, which binds them to the EU.

[7] Yaoundé is the capital of Cameroun.

[8] http://www.acp.int/en/archives/ACP_GROUP_en.html

Evolution of Europe ACP Partnership

Year	Event	No. of ACP Countries	No of European Countries
1957	Association System		
1963	Yaoundé I	18	6
1969	Yaoundé II	18	6
1975	Lomé I	46	9
1980	Lomé II	58	9
1985	Lomé III	65	10
1990	Lomé IV	68	12
1995	Lomé IV bis (1995–2000)	70	15
2000	Cotonou Agreement	77	15

Source: Dominique David: 40 Years of Europe-ACP Relationship, *The Courier* – September 2000 – Special Issue – Cotonou Agreement, p. 12.

The main objectives of the ACP Group are sustainable development of its Member-States and their gradual integration into the global economy, which entails making poverty reduction a matter of priority and establishing a new, fairer, and more equitable world order. Three other objective are "coordination of the activities of the ACP Group in the framework of the implementation of ACP-EC Partnership Agreements; consolidation of unity and solidarity among ACP States, as well as understanding among their peoples; and establishment and consolidation of peace and stability in a free and democratic society."[9]

In a real sense, Europe occupied the driver's seat in the formation of the ACP group of states. At the same time that Europe transferred hegemonic power to the US, including placing its former colonies under the US sphere of influence, it took steps that would lead to the resurgence of Europe as an imperialist bloc, rather than as individual countries, which would exercise control in the future over its former colonies. How did this happen?

Europe began almost immediately after World War II, the gradual process to establish the EU while engaging its Overseas Countries and Territories in an economic agreement. As the unity movement in Europe expanded to embrace more European countries, so did the

[9] http://www.acp.int/en/archives/ACP_GROUP_en.html

economic agreements to include the Overseas Countries and Territories of the newly joining members.

The ACP is merely the institutional agency that coordinates and represents the issues on the side of the Overseas Countries and Territories, in their agreements with the EU. Thus, when US-led globalization presented the opportunity for Europe to re-assert itself as an imperialist bloc, it is doing so through the economic partnership agreements with its former colonies. The EPAs will not only undermine US relations with the former European colonies, it will return them under Europe's imperialist control, indefinitely. However, Europe is re-emerging as a bloc imperialist power simultaneously that up-and-coming states such as China, Brazil, India, South Africa, Mexico, and Argentina lurk to varying degrees in the wings of global power, and are poised to become the nemesis to the European bloc imperialist designs of "global Europe." Furthermore, within the ACP Group, there are economic and political integration movements, such as Africa Union, the Economic Community of West African States (ECOWAS), the South African Development Community (SADEC), the Caribbean Community (Caricom) and the Caribbean Single Market Economy (CSME) that have the potential to act as buffers to European bloc imperialism.

US Hegemony Over the European Union

In this section, it will be observed that the evidence that the US-led globalization played an important role in the emergence of European bloc imperialism through the implementation of the economic partnership agreements is supplied by the US' successful struggle to force the EU to liberalize the Lomé Conventions. It presents a brief background to the EU-US power struggle, before undertaking an examination of some of the key events and processes concerning the open confrontation over the EU banana regime. It identifies some of the key activities of the dominant economic class forces in the US banana industry that influenced the US state to formulate its trade policy and take action in their class interest against the EU. Finally, there is an analysis of the process by which these corporations were able to force open the EU banana market to bananas produced in Latin America on the terms of the corporations, albeit not fully.

These actions, as will be shown in the following chapter, stimulated the EU's actions to gradually liberalize the Lomé Conventions through the formation and implementation of the Cotonou Agreement, followed by the EPAs. It is argued, however that in reality, the Cotonou Agreement and the EPAs represent a European bloc imperialist class project, a modern-day re-colonization the ACP states. They engage the emerging economies in the developing world in a "global Europe" imperialist strategy, and rival the US imperialism in the current period. This is all part of the aspiration of European bloc imperialism to establish fortress "global Europe" in the 21st century.

Background to US-EU Power Struggle

How did it transpire that a "banana war"[10] emerged between US capital as the adversary of the EU banana regime and the EU? In 1968, the United Nations Conference on Trade and Development (UNCTAD), an agency dominated by the former USSR and developing countries,[11] recommended that the industrialized states installed a "Generalized System of Tariff Preferences" (GSP) to grant preferential access to their markets to products from the developing countries. The General Agreement on Tariff and Trade (GATT) instituted a "waver" in 1971 that essentially allowed the industrialized countries to install the GSP within the then system of international capitalism.

The GATT rules, originally adopted for a ten-year period, became renewed indefinitely, in 1979. The implementation of the GSP nonetheless violated the GATT's Most Favored Nations (MFN) rule, an arrangement whereby one country confers specific trade advantages on another such as reduced tariffs on imported goods in order to increase its trade with that country. The World Trade Organization (WTO) that now enforces the MFN trade arrangement has agreements to the effect that as trading partners none of its members should normally discriminate against each other, and that if any member-country

[10] There are several books with the title banana wars. For example Langley, Lester D. 1983. *The Banana Wars: United States Intervention in the Caribbean, 1898–1934.* Lexington, KY: University Press of Kentucky. This book however, is not about the subject under discussion here; it is really an account of US military history told through US interventions in the Caribbean Basin. Josling, Timothy E. and Timothy G. Taylor, eds., 2003. *Banana Wars: The Anatomy of a Trade Dispute.* Cambridge, MA.: CABI Publishing; Striffler, Steve and Mark Moberg, eds., 2003. *Banana Wars: Power, Production and History in the Americas.* Durham, NC: Duke University Press.

[11] The US subsequently withdrew its financial support from UNCTAD because it could not get its way in the organization. In a sense therefore, the US struggle to liberalize the Lomé Convention is an attempt to settle an old score.

grants another a special favor it must also do the same for all other WTO members.

The GSP scheme implemented under the GATT granted preferential tariffs to all developing countries for a variety of products. With the evolution of the GATT into the WTO in 1995, any follow-up agreement to Lomé IV required either an extension of the "waiver" or had to be in conformity with WTO rules. This meant that the industrialized countries would have to end the preferential treatment of ACP goods in European markets, and the introduction of full reciprocity in future trade agreements.

Lomé I in 1975 gave a key function to the state in that it ascribes a central economic role for government through preferential trade arrangements. The Washington Consensus that drove US-led globalization from the 1980s is founded on neoliberal economic liberalization and democratization principles as preconditions for poor countries to attain economic and social development. The Lomé Conventions and the Washington Consensus represent therefore, incompatible ideological positions – the former based on an interventionist state that plays a greater role in economic development, and the latter anti-state interventionist and founded on neoliberal "free market" fundamentalist ideology.[12]

The principal actors in the drama that unfolded to transform the Lomé Conventions on the basis of the Washington Consensus, involved the US state representing the US banana multinationals and under the pretext of acting for a group of Latin American countries, the EU, and the ACP countries. The Lomé Conventions allowed the EU to maintain a great deal of influence and control over the ACP group of states. The Washington Consensus would seek to diminish that influence and transfer even more power to the US economic classes, in control of the transnational corporations, over the economic and political affairs of the ACP countries.

The US and the EU have been sparring with each other over a number of issues for many years. However their conflict over the liberalization of the Lomé Conventions has really left the Europeans bloodied-nosed and fighting back with the EPAs that would really diminish the US trade role in the ACP countries. The evolution of the Lomé Conventions into the CPA, and eventually the EPAs – that is the

[12] Montana, Ismael Musah. 2003. The Lomé Convention from Inception to the Dynamics of the Post-Cold War, 1957–1990s. *African and Asian Studies* (2) 1: 63–97.

liberalization process of the Lomé Conventions or the rise of European bloc imperialism in the current period of global capitalism was fairly rapid.

The EU Banana Regime[13]

The EU banana regime is a "Common Market Organization (CMO) for bananas" implemented by the EU that safeguard duty free preferential access for bananas from ACP states to the European market under the Banana Protocol of the Lomé Convention. It came into existence with the formation of the European single market economy in 1993. Hitherto, individual European nation-states pursued multiple arrangements in the banana trade with countries around the world. The primary outcomes of the banana regime were that it safeguarded EU banana production, guaranteed ACP access to European markets, and established higher prices for bananas in Europe thereby making the European banana market lucrative.

The banana regime was supposed to uphold trade liberalization in tropical products in line with the GATT, hold down average tariffs, and simultaneously allow ACP bananas continuous access to the European market in accordance with Lomé IV (1990). The EU also intended that the banana regime would not adversely affect banana production in EU states, namely France and Spain, and that the price for banana in Europe would be reasonably low.

The banana regime placed a tariff on all non-ACP banana imports into the European market the amount being EUC 100 per ton for Latin American bananas. EU banana importers are licensed under the banana regime that restricts them to specific quota quantities. This was intended as an incentive for importers to buy high-cost ACP bananas, but the policy simultaneously created an increase in supply of Latin American bananas in the European market and a lucrative trade in licenses.

The banana regime also created "a Special System of Assistance (SSA)" fund of (ECU95m) to help the ACP banana exporting states

[13] This section of the chapter draws heavily on the following works – Dickson, Anna K. 2003. The EU Banana Regime: History and Interests. *Banana Link*. Dearden, Stephen J.H. 1996. The EU Banana Regime and the Caribbean Island Economies. Manchester Metropolitan University, DSA European Development Policy Study Group Discussion Paper No. 1, December; and Sutton, Paul. 1997. The Banana Regime of the European Union, the Caribbean, and Latin America. *Journal of Interamerican Studies and World Affairs* (39) 2: 5–36.

cushion their losses due to its new measures. The fund was also intended to assist the ACP states to produce higher quality bananas, improve their marketing techniques, and enhance the quality of their bananas. The fund was nonetheless inadequate and could not help the ACP countries meet the costs of adjustment or the decline in the price of bananas in the UK the principal market for ACP bananas in 1992–93.

Banana Control Over US Trade Policy

Why did the US put up such a fight on behalf of its banana multinationals against the EU banana regime when the US is not a banana producing country? Chiquita Brands International the world's largest banana distributor was the principal beneficiary of the US struggle against the EU banana regime. Both the Democrats and the Republicans fought in Chiquita's corner in the struggle with the EU for free trade in the EU banana market that threatened to bring many losses to the ACP countries by destroying their banana industries, since they cannot compete with cheap Latin American bananas. Chiquita, however, had both the Democrats and Republicans in its deep pockets as the data revealed.[14]

Carl Lindner, then chairman and CEO of American Financial Group (AFG) a holding company for the Linder family's financial interests in the insurance and real estate sectors across the US, commanded nearly $20 billion in assets. Linder was also Board Chair of Chiquita Brands International, and the majority owner and CEO of the Cincinnati Reds. Linder raised "at least $200,000" for President Bush's reelection campaign in 2004 and "contributed $200,000 to Bush-Cheney inauguration ($100,000 from Lindner and $100,000 from American Financial Group)."[15]

Lindner and Chiquita Brands contributed $200,000 to each Bush and former Vice President Al Gore in their presidential bids. Linder gave another "$200,000 to the Bush-Cheney inauguration in 2001." The illegality of his excessive contributions forced the Bush-Cheney

[14] Hayes, Jack. 1996. Caricom Leaders Unlimber their Diplomatic Weaponry against White House Trade Onslaught. Council On Hemispheric Affairs. Washington: Memorandum to the Press 96.09, August.

[15] Common Cause, Bush and Kerry fundraisers: What have they gotten, and what do they want? Washington DC: http://www.commoncause.org/site/pp.asp?c=dkLNK1MQIwG&b=196963

inauguration committee to refund some of the money to Lindner, but he promptly re-funneled it to the Republicans through AFG. Then, for the 2002 Senatorial elections "Lindner and his family contributed $450,000 to Republicans," and again in the presidential campaign in 2004 "Lindner was one of the first 23 "Rangers" who raised at least $200,000 in bundled contributions for Bush." Furthermore, Lindner hosted a "fundraiser at his home in the Cincinnati suburb of Indian Hill," that "raised an estimated $1.7 million for Bush," in September 2003.[16]

Linder was therefore able to exert considerable influence over US trade policy. He pushed the US government to pressurize the EU to disband its quota system in bananas that he considered unfair and would cut Chiquita's European market share by half. However, Chiquita had 22 percent of the European market and the ACP only 8 percent within the quota system. The actions taken by the US political elites and Chiquita to open up the EU banana market to Chiquita nonetheless came at a high cost with serious consequences for US consumers and industries, as well as the ACP economies.

The actions by Chiquita and the US political elites put at risk, the economic stability of the economies of the Caribbean islands where there was a greater need for the European banana market due to the significance of bananas to their economies, and that of the ACP banana exporting states in general.[17] Meanwhile, there was an increase in prices of EU goods sold in the US in the amount of $191 million and this threatened to reduce the amount of jobs in US industries that consumed domestic steel.[18]

The trade conflict escalated as President Bush implemented a 30 percent tariff on imported steel from Europe, Asia, and South America, in March 2002.[19] The EU threatened to retaliate by imposing in excess of "$6 billion in tariffs, including $2.2 billion on goods produced in states that were crucial to Bush's re-election campaign (such as fruit

---

[16] Common Cause, Bush and Kerry fundraisers: What have they gotten, and what do they want? Washington DC: http://www.commoncause.org/site/pp.asp?c=dkLNK1MQIwG&b=196963

[17] Dearden, Stephen J.H. 2002. *The European Union and the Commonwealth Caribbean*. Aldershot: Ashgate.

[18] Common Cause, Bush and Kerry fundraisers: What have they gotten, and what do they want? Washington DC: http://www.commoncause.org/site/pp.asp?c=dkLNK1MQIwG&b=196963

[19] Shorrock, Tim. 2002. Bush Shrugs Off Trade War Over Steel Decision. Penang, Malaysia: Third World Network No. 275, February.

and nuts from California and Florida and textiles from Southern states) and another $4 billion in sanctions on products from U.S. corporations."[20] The EU threat and indications from the WTO that it would rule against Bush's 30 percent tariff caused the US to drop it in December 2003.

Chiquita is merely walking in the footsteps of its predecessor the United Fruit Company that took part in a *coup d'état* that ousted the democratically elected president Jacobo Arbenz Guzmán of Guatemala in 1954. The coup demonstrated the power of US multinationals over democratically elected governments in the developing states and added a new dimension to the term "banana republic" – a country in which the US multinational corporation could overthrow its democratically elected government. Chiquita's control over the US Congress, the White House, and US trade policy also gives a new meaning to the term "banana republic." Not only could the banana multinationals overthrow foreign governments they could also determine who occupies the US congress and White House, and the trade policies they formulate and implement.

US Banana Multinationals Force Open EU Banana Market

The "banana war" between the EU and the US erupted in earnest when right before the EU implemented its banana regime in 1993 the GATT had judged in response to a complaint lodged by the US in cahoots with the Latin American Banana producers – Columbia, Costa Rica, Guatemala, Nicaragua, and Venezuela – that the national import regimes of the European Community countries were incompatible with its rules.[21] The GATT found that the banana regime violated the MFN as well as the arrangement that the EU equalized its tariff rates for all members of GATT that exported bananas.

The US applied more pressure on the EU immediately after the implementation of the banana regime. The GATT declared in 1994 that the banana regime was illegal because it violated MFN and engaged in an unfair distribution of licenses to banana importers in

---

[20] Common Cause, Bush and Kerry fundraisers: What have they gotten, and what do they want? Washington DC: http://www.commoncause.org/site/pp.asp?c=dkLNK1MQIwG&b=196963

[21] Dickson, Anna K. 2003. The EU Banana Regime: History and Interests. *Banana Link*. See also Clegg, Peter. 2002. "From Insiders to Outsiders: Caribbean Banana Interests in the New International Trading Framework", in Stephen J.H. Dearden, ed., *The European Union and the Commonwealth Caribbean*. Aldershot: Ashgate, pp. 79-113

Europe. The GATT lacked the mechanism to enforce its rulings that could easily be blocked by a percentage vote of its members. The transition from the GATT to the WTO in 1995 changed that situation, since WTO rules could only be blocked by consensus.

The EU banana regime also faced internal dissent by Germany, the largest EU market for Bananas, and the Benelux – Belgium, Netherlands and Luxembourg – importers. They unsuccessfully challenged the banana regime in court on several occasions. The German banana importers argued that the EU banana regime cheated them.[22] However, Germany was fully within the ambit of the US' influence since it imported its bananas from the "dollar banana" exporting countries in Latin America controlled by the US multinationals.

The "dollar banana" countries in descending order of export volumes are Ecuador, Costa Rica, Colombia, Guatemala, Panama, Honduras, Nicaragua, and Venezuela. They got the name "dollar banana" because historically these countries are within the sphere of influence of the US dollar, and the US multinationals control either directly or indirectly about 60 percent of their banana exports. The multinationals own almost no lands in Ecuador, but still Dole, Del Monte and Chiquita account for a significant part of that country's banana exports. Ecuador, Costa Rica and Honduras rely heavily on bananas as an essential source of their national incomes.[23]

In response to the US-led challenge to the banana regime, the EU attempted to appease Colombia, Costa Rica, Nicaragua, and Venezuela, by negotiating with them a Framework Agreement in 1994. Essentially, the Framework Agreement increased the tariff quota for, and reduced the duty on, "dollar bananas" entering the EU market. It also conferred the authority on these states to issue export certificates in the determination of "dollar banana" suppliers that could exploit the EU's import licenses. The benefit of the Framework Agreement to the EU was that these "dollar banana" states would agree to hold back on their challenge to the banana regime until 2003.[24] Ecuador, Mexico, Honduras, the Dominican Republic, and Guatemala, one of the GATT complainants rejected the Framework Agreement.

---

[22] Banana Link, http://www.bananalink.org.uk/content/view/72/32/lang,en/

[23] Striffler, Steve and Mark Moberg, eds., 2003. *Banana Wars: Power, Production and History in the Americas*. Durham, North Carolina: Duke University Press.

[24] Dickson, Anna K. 2003. The EU Banana Regime: History and Interests. *Banana Link*.

The US banana multinationals that operate in Latin America argued that the EU banana regime and Framework Agreement combined to adversely affect them. Chiquita Brands International and the Hawaii Banana Industry Association in September 1994, filed a petition under Section 302(a) of the Omnibus Trade Act 1974 to find the EU banana regime guilty of unfair trading practices.[25] Their petition accused the EU's banana regime and Framework Agreement of discriminating against the US companies and decreasing their share of the EU market by more than 50 percent.

This was the first time that a petition was filed under Section 301 of the Trade Act of 1974, the main US law to enforce rights for US firms under existing trade agreements, to obtain increased foreign market access for US goods and services, and to respond to certain foreign practices such as infringement of intellectual property rights.[26] The complaint filed by Chiquita and Hawaii Bananas under the Clinton Administration became a test case on the use of US trade laws to protect US economic interests. The leadership in the US House of Representatives and fifty other members of the house sided with the US banana multinationals in a letter to the US Trade Representative, urging him to accept the petition by Chiquita and Hawaii Bananas. The case against the EU presented by the USTR was as follows:

> 1. The EU's assignment of import licenses for Latin American bananas to French and British companies (whose previous business had been limited to the distribution of European, Caribbean and African bananas only) took away a major part of the banana distribution business that US companies had developed over the past century; 2. the EU's assignment of import licenses for Latin American bananas to European banana ripening firms (which historically did not import bananas) further deprives US companies of market access; 3. the EU imposes more burdensome licensing requirements on banana imports from the Latin American co-complainants than for other countries; and 4. the EU's allocation of access to its market for bananas is discriminatory and trade-distorting because it departs from the fair share standard of the WTO which should be based on past levels of trade.[27]

[25] Hanrahan, Charles E. 1999. The U.S.-European Union Banana Dispute, *CRS Report for Congress*. Washington DC. December.

[26] US Department of Justice and Federal Trade Commission. 1995. Antitrust Enforcement Guidelines for International Operations. Washington DC., April.

[27] Hanrahan, Charles E. 1999. The U.S.-European Union Banana Dispute, *CRS Report for Congress*. Washington DC., December.

Support for the banana petition in the US House of Representatives and by the USTR shows the link between the US state and the US banana multinationals. Common Cause (2003) stated "Carl Lindner, chairman of Chiquita Brands and a longtime Republican donor, quietly gave $415,000 to about two dozen Democratic state parties … in April 1996, only hours after the [Clinton] administration formally challenged European Union trade sanctions against Central American bananas grown by Chiquita."[28] The Clinton Administration's actions had more to do with safeguarding the class interest of the US banana multinationals than to bring about fair play in the banana market. Indeed, Chiquita's operations are basically located outside of the US with non-US workers. It is difficult to fathom the US state acting in the interest of Latin American workers.

Failing to negotiate a settlement with the EU, the US adopted a different strategy by terminating its Section 301 case against the EU in September 1995 and in January 1996 forcing Costa Rica and Colombia under threat of trade sanctions to challenge the Framework Agreement that the two countries benefited from. Then, the US came together with Guatemala, Honduras, and Mexico, and Ecuador in February 1996, to take the matter to the WTO. Their WTO petition alleged that the EU regime violated several articles of the GATT 1994, as well as the Agreement on Import Licensing Procedures (AILP), the Agreement on Agriculture (AoA), the General Agreement on Trade in Services (GATS), and the Agreement on Trade-Related Investment Measures (TRIMs).[29] Also, Honduras, Guatemala, and Ecuador claimed that they had insufficient access to the European market.

The WTO ruled in favor of the complainants in May 1997, and the EU unsuccessfully appealed against the ruling, by challenging the ability of the US as a non-banana producing country to contest its banana regime. The US banana multinationals won and the EU was forced to accept the WTO's ruling, which meant that it had to revise its banana

---

[28] Common Cause and AARP. 2003. Brief of Common Cause and AARP as *Amici Curiae* in Support of the Constitutionality of the Bipartisan Campaign Reform Act of 2002, in the Supreme Court of the United States, No. 02–1674 & Consolidated Cases. Washington, DC: August 5. See also Archibald, George. 1997. *Banana Baron Peeled off Half a Mil; White House Paid Back in WTO Fight*, Wash. Times, Aug. 25. According to *Time*, "DNC officials instructed Lindner to give directly to state party coffers, which are subject to far less public scrutiny than federal election accounts." Weisskopf, Michael. 1997. *The Busy Back Door Men*, Time. March 31.

[29] Nolte, Stephan-Alfons. 2002. From Lomé IV to Cotonou and EBA – An Analysis of Trade Preferences and Redistribution of Economic Benefits. Abgabetermin: 20.11.

regime to bring it in line with WTO rules by January 1, 1999. Chiquita was unsatisfied with the revised banana regime and lobbied the US Congress to impose duties on EU exports, while Ecuador brought a new complaint in the WTO against the EU. The matter was then referred to the arbitration process within the WTO.

The US estimated that its banana multinationals lost $520 million annually in export and profit because of the EU's non-compliance with the WTO's ruling and proposed to impose tariff duties of 100 percent *ad valorem* on EU goods, in that amount. Meanwhile, in April 1999 the WTO's arbitrators held the view that the revised banana regime continued to breach its rules and awarded $191.4 million to the US for economic losses. The US imposed duties on the EU by that amount retroactive to March 3, 1999. Then, in May 2000, the WTO permitted Ecuador to impose duties on goods from the EU. Ecuador, however, did not impose the duty because of fear that they will increase the price of food in the country causing political unrest.[30]

The Bush Administration with Chiquita's prompting was still unsatisfied with the changes made to the EU banana regime. Claiming that the EU banana regime caused the company to suffer huge losses, Chiquita bananas filed a lawsuit against the EU for $525 million in the European Court for damages caused by the banana regime, January 25, 2001.[31] The US announced in March 2001 that it would impose further sanctions against the EU, and the EU threatened to retaliate.

The US' influence in the WTO was highlighted by the fact that several members decided they would bloc the EU's request in the WTO for a waiver for the new Cotonou Agreement, unless there was an agreement on the banana regime. Also, European companies were frustrated by the ongoing dispute that caused much damage to their businesses. The EU came to a settlement with Ecuador and the US on April 11, 2001 that allowed for a banana regime with both tariff and quota components. The EU caved in to the relentless pressure by the US banana multinationals and political elites. The EU decided in its self-interest to sacrifice the ACP banana exporting countries at the altar of the US banana multinationals and political elites on the

---

[30] Dickson, Anna K. 2003. The EU Banana Regime: History and Interests. *Banana Link*.

[31] Kenety, Brian. 2001. Chiquita Blames EU Banana Regime for Its Bankruptcy Woes. Geneva, Switzerland. *Third World Network*, North-South Development Monitor (SUNS 4819).

grounds that the US sanctions were going to hurt the EU much more than the political fall-out with the ACP group over a banana regime with both tariff and quota components.

Conclusion

The US won the trade liberalization battle, but as we shall see in the following chapter, Europe won and the US lost the war to exert control over the ACP countries. US hegemony prevailed over Europe only for a short while, as the Europeans bounced back with the EPAs. Europe used its trade dispute with the US as an opportunity to develop a new mercantilist trade arrangement with its former colonies under the pretext of adhering to US-styled free trade. The EPAs represent Europe's great deception of the US in modern times.

CHAPTER FIVE

THE EMERGENCE OF EUROPEAN BLOC IMPERIALISM

Introduction

The chapter seeks to deepen understanding about a hitherto unexplored dimension of imperialism termed "bloc imperialism" that emerged in the context of the attempt by US-led neoliberal globalization to liberalize the trade relations between Europe and the Africa, Caribbean and Pacific Group of States. Earlier, we outlined the struggle between the US and the EU over the liberalization of the Lomé Conventions, which paved the way for the emergence of EU bloc imperialism. Now, we examine the gradual liberalization of the Lomé Conventions that resulted from that struggle, and its consequences, namely the European bloc imperialist backlash. In this connection, we appraise the transitions to the partially liberalized Cotonou Partnership Agreement, and the divide and rule tactics of the EU a well-known ploy of imperialism, in the implementation of the fully liberalized economic partnership agreements with the ACP countries.

Next, there is a brief outline of the CARIFORUM-EU EPA, the first comprehensive EPA, as a concrete example of the workings of European bloc imperialism. This is followed by a discussion on the European bloc imperialist stranglehold over the ACP countries and the pushback against the economic partnership agreements.

European Bloc Imperialist Backlash to the Banana Trade War

The US banana multinationals and ruling elites used the WTO to force open the EU banana market to "dollar bananas," under the disguise of liberalizing the Lomé Conventions. The reality for the ACP bloc, however, from the liberalization of the Lomé Conventions, is that the EU has divided it into six regions for the purpose of negotiating comprehensive EPAs, and through this process tie these states to the EU bloc in a new mercantilism.

From The Lomé [1]to Cotonou[2]

The Lomé Conventions I to IV[3] represented a set of trade and aid agreements that the EU first signed with 48 of its former colonies in 1975, and lasted until 2000. Lomé I centered inter alia on trade, export earnings from commodities, industrial cooperation, financial and technical cooperation, and provisions relating to services, payments, and capital movements, and institutions. Lomé II contained innovations on Lomé I most significant of which were the guarantee system for ACP economies largely dependent on mineral exports, and a series of measures to develop the mining and energy potential of the ACP countries. Lomé III updated the agreement on agricultural cooperation and food security, drought and desertification, cooperation on agricultural commodities, fisheries development, industrial development, mining and energy potential development, transportation and communication, trade and services, regional cooperation, and cultural and social cooperation. Lomé IV negotiated in two parts for a period of 10 years from 1989 to 1999 (except finance reviewed in five years terms), included increases in EU resources to ACP countries, and a system of support for neoliberal structural adjustment policies. Lomé IV supposedly improved ACP-EU trade arrangements including the rules of origin, access for agricultural products, fisheries products, etc.

The Lomé trade arrangements involved both free access without reciprocity for almost all ACP's exports to EU markets and in particular favorable provisions for products such as sugar, rum, bananas, rice, beef and veal. Arguably, the Lomé Conventions brought security and reliability in ACP-EU relations over its period of validity, and their permanent and versatile nature, helped to forge close ties and discussion between the EU and ACP countries. The conventions operated

---

[1] Lomé is the capital city of Togo, a West African country.

[2] Cotonou is the capital city of Benin, a West African country.

[3] For more in-depth discussions on the Lomé Conventions see for example Hewitt, Adrian. 1984. The Lomé Conventions: Entering a Second Decade. *Journal of Common Market Studies* (23) 2: 95–115; Ravenhill, John. 1985. *Collective Clientelism: The Lomé Conventions and North-South Relations (The Political Economy of International Change).* New York: Colombia University Press; and Parfitt, Trevor W. and Sandy Bullock. 1990. The Prospects for a New Lomé Convention: Structural Adjustment or Structural Transformation? *Review of African Political Economy* (17) 47: 84–94. Frey-Woutera, Adele Ellen. 1980. *The European Community and the Third World: The Lomé Convention and Its Impact.* New York: Praeger.

on the principle that the EU and ACP states, accepted their economic and political differences, and subscribed to mutual respect for each other's sovereignty, cultural identity, and the type of development to which each aspires. The Lomé Conventions nonetheless helped to deepen state-led neocolonial relations in the ACP countries, and with the restructuring of global capitalism it took on the garb of neoliberal structural adjustment.

The EU and the ACP states signed the Cotonou Partnership Agreement in 2000 as a step towards market liberalization of the Lomé Conventions. The CPA in theory promoted and expedited the economic, cultural and social development of the ACP states, with the view to contribute to peace, security and a stable, democratic political environment. Its objectives were poverty reduction and eradication, sustainable development, and the integration of the ACP states into the world economy. The EU presented the Cotonou Agreement as a significant opportunity for developing countries to access European markets. The CPA nonetheless was merely a step along the way to implement the EU's bloc imperialist stranglehold on the ACP countries through the EPAs.

The EU Divides to Conquer through EPAs[4]

The EPA discussions, termed the all-ACP-EU phase of the EPA negotiations, commenced between the ACP and EU in September 2002, a year after the EU caved in to the relentless pressure by the US banana multinationals and political elites and came to a settlement with the US, sacrificing the ACP countries. The main issues in these discussions included the sequencing of the EPA negotiations in two phases – an all-ACP-EU level focusing on horizontal issues of interest to all

[4] See for example The Secretariat of the African, Caribbean and Pacific Group of States. 2008. President Kufuor says EPAs Divide ACP. Brussels: ACP Press Statement 3. October 2; Ameyibor, Francis. 2008. EPA Divides AU. Amsterdam, The Netherlands: African News. February 2; British Broadcasting Corporation. 2008. EPA: Caribbean Still Divided on Treaty. June 27; Brunsden, Jim. 2008. EPAs Pose Threat to ACP Regional Integration. EuropeanVoice.com. March 19; Roux, Wallie. 2008. EPAs: The New Game of Divide and Rule. Windhoek, Namibia. Labour Resource and Research Institute; Mutume, Gumisai. 2008. EU Undermining African Economic Stability: New EU Trade Deals Divide Africa. Afrik.com. November 13; and Jones, Emily. 2007. Signing Away The Future: How Trade and Investment Agreements between Rich and Poor Countries Undermine Development. Oxford: Oxfam Briefing Paper No. 101, March 2007.

parties, and in the ACP countries and regions concentrating on the specific commitments of the EU and ACP regions.[5]

The first phase negotiations ended in agreement that the CPA provides the basic principles and objectives of EPAs, and that the sustainable development of the ACP states, their smooth and gradual integration into the global economy, and poverty eradication were the overall objectives of the EPA. The specific objectives of the EPA are the promotion of sustained growth, the increase in the production and supply capacity of the ACP states, the structural transformation and diversification of ACP economies, and support for regional integration.

Undoubtedly, the EPAs divide rather than unite the ACP states, making it easier for European bloc imperialism to operate. Europe has had a long history of divide and rule tactics in the developing world. The EPA is the latest divide and rule strategy employed by Europe in the ACP region, but in this case it is not individual European states employing the strategy but Europe as a bloc. The EU bloc has divided the ACP group of countries into different regional groups under Article 37(5) of the CPA in order to facilitate the negotiation of EPAs. There are six such groups – the Pacific ACP (PACP), the Caribbean Forum (CARIFORUM), Central African, West African, Southern African Development Community (SADC), and Eastern and Southern African (ESA).

The ACP countries came together as a group in 1975 with the objective to negotiate and implement together, cooperation agreements with the European Community. However, the EU as a bloc decided that it would negotiate EPAs with regions within the ACP group of states. This means that the ACP cannot negotiate as a bloc but is broken-up in different groups or individual countries. The ACP countries therefore lose whatever advantage they had negotiating as a single entity. The division of the ACP group strengthens the EU's position in that the EU now negotiates EPAs with individual countries or smaller groups within the ACP, and not with the ACP as a whole. The ACP regions are at a disadvantage in that they cannot benefit from the inputs of their colleagues from other ACP regions, in their negotiations.

[5] Africa, Caribbean and Pacific Group and European Commission. 2003. ACP-EC EPA Negotiations Joint Report on the all-ACP-EC phase of EPA Negotiations. Brussels: ACP/00/118/03 Rev.1. European Commission Directorate General for Trade, 2006. Global Europe: Competing in the World. Brussels: Ref. 318/06.

The CRIFORUM is a case in point. Experienced Caribbean diplomats urged the Caribbean Regional Negotiating Machinery (CRNM) to tie its negotiations of the CARIFORUM-EU EPA to what the African countries were doing in order to broaden its support base, but of course the CRNM ignored the advise.[6]

The EPA divides groups engaged in regional integration movements both within and between member states, as is the case of the South Africa Development Community (SADC) and the Common Market for Eastern and Southern Africa (COMESA). The SADC is a typical example of how the divisiveness of the EPA works. The SADC group comprises Angola, Botswana, Democratic Republic of Congo, Lesotho, Madagascar, Malawi, Mauritius, Mozambique, Namibia, Seychelles, South Africa, Swaziland, Tanzania, Zambia and Zimbabwe. Countries that participated in two or three regional blocs by choice were, forced to choose one, for the purposes of negotiating EPAs. This is reminiscent of the partitioning of Africa at the Berlin Conference in 1884, where for example people belonging to the same ethnic group were divided by the drawing of arbitrary borders on the continent, and now are citizens of two different countries.

The EU forced SADC to divide into three splinter groups, SADC – 4 that is SADC countries also members of COMESA – Mauritius, Malawi, Zambia and Zimbabwe that negotiate an EPA as part of the so-called eastern and southern African configuration (ESA), and not as part of SADC. Second is the SADC – 7 negotiating an EPA as SADC. They include South African Customs Union (SACU) – 4 Botswana, Lesotho, Namibia and Swaziland, plus Mozambique, Angola and Tanzania.

SADC – 1 is South Africa that the EU accuses of being a stumbling bloc in the way preventing other African countries from signing-on to the EPAs. In sowing seeds of discord, Peter Mandelson, the EC Trade Commissioner said that South Africa does not "speak for the many African countries who do need" the EPAs "and who are signing up to them."[7] The EU strongly suggests that South Africa by its actions concerning the EPAs is impeding the economic development of

[6] This point was made by Sir Alistair McIntyre, senior Caribbean scholar and Diplomat at the Sir Arthur Lewis Institute of Social and Economic Studies (SALISES), conference in Jamaica in March 2008.

[7] Cronin, David. 2007. EPAs Signed "Under Duress," Says South Africa. *Inter Press Service News Agency* December 21.

Africa, while South Africa claims that the end result of the EPA negotiations would lead to Africa's disintegration.

In the Economic Community of West Africa (ECOWAS), for example, Nigeria, Ghana and Cote d'Ivoire, were at loggerheads over the fact that the latter two countries have initialed interim EPAs (IEPAs). The EU resorted to divisive tactic of IEPAs with individual ACP countries when it could not secure a deal with the ACP regions. Nigeria threatened to have Cote d'Ivoire and Ghana pay higher taxes and tariffs on the products they export to Nigeria if they did not align themselves with the ECOWAS in the EPA negotiations. Accounting for 61 percent of ECOWAS' gross domestic product, Nigeria is a significant market for countries in that sub-region. Nigeria also announced the suspension of talks for a common external tariff for ECOWAS, putting further pressure on Ghana and Cote d'Ivoire to back off from the IEPAs. The common external tariff that the West African states decided on in 2001 could collapse if either Ghana or Cote d'Ivoire goes through with their bilateral agreements with the EU, because each country would have individual tariff schedules. Rather than having a single ECOWAS common external tariff as the basis for market access for the EC, there will be multiple.[8]

In the Caribbean, for example, the Caricom countries could not negotiate EPAs as a part of Caricom, or the Organization of Eastern Caribbean States (OECS). At the behest of the EU bloc, they had to do so as part of CARIFORUM, a separate entity created specifically to negotiate the EPA. The CARIFORUM-EU EPA has already fractured the Caribbean at several levels. Regional governments, civil society, rank-and-file, and academics are not in one accord with the agreement. The EPAs are therefore undermining regional integration economic development strategies in the ACP regions.

Another problem that leads to further division, is that the policymakers negotiate and formulate the EPAs with hardly any reference to the peoples they are supposed to represent. This shows the class dimension of the EPAs and is the cause of further divisions and tensions between the goals of the policymakers and the aspirations of working people. The ruling elites who are in tune with the agenda of neoliberal global capitalism are on one side of the development spectrum, while working people are on the other.

[8] Kwa, Aileen. 2008. Nigeria 'Threatens' Neighbors in Wake of Bilateral EPAs. *Inter Press Service News Agency* June 2.

Imperialist divide and rule tactics require domestic collaborators to succeed and typically, there is no shortage in supply of these turncoats in the poverty stricken former colonies. The colonials used social, political and economic institutional structures to divide the people. For example, domestic support for colonial policies came from certain quarters of society, political parties, and economic organizations that reflected the class character of colonial society, in which the aspirants to neocolonial power took sides with colonial policy, and the working majority took a dissenting position. Thus, there is domestic support for the EPA by local ruling elites, although there is mounting opposition to it.

The EU bloc imperialist objectives are not obvious they are concealed from the ordinary people. The ruling elites behind the EU have the ability to hide their true objectives even from the European peoples.[9] Booker and North (2005) argue that the EU has secretly crept-up on the people of Europe. According to them, the ruling elites sold the EU to the European people as a trade arrangement among European states. Now, the European people have realized that the EU is really a political union representing a supra-national state imposed on all of Europe.[10] This in essence is the *modus operandi* of EU bloc imperialism. The ruling elites who negotiated the CARIFORUM-EU EPA told the Caribbean people that it was just a trade agreement with the EU to bring about good governance and sustainable development in the region, but when the agreement became public the people realize that it is a mercantilist agreement that ties the trade of the CARIFORUM states indefinitely to the EU, with no clear means by which these countries could free themselves from it.

The CARIFORUM-EU EPA

The CARIFORUM-EU EPA is a concrete example of the manifestation of European bloc imperialism through the EPAs. First, the EPA ties Caribbean trade indefinitely to the EU in a new-styled mercantilist arrangement. There is no clause in the EPA through which the

[9] Christopher Booker and Richard North, *The Great Deception: The Secret History of the European Union*, London, Continuum, 2005.

[10] John F. McManus, EU Déjà Vu in the Caribbean, *New American Magazine*, January 23, 2009.

Caribbean countries could opt out of the agreement. Second, the EPA grants EU products unhindered access into the Caribbean countries guaranteeing markets for the goods produced by EU multinational corporations. Third, the EPA secures for the EU multinational corporations unhindered access to raw materials from the CARIFORUM states, guaranteeing them of the necessary productive inputs that come from the Caribbean. Fourth, the EPA is also an instrument of political control. It has mechanisms for the Caribbean countries to police themselves to ensure that they do not renege on the agreement. The EU does not have to engage in the military or colonial occupation of the Caribbean region, as was the case when individual European countries held colonies in the area and fought wars with each other to capture and secure them.

European bloc imperialism exercises political control in the Caribbean by erecting new institutional mechanisms such as the supranational CARIFORUM Council that has political oversight over the implementation of the CARIFORUM-EU EPA. The EPA creates four new bodies, first, a ministerial level Joint CARIFORUM-EC Council that will deal with all policy and related decisions concerning Caribbean trade. This is incompatible with the Caricom Treaty that established the Caribbean Community and Common Market. Second, there is the CARIFORUM-EC Trade and Development Committee an implementing agency at the level of officials. Third, there is a joint CARIFORUM-EC Parliamentary Committee for political debate, on relevant issues. Finally, there is a CARIFORUM-EC Consultative Committee that aims to involve the private sector and other social partners in the EPA process.[11]

These institutional structures have bypassed the Caricom and the CSME two existing institutions that promote Caribbean integration as a development strategy in the region. However, there are even further problems with the governing structure of the EPA. The Caricom heads of government gave the mandate to coordinate Caribbean Member States' implementation of EPAs to the Caricom Secretary General at their meeting in Belize City on March 12–13, 2009.

The EPA also highlights the collaborative efforts between the local ruling elites and the European bloc imperialist. First, several of the

[11] Jessop, David. 2008. Understanding the EPA – Institutional Arrangements Raise Concerns – Supranational Council Seen as Infringing Sovereignty. *Jamaica Gleaner*, March 7.

negotiators had their training on EPA negotiations by European financed programs. The "benevolent" Europeans have been helping ACP governments, negotiators, and civil society organizations in their preparations to negotiate the EPAs. This is like hiring a man who wants to break-and-enter your house, as your night watchman. The Department for International Development (DFID) headed by the UK government's Secretary of State for International Development funded the Institute of Development Studies (IDS) at the University of Sussex, to the tune of £156,339 in its Technical Training for Scenario-Building on Reciprocity project from September 2005 to April 2006. The IDS engaged in building "trade datasets" and designing a methodology for each of the ACP states to help them in the EPA negotiation process.[12] Also, the DFID-UK funded training courses on trade negotiation skills, trade data and policy analysis for EPA negotiators in the EPA regions.

Second, the EPA negotiators were well versed in the neoliberal ideology concerning free trade and market liberalization, which the chief negotiator for example openly espoused in his writings.[13] Third, the CRNM, the principal negotiator of the EPA for the CARIFORUM countries, is not prepared to accept criticisms of the agreement. It arrogantly defends the EPA with perhaps even greater intensity than its European perpetrators. The behavior of the CRNM conjures-up Malcolm X's description of the relationship between the "house slave" and the "master" – when the master is sick the house slave says "Master we sick." For example, this is what the CRNM had to say in response to a Memorandum containing a well-taught out critique of the EPA by some highly respected and leading Caribbean scholars and diplomats,

> the Memorandum clearly does not represent the text of the EPA and the issues contained within it; is replete with errors and innuendos; dismisses the hard work of regional officials and stakeholders through the intense coordination process and well targeted analysis of relevant issues; and makes little or no contribution to the intended consideration

---

12 Department for International Development. 2006. Training the Trainers. United Kingdom, March 16.

13 See for example Bernal, Richard. 2007. The Globalization of the Health-care Industry: Opportunities for the Caribbean. *CEPAL Review* 92: 83–99, and Bernal, Richard. 2000. "The Caribbean in the International System: Outlook for the First 20 Years of the 21st Century", in Hall, Kenneth and Denis Benn, eds., *Contending with Destiny: The Caribbean in the 21st Century*. Kingston: Ian Randle, pp. 295–325.

of the regional negotiating process and recommendations for its improvement.[14]

The CRNM and the EU bloc imperialist agreed on a comprehensive CARIFORUM-EU EPA in October 2008. The EPA includes a WTO-compatible trade-in-goods agreement, an agreement on trade in services, rules on trade-related areas, as well as provisions for development cooperation. The CRNM pointed out that under the EPA the region would liberalize 86.9% of its trade with Europe, with 82.7% occurring within the first 15 years and the remainder within 25 years. Given the duty-free, quota-free access granted under the EC's market-access offer in 2007, some 92% of CARIFORUM-EU trade will be liberalized. The agreement includes a moratorium of three years on all tariff lines except for motor vehicles, parts and gasoline that benefit from a 10-year grace period.

In addition to the sugar-protocol access granted to Caribbean sugar exporters, an additional transitional quota of 60,000 tons will be made available, to be evenly divided between the Dominican Republic and traditional Caribbean sugar suppliers. The Caribbean has agreed to the EC's Most Favored Nation (MFN) clause, although some member governments have concerns over the provision. In a joint CARIFORUM-EU declaration on development there is stipulation of a commitment by the Caribbean countries and the EU to channel EPA support through a Caricom Development Fund. Liberalization commitments by the Caribbean region in the services sector cover 75% for non-LDCs and 65% for LDCs.

The objectives of the CARIFORUM-EU EPA are stated as follows

a. Contributing to the reduction and eventual eradication of poverty through the establishment of a trade partnership consistent with the objective of sustainable development, the Millennium Development Goals and the Cotonou Agreement; b. Promoting regional integration, economic cooperation, and good governance thus establishing and implementing an effective, predictable, and transparent regulatory framework for trade and investment between the Parties and in the CARIFORUM region; c. Promoting the gradual integration of the CARIFORUM States into the world economy, in conformity with their political choices and development priorities; d. Improving the

[14] Caribbean Regional Negotiating Machinery. "Response to the Memorandum entitled 'Problem Areas in the EPA and the case for Content Review' submitted for the consideration of the Reflections Group by Havelock Brewster, Norman Girvan and Vaughn Lewis." Kingston, Jamaica.

> CARIFORUM States' capacity in trade policy and trade related issues; e). Supporting the conditions for increasing investment and private sector initiative and enhancing supply capacity, competitiveness and economic growth in the CARIFORUM region; and f). Strengthening the existing relations between the Parties on the basis of solidarity and mutual interest.[15]

To this end, it is stated that the EPA would take into account the respective levels of development of the EU states and Caribbean countries, and

> consistent with WTO obligations enhance commercial and economic relations, support a new trading dynamic between the Parties by means of the progressive, asymmetrical liberalization of trade between them and reinforce, broaden and deepen cooperation in all areas relevant to trade and investment.[16]

These objectives should not come as a surprise given the neoliberal restructuring of global capitalism on the basis of free trade, the Caricom's embrace of free trade, the shift from the Lomé Conventions to the CPA with an agreement to transition to EPAs, and the agreements at all-ACP-EU phase of EPA negotiations. The CARIFORUM-EU EPA is an integral part of the process of the restructuring of global capitalism along the lines of European bloc imperialism that the Caribbean region signed on to.

The CARIFORUM-EU EPA excludes the Caricom, a juridical entity in the region, similar to the EU, as a party to the agreement. It is a legally binding international instrument of indefinite duration consisting of text, annexes, protocols and joint declarations in a document of over 1,000 pages. Nonetheless, although the EPA is legally binding its legal procedures are unclear for its amendment, revision or for withdrawing from it.[17]

The scope and depth of the EPAs are such however that they are establishing European bloc imperialism and mercantilist trade

---

[15] Caribbean Forum and European Union. 2008. Economic Partnership Agreement between the CARIFORUM States, of the One Part, and the European Community and Its Member States, of the Other Part. http://www.crnm.org/documents/ACP_EU _ EPA/epa_agreement/EPA_Text%20_11june08_final.pdf.

[16] Caribbean Forum and European Union. 2008. Economic Partnership Agreement between the CARIFORUM States, of the One Part, and the European Community and Its Member States, of the Other Part. http://www.crnm.org/documents/ACP_EU _ EPA/epa_agreement/EPA_Text%20_11june08_final.pdf.

[17] Girvan, Norman. 2008. Implications of the Economic Partnership Agreements. *South Bulletin* Issue 8, February 1.

practices that threaten to squeeze US trade with the ACP countries. The EPAs represent the new mercantilism in the sense that they are legally binding documents that tie ACP countries trade to the EU, indefinitely with little understanding of how the ACP countries could free themselves from them. The MFN clause makes it impossible for the ACP countries to have preferential trade amongst themselves, or for the Caribbean countries for example to enter into agreements such as the Caribbean Basin Initiatives (CBI) without the EU's involvement. In essence, "free trade" under the EPA becomes mercantilist free trade with European bloc imperialism.

The US-led globalization policies to benefit US banana multinationals have produced EU-led liberalization policies that counteract the US trade initiatives such as the CBI. Trade liberalization is therefore a myth, a ploy, and a means to bind poor countries to either US or European bloc imperialism. The EU-led liberalization policies are in competition with US-led globalization policies, and promote a kind of mercantilism and imperialism that is not of a single European country, but of the entire European geographic bloc. However, the nation-states in the EU imperialist bloc do not all have equal power. European bloc imperialism is driven by the more rich and powerful European states like the UK, France, Germany and the other European nation-states that stand to benefit the most from the comprehensive EPAs. This is how Europe averts imperialist competition and war among the European nations, and possibly fortifies itself for conflict with the US and the rest of the globe.

The US has awakened to the fact that the EU is using the EPAs to out-maneuever, it in the ACP countries. For example, the US regards the comprehensive CARIFORUM-EU EPA as undermining Caricom-US trade relations. Stephen Lande, a former Assistant US Trade Representative, who negotiated the Tokyo Round of the GATT in 1960, and developed and implemented the Caribbean Basin Initiative (CBI) in 1980, argues that by signing the EPA in its current form, the Caribbean will sacrifice continuing benefits from the US-led CBI. He argues that the US is the major market for the Caribbean while Europe is only a secondary one and that by entering into a full EPA with the EU the region will lose preferential trade access to its major US market. Lande believes that the Caribbean needs to resist EU pressure to enter into full EPAs, as the sub-Saharan African countries are doing that allows them to still receive the benefits of the Africa Growth and Opportunity Act (AGOA) that will now be extended by the New

Partnership Development Act (NPDA) recently introduced in the US congress.[18]

Lande identified three specific problems with the EPA in terms of Caribbean-US relations. The first is that the EPA "has made impossible the continuation of unilateral preferences with the US." In due course, he believes the US will "insists on replacing benefits under CBI with a comprehensive and reciprocal agreement similar to the EPA in scope and coverage." These changes will be made he believes because US exporters will not "allow unilateral preferences to continue for the CBI in the US market while" they "pay higher duties, receive less access for" their "services providers and face non-tariff barriers in Caraicom markets." Also, in Lande's view the EPA will undermine "successful efforts by Caricom countries and its friends in the US which made the CBI into a permanent program."[19]

Lande observed that the US is justifiably unhappy with the EPA because the agreement "requires that any concession given to a third party be automatically bestowed on the EU." The EU will therefore automatically benefit from any free trade agreement that Caricom enters into with the US. Lande noted that the US would continue, "to provide benefits under CBI unilaterally but have no promise of benefiting in any way from the EU agreement."[20]

Lander pointed out that in general and specific terms the CRNM "was unable to take advantage of opportunities to deepen and expand the more important relationship with the United States." Launder noted that the US Congress assigned Charles Rangel, Chairman of the Ways and Means Committee to meet with Caribbean leaders but after several meetings with them "he has not received any specific proposals as to what the region wants from the US in terms of improved trade relations."[21]

---

[18] Lande, Stephen. 2008. Caricom's Trade Relations with the European Union Undermining Its Relations with the United States. Manchester Trade Ltd. International Business Advisors, June 6.

[19] Lande, Stephen. 2008. Caricom's Trade Relations with the European Union Undermining Its Relations with the United States. Manchester Trade Ltd. International Business Advisors, June 6.

[20] Lande, Stephen. 2008. Caricom's Trade Relations with the European Union Undermining Its Relations with the United States. Manchester Trade Ltd. International Business Advisors, June 6.

[21] Lande, Stephen. 2008. Caricom's Trade Relations with the European Union Undermining Its Relations with the United States. Manchester Trade Ltd. International Business Advisors, June 6.

The EU, however, is now ahead of the liberalization game in that both the CBI and AGOA are preferential arrangements that the WTO ruled against concerning the Lomé Conventions. The US needed WTO waivers for both the CBI and AGOA but continued with their extension. The EU claims however that the EPA is a "major step forward in supporting development and industrialization efforts in CARIFORUM, more advantageous than the United States' "AGOA" scheme granted to a number of African countries, which is subject to conditions and limitations."[22] However, the EPA could result in improved access only for the EU, and trade diversion while not creating enough trade for the ACP countries.[23]

The EPAs are identified as instruments for development but they do not guarantee development, because they are not development ends in themselves. The ACP states must give up their revenue from tariffs imposed on imports from the EU but there is no guarantee that they will generate enough earnings from exports to the EU to recover the loss in revenue. The ACP states are on their own therefore, despite, the double-talk that the EPA is an instrument for development, which it does not guarantee.

European Bloc Imperialist Stranglehold

Smith (2008)[24] draws conclusions from his analysis of the CARIFORUM-EU EPA regarding financial liberalization, government procurement, intellectual property rights, services, competition and trade in goods that are quite instructive about the impending destructive effects of European bloc imperialism on ACP countries. According to Smith (2008), the new financial services due to the "movement of capital and entry of EU providers of financial services" will increase financial instability, simultaneously that the ACP countries embrace new rules and obligations in market access in investment, government

[22] Caribbean Forum and European Union. 2008. Information Paper Cariforum-EU Economic Partnership Agreement: An Overview. http://trade.ec.europa.eu/doclib/docs/2008/april/tradoc_138569.pdf.

[23] Berisha-Krasniqi, Valdete, Antoine Bouët and Simon Mevel. 2008. Economic Partnership Agreements between the European Union and African, Caribbean, and Pacific Countries: What Is at Stake for Senegal? *International Food Policy Research, (IFPRI)* Discussion Paper No. 00765, April.

[24] Smith, Sanya. 2008. EU's EPAs Can Spread Conditions for Finance Crisis to South Countries. *SUNS – South-North Development Monitor* #6559, October 2.

procurement, and competition policy, which were rejected as negotiating areas within the WTO. The EPA agreement on intellectual property has provisions beyond what the WTO requires, and would increase the costs of medicines and manufacturing, and augment the risk of biopiracy.

Smith (2008) noted that in this period of financial crisis, the financial fragility of the ACP countries could become worse due to the EPA. In addition, the financial instability in the ACP countries brought about by the EPA could become worse. He observed:

> the EPA can have serious implications for financial fragility in developing countries at a time of financial crisis. The possible magnification of financial instability induced by the EPA include the mandatory free movement of capital and current payments and an obligation to allow the entry of EU suppliers of new financial services if CARIFORUM states allow their own financial service suppliers to do so and these financial service activities have been liberalized under the EPA.[25]

The current financial crisis highlights the pitfalls of extreme deregulation and liberalization, obligations contained in the CARIFORUM-EU EPA despite the inadequate safeguards, which are quite limited. The CARIFORUM states cannot use the safeguards to restrict the movement of current payments, and can only use them if there is a balanced of payments or financial crisis, and only for six months.

In the area of services, the EPA commits the CARIFORUM states to a level of sectoral obligations that "exceeds the controversial benchmarks proposed by the EC in the GATS 2000 negotiations." The MDCs in CARIFORUM are committed to liberalize 75 percent of their services sectors, while for the LDCs the figure is 65 percent. The GATS have further narrowed the right to regulate, the universal service provision limited, "and the wording in special sections on courier, finance, telecommunications, maritime services etc. often copies word-for-word the EC sectoral proposals in the GATS 2000 negotiations and the optional Understandings and Reference Papers at the WTO" (Smith 2008).

The developing countries rejected the Singapore issues – investment, government procurement and competition – at the WTO but the CARIFORUM-EU EPA includes them as legally binding "for securing establishment rights and national treatment for foreign investment

---

[25] Smith, Sanya. 2008. EU's EPAs Can Spread Conditions for Finance Crisis to South Countries. *SUNS – South-North Development Monitor* #6559, October 2.

and investors." Government procurement is significant in stimulating national economies especially during recession and should be excluded from bilateral trade or economic agreements. The developing countries won the battle to exclude government procurement at the Doha round of negotiations, but European bloc imperialism forces it on the CARIFORUM countries. This is further evidence of the weakness of the ACP regions in negotiating with European bloc imperialism, compared with the ACP group as a whole doing so.

The EU requires the CARIFORUM states to implement specific competition laws within five years of the commencement of the EPA. The EU tried to introduce the competition issue at the WTO "to prevent advantages or preferences given by government to local firms on the ground that this would reduce 'effective market access' for foreign firms and goods." It is doubtful however that the competition framework of the developed economies fits the developing countries. Thus, the counterargument is that a competition law should suit the level of development of a country.

According to the South Centre,[26] the provision on competition "actually grants national treatment to EU nationals in Caribbean domestic markets." This means that the "scope of this measure is much larger than that of WTO rules, and ensures, in practice, much larger market penetration for EU companies or service providers." According to the South Centre, in practice state enterprises are prohibited by this provision

> to give preference to a national producer or a national service supplier. This is hence a direct restriction of policy space for the promotion of national productive or supplying capacity [and] curtails the capacity of developing countries to use the procurement operations of state enterprises to promote their own small and medium enterprises or services suppliers.[27]

There is extensive debate on the merits and demerits of protectionist import substitution industrialization measures. But, the evidence is clear however that the rich countries became rich by employing

[26] As quoted in Sanya Smith, "EU's EPAs Can Spread Conditions for Finance Crisis to South Countries," SUNS – South-North Development Monitor, #6559, October 2, 2008.

[27] Quoted in Sanya Smith, "EU's EPAs Can Spread Conditions for Finance Crisis to South Countries," SUNS – South-North Development Monitor, #6559, October 2, 2008.

protectionist measures,[28] while neoliberal globalization and the EPAs deny the poor countries the right to do the same thing – rights that the New International Economic Order (NIEO) sought to secure.

The provision in the EPA regarding intellectual property increases the cost for the ACP countries to gain access to "knowledge goods in the areas of public health, education and the environment," due primarily to the fact that the ACP countries are net importers of technology. Furthermore, the EPA exacts "stronger intellectual property protection" than required by the WTO's Trade-Related Aspects of Intellectual Property Rights (TRIPS) Agreement. In addition, the CPA has no requirement for an agreement on intellectual property in an EPA. The EPA ties the CARIFORUM states to harmonizing their intellectual property commitments up to whatever level a single member may attain by singing a bilateral trade agreement with another country such as the US. Also, it "could eventually require CARIFORUM countries to harmonize up to at least some European Union levels of intellectual property protection" (Smith 2008).

The CARIFORUM countries must now comply with two Internet treaties on Copyright that increase the difficulties of Caribbean citizens to gain access to information on the Internet. The World Intellectual Property Organization (WIPO) Copyright Treaty (WCT) limits the long-term access and substantially increases the cost of short-term access of developing countries to information for their development. For these reasons the Commission Report on Intellectual Property and Development by the British Government in 2002,[29] and an Oxfam supported report in 2008, advised the developing countries not to sign the WCT and WIPO Performance and Phonograms Treaty (WPPT), or to withdraw from them if they had already signed them.[30]

---

[28] Chang, Ha-Joon. 2008. *Bad Samaritans: The Myth of Free Trade and the Secret History of Capitalism*. New York: Bloomsbury Press; Chang, Ha-Joon. 2006. *Kicking Away The Ladder: Development Strategy in Historical Perspective*. London: Anthem Press.

[28] Reinert, Erik S. 2007. *How Rich Countries Got Rich ... and Why Poor Countries Stay Poor*. London: Constable and Robinson.

[29] Report of the Commission on Intellectual Property Rights, Integrating Intellectual Property Rights and Development Policy. 2002. London: September.

[30] Shabalala, Dalindyebo, Marcos Orellana, Nathalie Bernasconi-Osterwalder and Sofia Plagakis. 2008. Intellectual Property in European Union Economic Partnership Agreements with the African, Caribbean and Pacific Countries: What way Forward after the CARIFORUM EPA and the Interim EPAs? Washington: Center for International Environmental Law, April. For a more detailed analysis of CARIFORUM-EU EPA with respect to intellectual property rights see, Third World Network. 2009. EU

There is also the likelihood that more medicines will be patented in the CARIFORUM countries due the EPA's patent provision that requires these states to join the TRIPS-plus treaties. The patenting of other technology "will increase the cost of manufacturing, the cost of biotechnology research and foreign exchange losses." The conclusion by the TWN report is that in general "the treatment of genetic resources and traditional knowledge in the EC-CARIFORUM EPA adds little value and offer no major development benefit to CARIFORUM countries" (Smith 2008).

With respect to trade in goods the CARIFORUM states are committed to confer on the EU any tariff preferences they grant to any developed country or territory or state that accounts "for a share of world merchandise exports above 1 percent; or any group of countries acting individually, collectively or through a free trade agreement accounting collectively for a share of world merchandise exports above 1.5 percent" (Smith 2008). Brazil, India, South Africa among other developing countries have been severely critical of the MFN, but the CARIFORUM states have signed on to it.

The imposition of EPAs by European bloc imperialism takes place simultaneously with "the looming global recession and the triple crises of Finance, Fuel and Food" that hit ACP countries the hardest. For example, as food riots spread across Africa, millions there "are threatened with imminent famine, [and] food production is dealt another deathblow to make way for the artificially cheapened imports that are supposed to be the answer to the crisis."[31] Although the triple crises are at hand the European bloc imperialist continue to impose the EPAs that threaten to disrupt the export trade of the ACP countries. Indeed, the EU exploited the insecurities from these crises to ram through so-called interim economic partnership agreements, a stepping-stone to giving preferential privileges to EU businesses in perpetuity.[32]

EPAs: Economic and Social Development Implications: The Case of the CARIFORUM-EC Economic Partnership Agreement. Penang, Malaysia: Third World Network, February.

[31] Mustapha, Suleiman. 2008. Trade experts review EPA strategy. *The Statesman* 21/08: http://www.thestatesmanonline.com/.

[32] Mustapha, Suleiman. 2008. Trade experts review EPA strategy. *The Statesman* 21/08: http://www.thestatesmanonline.com/.

Pushback against European Bloc Imperialism

Resistance to the EPAs is essentially reformist in that civil society groups and individuals in the ACP regions and Europe seem more concerned with making the EPAs more compatible with the capitalist development process in the developing countries. The resistance therefore wants to make a deal with European bloc imperialism rather than reject it outright. The quarrel with the EPA is essentially over tactics about how the ACP region should go about implementing capitalist development. This reformist approach places those who resist the EPAs in the same category of the critics of free trade such as Ha-Joon Chang[33] and Erik Reinert[34] who oppose the current market liberalization approach to globalization preferring instead for the poor countries to implement protectionist measures to develop their manufacturing sectors before they embrace it. Their argument is that the poor countries must liberalize only those sectors that have been successfully protected to an age of maturity. This approach, which is associated with import substitution industrialization, may also be classified as "free trade through protection."

The anti-EPAs struggle is mainly reactive to the EPA negotiation process it does not put forward an alternative agenda for change. It merely seeks to reform the implementation of the agreement with European bloc imperialism but it does not provide an alternative plan that capitalizes on the potential reconfiguration of global power based on the emergence of Brazil, India, China and South Africa as significant players in international economic relations, and the role of alternative trade arrangements such as the Bolivarian Alternative for the Americas (ALBA), and Petrocaribe. Also, the trade union movements in the ACP states are hardly in the forefront of linking the EPA threat and job losses, degradation, and poor working conditions. In addition, the women's movement is not as vocal as a united front in the anti-EPAs struggle as an integral component of their fight for justice and equality (Mustapha 2008).

---

[33] Chang, Ha-Joon. 2008. *Bad Samaritans: The Myth of Free Trade and the Secret History of Capitalism*. New York: Bloomsbury Press; Chang, Ha-Joon. 2006. *Kicking Away The Ladder: Development Strategy in Historical Perspective*. London: Anthem Press.

[34] Reinert, Erik S. 2007. *How Rich Countries Got Rich ... and Why Poor Countries Stay Poor*. London: Constable and Robinson.

The elites, civil society groups, individuals, and academics in the ACP countries that because of their role in the negotiations process or ideological positions support the EPAs are mere collaborators with European bloc imperialism. They do not acknowledge the great opportunities to reorder the globe based on the emergence of the new global players mentioned above. They seem uniform in their belief that the EPAs are currently the "best deal" for the ACP countries, and that the rest of the society must embrace and collaborate with them uncritically, and work with the negotiators to secure agreements that are more development friendly.

The ACP states, however, have mounted major fights to dampen the effects of the impending European bloc imperialist stranglehold over them. The Third World Network (TWN) for example has placed considerable pressure on African governments and policy makers to refrain from signing EPAs. This pressure however seems not to be out of a need to completely reject the EPA, but an attempt to reform it to make it more palatable to the ACP countries.

The ACP states are awakening to the fraudulent nature of the comprehensive EPAs signed by the CARIFORUM states and the interim EPAs signed for example by Ghana and Cote d'Ivoire. The interim EPA is deceitful because it goes "beyond what it claims to do. Instead of focusing on trade in goods, the agreement actually captures the Singapore issues such as procurement, trade-related issues and intellectual property rights."[35] Furthermore, the interim EPAs are a framework for expansion into comprehensive EPAs, which include commitments such as universal liberalization and deregulation of services and investment rules that were rejected and thrown out by the WTO.

The ACP countries issued a statement that the EU brought "enormous pressure" on them to sign EPAs, and threatened to impose onerous tariffs often exceeding 10 percent on goods from ACP countries destined for EU markets should EPAs not be concluded by December 31, 2007. However, among the almost 80 ACP countries engaged in trade talks with the EU, only 35 accepted EPAs by 2007, the EU deadline for them to do so. Most agreements were restricted to trade in goods in which the ACP states have undertaken to remove barriers they impose on 80 percent of imports from the EU (Cronin, David. 2007).

[35] Daily Graphic. 2008. TWN To Mount Pressure On Government To withdraw From Signing EPA Pact, Fri. August 22.

Non-governmental organizations (NGOs) across the European continent launched a coalition to stop the EPAs. The stop EPA coalition wants EU member states to take action to withdraw reciprocity from the EPA negotiating mandate, since it could lead inter alia to the collapse of the manufacturing sector in West Africa and other developing regions. The Lomé Conventions granted unilateral preferences to ACP products in the EU markets, the CPA extended these preferences until 2007, while the EPAs abolish the non-reciprocal preferential trade regime. However, "the decline in import duties due to the preferential tariff elimination" is a major cause for concern since countries might not be able to recoup the lost revenue from trade. This would require the implementation of "complementary fiscal and economic policies... before or at the time the EPA come into force."[36]

The verdict pronounced on the EPAs by the NGO community is that while many people concur that cohesive and planned regional integration is a key development strategy, the EPAs will have an inevitable detrimental impact on regional economic integration, particularly in Africa.[37] The EPAs seek to ensure that African and Caribbean markets are extensively open to EU products, without real reciprocal opportunities for African and Caribbean products in Europe. Reciprocity is only in theory because African and Caribbean firms cannot compete with EU multinational corporations that would push them out of business and dominate African and Caribbean markets. The NGOs argue that the EPAs would damage farmers and fledgling industries in poor countries by exposing them to competition from a cascade of European imports. This in effect would squeeze out from the market uncompetitive companies in the ACP countries.

This is the reality of European bloc imperialism deceitfully clothed in the garb of sustainable development, poverty eradication, the Millennium Development Goals, the promotion of regional integration, good governance, integration into the global economy, increasing investment, solidarity and mutual interest, etc. Previously, the imperialist states in Europe pursued a "civilizing" mission in the developing

---

36 Busse, M. and S. Lüehje. 2007. Should the Caribbean Countries Sign an Economic Partnership Agreement with the EU? Challenges and Strategic Options. *Journal of Economic Integration* (22) 3: 598–618.

37 Cronin, David. 2007. EPAs Signed "Under Duress," Says South Africa. *Inter Press Service News Agency* December 21; Cronin, David. 2008. Africans Stuck with EU Deals. *Inter Press Service News Agency*. January 29.

countries, while under globalization the undertaking is to promote liberal democracy and to integrate these states into the global economy through free trade for them to achieve sustainable development and good governance. The EPA in this current period of US-led globalization is about opening and maintaining markets in the ACP countries to manufactured goods produced in the EU and securing the supply of raw materials produced in ACP countries that are utilized in the manufacturing process in the EU.

In the pushback against the EPA, the West African states for example, are working at collectively negotiating an EPA with the EU under the Economic Community of West African States (ECOWAS).[38] With the assistance of the West African Economic and Monetary Union (WEAMU), ECOWAS coordinated the region's negotiations with the EU until the target date for conclusion in, June 2009. This action had the effect of freezing the EPA text initialed by Ghana and Cote d'Ivoire.

The pushback in the Caribbean against the CARIFORUM-EU EPA has many faces but most importantly some regional governments – Guyana, Grenada and St. Lucia – had refused temporarily to sign the agreement although the other governments had signed it. Guyana, which has now caved in, had refused to sign the EPA on the grounds that the agreement threatens to impose higher tariffs on its essential exports such as rice, rum and sugar and would result in a loss of billions of dollars in revenue and unfair EU trading advantage in services. Guyana takes the position that there is very little it could export to Europe and that the result would be a negative impact on its balance of trade and balance of payments.

Furthermore, Guyana claims that the EPA would undermine the two-year old Caribbean Single Market Economy because the region would be obliged to give priority to implementing the EPA. In addition, the EPA has altered Caricom's foreign trade policy by compelling the region to offer similar trade agreements to the United States and Canada, and to give the EU the same treatment given to the large developing countries of India, China and Brazil. Also, the EPA would determine the foreign trade policy of the Caribbean for decades leaving these countries with little flexibility on the issue.[39]

---

[38] Kwa, Aileen. 2008. Nigeria 'Threatens' Neighbors in Wake of Bilateral EPAs. *Inter Press Service News Agency* June 2.

[39] Caribbean leaders to hold emergency summit on EU trade pact *21 August 2008*, http://www.eubusiness.com/news-eu/1219327347.04

Conclusion

In the light of the promise of the new global order, in which the ACP countries could permanently realign their economies in their self-interest, with the emerging economies in the developing world this is the worst possible time for them to enter into European bloc imperialist relationships through the EPAs. Furthermore, the food, gas, financial and economic crises indicate the failure of economic liberalization imposed on the ACP states and has generated major dissent among academics concerning the usefulness of the "free trade model," which is the foundation of the EPAs. Much of this dissent is taking place among scholars who work in the areas of trade and development, international finance, aid, development studies, and globalization. These are unique times that present a great opportunity for the creation of new development paradigms.

The promise of the new global order that reflects a power configuration in which Brazil, Russia, India, China (BRIC), and South Africa are major players must stimulate the anti-EPAs struggle and search for new development paradigms. The recent declarations of the first-ever BRIC summit in the Russian city of Yekaterinburg, in June 2009, are an indication of a possible march towards a new global order that would require new approaches to development.[40] Also, this struggle has already stymied the European bloc imperialist attempt to push through comprehensive EPAs on the ACP states by December 31, 2007. Furthermore, the anti-EPA struggle by progressive civil society, nationalist, and left leaning groups and academics has influenced the positions of some governments of the ACP states on the subject. For example, the widespread resentment of the EPAs has forced the European bloc imperialist to review and renegotiate interim EPAs in ACP regions in Africa.

[40] Joint Statement of the BRIC Countries Leaders, June 16 2009 Yekaterinburg. 2009. http://msdfli.wordpress.com/2009/06/25/joint-statement-of-the-bric-countries-leaders-june-16-2009-yekaterinburg/. June 25.

CHAPTER SIX

THE THEORETICAL FOUNDATIONS OF EUROPEAN BLOC IMPERIALISM

Introduction

This chapter reviews the theoretical foundations of European bloc imperialism, to purposely reinforce the argument that the economic partnership agreement, the conduit of European bloc imperialism, is established on failed conjectures that will bear little or no practical development fruits for the ACP group of states. It takes this position because of the underlying proposition of this book that development is not merely about technological change, industrialization, or human and sustainable development, but ultimately means the transformation of the wealth and power configurations historically associated with the system of capitalist production and exchange in which the ACP countries are entrapped.

The Caribbean region has been devoid of such structural transformation of wealth and power since its incorporation into the capitalist system. Since the 1970s the Caribbean countries became victims of neoliberal economic theory, which is associated with increasing inequality, higher levels of poverty, and economic decline in the ACP countries that slavishly embrace it. The Caricom countries for example, characterized by small open economies, have experienced on average "a declining growth trend and an increased disparity around that trend" since the 1980s,[1] while the sub-Saharan African economies encountered negative per capita income growth rates of -1.2 percent in the 1980s and -0.04 percent in the 1990s.[2]

---

[1] Economic Commission for Latin America and the Caribbean (ECLAC). 2005. Long Term Growth in the Caribbean: A Balance of Payments Constraints Approach. Port of Spain, Trinidad: Sub-regional Headquarters for the Caribbean.

[2] United Nations Industrial Development Organization (UNIDO). 2004. Industrialization, Environment and the Millennium Development Goals in Sub-Saharan Africa: The New Frontier in the Fight Against Poverty. Vienna, Austria: UNIDO Vienna International Center.

China and India, however, which steered clear of neoliberal economic theory pursuing an economic development strategy "of near autarky, industrialization, and the dominance of the state in the economy,"[3] enjoyed an "average rate of growth of GDP at around 10 percent and 6 percent respectively during the 1980–2000."[4] China began to emerge from insulation around 1978 while India implemented piecemeal reforms from the 1980s.[5] Also, Cuba did not implement neoliberal structural adjustment but the country continues to marvel the neoliberal ideologues who could only shower praise on the island for its remarkable performance in social welfare including health and education, and whose economy is making steady strides despite the US embargo against the country.[6]

The European imperialist powers have always pursued colonial economic policies in the Caribbean, which in appearance meant well for the region, but in reality failed to transform the structure of power in the region. Colonial policies were based on the Ricardian comparative advantage approach that basically deprived the region of its wealth, while simultaneously accumulating wealth in Europe. Although the Caribbean has evolved from "slavery-cum-capitalism"[7] to neoliberal globalization, the Ricardian free trade approach continues to be the most dominant theoretical framework that European bloc imperialism employs to the detriment of the region. The Ricardian free trade theory keeps the Caribbean subjugated in an international division of labor as suppliers of raw materials, and consumers of manufactured goods produced by the EU multinational corporations. The region also subsidizes the EU with professionals trained by Caribbean taxpayers' money. The region even subsidizes the EU in its proxy fight against so-called terrorism, by undertaking anti-terrorist measures paid for by regional taxpayers.

The underlying theoretical framework for the EPA is associated with centuries of European socio-economic domination of the Caribbean.

---

[3] Srinivasan, T.N. 2004. China and India: Growth and Poverty, 1980–2000. *Journal of Asian Economics,* (15) 4: 613–636.

[4] Srinivasan, T.N. 2004. China and India: Growth and Poverty, 1980–2000. *Journal of Asian Economics,* (15) 4: 613–636.

[5] Srinivasan, T.N. 2004. China and India: Growth and Poverty, 1980–2000. *Journal of Asian Economics,* (15) 4: 613–636.

[6] Lobe, Jim. 2001. Learn from Cuba, Says World Bank. Inter-Press Service, May 1.

[7] For an analysis of "slavery-cum-capitalism" see Thomas, Clive Y. 1984. *Plantations, Peasants, and State: A Study of the Mode of Sugar Production in Guyana.* Los Angeles: University of California, Centre for Afro-American Studies.

Thus, the EPA as a bundle of trade policies designed to bring about sustainable development and good governance in the Caribbean is the current apex of a number of failed theoretical approaches experimented with in the region. These theoretical approaches fall under the rubric of classical political economy, neo-classical economics, Keynesian economics and now neoliberal economics that have defined the economic relationship between the Caribbean and the European states, from since the region's incorporation into the mercantile capitalist world order beginning in the seventeenth century. They have dominated Caribbean-European economic relations in different historical phases of Caribbean development since the region's colonization by mercantile capital. The Caribbean has always been a recipient of socio-economic theory handed down to the area through the economic and social policies designed for the region by colonial powers.

However, we may extract from Thomas (1984), a theoretical formulation that periodizes Caribbean development into four distinct, but interrelated periods. These are characterized by what Thomas (1984) identifies as the colonial slave mode of production, the transition to dependency relations, and the rise of Caribbean nationalist economic experiments.[8] The principal neoliberal argument used against such and other[9] theoretical formulations about Caribbean-type socio-economic formations, is that social science theories must have universal applicability to be useful and that these approaches are not universally applicable. This criticism renders as useless any attempt by ACP scholars to formulate theories best suited to the internal conditions of their countries. Whereas, the development of capitalist theories were specific to particular European geographical regions, and as capitalism expanded across the globe it took its theories with it. The scientific idea about the universality of theory developed side-by-side with

---

[8] See Thomas, Clive Y. 1984. *Plantations, Peasants, and State: A Study of the Mode of Sugar Production in Guyana*. Los Angeles: University of California, Centre for Afro-American Studies; Thomas, Clive Y. 1974. *Dependence and Transformation: The Economics of the Transition to Socialism*. New York: Monthly Review Press.

[9] See for example Lewis, W. Arthur. 1950. The Industrialization of the British West Indies. *Caribbean Economic Review* 2: 1–39; Levitt, Kari. 2005. *Reclaiming Development: Independent Thought and Caribbean Community*. Kingston: Iran Randle Publishers; Beckford, George. 1984. *Persistent Poverty*. London: Zed Press; Best, L. 1968. Outline of a Model of Pure Plantation Economy. *Social and Economic Studies* (17) 3: 283–326; Girvan, Norman. 2006. Caribbean Development Thought Revisited. *Canadian Journal of Development Studies* (27) 3: 337–352.

capitalism. And as capitalism subordinated science to market production[10] and exchange for profit, it seized the notion of universality of theory to its self-defense. The universality of theory therefore became a capitalist project to defeat alternatives that could upturn the capitalist system as a whole.

The neoliberal counter-revolution rode on the idea about the universality of theory, in order to subordinate the opposition and threat to capitalism posed by state-led development alternatives. Thus, the principal line of attack by the neoliberal theorist against development economics is that development theories lack universal application. Also, they peddle the allegation that development economists regard orthodox economics as irrelevant.[11] The real problem with development economics however is that it operates within the mercantilist-classical political economy capitalist domain, and does not seek to alter the structures of power and capital accumulation in the ACP countries. Nonetheless, the neoliberal theorists regard development economics as posing a serious threat to the capitalist system, and therefore it must be defeated if capitalism is to remain in tack. This threat is seen to involve the heavy reliance by development economics and Keynesian theories on the state as an economic actor, and the alleged underplaying of the centrality and primacy of the market as the principal mechanism to allocate economic resources.

However, the current global financial and economic crises have demonstrated the folly of heavy reliance on market forces or market liberalization as the primary means of resource allocation. Nonetheless, there is serious pushback in defense of market liberalization, with argumentation to the effect that the current global financial and economic crises are due to too little market liberalization. For example, FreedomFeast the supposedly independent, non-partisan annual festival that annually celebrates great books, ideas, and minds in an open-society is quite clear about which system of economic production it wants to defend and maintain in the light of the current crises. The FreedomFeast 2009 televised debate on C-Span 2 Book TV (7/10/09) appeared to be a deliberate attempt to shift the cause for the current financial and economic crises from the failed neoliberal market

[10] See Braverman, Harry. 1974. *Labor and Monopoly Capitalism: The Degradation of Work in the Twentieth Century*. New York: Monthly Review Press.

[11] Lal, Deepak. 1983. *The Poverty of 'Development Economics'*. London: The Institute of Economic Affairs, Hobart Paperback 16.

liberalization policies to that of monopoly control exercised by the Federal Reserve Bank and the state over the financial and monetary sectors. According to the proponents of this view the Federal Reserve Bank and the state have monopoly control over the money supply, by their ability to manipulate the interest rate and print money, respectively, which is really the problem. The perceived solution is to abolish the Federal Reserve Bank, and allow market forces to determine the money supply, and the production of money, which is a commodity like any other commodity.

The historical dilemma of the ACP countries given their colonial past and possible future under the thumb of European bloc imperialism is that even the pushback against colonial policy and the economic partnership agreements embrace the very mercantilist/classical political economy or protectionist versus free trade theoretical frameworks that produce theoretical positions embraced by the neoliberals and debaters at FreedomFeast 2009. Perhaps, the strongest pushback, against colonialism but which was also acceptable to the colonial powers and the Caribbean ruling elites, came from Sir W. Arthur Lewis who chose Ricardian comparative advantage as a basis to argue a case for the industrialization of the Caribbean in opposition to the then standard colonial belief that because of its factor endowments the region should specialize in agriculture. Girvan (2008) noted however that

> The thrust of Lewis's conclusions, which have been amplified in the UNDP Report, is that trade expansion is not an end in itself, but must be made to serve the ends of development, and that to do so there must be strategic and targeted policy interventions; to raise productivity in the case of one, to promote human development in the case of the other.[12]

The Marxist and plantation dependence frameworks did not resolve the aforementioned development dilemma. Caribbean Marxists were never in power except for short periods in Guyana under Cheddi Jagan in 1953, Jamaica under Michael Manley, and Grenada under Maurice Bishop. Their policies nonetheless did not bring about the desired structural transformations in support of development. The plantation dependence school operated more or less within a Keynesian framework and as such does not seek the kind of structural change that is typically associated with the Marxists.

[12] Girvan, Norman. 2008. Lewis and the New World Economists. Georgetown, Guyana. *Guyana Review*, May 28. http://www.stabroeknews.com/2008/guyana-review/05/28/people-2/print/

The chapter is organized along the following lines – first there is a discussion on the theoretical lineage of the CARIFORUM-EU EPA, focusing on mercantilism as the handmaiden of the nation-state, and the free trade critique of mercantilism. Second, there is an analysis of the persistence of the mercantilist/free trade dichotomy in the Caribbean. Third, there are some definitional considerations of key concepts in everyday usage, such as Washington Consensus, neoliberal economics, Keynesian Consensus, structural adjustment, economic liberalization, market liberalization, and neoliberal political principles. Fourth, there is a brief description of selected neoliberal policies in specific Caribbean countries to demonstrate the one-size-fits-all nature of structural adjustment. Finally, a brief outline is provided of structural adjustment and economic liberalization in the Caribbean, and the emergence of the EPA.

The Theoretical Lineage of the EPAs

The EPA is the latest in a litany of failed development approaches couched within the free trade-mercantilism theoretical framework. Mercantilism was a pre-industrial capitalist trade system organized by European city- and nation-states enforced by their naval and military power. It was not a unified theory as such at the time of the colonization of the Caribbean between 1500 and 1750. The mercantile system comprised a package of government policy founded on an economic theory that capital in the form of precious metals (gold and silver) determine the development of a country, and that the volume of the world economy and international trade is fixed. The gold, silver, and trade value held by a country represented its economic assets or capital. The mercantilists believed that a positive balance of trade would increase a country's economic assets, and that the best way to advance that goal was for the government to pursue protectionist policies in the economy through measures to restrict imports and stimulate exports. Tariffs were the most effective government policy instruments employed in the restriction of imports.[13]

---

[13] For detailed analyses of the mercantile system see for example Vaggi, Gianni and Peter Groenewegen. 2006. *A Concise History of Economic Thought: From Mercantilism to Monetarism*. New York: Palgrave Macmillan; Ekelund Jr., Robert B. and Robert D. Tollison. 1997. *Politicized Economies: Monarchy, Monopoly, and Mercantilism*. College

Mercantilism as Handmaiden of the Nation-State

Mercantilism represented the early stages of capitalism from the 16th to the 18th centuries that coincided with the emergence of the nation-state, created by the Treaty of Westphalia in 1648, a political and economic entity and unit for analysis of development. The emergence of the nation-state stimulated the need for a power greater than the strongest individual or group within it. Today, we recognize that power as the state – government, military and para-military forces, and the judiciary. There also arose the need for mechanisms of revenue generation and collection in the form of taxes, excise duties, licensing fees, and the different forms of state revenues that we know today, to finance the state.

The nation-state needed to accumulate wealth to build a strong army and navy to defend itself against its neighbors and rivals, erect a strong internal security apparatus to suppress internal descent, and establish a well-oiled diplomatic service to negotiate international settlements on its behalf to avert war. By accumulating wealth the state could maintain the social contract with its subjects in the nation-state to fulfill their economic, social, and political welfare, and defend them from foreign aggression and domination. In essence, the nation-state needs to accumulate wealth for its independent development and survival, free from foreign aggression and domination, and taking proper care of the welfare of its citizens.[14] Mercantilism was the economic system of choice by the nation-state to achieve those goals. The rise of the nation-state coupled with mercantilism brought to the fore the issue of government intervention and control over national economies and markets.

The European nation-state became the curse of Africa, Asia and the Americas, which became the objects of conquest, plunder and settlement by European powers in pursuit of bullion, silver, raw materials and markets. European imperialism was a product of the emergence of the nation-state, and a means by which the nation-state would acquire wealth. The European nation-states continue to pursue wealth accumulation as their principal goal in the twenty-first century. The ACP countries are latecomers to the game of wealth accumulation. Their

---

Station, Texas: Texas A & M University Press; Magnusson, Lars, ed., 1996. *Mercantilism: Critical Concepts in the History of Economics*. London: Routledge.

14 Spechler, Martin C. 1990. *Perspectives in Economic Thought*. New York: McGraw-Hill.

principal dilemma is that as they seek to become the subjects of development for themselves, they remain objectives of development of Europe currently as a single entity and not necessarily, as individual nation-states.

The EPA, a legal trade document, is a throw back to the Navigation Act of 1651 in response to Holland's proposal for a free trade agreement with England. Britain felt it was not strong enough economically to compete in a free trade agreement with Holland, hence it chose the Navigation Act, the mercantilist protectionist option. The ACP countries, which are not in an economic position to compete in a free trade agreement with the EU are forced into EU proposed EPAs, which are classified as new forms of mercantilism. However, the classical political economists mounted major criticisms against mercantilism in the late eighteenth century.

Free Trade Critique of Mercantilism

The French physiocrats in the 1760s were among the first to completely reject mercantilism.[15] In their view it was only the land and agriculture that could increase and multiply wealth, not the pursuit of precious metals, industry and commerce promoted by the mercantilists. The physiocrats believed that only agriculture yielded a surplus and that manufacturing took up much value as inputs into production as it created in output, and therefore does not create a net product. In the physiocratic doctrine the wealth of a nation lies not in its stocks of gold and silver as the mercantilist believed, but rather in the size of the net agricultural product. The physiocrats believed that free trade was essential to keep prices stable and fair, and was the fountain of prosperity.

Adam Smith's *Wealth of Nations* influenced by the physiocrats represents a formidable challenge to the mercantile theory about what nation-states must do to develop and maintain their developed status. According to Adam Smith the proponents of mercantilism argued,

> the wealth of a country consists, not in its gold and silver only, but in its lands, houses, and consumable goods of all different kinds, but in the

[15] See for example Higgs, Henry. 1989. *The Physiocrats: Six Lectures on the French Économistes of the 18th Century*. Fairfield, New Jersey: A.M. Kelley; Beer, Max. 1966. *An Inquiry into Physiocracy*. New York: Russell and Russell, Inc.; Meek, Ronald L., ed., 1962. *The Economics of Physiocracy*. London: Macmillan.

> course of their reasoning, however, the lands, houses, and consumable goods seem to slip out of their memory, and the strain of their argument frequently supposes that all wealth consists in gold and silver, and to multiply those metals is the great object of national industry and commerce (Smith 1992: 342).[16]

In Smith's (1991) view the pursuit of the mercantilist objective to multiply wealth led to the view that the "two great engines for enriching" a country "were restraints upon importation, and encouragements of exportation."

This means that the mercantile system sacrificed domestic consumption, punishing the consumer by restricting imports, in favor of pleasing the producer by encouraging exports. Smith (1991) noted that the system of laws established to manage Britain's American and West Indian colonies sacrifices the interest of the home consumers to that of the producer "with a more extravagant profusion than in all our other commercial regulations." Smith (1991) regarded mercantilist monopoly of colonial trade as "mean and malignant expedients," which not only depress the industry of all other countries especially those of the colonies, but also diminishes those of the country in whose favor it is established.

David Ricardo (1996)[17] embraced Smith's criticism of the mercantile system, who he argues fully exposed the weaknesses of the system. Ricardo (1996) noted that the mercantile system aimed to increase commodity prices at home by restricting competition abroad. It reduced the quantity of commodities produced by forced capital into areas where it would not otherwise flow. Commodities were sold at higher prices sustained by the difficulty of production and not by scarcity. Thus, although goods fetched higher prices their production lacked the requisite quantity of capital to produce them (Ricardo 1996).

Thus, the assessment of mercantilism by Smith (1991) is both right and wrong in the sense that mercantilism depresses the manufacturing sector in the Caribbean confining the region to the role as producer of raw materials and importers of finished manufactured products. However, mercantilism did not diminish the industries of the countries

---

[16] Smith, Adam. 1991. *An Inquiry in to the Nature and Causes of the Wealth of Nations*. New York: Prometheus Books.

[17] Ricardo, David. 1996. *Principles of Political Economy and Taxation*. New York: Prometheus Books.

that established the system, to the contrary it strengthened their industries. Indeed, the ACP countries experienced higher levels of industrialization under the state-led development strategy, and were de-industrialized under the so-called "free trade" approach associated with US-led globalization.[18]

Although Smith (1991) and Ricardo (1996) criticized the mercantile system and proposed free trade as an alternative, the effects of trade relations between the Caribbean and Europe have remain the same. They argue that both the colonizer nation-states and the colonies (later independent nation-states) will benefit, since wealth would accumulate in both sets of nation-states engaged in free trade. Ricardo (1996) argued on the basis of absolute and comparative advantage that free trade is more beneficial to nation-states compared with mercantile protectionist policies. Countries would be better off even if they had the absolute advantage in the production of a single commodity as long as they specialize in its production and engage in free trade. The flip side to this argument is that countries will become poorer if they impose import restriction and tariffs.

From the perspective of the European ACP colonies, mercantilism had debilitating effects on the self-respect, dignity, and social, political and economic wellbeing of the colonized. Mercantilism meant only one thing to the colonized – exploitation of human and natural resources in the colonies to accumulate wealth in the European nation-states. This exploitation could not coexist with wealth accumulation in the colonies – it generated happiness and prosperity in the European nation-states, simultaneously that it produced misery and comparative backwardness in the colonies.

The classical political economy free trade theoretical framework based on specialization determined by comparative advantage in factor endowment is the foundation of the CARIFORUM-EU EPA. According to this theory if tiny Montserrat with 12,000 inhabitants specializes in tourism because nature bestows the island with sandy beaches, turquoise water, and a volcano that attracts tourists, and engages in free trade with the EU then that country will develop on an equal footing with the EU states. Reinert (2007) observed however,

[18] For more on the deindustrialization of the poor countries see Reinert, Erik S. 2007. *How Rich Countries Got Rich ... and Why Poor Countries Stay Poor*. London: Constable and Robinson.

that comparative advantage by its claim that all participating countries in free trade stand an equal chance to develop merely helped to mask the guilt of the imperialist states that plundered their colonies.

If the ACP countries collectively refuse to enter into EPAs, it is doubtful that a EU flotilla or armada would enter the waters of Africa, the Pacific Islands, and the Caribbean to forcefully make the ACP countries sign them. The US imperialists however still send their military ahead of their multinational corporations in their particular brand of market conquest and maintenance. This is evident in Iraq, and in the recent decision by the US to resuscitate its naval patrol of the Caribbean in an attempt to threaten Venezuela, and possibly to send a signal to its competitors in the region, namely China and the EU. The EU uses other methods including divide and rule tactics, to bring about "voluntary" complicity on the part of the ACP states with the modern Navigation Act termed the EPA.

Neoliberal Theoretical Foundation of EPAs

The EPAs are constructed within the broad mercantilist-free trade theoretical framework bequeathed to present generations by the framers of the idea of the nation-state and how it might accumulate and maintain wealth. Academics and policymakers in both the rich and poor countries continue to formulate their development theories and policies within the mercantilist-free trade theoretical framework. Marxists and the alternative socialist/communist system that they seek to establish are an exception. Today, the theoretical agenda within the mercantilist-free trade framework about the development of the nation-state is referred to as neoliberalism. The neoliberal theoretical agenda is on the free trade side of the mercantilist-free trade theoretical divide. In the tradition of Adam Smith and David Ricardo, perfected by the neo-classical economists such as Alfred Marshall,[19] the neoliberal theorists represent their free trade agenda both at the level of theory and policy.

The theoretical tradition from which the EPA emerged took the neoliberal turn in the 1970s. Economic growth associated with state-interventionist models in what scholars describe as the "golden age of capitalism" in the post-World War II period ran into trouble as profit

[19] Marshall, Alfred. 1910. *The Principles of Economics*. London: St. Martin's Press.

began to fall in the 1970s.[20] The diagnosis was that the crisis was caused by too much state-intervention in the economy and worker control through labor unions. Neoliberalism, or the swing back to free market fundamentalism was the preferred theoretical solution to the crisis.

A plethora of theoretical writings emerged on the virtues of free trade, and policy prescriptions surfaced under the rubric of structural adjustment in support of the neoliberal theoretical objective to extricate the state from the economy, establish free trade, and curtail the strength of trade unions. The key concepts associated with neoliberal theory and policy that have dominated the academic and policy landscapes since the 1980s include neoliberal economics and economic and market liberalization, structural adjustment, divestment, privatization, free trade, globalization, civil society, governance, democratization, etc. These theoretical and policy objectives became known as the Washington Consensus that replaced the Keynesian Consensus[21] on the interventionist state that was formulated as a solution to the Great Depression.

The "Washington Consensus" had its precursor in the free trade era that prevailed in the late 19th century from 1850 to 1900. Then, colonialism and gunboat diplomacy of the imperialist hegemonic powers supported a system of international finance, bond markets and the gold standard foisted on the rest of the world. That era of free trade stimulated World War I, the Great Depression, and World War II.

Neoliberal economics is a set of economic ideas piggybacking on classical and neoclassical economic theory and adapted to a US-dominated global order, designed to bring about free trade in all markets. It rejects the idea that developing countries require special theories of development that catered to the needs of the peoples in those areas. Lal (1983)[22] argues that these special development theories are irrational because they seek to promote an alternative economics based on the peculiarities of the developing countries. According to the neoliberals there is only one economics with universally applicable laws without bias to both the developed and developing countries. This is the key criticism that the proponents of neoliberal economics level

---

[20] See Petras, James and Henry Veltmeyer. 2007. *Multinationals on Trial: Foreign Investment Matters*. Aldershot, Hampshire: Ashgate

[21] Singer, Hans W. 1997. The Golden Age of the Keynesian Consensus: The Pendulum Swings Back. *World Development* (25) 3: 293–295.

[22] Lal, Deepak. 1983. *The Poverty of 'Development Economics'*. London: The Institute of Economic Affairs, Hobart Paperback 16.

against development theory classified as falling within the ambit of the Keynesian Consensus.

This criticism of development theory is the foundation of neoliberal mono-economic theory and structural adjustment[23] policies regarded as relevant to any country whether developed or developing. It is the basis of the vilification of the state whose very mechanisms played a central role in the socio-economic development of the rich countries, and on which the developed countries are banking for a bailout from the current global financial and economic crises. Nonetheless, structural adjustment the panacea for curing all economic ills in developing countries is premised on the neoliberal ideal that the self-regulating market allocates scarce economic resources much more efficiently than the state. On this basis the state must be removed from direct economic activity, and confined to providing the macro-economic and legal institutional frameworks for the operations of the free market system whose activities are the domain only of private enterprises.

Proponents of structural adjustment hold the monetarist view that excessive state involvement in the economy increases the money supply and the velocity of money circulation. In turn, this expands aggregate demand and raises the general price level thus making the economy inflationary. They argue that increased government involvement in direct production is one of the causes of the debt crisis,[24] inflation, and the escalation in rent extraction by state bureaucrats in the developing world. Furthermore, they contend that the monopsonistic behavior of trade unions puts an upward pressure on wages, increases production costs, contracts economic activity, aggravates inflation, and thereby hinders development. The state and labor unions are identified as the chief culprits responsible for inflation, the debt crisis, decreasing profits, economic contraction, and the persistence of underdevelopment. Neoliberal economics shifts the blame for the persistence of

---

[23] There is a vast literature on structural adjustment. The discussion on adjustment and privatization is going on under the general rubric of "globalization." See for example, Mhone, Guy. 1995. Dependency and Underdevelopment: The Limits of Structural Adjustment Programs and Towards a Proactive State-led Development Strategy. *African Development Review* 7: 51–85; Savas, Emanuel S. 1987. *Privatization: The Key to Better Government.* London: Chatham House; Kent, Calvin A., ed., 1987. *Entrepreneurship and the Privatizing of Government*, Westport, Connecticut: Quorum Books.

[24] See Canterbury, Dennis C. 1991. "Guyana's Debt Crisis: Its Meaning and Effect", in Jack Menke and Henry Jeffrey, eds., *Problems of Development of the Guianas.* Paramaribo: Anton de Kom University of Suriname, pp. 184–194.

underdevelopment from the exploitative mercantilist economic relations between the developed and the underdeveloped economies to the state and labor unions in the poor countries.

Structural adjustment is the process of deliberately adjusting or changing the structure and operation of the economy to mitigate the effects of negative internal and/or external shocks.[25] It is the comprehensive restructuring and coordination of a country's public and private sector organizations to make them more effective in the national and sectoral management of the economy.[26] While SAPs concentrate on changing the structure and operation of the economy, stabilization programs focus on restoring and maintaining the interactive balance between aggregate demand and supply, price-cost relationships, in the external accounts, and in the financial markets. A major goal of structural adjustment is macroeconomic stabilization, which means that the foreign sector payments are balanced.[27] Macroeconomic stabilization is achieved through fiscal and monetary reform, and devaluation. Structural adjustment involves resource mobilization, public sector allocation, and institutional reform. These other structural adjustment policies are merely auxiliaries to the prime goal of macroeconomic stabilization.

Neoliberal theorists believe that stabilization must be achieved before the auxiliary programs are implemented. This sequencing is advocated due to the belief that the public and private sectors would be adjusting to an unstable macroeconomic framework, which is totally undesirable and unacceptable (Toye 1995: 5–6).[28]

An assumption of structural adjustment is that the functions of the state must be reformed particularly in the areas of production and finance. The state must extricate itself as an active producer of goods

[25] Downes, Andrew. 1992. The Search for a Sustainable Labor Market Response to Structural Adjustment Programs in the Caribbean. Paper presented at Regional Seminar for Senior Trade Unions Officials on "The Role of Trade Unions in Periods of Structural Adjustment Programs." Bridgetown, Barbados: Barbados Workers Union Labor College.

[26] See Downes, Andrew. 1992. The Search for a Sustainable Labor Market Response to Structural Adjustment Programs in the Caribbean. Paper presented at Regional Seminar for Senior Trade Unions Officials on "The Role of Trade Unions in Periods of Structural Adjustment Programs." Bridgetown, Barbados: Barbados Workers Union Labor College.

[27] This means that the monies leaving the economy for other countries must be equal to those coming into the economy from abroad.

[28] See Toye, John. 1995. Structural Adjustment and Employment Policy: Issues and Experiences. Geneva. International Labor Office.

and services including financial services, such as commercial banking and insurance, etc. Also, it must deregulate the productive and services sectors. Given the potential for political instability that the dismantling of the state sector may cause, a political assumption of structural adjustment is that its successful implementation requires a strong state.[29]

Lal (1983) provided the justification for this assumption in his recommendation on how countries on their path to more efficient domestic policies could minimize political difficulties. In response to the political opposition to structural adjustment, Lal (1983) argues, "a courageous, ruthless, and perhaps undemocratic government is required to ride roughshod over the newly created special interest groups" (Lal 1983: 33). It is not surprising, therefore, that structural adjustment was first implemented by the dictatorship government of General Augusto Pinochet in Chile.

The IMF and World Bank, which were given the responsibility of enforcing structural adjustment, employed different policy-measures to achieve their respective goals. IMF policies focus on monetary restraint, interest rate manipulation, reduction of the fiscal deficit, exchange rate actions, reducing the external debt, and structural reform. World Bank policies concentrate on trade, resource mobilization, efficient use of resources and institutional reform.

Economic liberalization the opening up of hitherto closed economies and the removal all hindrance to free trade, is the cornerstone of neoliberal theory. It is inevitably a political process that requires state action to remove all trade barriers.[30] The OECD (1998) postulates that the open market brings greater freedom of choice, specialization and exchange, and economic benefits from comparative advantage. Liberalization promotes competition, productivity gains and encourages best practice production methods, compared with protection that operates like a tax hike, and shrinks the domestic economy (OECD, 1998). It is believed that free trade in open markets brings

---

[29] Toye. John. 1993. *Dilemmas of Development: Reflections on the Counter-revolution in Development Economics.* Oxford: Blackwell; Lal, Deepak. 1983. *The Poverty of 'Development Economics'.* London: The Institute of Economic Affairs, Hobart Paperback 16.

[30] Note that "free trade" and "*laissez faire*" are not the same things. Free trade concerns the exchange of goods and services across countries. "*Laissez faire*" is associated with Adam Smith's idea of the "invisible hand" of the market. See Lal, Deepak. 1983. *The Poverty of 'Development Economics'.* London: The Institute of Economic Affairs, Hobart Paperback 16. See Smith, Adam. 1991. *An Inquiry in to the Nature and Causes of the Wealth of Nations.* New York: Prometheus Books.

more benefits to firms, individual households, and governments. The theoretical tradition that free trade is the solution and alternative to economic stagnation could be traced back to the classical political economists.[31]

Neoliberal theorist argue that the evidence from the underdeveloped countries in the post-World War II period strengthens the case for free trade although "the case for *laissez faire* may have been undermined" (Lal 1983: 48). Lal (2003) noted that free trade and *laissez faire* developed in the classical liberal phase in the 19th century, and "free trade was really a special case of the argument for *laissez faire*"[32] – *laissez faire* being a broader concept referring to a governmental system that does not interfere in the affairs of other countries or the conduct of individual freedom. It also refers to an autonomous economic system in which there is little government intervention in the economy. Free trade and not *laissez faire* is the goal of economic liberalization.

Market liberalization refers to a variety of economic and political conditions including free trade in goods, services, finance, capital, and factor markets in general. It involves policy measures that promote a market-determined price system; the removal of quantitative restrictions; the promotion of private sector operations, such as divestment and contracting out; and placing restrictions on the economic role of government. The Pareto theorem "that a general equilibrium of markets brought about by freely adjusting prices maximizes economic welfare (assuming that the existing distribution of assets and income is optimal)" (Toye 1993: 87) is the basis of both economic liberalization and structural adjustment. The policy prescriptions of the Washington Consensus therefore are decidedly market oriented.

The Washington Consensus also represents a set of neoliberal political principles concerning democracy and its implementation globally. The liberal democratic principles include freedom of speech – including a free press, which arguably is necessary to ensure transparency, make leaders accountable and allow citizens to voice their concerns and frustrations. They involve the freedom of assembly, to create a venue for organization and dissent, and the formation of a loyal opposition that provides citizens with real choices. They involve a free

[31] See Dobb, Maurice. 1973. *Theories of Value and Distribution*. Cambridge: Cambridge University Press.

[32] Lal, Deepak. 2003. Free Trade and Laissez Faire: Has the Wheel Come Full Circle? *The World Economy* (26) 4: 471–482. The latter quote in Lal came from Corden, W. Max. 1997. *Trade Policy and Economic Welfare*. Oxford: Clarendon Press, p. 2.

economy, to create opportunity and free people from dependence on the state. Furthermore, an independent judiciary is necessary to guarantee the rule of law, equal justice and a check on the power of the executive. The liberal democratic principles also include the freedom of worship, to ensure respect for the beliefs of others and a tolerant, compassionate society.[33]

In the neoliberal perspective, there are other components of democracy that are necessary to ensure the democratization of society. These include free and fair elections with active political participation by diverse elements of society. In addition, there is the enumeration of inalienable rights and the protection of minorities. Furthermore, there is the building of essential democratic institutions, including a functioning legislative body, and a capable civil service – all held to a high standard by disincentives for corruption. Also, there are the fostering of a vibrant civil society, and the protection of the key freedoms that are the essential pillars of democracy.[34] Nonetheless, these are just lofty ideals used as pretexts for imperialist intervention and domination.[35]

US-led globalization characterized by the Washington Consensus has produced its anti-thesis described as the anti-globalization movement in search of alternatives to neoliberalism. The resistance to the globalization of capitalism however has a long history that goes back to the anti-colonial movements involving the nationalist struggles in the former European colonies, one of the factors that eventually led to their political independence. In recent times, the anti-globalization struggles involved anti-IMF rioting and strikes, in poor countries. Globally, it involves protests against the World Bank, IMF, WTO, G-8, World Economic Forum, etc.[36]

There is also a notion of globalization from below amongst the anti-globalization activists representing the poor and powerless.[37] The

---

[33] These points on democracy were taken from the inauguration speech of President George Bush, January 20, 2005, available at http://www.whitehouse.gov/inaugural/index.html

[34] These points on democracy were taken from the inauguration speech of President George Bush, January 20, 2005, available at http://www.whitehouse.gov/inaugural/index.html

[35] Petras, James and Henry Veltmeyer. 2001. *Globalization Unmasked: Imperialism in the 21st Century*. London: Zed Press.

[36] See Veltmeyer, Henry, ed., 2008. *New Perspectives on Globalization and Anti-Globalization: Prospects for a New World Order*. Aldershot, Hampshire: Ashgate.

[37] Brecher, Jeremy, Tim Costelo and Brendan Smith. 2000. *Globalization from Below: The Power of Solidarity*. Cambridge, Massachusetts: South End Press; Della Porta, Donatella, Massimillano Andretta, Lorenzo Mosca, and Herbert Reiter. 2006.

tactics and strategies of the anti-globalization movement involve the activities of organized labor, social classes as change agents, and peasants and landless workers' movements.[38] In the Caribbean for example anti-globalization activities spearheaded by the Oil Field Workers' Union bloc the sale of Trinidad and Tobago Cement Limited (TCL) a regionally owned newly emerging cement transnational to Cemestos Mexicanos (CEMEX) the world's number one cement producer.[39]

There are several theoretical classifications for globalization such as it being a technologically driven process, which strengthens markets and market actors, simultaneously that nation-states are weakened and have to adapt to market imperatives. Also, globalization is seen as a "myth" – it has not weakened the national basis of economic activity, and the significance of nation states, and it is not an objective description of contemporary capitalism. In addition, globalization is regarded as imperialism – some states are weakened by globalization while it strengthens others. The globalization process is a strategy designed to enhance the interests of imperial powers by opening up the markets of weaker countries. Globalization is regarded as an inadequate descriptor of the economic and political processes currently underway – regionalization and/or regionalism are better explanatory variables of the phenomenon.[40]

Neoliberalism in the Caribbean

The Caribbean countries embarked on state-led nationalist economic policies to complement the struggle that led to their political independence. The goal of the nationalist economic model was to establish the economic independence of the Caribbean countries. The free marketers argue that the state-led model was the cause that the Caribbean

---

Globalization From Below: Transnational Activists And Protest Networks (Social Movements, Protest and Contention). Minneapolis: University of Minnesota Press.

[38] Petras, James and Henry Veltmeyer. 2003. *System in Crisis: The Dynamics of Free Market Capitalism*. London: Zed Books.

[39] Canterbury, Dennis C. 2007. Market Liberalization: The Struggle between Foreign and Domestic/Regional Capital in the Caribbean. Paper presented at the Canadian Association for the Study of International Development (CASID) under the theme 'Bridging Communities: Making Public Knowledge-Making Knowledge Public' University of Saskatchewan, Saskatoon, Arts Building May 31-June 2.

[40] Bowels, Paul. 2008. "Globalization: A Taxonomy of Theoretical Approaches", in Henry Veltmeyer, ed., *Globalization and Anti-Globalization: Prospects for a New World Order*. Aldershot, Hampshire: Ashgate, pp. 13–34.

countries failed to achieve economic growth. But, the historical evidence demonstrates quite clearly that state-led economic models dominated the Caribbean region even before the nationalist experiments in the post-independence period. All hitherto economic models in the Caribbean were state-led, even to the so-called "free market" model that the imperial states push on the region. The colonial economic model is a state-led model. The accusation that the state-led model was the cause of the economic crisis in the 1970s, was just a ploy to establish the new imperialism called "globalization" in the Caribbean of which the EPA that re-establishes European imperialist domination of the region is its latest bi-product.

The nationalist economic development model in the Caribbean was a direct outgrowth of the anti-colonial movement for Caribbean political and economic independence. Wanting to fashion a development path that was different to that imposed by colonial economic relations, Caribbean governments pursued six broad strategies to secure their economic independence. These strategies were the "industrialization-by-invitation" model, natural resource development, restructuring the agricultural sector, economic diversification, economic institutional reform, and regional economic integration (Thomas 1988: 72–73).[41]

Grenada, Guyana, and Jamaica undertook nationalist experiments in the post-colonial period labeled "non-capitalist development/socialist orientation," "cooperative socialism," and "democratic socialism," respectively.[42] A major characteristic of economic nationalism in the Caribbean was state domination of the economy, referred to as structuralism,[43] achieved by different methods in the region.

Trinidad and Tobago had the largest state sector in the Caribbean[44] created by government direct investment in the economy, along the lines of Lewis' state-led model of industrialization. The development model in Trinidad and Tobago therefore represented a classic case of

---

41 Thomas, Clive Y. 1988. *The Poor and the Powerless, Economic Policy and Change in the Caribbean*. New York: Monthly Review Press.

42 For an elaboration on these nationalist social experiments, see Thomas, Clive Y. 1988. *The Poor and the Powerless, Economic Policy and Change in the Caribbean*. New York: Monthly Review Press.

43 Structuralism refers to the economic policy options associated with import substitution industrialization and the Lewis (1950) strategy of industrialization.

44 See Odle, Maurice A. 1972. *The Significance of Non-Bank Financial Intermediaries in the Caribbean: An Analysis of Patterns of Financial Structure and Development*. Kingston, Jamaica: Institute of Social and Economic Research, University of the West Indies.

state capitalism. In Guyana, however the state dominated the economy through mortgage-financed nationalization of foreign and local private assets. The Guyana government claimed that it was building a "co-operative socialist republic," but the results however were authoritarianism and a crisis-ridden state capitalist economy. The state sector in Jamaica was also based on nationalization, but compared with Trinidad and Tobago and Guyana however its state sector was the smallest. The Jamaican economy depended primarily on private enterprises, while the Jamaican state controlled the economy through government regulation.

Economic nationalism however failed to bring about the desired socio-economic transformation and independence in the Caribbean states. Instead, it was associated with deficits in the foreign and public sector accounts, stagnation in the productive sectors, increasing domestic and foreign debt, and high unemployment.[45] These internal failures blamed on the state are seen as the major causes for the shift from economic nationalism to structural adjustment and economic liberalization.

Caribbean scholars identified the oil crisis, the collapse in export earnings, recession in the US and world economies, and bad weather, as some of the key external causes of serious financial and real sector disequilibria in regional economies in the 1970s and 1980s.[46] Another major external factor was the concerted attack on development theory in the form of the revival of mono-economics. The swing from structuralism to mono-economics was also characterized by the abandonment of the state-led Keynesian Consensus, and its replacement by the market-driven Washington Consensus in the 1970s.[47]

IMF and World Bank inspired economic liberalization and structural adjustment were resorted to as a means of restoring acceptable levels of macroeconomic balance in Caribbean economies. Although

[45] See Downes, Andrew. 1992. The Search for a Sustainable Labor Market Response to Structural Adjustment Programs in the Caribbean. Paper presented at Regional Seminar for Senior Trade Unions Officials on "The Role of Trade Unions in Periods of Structural Adjustment Programs." Bridgetown, Barbados: Barbados Workers Union Labor College.

[46] See Downes, Andrew. 1992. The Search for a Sustainable Labor Market Response to Structural Adjustment Programs in the Caribbean. Paper presented at Regional Seminar for Senior Trade Unions Officials on "The Role of Trade Unions in Periods of Structural Adjustment Programs." Bridgetown, Barbados: Barbados Workers Union Labor College.

[47] Singer, Hans W. 1997. The Golden Age of the Keynesian Consensus: The Pendulum Swings Back. *World Development* (25) 3: 293–295.

there were differences in the internal causes of their economic imbalances, the identical economic liberalization and structural adjustment program was implemented in each of them. The basics of stabilization programs in four different economies - Barbados, Guyana, Jamaica, and Trinidad and Tobago between 1985–1998,[48] are cases in point.

The main elements of structural adjustment in Barbados, Guyana, Jamaica, and Trinidad and Tobago between 1985 and 1998 reveal the similarities in their market economic reform programs. Barbados focused on fixed exchange rate with income restraint, and diversification into high-end tourism. Guyana, concentrated on reducing state participation in the economy, encouraged foreign investment, and secured external debt relief. Jamaica engaged in rapid trade and financial liberalization and from 1993 gave attention to low inflation. Trinidad and Tobago, engaged in trade liberalization supported by devaluations and diversification into natural gas based industries. Furthermore, each country undertook IMF standby programs in support of their balance of payments.

A prime goal of fiscal policy in each country was to compress capital spending, and they all took steps to bring about a shift from direct to indirect taxes. Barbados and Trinidad and Tobago reduced wages in the public sector, while Guyana, Jamaica, and Trinidad and Tobago cut the size of their work force. Trinidad and Tobago introduced a voluntary retrenchment program unlike Guyana and Jamaica that engaged in forced layoffs.

Barbados and Trinidad and Tobago introduced value-added tax (VAT) in 1997, and 1993, respectively. Guyana streamlined its consumption tax, and introduced the VAT in 2007, while Jamaica introduced a general consumption tax and VAT in 1991.

Monetary policy in each country focused on improving the reserve requirements, while Barbados concentrated additionally, on minimum deposit rate, and Guyana engaged in limited open market operations. Jamaica pursued aggressive base money targeting from 1995, using open market operations, while Trinidad and Tobago moved slowly from direct to indirect instruments of economic regulation.

The major goals of trade policy were the reduction in Caricom's common external tariff (CET), reduced import quantity restrictions (QRs), and the introduction of temporary import surcharges.

[48] See Hilaire, Alvin D. L. 2000. Caribbean Approaches to Economic Stabilization, IMF Working Paper, WP/00/73, for more details in this connection. This section is based on Table 2 in Hilaire (2000).

Barbados pursued fixed exchange rate policies, and exercised controls on capital outflows. Guyana and Jamaica adopted a variety of exchange rate regimes. They, along with Trinidad and Tobago employed discrete devaluations, and floating rates. In addition, Guyana adopted single peg, basket peg, and cambios, while Jamaica engaged in auctions. Guyana and Jamaica undertook complete liberalization of capital controls in 1996 and 1991, respectively. Trinidad and Tobago engaged in full capital account liberalization in 1993.

The Prospects of the CARIFORUM-EU EPA

The CARIFORUM-EU EPA is an extension and consolidation of structural adjustment and economic liberalization in the Caribbean. Economic liberalization provides the direct link between the EU bloc imperialist EPA and structural adjustment spearheaded by US-led globalization. The EPA is a trade agreement to foster economic and market liberalization in the Caribbean. Girvan (2008) observed that the EU proposes "to make radical changes in its trade and aid relationship with the ACP," and that these changes "are in line with neoliberal thinking and the requirements of WTO compatibility."[49] Since the advent of neoliberal theory however there has been more deprivation, misery, inequality and less economic growth in the countries that wholeheartedly embraced it. The chances of success of the EPAs are rather slim not only because of its flawed theoretical basis. Girvan (2008) noted, "Studies commissioned by the EU show that the proposed" EPAs "will at best lead to marginal increases in ACP exports to the EU, with more significant increases in EU exports to ACP countries."[50]

Conclusion: Weaknesses of Neoliberal Theory

The idea that "free trade" is the best means by which a country could achieve economic prosperity is at the center of neoliberal theory. The results of the free trade doctrine foisted on the developing countries

---

[49] Girvan, Norman. 2008. "Globalization and Counter-Globalization in the Caribbean", in Henry Veltmeyer, ed., *New Perspectives on Globalization and Anti-globalization*. Aldershot, Hampshire: Ashgate, pp. 113–127.

[50] Girvan, Norman. 2008. "Globalization and Counter-Globalization in the Caribbean", in Henry Veltmeyer, ed., *New Perspectives on Globalization and Anti-globalization*. Aldershot, Hampshire: Ashgate, pp. 113–127.

by the international financial institutions have not been encouraging. In Mexico, for example, free trade policies associated with the North American Free Trade Agreement (NAFTA) led to per capita GDP growth at about 1.8 percent per annum between 1994 and 2002, compared with 0.1 percent between 1985 and 1995. However, Mexico embraced neoliberal economic policies before it entered into NAFTA, meaning that market liberalization only brought about a growth rate of 0.1 percent between 1985 and 1995. The costs of this slender growth however, far outweigh the benefits, and this seriously brings neoliberal economic theory into disrepute.

Market liberalization "wiped out whole swathes of Mexican industry that had been painstakingly built up during the period of import substitution industrialization (ISI)."[51] This resulted in a downturn in "economic growth, lost jobs and falls in wages (as better-paying manufacturing jobs disappeared)." Mexico's "agricultural sector was also hard hit by subsidized US products, especially corn, the staple diet of most Mexicans."[52] Furthermore, between 2001 and 2005, Mexico experienced "an annual growth rate of per capita income" of 0.3 percent, compared with an annual average growth rate of 3.1 percent per annum during the ISI years between 1955 and 1982.[53]

The results of the implementation of neoliberal economic theory in the Caribbean – "low and stagnant growth rates, inadequate inflow of investment, and declining share of world trade" have called that theory into question and highlight the vulnerability of small states.[54] Indeed, Levitt (2005) pointed out that IMF/World Bank neoliberal theory imposed on the Caribbean are "taking us off course towards a black hole of social disintegration and dependence on begging scraps of favors from the so-called donor communities."[55] Furthermore, in this

---

[51] Chang, Ha-Joon. 2008. *Bad Samaritans: The Myth of Free Trade and the Secret History of Capitalism.* New York: Bloomsbury Press.

[52] Chang, Ha-Joon. 2008. *Bad Samaritans: The Myth of Free Trade and the Secret History of Capitalism.* New York: Bloomsbury Press; Bello, Walden. 2008. Globalization, Development, and Democracy: A Reflection on the Global Food Crisis. CASID 2008 Keynote Address: University of British Colombia, Vancouver BC, Canada

[53] Chang, Ha-Joon. 2008. *Bad Samaritans: The Myth of Free Trade and the Secret History of Capitalism.* New York: Bloomsbury Press.

[54] Gonzales, Anthony Peter. 2002. "Globalization and Adjustment in the Caribbean: An Assessment", in Ramesh Ramsaran, ed., *Caribbean Survival and the Global Challenge.* Kingston: Ian Randal, pp. 299–336.

[55] Levitt, Kari. 2005. *Reclaiming Development: Independent Thought and Caribbean Community.* Kingston: Iran Randle Publishers.

process "the banks have been able to operate as a creditor cartel" in a new form of colonialism as "an effective mechanism for transferring real resources from poor debtor countries to creditor banks of the industrialized world." The implementation of neoliberal theory has led to a negative net transfer of resources to creditor countries. In Mexico for example, the "commercial banks pulled out" $10 billion in 1983, $20 billion in 1984, $30 billion in 1985 "and in every year since, another $30 billion."[56]

The application of neoliberal theory in the developing countries has created many ills. Levitt summarized some of the major ills as follows.

> Restrictive credit policy leads to output contraction, and reduction in investment. High interest rates may encourage saving, but borrowers are more likely to be traders and speculators, than productive entrepreneurs. Whatever advantages are derived by exporters who get windfall gains from heavy devaluations, are negated by failure to reduce imports, and by their inflationary effects. Trade liberalization is not a feasible policy in view of protectionist practices of industrial countries and adverse effects on infant industries. Privatization is indiscriminate and doctrinaire. The presume superiority of private over public enterprise has no theoretical foundation, and the substitution of profitability criteria for social welfare criteria in vital areas like water supply is not acceptable. Indiscriminate liberalization, deregulation and minimization of the role of the state does not take into account the need for selective government intervention which may be indispensable in countries experiencing skewed income distribution. Across-the-board reductions in deficits are deflationary and the consequent reductions in social expenditure on education, health, sanitation and water have adverse effects on the wellbeing and the productivity of the population (Levitt 2005: 226–227).

Thomas (2007) noted, "The evidence is strong that for many developing countries the initial benefits" of the application of neoliberal theory "reached a plateau, as growth leveled off," bringing about "a strong challenge within official circles and institutions against the rigid orthodoxies" of neoliberal theory.[57] This challenge is probably an indication that underway is "another sea-change in economic ideas and development practice" (Thomas 2007).

---

[56] Levitt, Kari. 2005. *Reclaiming Development: Independent Thought and Caribbean Community*. Kingston: Iran Randle Publishers.

[57] Thomas, Clive Y. 2007. International Development Policy, Macroeconomic Management, Debt and Trade, in The Eastern Caribbean Central Bank, *Economic Theory and Development Options for the Caribbean: The Sir Arthur Lewis Memorial Lectures 1996–2005*. Kingston: Ian Randal, pp. 165–190.

Finally, US-led globalization has several negative outcomes for the people in both the rich and poor countries. It contributed towards to emergence of European bloc imperialism that now competes with it for global dominance. It increased inequalities between and within the rich and poor countries. It produced the worse global financial crisis since the Great Depression. It created a global food crisis and rising oil prices that negatively impacted both rich and poor countries. It resulted in unwinnable wars in Iraq and Afghanistan that has cost many American, Iraqi and Afghan lives and wasted billions of dollars on arms and ammunitions, and caused wanton destruction of property, rent collection, and other forms of corruption that enriches only a few.

CHAPTER SEVEN

THE CARIFORUM-EU EPA AND DEVELOPMENT THEORY

Introduction

The EU-EPA is not a development plan but a trade agreement that would stimulate sustainable economic development. Thus, the CARIFORUM-EU EPA states that although it is a trade agreement, its foundation is the sustainable development of the Caribbean. It is a European bloc imperialist trade arrangement with neoliberal sustainable development as its foundation. On this basis therefore, the EPA could be classified as a trade arrangement sufficiently concerned with development to contain within it a theory of development. Essentially, the theory of development of the EPA is that the CARIFORUM states will experience sustainable economic development by participating in an economic partnership agreement with the EU. It is development stimulated by free trade, the same old classical political economy idea that trade founded on comparative advantage, brought more progress or prosperity to nation-states than mercantilism. According to this theory, the economic development of the CARIFORUM states in the current period of US-led globalization and European bloc imperialism depends on their participation in the CARIFORUM-EU EPA.

The flip side to that view is that if these states do not participate in the CARIFORUM-EU EPA then they would perish experiencing economic hardships rather than sustainable development because the EU would impose tariffs on their exports to Europe causing the CARIFORUM states to earn less from their export trade. Indeed, the EU threatens to punish any country that does not sign-on to an EPA with it. The Caribbean states would also perish because they would not benefit from the virtues of free trade identified in the previous chapter. The CARIFORUM-EU EPA therefore qualifies for critique as a development theory, since in the view of its negotiators the CARIFORUM states could experience sustainable development by signing it, or perish if they do not.

This chapter assesses the CARIFORUM-EU EPA in the context of a variety of failed development approaches foisted on the Caribbean since the region was incorporated into the global capitalist system.

These approaches are all within the mercantile/classical political economy framework of development as wealth accumulation by nation-states through the implementation of protectionist or free trade economic policies. The argument is that the CARIFORUM-EU EPA must be understood in the contexts of the restructuring of global capitalism and the re-emergence of Europe as an imperialist bloc, which undoubtedly has very little or nothing to do with sustainable development. The idea about sustainable development it embraces is really about promoting free trade, expanding the capitalist world order, the management of the capitalist world order in its environmental aspects, and not about putting food on the table of ordinary people, or transforming the power relations within the ACP countries and between them and the rich capitalist states. In essence, sustainable development is a code phase for European bloc imperialism manifested through the CARIFORUM-EU EPA.

False Origins of Development Theory

A review of the general surveys of the origins and evolution of development theory reveals the following approaches. First, they are those written from the perspective of different disciplines such as economics, political science and sociology that identify the theoretical contributions made by each discipline to the subject (Hettne 1995; Levitt 1992; Rist 1997). Many of these surveys overlap in that they recognize the interdisciplinary nature of development theory. The common storyline is that economist first started to theorize about development, but that they overlooked the social factors subsequently added by political scientists, sociologists, anthropologists, geographers, and psychologists. Second, invariably, the surveys place the origins of development theory, due to various historical events and processes at sometime, around the 1940s after World War II. Some of these events and processes are identified as the collapse of colonialism and the transition of former colonies into newly independent states. The leadership of newly independent states wanted their countries to become like the European states in their socio-economic aspects. Finally, there was President Truman's Point Four in his inauguration speech that divided the world into developed and underdeveloped countries. It is believed that these events and processes combined to launch development as a subject for study and a national goal for nation-states, necessitating a role for development theory.

Because of these events, the 1940s are mistakenly regarded as the pioneering years of development theory. There are even arguments that mercantilist and classical political economists were not development theorists, and that development theory is outside of the mainstream of economic theory and therefore should be expunged from the discipline. These mistakes are made because of the failure to establish the correct link between the simultaneous advent of the nation-state and the development problem. The development problem never existed until nation-states emerged.

The view that the new nation-states in the Third World posed a new development problem different to the development problem experienced by the European nation-states is ludicrous. The introduction of the new nation-states brought to the fore an old development problem that the mercantilist and classical political economists debated – how best a nation-state could accumulate wealth – by insulating itself through protective measures or engaging in free trade. That is the development problem faced by all nation-states pursuing capitalist development, whether they are old or new. The rush to find theories to modernize the newly independent nation-states that the development literature classifies as a new discipline was therefore misguided. The true development pioneers were the mercantilist and classical political economists, while the "pioneers" in the 1940s were merely chewing over old bones but failing to recognize it.

Development theory was not written specifically for the Caribbean, but when independent nation-states emerged in the region these theories were immediately applied to the new countries. The Caribbean countries nonetheless did play a major role in development theory even during the period that it did not apply to them (before they became countries) in terms of the expansion of their productive forces. The Caribbean's role was that of a location from which European nation-states accumulated wealth. The mercantilist/classical political economist debate on protection versus free trade only affected the Caribbean insofar as it confined regional trade to specific European nation-states or free trade with any European nation-state in order that wealth accumulated in Europe. The debate on free trade versus protection or outward-versus inward-looking approaches became directly applicable to Caribbean states in terms of their accumulation of wealth only at the onset of their political independence.

Wealth accumulation was the essence of the contributions of the "development pioneers" Rosenstein-Rodan (1943), Ragnar Nurkse (1953), W. Arthur Lewis (1954), Raul Prebisch (1950), Hans Singer

(1949; 1950), and Gunnar Myrdal (1944; 1956), and others. This was also the essence of the Caribbean contribution to development theory (Best 1969), Girvan (1973), Beckford (1972), Demas (1965), and Thomas (1974). They may have plotted different paths to get there but the goal was the same – wealth accumulation in nation-states that translates into economic growth, increases in national income, industrialization, and social development through redistribution with growth. The same is true of the Marxist, neo-Marxist, dependency, and neoclassical critique of the "development pioneers" including its Caribbean variation. The Marxist envisioned an alternative socioeconomic system to capitalism in which accumulated wealth is distributed evenly among its producers. The neo-Marxist advocated state ownership of the commanding heights of the economy to allow wealth produced domestically to remain in the country rather that be expatriated abroad. Dependency theory promoted structural transformation to allow more wealth to accumulate where it is produced. However, neoclassical theory also favours wealth accumulation through free trade.

The "development pioneers" and others mentioned above intensified the manufacture of development theory from the 1940s until the 1970s. Ideas on wealth accumulation in that period ranged from modernization to its dependency critique. There is on the modernization side a plethora of theories such as Rosenstein-Rodan's "big push," Rostow's "take-off," Gerschenkron's "great spurt," Hirschman's "backward and forward linkages," and "two-gap" theory, Prebisch's "centre-periphery" model, and Lewis's "two-sector" model (Levitt 1992). On the dependency side are ideas generated by writers such as Dos Santos (1970), Cardoso (1977), Frank (1966), Baran (1957), Magdoff (1969), and Sunkel (1973). The Caribbean produced a variation of dependency analysis in large measure in critique of Lewis' industrialization by invitation approach. Contributions in this regard came from Demas (1965), Best (1969), Beckford (1972), Thomas (1967; 1974), Girvan (1973) and Girvan and Jefferson (1971).

Prevailing Ideas on Caribbean Development

The survey of Caribbean thought ably undertaken by Benn (2004) presents the different perspectives on development that emerged in the region overlooking nonetheless, the contributions in the areas of the 'posts' and 'cultural studies' theories in the 1990s and early 2000s. Girvan (2006) also provided a useful overview of Caribbean dependency theories identifying the authors and the related themes in their works from the 1960s to the 1970s, and placing Sir Arthur Lewis as a forerunner to that body of literature. Bolland (2004)[1] took a broader view on Caribbean thought by focusing his review on ideas of nationhood emanating from intellectuals in the Hispanophone, Francophone, and Anglophone Caribbean.

There seems to be a consensus in the region around a false belief that Caribbean development theory is separate from development theory in general – the former having specific application to the Caribbean, and the latter having universal application to the entire underdeveloped world. This is the cause for classifying Sir Arthur Lewis outside of Caribbean development theory, and placing him in the category of development theory in general (Eastern Caribbean Central Bank 2007). Such classification nonetheless falls short of recognizing the identity between so-called general and specific development theory. Lewis was as much concerned with the economic development of the Caribbean as any other Caribbean development theorist. Furthermore, the works identified as fulfilling the conditions to qualify as Caribbean development theory could stand on equal footing with Lewis' work in the so-called category of general development theory.

Thomas' (1974) theses on the economics of the transition to socialism, and the works by Best (1969), Beckford (1972), Girvan (1973), and others that make up the Caribbean dependency school have application to the rest of the underdeveloped world, as does the Lewis industrialization model. They all have the same goal namely wealth accumulation by nation-states. The exception is Thomas (1974) whose goal includes the establishment of socialism in the developing countries. Lewis' work enjoyed greater global success due perhaps to ideological reasons during the cold war. At the end of the cold war and the ascendancy of neoliberalism however Lewis' work became *persona non grata* a status enjoyed by the radical development literature – dependency and Marxist – during the cold war. Neoliberal theory now lumps Lewis, Keynes, socialist, dependency theory, etc. in the same category as advocates of state-led development.

---

[1] Bolland, O. Nigel. 2004. *The Birth of Caribbean Civilization: A Century of Ideas about Culture and Identity, Nation and Society*. Oxford: James Currey Publishers.

Theorizing on Caribbean development emerged in the context of the transition of these countries from colonies to independent states. Poor socio-economic conditions internally, European imperialism, the cold war, and the ascendancy of the US to super-power status were, defining characteristics of the period that the region launched its initial quest for socio-economic development[2] in its own behalf. The principal ideas to split the development atom to break out from colonial underdevelopment involved the pursuit of independent self-reliant development that either supported variations of the colonial approach, promoted a brand of Caribbean nationalism based on state and market-led strategies, advocated socialism/communism, or argued for "another development."

The rethinking of Caribbean development in the 1990s[3] focused on the shift from economic nationalism towards structural adjustment. There is need however to rethink this rethinking of Caribbean development. The failure of structural adjustment and the rise of the new imperialism, described as 'reluctant,' 'ethnical,' or 'nascent' imperialism,[4] demand that the rethinking of development be extended into the current period of imperialist rivalry with a view to reviving the search for alternative development to capitalism.

The call to "reclaim development" with "independent thought"[5] – probably a code phase to update plantation dependence analysis to the current conditions of global capitalism i.e., plantation economy "further modified" – is a step in that direction. Plantation dependence theory "further modified" would diversify the analysis of current globalization, but like its predecessors – the pure plantation economy and the plantation economy modified – it will maintain its analytical capabilities and inadequacies in terms of effecting Caribbean socio-economic development and to change the power dynamics in the region in favour of working people. The reason is that the plantation model possesses analytical but not transformative capabilities.

---

[2] Girvan, Norman. 2006. Caribbean Development Thought Revisited. *Canadian Journal of Development Studies* (27) 3: 337–352; Benn, Denis M. 2004. The Caribbean an Intellectual History 1774–2003. Kingston: Ian Randal.

[3] Girvan, Norman, ed., 1997. *Poverty, Empowerment and Social Development in the Caribbean*. Mona, Jamaica: Canoe Press.

[4] Mallaby, Sebastian. 2002. The Reluctant Imperialist: Terrorism, Failed States, and the Case for Empire Building. *Foreign Affairs* (81) 2: 2–7.

Simes, Dimitri, K. 2003. America's Imperial Dilemma. *Foreign Affairs* (82) 6: 91–103.

[5] Levitt, Kari. 2005. *Reclaiming Development: Independent Thought and Caribbean Community*. Kingston: Iran Randle Publishers.

Since the 1990s, various ideas have emerged on Caribbean development within the context of Euro-American globalization. They emphasize inter alia new forms of regionalism and economic integration,[6] "free trade" and preferential trade areas, foreign direct investment, "inserting" and "repositioning" the region in global capitalism, "collective lobbying," "good governance," and services promotion. Now, the CARIFORUM-EU EPA must be added as the latest externally driven approach to develop the region. The historical basis for judging these ideas will be the extent to which they place the Caribbean deeper in the clutches of US-led globalization and EU bloc imperialism, or transform the power dynamics in the region to favour working people, and reinforce regional economic and political independence.

Development through Integration and Trade Arrangements

The Caricom states have positioned "free trade" as the principal engine of regional economic growth and development, but historical and current evidence indicate that the state is what guides the process of economic development both in the region and abroad. There is need however for a few comments to clarify the term "free trade." First, all "free trade" arrangements are state-directed since they are agreements entered into by nation-states and not private individuals. Trade in the so-called "underground economy" is perhaps the only non-state-driven free trade arrangement in the region but the state represses this activity on the bases that it does not contribute to state revenue and increases corruption. Second, the exogenous Euro-American "free trade" models based on neoclassical economic theory further Euro-American imperialist interests globally – a model pushed on the Caribbean through the EPA and FTAs. Third, the endogenous state-driven "free trade" development strategy that is regional in character focuses on a Caribbean approach to the globe and intra-regional affairs.

In the past two decades, the region entered into three varieties of "free trade" arrangements – Free Trade Agreements (FTAs), trade and development assistance, and preferential agreements. Ten of these arrangements fall into the exogenous "free trade" category and two

[6] Girvan, Norman. 2007. Reinterpreting Caribbean Development, in The Eastern Caribbean Central Bank, *Economic Theory and Development Options for the Caribbean: The Sir Arthur Lewis Memorial Lectures 1996–2005*. Kingston: Ian Randal, pp. 16–35.

are in the endogenous regional state-driven "free trade" development strategy.[7]

CaribCan is a non-reciprocal economic and trade, development assistance program that provides duty-free access to the Canadian market for most Caricom goods exports. Under WTO rules, however, such non-reciprocal preferential agreements require a waiver. CaribCan has secured an extended WTO waiver until year 2011. Caricom and Canada undertook the first round of negotiations on a new trade deal to replace CaribCan in September 2008. The CRNM had intended the Caribbean to sign a new reciprocal trade agreement with Canada within a year of those talks, but it never materialized. The scope of the negotiations was around trade in goods, services, and investments including competition policy, government procurement and innovation and competitiveness, as well as side agreements on labor and the environment.[8] Caricom has already signalled that it plans to push for concessions for low-skilled workers under the agreement on services. The Office of Trade Negotiations (OTN) that has replaced the CRNM is now charged with taking up the negotiations with Canada.

Arrangements in the US "free trade" category has three essential features, the first being the centrality of the private sector as stimulant to growth and development. In reality, the US imperialist state drives this "free trade" process on behalf of US private capital. The empirical evidence suggests that the Caribbean private sector focuses on short-term profit rather than long-term investment necessary for development[9]

[7] In the first category are the Caribbean Basin Initiative (CBI) 1983, Caribbean-Canada Trade Arrangement 1986 (CaribCan), Caricom-Colombia Preferential Agreement 1994, Association of Caribbean States (ACS) 1994, Caricom-Dominican Republic FTA 1998, Caricom-Costa Rica FTA 2004, Free Trade Area of the Americas (FTAA) 1994, and currently negotiated Economic Partnership Agreement (EPA) and Caricom-Canada Free Trade Area. There is talk about a Caricom-US Free Trade Area that if comes to fruition fits in this category. In the second category are the Caricom and its institutions, Petrocaribe in 2004 that replaced the Caricom-Venezuela Preferential Agreement 1992, and the China-Caribbean Economic and Trade Cooperation Forum 2005.

[8] Rose, Dionne. 2008. CaribCan Negotiations Set for September. *Jamaica Gleaner*, July 4.

[9] Bourne, Compton and Marlene Attzs. 2005. The Role of Economic Institutions in Caribbean Economic Growth: From Lewis to the Present. *Social and Economic Studies* (54) 3: 26–49; Thomas, Clive Y. 1996. "The Crisis of Development Theory and Practice: A Caribbean Perspective", in Kari Levitt and Michael Witter eds., *The Critical Tradition of Caribbean Political Economy: The Legacy of George Beckford*. Kingston: Ian Randle Publishers, pp. 223–239.

meaning that private foreign capital through foreign direct investment will dominate regional growth and development generated through the FTAs. Foreign capital however has a very poor historical record of accomplishments in promoting growth and development in the Caribbean.

A second feature of FTAs is that they seek to protect private investments through para-military militias, police repression, military invasion and economic and political sanctions. Latin America is rich with examples of these experiences. Third, the FTAs commit to measures that repress anti-competition activities. This feature has the capacity for potential and actual political repression of people and institutions that oppose the US "free trade" model, as witnessed during anti-globalization protests in Europe, Latin America, Canada, and the US.

The endogenous regional state-driven "free trade" development strategy has the following two essential features. First, it is explicitly or implicitly state-driven – the state seeks to effect development by implementing trade arrangements that redistribute wealth and income in favour of the less privileged. Second, it deliberately seeks to counteract the US "free trade" model for which it represents a credible alternative. This state-driven "free trade" model takes the form of state institutions such as the Caribbean Community (Caricom), its organs, and the Caricom-established Caribbean Single Market Economy (CSME).

Foreign Direct Investment

Foreign direct investment (FDI) is a major plank in the Euro-American "free trade" models. The Caricom countries need however to regulate the movement of domestic capital to prevent capital flight,[10] since the region is not a favoured location for foreign capital.[11] The Caricom countries attracted nine FDIs between the period 2002 and 2005

[10] On capital flight from the region see Bennett, Karl. 1995. "Capital Flight and Caribbean Economic Policy", in Ramesh F. Ramsaran, ed., *The Savings/Investment Environment in the Caribbean: Emerging Imperatives*, St. Augustine, Trinidad: Caribbean Centre for Monetary Studies, The University of The West Indies, pp. 43–59; Bennett, Karl. 1991. "Capital Flight and Its Implications for Caribbean Development", in De Lisle Worrell, Compton Bourne and Dinesh Dodhia, eds., *Financing Development in the Commonwealth Caribbean*. London: Macmillan, pp. 289–310

[11] As gleaned from United Nations Conference on Trade and Development. 2006a. Top TNCs Present in 40 Host Countries on Average. *UNCTAD Investment Brief*, Number 5, 2006.

according to the Greenfield FDI projects data by investor/destination for 2002–2005. The wider Caribbean attracted an average of 24 FDIs between the period 2002 and 2005. In 2002 Jamaica, Puerto Rico and Trinidad and Tobago each attracted one, while 14 went to Bermuda. A similar pattern obtained for 2003 with one each to Antigua and Barbuda, Cayman Islands, Cuba, Dominican Republic, Guyana, and Puerto Rico and 22 to Bermuda. In 2004, there was one in Cayman Islands, 4 each in Jamaica and Puerto Rico, and 17 in Bermuda. In 2005, there was one each in Bahamas, Dominican Republic, Saint Lucia and Dominican Republic, 2 in Cayman Islands, and 21 in Bermuda.

In 2005, Bermuda had the highest number of parent corporations 362, followed by Netherlands Antilles 101, Cayman Islands 84, and the Bahamas 44. In 2005, Cayman Islands had the highest number of foreign affiliates located in its economy 539, followed by Bermuda 348, Netherlands Antilles 179, Bahamas 165, Dominican Republic 147, Barbados 145, and Jamaica 78. Trinidad and Tobago had 61 in 2004.[12]

The data also showed that the Caribbean is not among the 25 most favoured locations for the largest 100 TNCs in the world and from TNCs in developing economies. In the Western Hemisphere, the US is number one with a location intensity of 92, followed by Brazil 81 and Mexico 78. The countries in the hemisphere among the twenty-five most favoured locations of TNCs from developing economies were the US with a location intensity of 50, followed by 16.2 in Canada, 13.7 in Cayman Islands, 11.2 in Virgin Islands (UK) and Bermuda, 10.4 in Brazil, and 9.5 in Mexico.

These trends in FDIs increase the importance of a development alternative vision focusing on regional cooperation with countries such as Venezuela, Cuba, Bolivia, Russia and China among others. It is perhaps for good reasons that the Caricom is not a favoured destination for FDIs. The region has the opportunity as the East Asian countries did to save more towards its own long-term investments, implement state-coordinated development programs, engage in capital controls, and promote educational, health and other social programs. Through the implementation of these state-coordinated policies, the East Asian countries "followed pretty much the developmental paths of the currently wealthy countries, which are radically different from the rules

[12] United Nations Conference on Trade and Development. 2006. World Investment Report 2006 FDI From Developing and Transition Economies: Implications for Development. New York and Geneva: United Nations.

that are being imposed on the South."[13] The development path being suggested here however is one that is an alternative to capitalism.

Perspectives on the Caribbean and Globalization

Complementing the foci on trade and integration, and FDI are ideas put forward to competitively insert and strategically reposition the region in the current global capitalist system, collectively lobby in the appropriate global institutions for development assistance and deals, and the pursuance of good governance. These ideas represent the current new visions for Caribbean development in the twenty-first century.[14]

The "competitive insertion" (CI) view hypothesizes that the Caribbean will achieve economic development if the region abolishes state-led approaches to economic integration and cooperation employed by the Caricom and Association of Caribbean States (ACS), and replace them with the US-led "free trade" model. It regards state-led models as anachronistic and surpassed by new forces of globalization and the move towards a hemispheric free trade bloc. The challenge identified for the region is its determination of the role for the Caricom and ACS to bring about the "competitive insertion" of Caribbean states into the new global economy dominated by trading blocs. According to the CI view "education," "enabling government," and "export diversification," are three missing ingredients necessary to competitively insert the region into current global capitalism.[15]

The view is that although historically the region achieved considerable success in education, currently there is a substantial decline in education expenditure and the quality of education. Enabling government entails state reforms around a new consensus idea that government is not the engine of growth, or the custodian of the people, but the facilitator and channel for the effective operation of the private

[13] Chomsky, Noam. 2006. Historical Perspectives on Latin American and East Asian Regional Development. *The Asia-Pacific Journal: Japan Focus*. December 20.

[14] Caribbean leaders also outlined various strategic perspectives to chart the direction of the region in the current century in Hall, Kenneth and Benn, Denis, ed. 2000. *Contending With Destiny: The Caribbean in the 21st Century*. Kingston: Ian Randle.

[15] Nogueira, Uziel Batista. 1997. The Integration Movement in the Caribbean at Crossroads: Towards a New Approach of Integration. Working Paper Series 1, Buenos Aires, Argentina: Inter-American Development Bank, Integration and Regional Programs Department, Institute for the Integration of Latin America and the Caribbean.

sector in every respect. Export diversification requires the Caribbean to rely less on commodity-based exports and more on products/services that enhance their comparative advantage and increase value-added.

Transitioning from commodity-based exports to services involves abandoning the view that Caribbean economies cannot compete in international markets, and embracing the ideas that small economies can be big and dominate specific niche markets, and that Caribbean labor can compete effectively with others around the world. Niche and competitive labor markets would set the foundation for future sustainable Caribbean economic growth in the global capitalist system. The Caribbean has the capacity to attract FDI with a high technological content, a key factor in inducing change in the region's state-led economic development model (Nogueira 1997).

Strategic global repositioning (SGI) is the "process of repositioning a country in the global economy and world affairs by implementing a strategic medium-to long term plan formulated from continuous dialogue of the public sector, private sector, academic community and the social sector."[16] Regarded as different to structural adjustment, it involves improving among other things the "competitiveness and productivity in existing export sectors" in Caribbean industries. The premise of SGI like its counterpart CI is that globalization is a "process in which national barriers to the international flow of goods, services, capital, money and information are being increasingly reduced or eliminated is well advanced and in many respects irreversible."[17]

[16] Bernal, Richard. 2000. "The Caribbean in the International System: Outlook for the First 20 Years of the 21st Century", in Kenneth Hall and Denis Benn, eds., *Contending with Destiny: The Caribbean in the 21st Century*. Kingston: Ian Randle, pp. 295–325. See also Bernal, Richard. 1996. Strategic Global Repositioning, and Future Economic Development in Jamaica. *The North-South Agenda* (18). Florida: University of Miami North-South Centre; Davenport, M., C. Kirton, N. Plaisier, and H. Poot. 2000. Caribbean Perspectives: Trade, Regional Integration and Strategic Global Repositioning Final Report. European Commission, ECORYS-NEI Macro and Sectoral Reform, Rotterdam.

[17] Bernal, Richard. 2000. "The Caribbean in the International System: Outlook for the First 20 Years of the 21st Century", in Kenneth Hall and Denis Benn, eds., *Contending with Destiny: The Caribbean in the 21st Century*. Kingston: Ian Randle, pp. 295–325. See also Bernal, Richard. 1996. Strategic Global Repositioning, and Future Economic Development in Jamaica. *The North-South Agenda* (18). Florida: University of Miami North-South Centre; Davenport, M., C. Kirton, N. Plaisier, and H. Poot. 2000. Caribbean Perspectives: Trade, Regional Integration and Strategic Global Repositioning Final Report. European Commission, ECORYS-NEI Macro and Sectoral Reform, Rotterdam.

In other words, Euro-American-led globalization is inevitable, so the Caribbean has to reposition itself within it.

"Collective lobbying" (CL), emphasizes the need for Caribbean states to take collective action in global institutions to squeeze development opportunities from globalization. First, CL allows small states to speak with one voice in the global arena that gives them greater influence in international institutions compared with if each country goes it alone. Second, the Caribbean must engage CL "partly on the power of ideas, i.e. the quality of their concepts and philosophies" and on the ability of Caribbean peoples "to disseminate these effectively in the communities of the wealthy and powerful."[18] Third, the region must base CL on its ethnicity in the same way that within the US there are pro-Israeli, Cuban-, Irish-, Armenian-, Arab-, and Polish-American lobbies. These groups gain access to the highest level of decision-making in the US Congress and certain markets that benefit their communities in the US and their countries of origin.[19]

Three other justifications for CL are first, Caribbean governments have lost their autonomy as steering institutions,[20] and second that in recent decades two poles of power have emerged – the mega-corporations and the US government that determine and dominate governance and economic policies in developing countries (Bourne 2003). Third, the Caribbean exists in a post-national world in which "The nation state may still be important for political and emotional reasons, but economically it is all but dead" (Patterson 2000). These prognoses demand that the region engages in CL for its development.

"Good governance" (GG) is a condition for human development leading to increases in income, decreases in poverty, and improvements in social indicators such as literacy or infant mortality.[21] Competitive political party politics however it destructive, in that it

---

[18] Bourne, Compton. 2003. Small States in the Context of Global Change. Presented at 4th Annual Conference of Sir Arthur Lewis Institute of Social and Economic Studies (SALISES), University of the West Indies. Barbados: Sherbourne Conference Centre.

[19] Patterson, Orlando. 2000. "Reflection on the Caribbean Diaspora and Its Policy Implications", in Kenneth Hall and Denis Benn eds., *Contending with Destiny: The Caribbean in the 21st Century*. Kingston: Ian Randle, pp. 500–510.

[20] Lewis, Vaughn. 2000. "Looking from the Inside Outwards: The Caribbean in the International System after 2000", in Kenneth Hall and Denis Benn, eds., *Contending with Destiny: The Caribbean in the 21st Century*, Kingston: Ian Randle, pp. 326–346.

[21] Caribbean Group for Cooperation in Economic Development (CGCED). 2000. Governance and Social Justice in Caribbean States. Development Research Group, The World Bank Report No. 20449-LAC.

deepens political tribalism, perpetuates a patronage and spoils system, and increases the focus on immediate partisan gains, rather than forging long-term strategic developmental goals in the region. Additionally, the current political system in the region concentrates power in the hands of the ruling elites resulting in "alienation, cynicism and marginalization."[22] The solution to these political, social, and economic problems is GG founded on decentralization, transparency, accountability, participation, consensualism, regionalism and globalism, and influenced-based, rather than authority-driven leadership (Arthur 2000). Furthermore, good governance requires decision making free from ideology and hard-line positions, and based on a common sense approach driven by "Principles Proactive Pragmatism" (PPP).[23] Founded on cost-benefit analysis the PPP implements policies that maximize benefits and minimize costs.

Progressively since the 1950s, the Caribbean labor force shifted from agriculture into other areas, and the services sector gradually took over from agriculture as the main contributor to gross domestic product (GDP) in Barbados, Jamaica, Saint Kitts, Antigua, etc. Recent growth experiences in the Organization of Eastern Caribbean States (OECS) suggest a decline in agriculture and rise in services.[24] Based on this evidence some Caribbean politicians, academics, and policy makers, argue that the region must reallocate resources from agriculture to services as the lead sector in regional economic growth and development.[25]

Deepening Euro-American Domination

The Euro-American "free trade" model is the premise of the foregoing strategies that appear to be development alternatives to the current

---

[22] Arthur, Owen. 2000. "Economic Policy Options in the Twenty-first Century", in Kenneth Hall and Denis Benn, eds., *Contending With Destiny: The Caribbean in the 21st Century*. Kingston: Ian Randle, pp. 12–25.

[23] Panton, David. 2000. The Politics of Principles Proactive Pragmatism. In *Contending With Destiny: The Caribbean in the 21st Century*, edited by Kenneth Hall and Denis Benn 286–292. Kingston: Ian Randle.

[24] Lazare, Alick, Patrick Antoine, Wendell Samuel. 2001. Regional Negotiating Machinery/Organization of Eastern Caribbean States Country Studies to Inform Trade Negotiations: Overview. March.

[25] Kendall, Patrick and Marco Petracco. 2003. The Current State and Future of Caribbean Agriculture. Economics Department: Caribbean Development Bank, January.

economic and political situation in the region. The strategies represent nonetheless a search for a Caribbean way within the framework of the new imperialisms. Rather than drawing on the Caribbean's historical experiences and the current concrete global reality characterized by the rivalry between the US-led globalization and European bloc imperialism, and the challenges posed to the global order by the emerging economies (BRIC), to forge measures that strengthen the region's political and economic independence the foregoing strategies draw the region deeper into the clutches of Euro-American imperialist domination. Contrary to the view that there is no alternative to US-led globalization and European bloc imperialism, the opportunity for independent choice by Caribbean states is stronger now in the post-cold war era. This is because of the contradictions between US-led globalization and European bloc imperialism and between themselves and emerging powers in a scramble to reorder the globe. The Caribbean should stake a claim in the reordering the globe by economically realigning the region with BRIC, ALBA and Petrocaribe.

There are major problems with CI that must be pointed out. Experiences with the Caribbean Basin Initiative (CBI) and the NAFTA have taught the region to be wary of such deals with the US, whose companies are their prime beneficiaries. Regarded as "gunboat economics" in the US' national security interest, the "CBI turned a US trade deficit with the beneficiary countries of the, Caribbean into a sustained surplus."[26]

The setbacks in the Mexican agricultural sector from Mexico's participation in NAFTA must sound a warning that should dissuade Caricom countries from joining the US-envisioned FTAA, and the EU-EPA. The Caricom must take heed from the widespread demonstrations against the US dominated Dominican Republic – Central American Free Trade Area (DR-CAFTA) that the ruling elites implemented against the wishes of their respective peoples.[27] The

[26] Grant, Cedric. 2005. US-Caribbean Relations. *Foreign Policy in Focus* (5) 19: 1–3.

[27] Ribando, Clare. 2005. DR-CAFTA: Regional Issues. CRS Report for Congress. Washington; Network in Solidarity with the People of Guatemala. 2005. Popular Opposition to DR-CAFTA in Guatemala. NISGUA: Oakland, California; Oxfam America. 2005. Road Show of Central American Presidents Can't Prevent Growing Opposition to DR-CAFTA. Washington, DC., May 12; Hansen-Kuhn, Karen. 2005. Central Americans Speak Out Against DR-CAFTA: Major Issues and Mobilizations. Alliance for Responsible Trade: Washington, DC., March.

problematic FTAA ran into serious opposition in Latin America – Brazil and Argentina are sceptical, about the US' commitment to "free trade" given among other things the US' subsidies to its farmers that hurt the agricultural sector in the region. The Caribbean banana[28] and sugar industries experience major setbacks due to Euro-American "free trade" policies, which are indicators of what is to come if Caribbean countries join the FTAA, and sign on to the EPA, goals to which Caribbean states are firmly committed.[29]

"Export diversification" a central plank of CI requires the Caribbean to downplay commodity-based exports and promote products/services to enhance its comparative advantage and increase value-added. This strategy will effectively break-up the agricultural, manufacturing and mining bases of regional economies and increase their dependence on precarious services. A useful export diversification strategy to enhance Caribbean independence would be to develop policies to fix the problems in the productive sectors with a regional focus complementary to services.

CI seeks to insert the Caribbean into a system of global capitalism to which it already belongs. The idea treats with globalization, a historical phenomenon[30] in an ahistorical manner. Undoubtedly, "globalization has been a cyclical phenomenon for millennia, being associated with the rise and fall of empires."[31] The Caribbean has always participated in globalization – the "process of integrating previously loosely linked or even autarkic countries and regions through freeing flows of goods, services and capital" (Lal 2000) – from since the region's incorporation into the global capitalist system (Lewis 2000). Furthermore, "National

[28] Rush, Rebecca. 2005. Banana Wars Continue – Chiquita Once Again Tries to Work Its Omnipotent Will, Now Under New Management: Likely Big Losers Will be Caricom's Windward Islands. Washington DC: Council on Hemispheric Affairs Memorandum to the Press, May 16; Lewis, Vaughn. 2000. "Looking from the Inside Outwards: The Caribbean in the International System after 2000", in Kenneth Hall and Denis Benn, eds., *Contending with Destiny: The Caribbean in the 21st Century*, Kingston: Ian Randle, pp. 326–346.

[29] Richard Bernal, the Director-General of the Caribbean Regional Negotiating Machinery (CRNM) observed, 'The region is actively positioning itself to re-shape the 'vision' of the FTAA, in accordance with the regional development goals and priorities,' CRNM News Release No. 03/2005.

[30] Sen, Amartya. 2001. Ten Theses on Globalization. *New Perspectives Quarterly* (18) 4: 9–15.

[31] Lal, Deepak. 2000. Globalization, Imperialism and Regulation. *Cambridge Review of International Affairs*. (14) 1: 107–121.

states are already in the international system, so much so that they do not have the ability to be outside of the system."[32]

Finally, while according to CI the Caribbean must deepen free market economic reforms, to strategically insert itself into the global capitalist system, "increasingly Washington is moving toward import controls, quotas and tariffs to protect non-competitive local industries, from steel to shrimp"[33] and agriculture.[34] Through these actions, the US is creating a new mercantilism "based on unilateral state decisions and military supremacy designed to impose policies on international, regional, and national competitors" (Petras 2003).

SGR and CI preach the inevitability of capitalist globalization, but nothing is inevitable about capitalism other than its demise. Capitalism is not a natural phenomenon but an economic system invented by humans that will rise and fall, as hitherto economic systems. SGR and CI assume a homogenous globe based on the Euro-American "free trade" models, and ignores existing competitive alternatives around the globe.

Furthermore, the claim that SGR is different to structural adjustment is highly questionable because in reality, SGR belongs to the neoliberal scheme of thinking similar to CI. First, they are both reacting to the current restructuring of global capitalism by trying to identify ways that Caribbean states could derive maximum benefits from US-led globalization, and European bloc imperialism. Second, they both focus on improving competitiveness in the region, which in essence means reducing production costs, and increasing productivity focal points of neoliberal structural adjustment. The belief is that low production costs and high productivity would attract foreign direct investments to the region and increase its exports.

Third, they are both integral components that seek to reform and not transform the neoliberal economic framework. Their concern is with how to make the Caribbean participate more efficiently in a system that has historically deprived the region of its wealth. Fourth, they

---

[32] Watson, Hilbourne A. 2000. "Global Neoliberalism, The Third Technological Revolution and Global 2000: A Perspective on Issues Affecting the Caribbean on the Eve of the 21st Century", in Kenneth Hall and Denis Benn, eds., *Contending with Destiny: The Caribbean in the 21st Century*. Kingston: Ian Randle, pp. 382–446.

[33] Petras, James. 2003. *The New Development Politics: The Age of Empire Building and New Social Movements*. Aldershot: Ashgate.

[34] Atkins, Vincent J. 2002. The US Farm Bill of 2002: Implications for Caricom's Agricultural Export Trade. Caribbean Regional Negotiating Machinery, Staff Papers.

are both oriented towards the promotion of growth through "free trade" in capitalist markets. Experience shows however, that "free trade" without deliberate state control is ruinous to small island developing states (SIDS) such as those in the Caribbean. Fifth, in essence SGR and CI are about the deepening of the failed neoliberal economic reforms in the region implemented from the outside and from the top by the international financial institutions (IFIs) – the IMF and World Bank. Even the World Bank officials now embrace the criticisms of structural adjustment emanating from the poor countries.[35] Moreover, the current global financial and economic crises have the neoliberals fleeing from their own free-market policies and embracing state-led solutions.

Sixth, although SGI accords a role to the masses in policy formation, there is no mechanism for this to take place, and along with CI, the regional elites must carry out the processes of SGI and CI. Thus, SGI and CI may not necessarily lead to democracy, and will promote the same old top-down authoritarian approach to political and economic decision-making and resource allocation that has plagued the Caribbean over centuries of capitalist globalization.

The significance of CL is undeniable but it is restricted to bureaucratic actions in global institutions and the US Congress. Instead, collective actions against Euro American "free trade" models must be the overall strategy of which CL is only an integral component. Historically, collective action by Caribbean people against colonialism has brought about improvements in their living conditions. CL cannot substitute for collective mass action.

The CL view on the nation-state wishes away the resolve by Caribbean people to acquire genuine political and economic independence. The overwhelming evidence is that the nation-state in the Caribbean is not dead in any sense. The existence of the Caricom and other regional institutions such as the CSME, demonstrate the resolve of Caribbean people to secure their economic and political sovereignty. The Caribbean people engaged imperialist forces continuously, an effort in which they have made significant gains since the social unrests in the 1930s.

The mega-corporations and the Euro-American imperialisms are not mutually exclusive poles of power, there is great overlap between

[35] Stiglitz, Joseph E. 2003. *Globalization and Its Discontents*. New York: Norton and Company.

them that makes them a single capitalist power center. For example, US shareholders dominate the 100 most powerful corporations in the world, and there is a very close relationship between the US Congress and these corporations. Indeed, these corporations help to write and determine US legislation and foreign policy.[36] The data showed that the 25 most-favoured locations of the largest 100 TNCs in the world in 2005 were the United States (92.0), the United Kingdom (91.0), the Netherlands (89.6), Germany (87.4), and France (83.5). The 25 most-favoured locations of the largest 100 TNCs from developing economies in 2005 were United States (50.0), Hong Kong, China (33.9), United Kingdom (33.7), China (30.0), and Singapore (26.4) (UNCTAD 2006a). The real poles of power that compete with Euro-American imperialism are China, Russia, and an emergent Latin America.

The Caribbean states have been engaged in collective actions globally in organizations like the Non-Aligned Movement, the G-77, the Africa, Caribbean and Pacific (ACP) countries, and in the call for a New International Economic Order (NIEO). They remain active in various groupings engaged in a struggle for fair trade and WTO reform. It is noteworthy that although the Caribbean became involved in these actions, the problems of growth, inequality, and poverty continue to persist in the region.

The potential developmental role of the Caribbean Diaspora in CL is a complex issue. The Caribbean Diaspora is not a homogeneous or unified entity, and factors such as small island insularity, colour, class, and race differences that divide the region remain a problem among Caribbean peoples abroad. This makes it difficult for them to form an effective collective lobby in the US for example, to reverse the trends in decline in US economic assistance to the region including Development Assistance, Economic Support Funds, and P.L. 480 food aid.[37]

US assistance to the Caribbean in the 1980s amounted to approximately US$3.2 billion, but declined to US$2.0 billion in the 1990s, at

---

[36] Petras, James. 2007a 'Who Rules America?' *Third World Traveller*. www.dissidentvoice.org, January 13.

[37] The problem with food aid is that it causes producer disincentives in low-income countries and disrupts commercial trade, and pushes genetically modified foods on underdeveloped countries. Furthermore, the rich countries use food aid to support domestic farm prices, promote commercial agricultural exports, advance their geostrategic goals, and maintain a viable maritime industry. See Barrett, Christopher B. and Daniel G. Maxwell. 2004. PL480 Food Aid: We Can Do Better, *Choices (The Magazine of Food, Farm, and Resource Issues)*, 19: 3.

an annual average of $205 million. Haiti received the most assistance from the US in the 1990s about US$1.1 billion, or 54 percent of the total, followed by Jamaica with about $507 million, almost 25 percent, and the Dominican Republic, about $352 million, or 17 percent. The Eastern Caribbean nations received about $178 million, almost 9 percent. Military assistance to the region amounted to less than $60 million during the 1990s.[38]

Through remittances, however the Caribbean Diaspora continues to play an important role in the economic affairs of the region. Remittances to selected Caricom countries reached US$14.6 billion between 2002 and 2005, averaging US$3.4 billion per annum. Remittances increased from roughly US$2.9 billion in 2002 to approximately US$4.5 billion 2005, or by 48.1 percent over the period. Remittances as a percentage of GDP averaged 48.6 percent in Haiti, 20.0 percent in Guyana, and 17.2 percent in Jamaica between 2002 and 2004.[39]

The problem with remittances in the Caribbean however is that they do not contribute as much to capital accumulation, but are mainly for consumption purposes of commodities imported from Europe and the US. Furthermore, highly skilled Caribbean professionals migrate to the US and find jobs way below their skill-level. They are then able to remit money and barrels with commodities back to the region. However, to arrive at a proper understanding of the gains from remittances, we have to discount from the cost to the Caribbean for the training of these professionals, combined with their loss in income due to their underemployment in the US. This has not been done although regional scholars argue that remittances are a main means of development and sustenance in the Caribbean. They are not really in a position to arrive at such conclusions because they omit to consider all appropriate costs. Furthermore, remittances are under serious threat due to the current global economic and financial crises.

The struggle for GG in the Caribbean goes back to the social unrest during the 1930s, and even before that period. Nowadays, GG is a tool of the elites in the global institutions that are not themselves

---

[38] Veillette, Connie, Clare Ribando and Mark Sullivan. 2006. U.S. Foreign Assistance to Latin America and the Caribbean. Washington DC: Congress Research Service (CRS) Report for Congress.

[39] Kirton, Claremont and Georgia McLeod. 2006. Remittances to Caricom Countries: Policy Issues and Options paper presented at the 38th Annual Conference of the Caribbean Centre for Monetary Studies (CCMS), Barbados, November 2006.

accountable to any Caribbean constituency. The difference between the two is that the former represented a people's movement, while the latter is an instrument of US-led globalization and European bloc imperialism. Indeed, nowadays, "political independence has been subordinated to the more abstract and obfuscating trope of 'governance.'"[40] Nation-states are now "compelled under the guise of governance, to embrace financial reforms to improve global market access."[41] GG conceived along the lines of neoliberal political ideology is more about external political control than it is about the creation of popular bottom-up democracy in the region through mass collective action.

Based on the neoliberal view of "democracy promotion," GG is the political arrangements to facilitate current capitalist growth and development. It does not matter that recent research established that there is no correlation between economic growth and type of political system.[42] Rather than instituting popular democracy, GG strengthens neoliberal democratization, a new form of authoritarianism[43] that guarantees the smooth operations of the US owned and controlled mega-corporations in their extraction of the economic surplus from the Caribbean and Third World locations. The colonial authoritarian state performed this facilitative function of global capitalism in the past that GG does today.

The advocates of services promotion also fit nicely within the scheme of global capitalism. Rather than finding the cause of labour's migration from agriculture, they advance services as the new growth sector. The major problems with this idea are discussed in a separate chapter.

CARIFORUM-EU EPA as a Development Strategy

The mercantile/classical political economy tradition founded on the protection-free trade dichotomy, bequeathed to subsequent

---

[40] McMichael, Philip. 2006. Reframing Development: Global Peasant Movements and the New Agrarian Question. *Canadian Journal of Development Studies* (27) 4: 471–483.

[41] McMichael, Philip. 2006. Reframing Development: Global Peasant Movements and the New Agrarian Question. *Canadian Journal of Development Studies* (27) 4: 471–483.

[42] Przeworski, Adam. 2003. A Flawed Blueprint: The Covert Politicization of Development Economics. *Harvard International Review* (25) 1: 42–47.

[43] Canterbury, Dennis C. 2005. *Neoliberal Democratization and New Authoritarianism*. Aldershot: Ashgate Publishing.

generations the idea that development is about the nation-state accumulating and distributing wealth to various economic classes within its borders. This tradition advocates two distinct methods by which a nation-state could accumulate wealth – protectionist measures and free trade. The EPA has pretensions as a direct descendant of the free trade variant of the mercantile/classical political economy tradition, which arguably possesses the capability to assist Caribbean and EU states to further the accumulation and distribution of wealth in their respective geographic areas.

Its essence however is the protection of the global economic status quo that keeps Europe at the top and the ACP countries at the bottom. Its perpetuators present it as the vehicle through which Caribbean and EU countries could accumulate and distribute wealth in the current era of capitalist globalization and European bloc imperialism. Its premise therefore is that through the EPA these two historically bound regions – one (the EU) that violently incorporated the other (the Caribbean) into the global capitalist system to produce wealth for accumulation in the former – will transform that relationship such that each region will derive proportionate benefits from their participation in the CARIFORUM-EU EPA. Thus, through the CARIFORUM-EU EPA wealth will accumulate in both the EU and the Caribbean, rather than only in the EU, which was the case in hitherto models of EU-Caribbean economic relations. By some strange twist of logic the CARIFORUM-EU EPA will transform centuries of asymmetrical economic relations between Europe and the Caribbean into economic relations that are equal.

The Ricardian trade theory that maintained the mono-crop agricultural system in the Caribbean and restricted the region to the position of producer of raw materials, primary causes of its poverty, will suddenly have the opposite effect by expanding wealth in the region through the CARIFORUM-EU EPA. It is known however that the EPA is about trade and not about improving the productive capabilities of the Caribbean. Moreover, the classification of the Caribbean as a middle-income region will have the effect of lessening the efficacy of the Caribbean in its ability to push the EU to help the region in its bid to improve its productive capabilities. The World Bank classifies Antigua and Barbuda, the Bahamas, Barbados, and Trinidad and Tobago as "High Income Countries." It places Belize, Dominica, Grenada, St. Kitts and Nevis, St. Lucia, and St. Vincent and the

Grenadines in the category of "Upper Middle Income Countries," while Guyana and Jamaica are in the category "Lower Middle Income Countries."[44]

This means that the EU will not be prepared to give much assistance to the Caricom countries because of their so-called "Middle Income" status. The CARIFORUM-EU EPA is therefore a trade deal to further the sustainable development of middle-income and not low-income countries. It is a so-called sustainable development strategy for middle-income states. Do middle-income and low-income countries require different economic development strategies? The CARIFORUM-EU EPA does not address this question but it does distinguish between middle- and low-income countries, as is the case with EPAs in Africa.

The CARIFORUM-EU EPA purports to be something new, but in reality it locks Caribbean development into the same old way of thinking, which is that the region must strive to become like the European nation-states through engaging in "free trade." It reinforces the subordinate status of the Caribbean as imitator of Europe. It strengthens the capitalist mode of production as the primary economic system for the Caribbean and globally. It fortifies the traditional ideas about free trade that say the Caribbean needs to find its *niche* in which to specialize for export. The EPA fastens the region in the mercantile/classical political economy tradition of the development phenomena associated with nation-states, the very tradition that is the cause of the region's underdeveloped, and existence in the global capitalist system. The main goal of that tradition is wealth accumulation in nation-states either by the state itself or individuals or classes in them.

The CARIFORUM-EU EPA does not create the conditions for alternative development – alternative to capitalist accumulation or alternative to the nation-state system for which the mercantilist/classical political economy system evolved. Alternative development must mean the dismantling of nation-states that would remove the idea of wealth accumulation as the primordial goal of humans.

---

[44] See Brewster, Havelock. 2007. Understanding Development Challenges in the Caribbean: Time to Take in the Begging Bowl. Available at http://www.normangirvan.info/understanding-developmentchallenges-in-the-caribbean/.

Alternative Development Visions to the CARIFORUM-EU EPA

The purpose here is to present some sketches of tentative ideas on an alternative development vision for the Caribbean. Alternative development is characterized by two sets of ideas first those that seek to replace capitalist commodity production for exchange and accumulation with socialism, and second, the adoption of different policy approaches within the capitalist framework of commodity production. The ideas on alternative development presented here are located with those that seek to transcend the capitalist system. Specifically, the view is that alternative development entails the deliberate dismantling of the nation-state and its replacement with "autonomous communities" that may take the shape of regional unions such as the ALBA and Petrocaribe, which may not be end-goals of Caribbean alternative development, but the means by which the region could achieve greater equality and form a buffer against Euro-American imperialism.

The idea about the dismantling of the nation-state is rooted in Marx's notion of the "withering away of the state." The view is that the nation-state is the basis for the state, which means that the state would only disappear after the nation-state does. The nation-state is not only the basis of the state it is also the foundation of capitalist economic development and its accompanying social relations. The mercantile/classical political economy vision of development as progress emerged specifically to address the problem of nation-state building. It is the only theory of development that exists that has become manifest over the centuries as neoclassical, Keynesian, and neoliberalism approaches. Also, so-called development theory from the 1940s fit squarely within the mercantile/classical political economy tradition of protectionism versus free trade in the building of capitalist nation-states. If development is about building capitalist nation-states, then alternative development must dismantle the capitalist nation-state.

"Another Development" in the Caribbean

Hitherto conceptualizations of alternative or "another development" in the Caribbean focused on replacing the private and state-capitalist development approaches experimented with in the region since political independence. Thomas (1988) outlined eight requirements for "another development" in this context. First, "development requires a system of ownership, control, and production oriented towards satisfying the basic needs of the masses." Second, "there can only be real development in the region if these basic needs are satisfied through planned and effective implementation of the right to work." Third, "to reverse the region's authoritarian tradition, the material conditions of life should be reproduced within a self-reliant and endogenous pattern of growth." Fourth, "development also implies that work, politics and social organization are based on democratizing power in society and on the effective (as opposed to nominal) exercise of fundamental rights, such as those to free expression and organization, respect for an individual's privacy and the abolition of repression and torture." Fifth, "development also implies preserving the stability of the environment and putting an end to the degradation it has suffered through the growth of national production in Caribbean societies." Sixth, "it is important to recognize that because of the polarity between the state and the private sector, the state would have to play an important part in the development of the region, but only within the context of a participatory political process in which the ordinary West Indian's status as a citizen, producer and consumer of wealth was enhanced." Seventh, "a realistic approach to development in the region must begin by recognizing the stark reality of the hostile environment created by living in imperialism's backyard." Eight, the external context is relevant to the region's development (Thomas, 1988: 356–362).

Thomas (1988) identified an alternative conception of development to tackle three principal problems. First, "that the pattern of consumption in the region fails to satisfy the basic needs of the broad mass of the population (instead it reflects the unequal distribution of wealth and income, disparities in urban and rural development and the poverty and dispossession of large social groups, particularly the peasants and urban poor." Second, "that because imperatives for bringing resources into production in the past derived largely from the needs of international capitalist expansion, the pattern of resource use and resource endowment are improperly reconciled." Third,

> reflecting the situation in 1 and 2 above, the pattern of property ownership and the social relations centring on this, show sharp and worsening inequalities both at the national/international level within each national territory. Because of the systemic nature of these problems, it follows that the configurations of a transformed regional economy must be based on the *construction of a process of accumulation founded on the priorities required to ensure the eventual reversal of these divergences.* In other words, accumulation has to be founded on the logic of a dynamic convergence between social needs and the use of domestic resources (Thomas, 1988: 363–364).

While Thomas' (1988) alternative development proposal is sound and founded on notions about delinking from capitalism, its basis remains capital accumulation by nation-states. This is gleaned from Thomas' (1988) view that the foundation of economic transformation or alternative development in the Caribbean is a process of accumulation that puts an end to the patterns of capitalist property ownership and the social relations they produce. Furthermore, the imperialist expansion of the capitalist system must not be the basis for bringing Caribbean resources into production. The region needs to produce to fulfill its social needs, based on what its resources would allow. This is a form of sustainable development, unlike the neoliberal sustainable development of the CARIFORUM-EU EAP.

From a practical perspective, it is easy to see why the nation-state figures so prominently in the alternative development proffered by Thomas (1988). The nation-state is so dominant that it is difficult to visualize human political and economic organization outside them. This might have very well been the case in the heyday of the city-state – the failure to see its transition into the nation-state. The growing number of regions globally however seems to indicate that the potential is there for a transition from the nation-state to something else. In the Caribbean, the trajectory of the regional integration process leads towards a single political and economic space in the region, similar to that of the EU. The same is true of Africa Union. The emergence of these broader political and economic spaces characterized by nation-states that act more in unison politically and economically, would signal the downplaying of the nation-state. Of curse this would be different to the false neoliberal idea that the nation-state is losing sovereignty to the multinational corporations.

Inevitably, regional blocs will eventually remove the nation-state as the entity that needs to accumulate wealth. The development of the bloc will take precedence over the nation-state, as is being witnessed with the EU. Furthermore, it would be possible to replace capital accumulation in the nation-state by accumulation in regional blocs, which take care of the socio-economic needs of its member-state.

Method for Conceptualizing Alternative Development

The arrangement of Caribbean political economy in historical sequence helps to clarify the roles played by actually existing individuals and groups (classes) in the economic sphere of production and distribution, and in the social ideological sphere of Caribbean society. Historical method helps to identify the positions of these individuals and groups in the trajectory of the mercantilist/classical political economy vision of development. The relevant Caribbean literature reveal certain specific classifications in that trajectory – mercantile and free trade economies, plantation and post-plantation economies, the slave and colonial slave mode of production societies, centre periphery relations (dependency societies), and neoliberalism.

Caribbean society could be analyzed in two broad historical periods the first being pre-mercantilist/pre-free trade, and the second the mercantile/classical political economy period. The first period was characterized by a lack of private property, states, and nation-states. Then, if there was a value known as happiness to humans in the region, it had a different meaning, compared with its meaning in the second historical period, in which accumulated wealth is regarded as the source of happiness.

The actually existing life-processes of humans in the Caribbean in the second epoch involve the creation and evolution of mercantilist colonies and nation-states formed for the specific purpose to accumulate wealth for mercantile/industrial capitalist nation-states in Europe. The Caribbean was created to fulfill the happiness of the inhabitants of European nation-states. Caribbean people only began to pursue happiness for themselves after Caribbean colonies became nation-states, due to their political independence.

The social laws of production and distribution in the Caribbean – the ideological relations that actually evolved into those that currently exist in the region had their beginnings in a system of physical production and distribution for the happiness of European nation-states. There is therefore a tension in these relations in the region in the sense that their origins are to enrich Europe, but Caribbean people now want them to serve the interest of the region. The other aspect of this tension is that Caribbean people took their schooling in those ideological relations but evolved ideological relations of their own that conflict with the original purpose for which Europeans created the region.

Thus, while the progress of European nation-states was the prime reason for the creation of Caribbean colonies, Caribbean countries now want to use their economies to develop themselves in the image of the European nation-states. Caribbean nation-states have the identical goal as the European nation-states that created them – wealth accumulation. Caribbean ideological relations must therefore serve two masters the rich countries that continue to enrich themselves off of the region through state-protection or free trade arrangements like the economic partnership agreement, and the Caribbean people that want to become rich off the same trade.

The mercantile/classical political economy vision of progress as wealth accumulation however represents a perfect state of development that can only exist in the imagination. Nonetheless, there are several imaginations on development since nothing, including development as wealth accumulation and its ideological relations, is perfect, absolute, or permanent. This means that development is transitory and we do not have to think, operate, or believe that we are pursuing something that is absolute or permanent. Caribbean society is transitory within the framework of mercantilist/classical political economy vision of development as progress. That is why Thomas (2005) for example identifies the development glass in the region as half-empty or half-full depending on the observer's perspective. Caribbean states can also transition out of the mercantile/classical political economy framework, which itself is not permanent or final but also transitory.

Tentative Ideas on Development Alternatives to the EU EPA

An appreciation of alternative development therefore involves first recognition of the mercantile/classical political economy framework that entraps Caribbean countries. The most important ingredients of that vision are the nation-state and wealth accumulation. If you take away the nation-state as a development entity, then the mercantilist/classical political economy vision of development cannot stand-up. It is because of the existence of the nation-state that the mercantile/classical political economy development vision emerged and remains dominant.

Second, humans lived for a much longer period outside of nation-states than they lived in them. In the periods of human history where they lived outside of the nation-state, they did not have a development problem as outlined by the mercantile/classical political economy tradition. The dialectics of history therefore does not augur well for the survival of the nation-state as the primary means of human organization, and development in the mercantile/classical political economy tradition. Marx's idea about the "withering away of the state" is essentially a prediction of the dismantling of the nation-state. The state and development are both creatures of the nation-state, and they will only disappear when the nation-state does. In essence, the alternative vision of development must visualize human existence outside of the confines of the nation-state possibly as forms of autonomous communities.

Third, there is need for a reconfiguration of the post-World War II idea of development as technical change or industrialization, and poor countries "catching-up" technologically, economically, politically, and socially with the rich capitalist countries. The Caribbean countries bought into that development idea and have since been struggling to "develop" by creating and implementing economic measures to institute technical change or industrialization. Technical change is not the only condition for development – sustainability in terms of the environment, production (agricultural, manufacturing, mining, and services), economic growth, equality, fair income distribution, employment, democracy, health care, education, etc. – informed by natural and human resources and ability to export and import must be its backbone.

Furthermore, alternative development means conquering the psychological state imposed on the region by the post-World War II development vision that places the Caribbean in a state of mental self-oppression of always playing "catch-up" with the rich capitalist countries. Playing "catch-up" ensnares the region in a vicious cycle of domination that entraps rather than liberates its future generations. Under such conditions, the present generation leaves nothing for future generations other than the sorry mental state that implies Caribbean peoples are not good enough to build societies to their liking with the resources at their disposal and those obtained through trade, but must strive to become like somebody else.

Fourth, alternative development is finding a Caribbean dynamic optimum or level of satisfactory living conditions acceptable to Caribbean people. What do the Caribbean people accept as a satisfactory level of human development? This information is a desirable starting point for an alternative development strategy. This would require the mammoth task to gather information across the region from working people themselves and through their institutions as the first act to involve them in the decisions on alternative development. The people must determine the goals of alternative development, and the institutional framework to deliver on their stated needs.

A lead role is carved-out here for workers' institutions including trade unions and civil society agencies. Trade unions and civil society agencies were at the very centre of the struggle for better living conditions and alternatives to colonial development, and played a key role in helping to shape the nationalist alternatives to colonialism. This is the historical basis for the involvement of civil society in alternative development, and not the role neoliberal capitalism prescribes for non-governmental organizations (NGOs). Neoliberal capitalism hijacked civil society agencies in the 1990s converting them into tools of US-led globalization and EU bloc imperialism. Now that the NGOs did their job to pacify people into believing that there is no alternative but to work within the neoliberal globalization framework, their external bankers are gradually disappearing leaving NGOs in dire financial problems that caused many of them to fold-up. Caribbean civil society agencies need to return to the role they played in the nationalist movement in search of development alternatives, to European imperialism.

Fifth, the historic struggles by Caribbean people for better living conditions must be separated from the academic study of "development" as a subject. The former is a political process to democratize Caribbean society in all its aspects in which the masses win through struggle a greater share and control of the wealth they produce. The latter is a process that creates theories and policy measures to bring about technical change or industrialization to generate economic growth. Although separate, we cannot deny the inextricable link between the two even though at times they work against each other, such as oppressive liberalization policies that cause mass poverty and dissent.

There is a false view that "development" as a subject for study and national goal is a post-World War II invention. This view of course discounts the practical struggle for democracy conducted by Caribbean working people, historically. This false conception is discussed above, although in the post-World War II period "development" re-emerged in the context of the US strategy to dismantle European colonialism and establish itself as the new global hegemon. The US strategy aimed to reconstruct Europe through the Marshall Plan and simultaneously with the break-up of the colonial system "develop" the former European colonies. This strategy served the ideological function to combat socialism/communism in Europe and its former colonies, concurrently. "Development" theory and practice became at that time an ideological contest between capitalism and socialism/communism.

The struggle by Caribbean peoples for better living conditions commenced long before the false view emerged about when "development" became a subject for academic study. The Caribbean people must continue their struggle for better living conditions simultaneously with the pursuit of "development" recognizing where they differ and overlap. The trajectory of the Caribbean struggle for betterment involved revolts, and industrial and social unrest that brought the region significant political and economic gains since the 1840s. Seemingly, "development" has taken this combative spirit out of the region's psyche and replaced it with a more acceptable academic search for theories of "development."

Sixth, there is need for a rethinking of the underlying assumptions of the so-called pioneers of "development" theory[45] about the link between economic development as industrialization, and increased social and political participation. The prevailing idea is that economic prosperity inevitably increases democracy because it eventually alters living conditions for the better increasing social and political participation. Empirical research established however that there is no correlation between economic prosperity and type of political system.

Some critics observed that too much democracy gives the populace excessive rights that could cause it to take political action that thwarts economic progress. They posit instead the need for strong states to counteract political and economic activities that thwart development. Their position suggests that political repression is a necessary condition for increased economic prosperity. The evidence presented in support of this position includes Stalinism in the industrialization of Russia, and the role of strong states in the newly industrializing

---

[45] These early pioneers included Rosenstein-Rodan, Paul N. 1943. Problems of Industrialization of Eastern and South- Eastern Europe. *Economic Journal* (53) 210/211: 202–211; Rosenstein-Rodan, Paul. 1944. The International Development of Economically Backward Areas. *International Affairs* 20: 157–65. Prebisch, Raul. 1950. *The Economic Development of Latin America and Its Principal Problems*. New York: United Nations; Lewis, W. Arthur. 1954. Economic Development with Unlimited Supplies of Labor. *The Manchester School* (22) 2: 139–91; Myint, Hla. 1954. An Interpretation of Economic Backwardness. *Oxford Economic Papers* (6) 6: 132–66. The early pioneers of development theory in the Caribbean include Lewis, W. Arthur. 1950. Industrialization of the British West Indies. *Caribbean Economic Review* 2: 1–39; Best, L. 1968. Outline of a Model of Pure Plantation Economy. *Social and Economic Studies* (17) 3: 283–326; Levitt, Kari and Best, Lloyd.1969. Export Propelled Growth and Industrialization in the Caribbean, 4 Volumes. Montreal: Mc Gill University. Beckford, George. 1984. *Persistent Poverty*. London: Zed Press; Thomas, Clive Y. 1974. *Dependence and Transformation: The Economics of the Transition to Socialism*. New York: Monthly Review Press; Demas, William. 1965. *The Economics of Development in Small Countries, with Special Reference to the Caribbean*. Montreal: Mc Gill University Press; Girvan, Norman. 1976. *Corporate Imperialism, Conflict and Expropriation*. New York: Monthly Review Press.

countries (NICs) in Southeast Asia. Proponents of the US "free trade" model and EU bloc imperialism argue that democracy enhances economic development and consequently they launched a "good governance" crusade to democratize the globe.

These three dominant frameworks – economic development leads to increased participation and democracy, authoritarian states stimulate economic development by restraining liberty, and democracy as a first principle in inspiring economic development – within which theorizing about development has taken place must be challenged from the perspective of alternative development. In essence, these frameworks are about the evolution of capitalism as an economic system and its relationship with politics – the very understanding of economics and politics for which alternatives are sought. Caribbean alternative development cannot centre on ideological apprehensions that seek to link economics and politics in any particular sequence of significance, which suits society best.

Seventh, the Caribbean cannot pursue development purely from a self-reliance perspective, the region's future lies in its collaboration with alternative movements to counteract Euro-American domination and achieve greater political and economic independence. The extent to which this alliance goes depends on the ability of regional leaders to take advantage of existing global competitive arenas such as the ALBA and the BRIC.

A lingering problem with this alternative vision of development is the issue of power the domain of the state. The US, and European bloc imperialists have the greatest power. How can the SIDS in the Caribbean implement an alternative development vision in their own image when these countries do not possess comparable power? An examination of Caribbean history reveals however that there were numerous ways Caribbean peoples contributed towards the break-up of the most powerful European Empires. The Caribbean countries may not be able to go it alone but they can do their part in collaboration with others.

CHAPTER EIGHT

THE CRITICS OF THE CARIFORUM-EU EPA

Introduction

EU bloc imperialism secures the support of domestic elites in the ACP regions that it seeks to plunder through economic partnership agreements. This is a key part of the strategy in the arsenal of EU bloc imperialism. These elites are the negotiators, public sector officials, key private sector agencies, trade union leaders, and civil society operatives. These groups vary between the two points of complete support for the EU EPA and conditional support for it. Prominent academics may formulate important critiques of the EU EPA, but do not call for its outright rejection. The purpose of this chapter is to provide direct evidence, which highlights these tendencies among the critics of the EU EPA, focusing on the CARIFORUM-EU EPA, as the example.

The negotiators of the EU EPA and their allies among the academics, and in the private and public sectors, and civil society defend the EU EPA as the best possibly deal for the ACP countries. On the opposite side to the proposers of the EPA, are the academics, civil society agencies, and private and public sector officials who oppose it on different grounds but merely from perspectives of wanting to change some of its provisions to the benefit of the ACP regions. Thus, the dispute really concerns the manner in which the region pursues the EPA and not whether the European bloc imperialist EPA is good or bad for the CARIFORUM countries at this stage of their capitalist development.

The debate is not about alternative development models to replace the neoliberal EPA. Furthermore, there is hardly any comparative analysis of the alternative ALBA trade model and the EPA, or between the EPA with the Chinese model, which has upturned neoliberal theories about direct foreign investment. It is difficult to locate any group in the region that wants to abolish the EPA, altogether.

The current chapter presents the positions adopted by the different groups concerning the CARIFORUM-EU EPA, the only comprehensive EPA signed by an ACP region with European bloc imperialism at the time of writing. Its central contention is that the critics of the EPA merely want to see its reform, but not its overthrow, and are prepared to enter into a trade deal with EU bloc imperialism, and as such are tacit or open supporters of European bloc imperialism. The major positions adopted on the EPA by these diverse sources are outlined, in support of this assertion.

The leaders of the CARIFORUM and the EU bloc imperialist signed the EPA in October 2008. The CARIFORUM parliaments have ratified the EPA but it is still pending in the European parliament. When the contents of the EPA became public there was public outcry against it by the various constituencies identified above. A central feature of the *ex post facto* debate on the CARIFORUM-EU EPA is the bringing to the foreground the issue of secrecy surrounding negotiations of the EPA. The Caribbean Regional Negotiating Machinery (CRNM), which negotiated the CARIFORUM EPA with the EU, claims, nonetheless that the critics of the EPA had the opportunity to participate in its negotiations but failed to do so.

EU Bloc Imperialism Defines Civil Society

The neoliberal theoretical tradition that underlies EU bloc imperialism fosters the view that the state does not possess the capacity to adequately address the needs of its citizens. The proffered solution is for civil society to step in to fill the void created by the absence of government in the development process. It is argued in this chapter however that the promotion of civil society within the framework of EU bloc imperialism is a class project designed to cultivate support for the political and economic objectives of the European Union. The evidence in support of this view is provided by the role and response of civil society in the Caribbean to the CARIFORUM-EU EPA. Caribbean civil society organizations were critical of the CARIFORUM-EU EPA but they join in chorus to advocate its reform rather than to reject it outright for what it truly is – a EU bloc imperialist mercantilist project.

EU bloc imperialism accords a superficial role to "civil society," a concept for which it is claimed there is no commonly accepted or legal definition. The European Communities' (EC) White Paper on European Governance provides a broad summary of what is its understanding of the role of civil society. In the first instance civil society, in which is located churches and religious communities, non-governmental organizations, trade unions and employers' organizations, is seen to play an important role "in giving voice to the concerns of citizens and delivering services that meet people's needs." These organizations mobilize people and support including those "suffering from exclusion or discrimination." They may "play an important role at global level in development policy," and even "act as an early warning system for the direction of political debate," and exercise considerable influence.[1]

According to the EC civil society organizations are facilitators of a broad policy dialogue.[2] Their specific role in modern democracies "is closely linked to the fundamental rights of citizens to form organizations in order to pursue a common purpose."[3] The EC's view is that by belonging to an association citizens can find ways to participate actively in society, in addition to becoming involved, in political parties or through elections.[4] The EU asserts that the term "civil society organization" is the shorthand descriptor for three broadly defined categories of organizations, that form the principal structures of society outside of government and public administration, including economic operators not generally considered to be "third sector" or non-governmental organizations (NGOs).[5]

The first category is trade unions and employers' federations, what are termed the "social partners" that operate in the labor-market. Second, there are consumer organizations which are not social partners as such, but do represent social and economic players. Third, there are NGOs that unite people around a common cause, such as the environment, human rights, charity, education, and training, etc. Fourth, there are community-based organizations (CBOs), established at the grassroots level to pursue member-oriented objectives. The EC identified, as CBOs "youth organizations, family associations and all

---

1 Commission of the European Communities, European Governance: A White Paper, Brussels, 25.7.2001COM(2001) 428 final p. 14.

2 The European Commission and Civil Society, General Principles and Minimum Standards for Consultation of Interested Parties by the Commission, COM (2002) 704.

3 The European Commission and Civil Society, General Principles and Minimum Standards for Consultation of Interested Parties by the Commission, COM (2002) 704.

4 The European Commission and Civil Society, General Principles and Minimum Standards for Consultation of Interested Parties by the Commission, COM (2002) 704.

5 The European Commission and Civil Society, General Principles and Minimum Standards for Consultation of Interested Parties by the Commission, COM (2002) 704, pp. 4–5.

organizations through which citizens participate in local and municipal life; and religious communities."

The EU bloc imperialism model ascribes to civil society the role of democratizing the society through their participation in the decision-making processes at all levels. This position belongs to the idealist framework that regards the state as the basis of civil society meaning that civil society is a part of the state – the citizens of the state are members of civil society. Marx (1970) observed however that civil society is the basis of the state since the state is an abstraction and only the people alone are concrete.[6]

Caribbean civil society agencies, nonetheless, many of which are products of the EU bloc imperialist model through their funding and stated goals to democratize society, and operating as members of the state, formulated critiques of the CARIFORUM-EU EPA merely to put pressure on the state to – reform the EPA to the benefit of the Caribbean, rather than to transform it.

Reformist Views from Caribbean Civil Society

Consideration is given below to the reformist views expressed by the Caribbean Banana Exporters Association (CBEA), the Federation of Independent Trade Unions and NGOs (FITUN), the Group of Concerned Caribbean Citizens (GCCC), the International Trade Union Confederation (ITUC), and the Caribbean Association of Industry and Commerce (CAIC).

The Caribbean Banana Exporters Association

The Caribbean Banana Exporters Association (CBEA) represents banana-exporting interests in Belize, Dominican Republic, Jamaica, Suriname, and the Windward Islands. It has counterparts in Cameroon and Cote d' Ivoire. The first point to note about the CBEA and its counterparts is that they welcomed the EPA although they expressed misgivings about it. A CBEA press release[7] on the matter states that the

---

[6] Karl Marx, *Critique of Hegel's Philosophy of Right* (Translated and edited by Joseph O'Malley), Cambridge, Cambridge University Press, 1970.

[7] The Caribbean Banana Exporters Association (CBEA) Press Release, February 12th, 2008.

organization welcomed various EPAs between "the Caribbean region, Cameroon, Cote d'Ivoire, Ghana and the European Union" within "a WTO compatible framework for preference for the ACP banana trade."[8] Second, the CBEA took the position that although the EU had promised to do otherwise it appears that the bloc was now "willing to dilute or nullify the benefits" to the Caribbean even before the EPAs are formally signed and ratified.[9]

Third, the CBEA demanded that the EU entered into substantive dialogue as required by the EPAs before making proposals for other bilateral free trade agreements or in the WTO arena. Specifically, the CBEA wants the EU to do four things. The first is for the EU to "recognize the structural, social and economic factors that justify the long standing preference granted to banana industries of the ACP."[10] Second, recognition must be given to the situation that "under the current EU tariff structure, from January 2006 to November 2007, ACP exports have grown by 74,000 tonnes while Latin American exports have grown by 635,000 tonnes."[11] Third, the EU should "not make a premature offer for bananas in their negotiations with Central America or other non-ACP regions." Fourth, the EU should "vigorously defend the existing tariff preference for bananas in the WTO Doha Round negotiations."[12]

The fourth general point to be gleaned from the CBEA's position is its argument that the EU's recognition of the above factors is the critical test as to whether the ACP banana trade will flourish or die under the EPA. It is obvious however that the CBEA's actions are not furthering the democratic process as the EU claims for the role of civil society. The CBEA is not operating from a position of strength but is more or less on its knees begging for concessions from the EU. That is far from promoting democracy and is more about fostering dependency and subordination to EU bloc imperialism.

---

[8] The Caribbean Banana Exporters Association (CBEA) Press Release, February 12th, 2008.

[9] Caribbean Net News, "Suriname to defend ACP banana trade at WTO," February 26, 2008.

[10] The Caribbean Banana Exporters Association (CBEA) Press Release, February 12th, 2008.

[11] The Caribbean Banana Exporters Association (CBEA) Press Release, February 12th, 2008.

[12] The Caribbean Banana Exporters Association (CBEA) Press Release, February 12th, 2008.

The Federation of Independent Trade Unions and NGOs

The Federation of Independent Trade Unions and NGOs (FITUN) is an umbrella organization that has amongst its membership trade unions that represent some 40,000 working people; major farmers' organizations, NGOs representative of youth and the differently able, and important community and land-based organizations in Trinidad and Tobago. The FITUN takes a position not dissimilar from that expressed by business, civil society, academics, and persons knowledgeable about international trade agreements and the state of Caribbean integration.[13] That position is that it is better for the Caribbean "not be pressured – by the EU threat of invoking GSP arrangements after December 31st 2007 – into signing an EPA that would be deleterious" to its interests. The FITUN's view is that if necessary, the region should "utilize several months in 2008 to get the agreement 'right,'" since that would be more advantageous to the Caribbean people in the medium to long run.[14] In its letter to Prime Minister Patrick Manning of Trinidad and Tobago dated December 5, 2007, the FITUN advanced several reasons why it takes the position it does on the CARIFORUM-EU EPA.

Its first point is that the EPA will lock the Caribbean into trade and economic arrangements with the EU indefinitely. This means that the region will have to live with a "bad" agreement that may cost it dearly. The possible costs to the region identified by the FITUN included the loss in profit and closures of businesses, and increase in unemployment. Also, the EPAs would have a negative impact on the Caribbean's ailing agricultural sector, and reduced government revenue, would result in major challenges with respect to fiscal deficits and increasing debt burdens. This is especially important for the countries that comprise the Organization of Eastern Caribbean States. In addition, the FITUN pointed out that the region's balance of payments would come under pressure as imports from the EU rise while Caribbean exports decline.[15] The FITUN envisages that a bad EPA deal would increase

[13] Federation of Independent Trade Unions and NGOS (FITUN) Letter to Prime Minister Patrick Manning dated December 5, 2007.

[14] Federation of Independent Trade Unions and NGOS (FITUN) Letter to Prime Minister Patrick Manning dated December 5, 2007.

[15] Federation of Independent Trade Unions and NGOS (FITUN) Letter to Prime Minister Patrick Manning dated December 5, 2007.

the difficulties of the Caribbean to pursue future development policies to foster improvements in domestic industry, agriculture and small and medium sized businesses.[16]

Second, the FITUN argues that "The EC negotiators do not seem to be appreciative of how "special and differential" treatment should apply to the region and in particular to the economies of the OECS." In its view the rejection by the EU of the CARIFORUM negotiators' timelines for the phasing in of lower tariffs is one manifestation of this lack of appreciation. The FITUN opposed the 10 to 15 years time frame to reduce tariffs to zero on the grounds that the period is unrealistic. Its argument is that "given the many constraints and vulnerabilities of small island developing states," 10 to 15 years "is an impossibly short time within which to transform" their "economies to meet the requirements of deep liberalization."[17] Note that this is not an argument against "deep liberalization" but a plea by the FITUN for more time to implement deeper market liberalization in the Caribbean.

Third, the FITUN noted that in the light of new international trading rules, particularly the WTO's framework, the Caribbean could find itself in a situation where the EPA agreement ties its hands "in future negotiations for Free Trade Agreements (FTA) with other countries and/or trade blocks and becomes the floor below which none is prepared to go beneath."[18] The FITUN warned that in the Caricom-Canada FTA negotiations for example, Canada could adopt an "EPA plus stance," and that the US could take a similar position in future trade deals with the region. The EPA will therefore treat Canada and the US less favorably than the EU with regards to trade with the Caribbean. At the multilateral level, the FITUN envisages that the EPA will impact on offers made by the Caribbean at the WTO. In connection with this point, the FITUN concludes that the region's "EPA negotiations are establishing benchmarks for [Caribbean] trade and economic arrangements with the rest of the world, and these for an indefinite time!" In its final assessment the FITUN states that a good EPA will assist the

[16] Federation of Independent Trade Unions and NGOS (FITUN) Letter to Prime Minister Patrick Manning dated December 5, 2007.

[17] Federation of Independent Trade Unions and NGOS (FITUN) Letter to Prime Minister Patrick Manning dated December 5, 2007.

[18] Federation of Independent Trade Unions and NGOS (FITUN) Letter to Prime Minister Patrick Manning dated December 5, 2007.

Caribbean in its future negotiations, while a bad one will put the region at very serious risk.[19]

The FITUN opined that given the distance between the CARIFORUM and EU negotiators and the apparent intransigence of the latter, the option of further amending the region's offers to bring them closer in line with the EU's would result in a bad agreement. Indeed, the FITUN argues that the Caribbean has conceded too much and that the region's offers could result in very substantial costs to local businesses, workers, farmers, fisher folk, women and youth.[20]

The FITUN therefore called on the Trinidad and Tobago government to adopt a position that a bad EPA is worse than no EPA. Furthermore, it admonished the Caricom not to be rushed into signing the CARIFORUM-EU EPA to satisfy the EU's deadline for the agreement. It urged the Caricom to maintain its position on the application of 'special and differential treatment', and to engage in a major dialogue with Caribbean business, labor, NGOs, and farmers' organizations to arrive at a consensus of a good agreement before it signs off on the CARIFORUM-EU EPA.[21] The FITUN called for "a participatory process through which the citizens of the region and their civil society organizations can participate in the discussion of the problem and search for solutions."[22]

These are very commendable points that the entire Caribbean region should support, but they fall short nonetheless of a call for the total abandonment of the EPA in the light of its farcical nature and failed theoretical foundations. The real question however is: Is the "participatory" process envisaged by the FITUN really a democratic one, or it is merely an attempt to foster discussion within a framework predetermined for the Caribbean by European bloc imperialism? The answer is that the "participatory" process promotes limited or constrained democracy. It fosters a democracy that is constrained by the parameters established by EU bloc imperialism. The real challenge to democracy in the Caribbean is for the region to breakout from the framework of constrained democracy.

[19] Federation of Independent Trade Unions and NGOS (FITUN) Letter to Prime Minister Patrick Manning dated December 5, 2007.

[20] Federation of Independent Trade Unions and NGOS (FITUN) Letter to Prime Minister Patrick Manning dated December 5, 2007.

[21] Federation of Independent Trade Unions and NGOS (FITUN) Letter to Prime Minister Patrick Manning dated December 5, 2007.

[22] Federation of Independent Trade Unions and NGOS (FITUN) Letter to Prime Minister Patrick Manning dated December 5, 2007.

Group of Concerned Caribbean Citizens

A group of concerned Caribbean citizens comprising prominent academics, civil society personnel, and individuals issued a statement that called for a full and public review of the CARIFORUM-EU APA. The main issues that the GCCC has with the CARIFORUM-EU EPA are gleaned from a statement it issued dated January 20, 2008.[23] First, the GCCC states that "the Caribbean public was not kept fully abreast of the potential implications of the EPA for the course of the region's economic relations," with Europe and other trading partners. It observed that the EPA could "become a blueprint for future trade negotiations." Second, the GCCC accused the "Caribbean governments and responsible officials" of not keeping "the public better informed about the progress of the negotiations and the 'bullying' and 'broken promises' by Europe." Third, the GCCC believes that the authorities should find "opportunities" to "remedy this deficit in the future" through "full disclosure," "public explanation of the shortcomings as well as any anticipated benefit of the EPA, and for open participation in a discussion of its implications" for the economies and livelihoods of Caribbean peoples.

Fourth, the group argues that after the EPA is signed the "Caribbean countries will be locked in for all time to the provisions of this legally binding instrument." Fifth, the GCCC argues that it would "be very difficult, and in all likelihood very costly, to amend the EPA after it comes into force." Sixth, in the light of these issues, the GCCC urgently proposed, "that more time and opportunity be provided for a full and public review of the EPA in order that all its aspects are explained and understood and relevant objections taken into account."[24]

The Business Community

The Caribbean business community represented by the Caribbean Association of Industry and Commerce (CAIC) [25] is in full support of

---

[23] Statement by a Group of Concerned Caribbean Citizens Calling for Full and Public Review of the CARIFORUM-EC Economic Partnership Agreement (EPA), January 20, 2008.

[24] Statement by a Group of Concerned Caribbean Citizens Calling for Full and Public Review of the CARIFORUM-EC Economic Partnership Agreement (EPA), January 20, 2008.

[25] CAIC Statement on the CARIFORUM-EU Economic Partnership Agreement, *CAIC Newsletter*, Volume 5, Issue 2, February 2008.

the EPA, although it has certain areas of concerns. The CAIC argues that the EPA ushers in a "new era in trade relations" between the Caribbean and the EU. It commended the negotiators of the EPA, and praised them for successfully completing a comprehensive EPA that "covers services, investment, and intellectual property." The CAIC was happy at the negotiators' "efforts to seek consultation with the region's private sector and the inclusion of representatives from the sector in preparatory meetings and working groups throughout the negotiating process." The CAIC warns, however, that the Caribbean' "history is replete with examples which prove that the signing of a trade agreement do not necessarily translates into export growth and diversification" (CAIC 2008).

The CAIC, nonetheless, sees the EPA as providing opportunities for the region's exports and "development assistance" to help the area to meet its "costs of adjustments necessary for implementation" of the agreement. The CAIC applauds the recognition in the EPA that the EU and the CARIFORUM states, "differ significantly in size and level of development," which necessitates "asymmetrical commitments" by the two sides that "include complete duty free, quota free access for CARIFORUM goods entering the EU markets whilst CARIFORUM will liberalize access to markets for a period as long as 25 years in the case of some products" (CAIC 2008).

The CAIC believes that the Caribbean private sector must urgently position itself to seize the future opportunities that the EPA presents, and that the authorities must implement the necessary policies and put in place the infrastructure "to facilitate export to the EU under stated terms and conditions." The CAIC considers that some of the major opportunities for the Caribbean lie in the areas of services, intellectual property, and the movement of persons in the performing arts.

In this connection, however, the CAIC seems to overlook the brain drain from the Caribbean region and its sure escalation with the EPA. Also, the CAIC hedges its bet on cultural exports in terms of the performing arts and not on production the foundation of sustainable economic development.

The CAIC identified several objectives and achievements concerning gains in market access due to the EPA (Table 8.1). The first objective was to "secure effective market access into the European Union for new products and expanded access for current products." The achievement in this regard is that "The EU has offered to remove all remaining tariffs and quotas from 1 January 2008 with the exception of rice and

Table 8.1 Gains in Market Access through the CARIFORUM-EU EPA

Objectives	Achievements
Secure effective market access into the European Union for new products and expanded access for current products	The EU has offered to remove all remaining tariffs and quotas from 1 January 2008 with the exception of rice and sugar (until 2010 and 2015 respectively). This translates into Duty-free and quota free access for almost all products into the 27 markets of the EU
Gradual liberalization of import duties to minimize the revenue effect and provide sufficient timeframe for industry competitiveness.	Liberalization in CARIFORUM is gradual, taking place over many years. Where trade is liberalized at once, tariffs for the products are in many cases already set at 0 percent. CARIFORUM has an overall 25 year timeframe for liberalization of 86.9 percent of EU imports into its market
Exclusion from tariff reduction of CARIFORUM's sensitive sectors	Achieved with an Exclusion List for 13.1 percent of EU imports into CARIFORUM. CARIFORUM opted not to liberalize most agricultural products and other important locally produced products
Provision of shelter for growing industry from external competition	Sensitive industrial sectors have been excluded and an "infant industry clause" has been agreed where CARIFORUM will be allowed to reinstate tariffs in the future to protect growing industry and/or industries

(Continued)

Table 8.1 *(Cont.,)*

Objectives	Achievements
In order to provide some solution to the negative impact of the inability of CF to use sugar from other CARIFORUM States in export of sugar and sugar related products until 2015, a new Article was inserted into the Rules of Origin Protocol	Simplification of Rules of Origin and wider accumulation of inputs to allow producers from CARIFORUM to increase their exports to the EU
Favorable concessions on sugar	CARIFORUM received an additional Tariff Rate Quota (TRQ) of 60,000 tonnes - 30,000 for the Dominican Republic (which previously was not a party to the Sugar Protocol) and 30,000 to be shared between Caricom sugar producing countries
Technical assistance towards developing the capacity to export successfully in EU markets	Achieved with agreement on the Trade Partnership for Sustainable Development (Development Chapter), which includes support for infrastructure and the Caricom Development vision. The Joint Declaration on Development Cooperation includes a commitment to channel EPA support through the Caricom Development Fund. Joint Declarations were agreed to on bananas, sugar allocation, and traditional agricultural products.

Source: CAIC. 2008. Statement on the CARIFORUM-EU Economic Partnership Agreement, *CAIC Newsletter* 5: 2.

sugar (until 2010 and 2015 respectively). This translates into duty free and quota free access for almost all products into the 27 markets of the EU."

A second objective was the "Gradual liberalization of import duties to minimize the revenue effect and provide sufficient timeframe for industry competitiveness." According to the CAIC, the accomplishment here is that "Liberalization in CARIFORUM is gradual, taking place over many years. Where trade is liberalized at once, tariffs for the products are in many cases already set at 0 percent. CARIFORUM has an overall 25-year timeframe for liberalization of 86.9 percent of EU imports into its market."

A third objective was that CARIFORUM wanted the exclusion from tariff reduction of its sensitive sectors. According to the CAIC the EPA achieved this by having an "Exclusion List for 13.1 percent of EU imports into CARIFORUM." The CARIFORUM countries "opted not to liberalize most agricultural products and other important locally produced products."

A fourth objective was that the region wanted "shelter for growing industry from external competition." The CAIC pointed out that the EPA attains this by excluding "sensitive industrial sectors" and including an "infant industry clause" through which "CARIFORUM will be allowed to reinstate tariffs in the future to protect growing industry and/or industries." However, the CARIFORUM-EU EPA does not define what it means by "infant industry," and although the "clause looks good," it "does nothing that cannot be done under the normal bilateral safeguards clause."[26]

A fifth objective was that "In order to provide some solution to the negative impact of the inability of CF to use sugar from other CARIFORUM States in export of sugar and sugar related products until 2015, a new Article was inserted into the Rules of Origin Protocol." The achievement here in the view of the CAIC is the "Simplification of Rules of Origin and wider accumulation of inputs to allow producers from CARIFORUM to increase their exports to the EU."

A sixth objective was to have favorable concessions on sugar. The achievement here is that the "CARIFORUM received an additional Tariff Rate Quota (TRQ) of 60,000 tones - 30,000 for the Dominican

---

[26] CARIFORUM-EU Economic Partnership Agreement Comments by Dr Lorand Bartels (Trinity Hall, University of Cambridge), European Commission, 13 February 2008.

Republic (which previously was not a party to the Sugar Protocol) and 30,000 to be shared between Caricom sugar producing countries."

A seventh objective was for the CARIFORUM to attain "Technical assistance towards developing the capacity to export successfully in EU markets." According to the CAIC, the EPA achieved this objective with agreement on the Trade Partnership for Sustainable Development in the Development Chapter. This Chapter includes "support for infrastructure and the Caricom Development vision." In addition, the Joint Declaration on Development Cooperation "includes a commitment to channel EPA support through the Caricom Development Fund." Furthermore, "Joint Declarations were agreed to on bananas, sugar allocation, and traditional agricultural products.[27]

Also, it is believed that there are new opportunities for Caribbean vegetable farmers under the EPA.[28] The view is that the EPA could facilitate the exports of Jamaican smallholder vegetable production to the EU. In the light of these so-called "opportunities" the Caricom countries are encouraged to welcome the CARIFORUM-EU EPA. The argument is that small farmers need "all the technical and financial help they can get to meet the demands of the new market."

The Caribbean private sector is not all satisfied however, with its role in the negotiations of the EPA and its benefits from the agreement. It is evident that the CAIC does not speak for the entire private sector in the Caribbean region, since sections of it did not participate in the EPA negotiations. The private sector came in for severe chastisement by Carlos Wharton[29] for its non-involvement in the EPA. Wharton, a trade consultant with the Barbados private sector trade team, who attended EPA negotiations on behalf of the private sector, chided it for not playing an active role in constructing the relevant policies for their own future and survival that would benefit the sector.[30] In Wharton's view had the private sector played a more active role, it would have achieved more from the EPA. Wharton argues that because they were

---

[27] CAIC Statement on the CARIFORUM-EU Economic Partnership Agreement, *CAIC Newsletter*, Volume 5, Issue 2, February 2008.

[28] Manning, Gareth. 2007. New Markets for Regional Farmers. Jamaica Gleaner, April 1.

[29] "Consultant chastises private sector for EPA non-involvement," The Nation Newspapers (Barbados), January 30, 2008 Nationnews.com

[30] "Consultant chastises private sector for EPA non-involvement," The Nation Newspapers (Barbados), January 30, 2008 Nationnews.com

not a part of the negotiation process, it was a challenge to explain the mechanics of the EPA to private sector members.

The private sector identified four other areas of primary concern with the EPA, as represented by David Jessop the executive director of the Caribbean Council for Europe (CCE).[31] The first was the absence of a publicly available text of the agreement. It took weeks before the text of the CARIFORUM-EU EPA became available to the public, and when it did its source was the EU. This prevented the business community "from evaluating the impact of the agreement on specific areas of concern to their operations." The absence of a publicly available text of the CARIFORUM-EU EPA pointed to two seemingly important factors. The first is that there was either a lack, or low level of participation by the Caribbean private sector in the EPA negotiations that its members did not even know what the final agreement looked-like, and second there was a shroud of secrecy surrounding the EPA negotiation process.

The second area of primary concern to the private sector related to the attitude of public-sector officials and the perceived absence of an appreciation of a need for a paradigm shift, "with governments shifting from directing economic development to facilitating private-sector economic development." It would seem that although the EPA purports to favour private sector-led development the state was in the driving seat during the negotiations, since the CRNM is a state agency.

A third area of apprehension related "to the 'deep concern, verging on anger, about the ability of the EU and its representatives to deliver development assistance to the private sector'" in the Caribbean. The CCE executive director noted that private sector funding by the EC is widely viewed as virtually inaccessible. The EC system does not even deliver modest levels of support to affect change, because of the accompanying rules that are "at odds with individual corporate success." In Jessop's view this has led to deep cynicism about the real meaning of the EPA.

---

[31] A Comparison of the Experience of Agricultural Sector Trade and Production Adjustment Support in the French Overseas Territories of the Caribbean and the Caribbean Sugar Protocol Accompanying Measures Program Beneficiaries. Paper commissioned for the CTA-ECDPM dialogue meeting on 'Challenges of changing agricultural markets in the context of ACPEU trade: Identifying an Aid for Trade agenda for the agricultural sector' Brussels, 14–15 April 2008.

The fourth area of concern had to do with the uncertainty about when change would occur or how much time might be available in which to adapt. In this connection, there are concerns about the "continued existence of EU non-tariff barriers and the rules of origin to be applied." The CCE executive director advised that an electronic summary of the EPA by country and sector, should be produced, and that there be established "a virtual centre where manufacturers and others can explore the schedules by tariff line or by the area of services activity."

Views from the Public Sector

Several officials of Caribbean governments and public agencies have taken different positions in opposition to the CARIFORUM-EU EPA, but like civil society they do not reject it outright but are mostly accommodative of it. Bharrat Jagdeo the President of Guyana observed that the Caribbean stood to gain little from the EPA, noting that the agreement was concluded against the backdrop of a threat that tariffs would be imposed on Caribbean exports of sugar, bananas and manufactured goods to the European community as of January 1st 2008 if the region did not sign the EPA by December 31, 2007, the date when the WTO waiver for the trade arrangements under the Cotonou Agreement was set to expire. The President suggested that the shift from the principle of preferential trade to one of reciprocity incorporated in the EPA introduces a new set of challenges that the Caribbean is ill equipped to face.[32] Mr. Jagdeo expressed concerns about the double standards of the EU concerning safeguards that kept Caribbean sugar and rum out of EU member states overseas territories in the Caribbean region, "while themselves being prevented from applying similar safeguards." Also, he expressed apprehensions "about the rules of origin to be applied on sugar-based value-added products," which led him to complain that the EC was "consistently bullying the ACP countries."

The President argued that the Caribbean was forced into the EPA following a "well thought-out ploy by Europe to dismantle the

[32] Jagdeo, Bharrat, "The Caribbean Lost in the Negotiation with Europe," *South Bulletin*, Issue 8, February 1, 2008.

solidarity of the ACP... and play one off against the other, which they did very effectively." According to Jagdeo, not only is the EC acting in bad faith, all along it had plans "to dismantle the preferences and to basically bully the countries into meeting the deadlines," which could have been easily be adjusted. Although problems might not surface right away, the President argued that "they would soon arise, notably in terms of reduced government revenues and with regard to negotiations with other developed countries." Also, the President "highlighted issues in regard to regional cumulation in the sugar value chain and the application of the special safeguard measures."

After all of this ranting, however, President Jagdeo signed the EPA. There seems to be a lack of courage of the part of the Caribbean leaders to totally reject the EPA for what it really is, a new mercantile trade agreement fostered by EU bloc imperialism.

Jagdeo's signing of the EPA, however is reflective of a broader sentiment among the Caribbean ruling elites, as expressed by the Prime Ministers of Trinidad & Tobago and Jamaica that "although the agreement may not be ideal it is the best that could be obtained." The Prime Ministers of Barbados and Grenada however, "have undertaken reviews of the text and called on the EU to 'listen to the concerns of the region.'" The deputy-director of foreign trade in Belize nonetheless was more in praise of the EPA pointing out that it "allows for protection of our agricultural products, for example chickens, beans, papayas and manufactured goods, for example beer."

The secretary-general of the Caricom stressed however that due to "reciprocal preferential access for EU goods" under the EPA there is a pressing need for CARIFORUM producers to become more competitive, if they are to survive. The achievement of this competitiveness is seen as the "tri-partite responsibility" of government, business and labour.

Meanwhile, the Minister of Finance for Antigua and Barbuda Dr Errol Cort took the position that the region has done quite well with regards to EPA.[33] In an address at the Monetary Council of the Eastern Caribbean Central Bank, St. Kitts in early 2008, Cort claimed that the EPA would bring about economic growth in the Caribbean because of the region's "wider access to global markets." Cort remarked that the

[33] Mills, Precious, "Region has done quite well with regards to the negotiations of the EPA: Cort," *Sun* St. Kitts & Nevis, February 12, 2008.

negotiations were difficult because the Caribbean had to enter the new arrangement at a time when the EU seeks to establish a free trade system. According to him, this situation made it difficult for the region to negotiate for preferential treatment.

Cort said, "We live in a globalized world where access to markets has become more readily available. It seems to me that we did as best as we could in terms of negotiating the EPA" (Mills 2008). However, the Antiguan Government Minister outlined two main challenges with regard to the EPA. The first is that the public needs to understand the EPA and second, "there has to be evaluations in finding areas where the region can directly gain benefits." Unsurprisingly, the Minister argued that now that the region has negotiated an EPA it must search it to find benefits, in other words "placing the cart before the horse." Minister Cort then appealed to the private sector to support the EPA to help the region to effectively secure and execute the agreement (Mills 2008).

Addressing the same meeting the Prime Minister and Minister of Finance in Commonwealth of Dominica Roosevelt Skerrit said "one recognisable positive outcome [of the EPA] is that the region still has access to European markets, adding that Caricom should hold this access in high regard especially in this time when the US dollar is falling" (Mills 2008). Prime Minister Skerrit claims, "Now is the time for us to capitalise on that agreement and get our products and services to the markets in Europe and elsewhere" (Mills 2008). The Prime Minister "expressed satisfaction with the EPA negotiations" saying that "the decision for the EPA is based on what is compatible with the WTO" and that "the shift has allowed Caricom to get in the open market since that is where more people are located" (Mills 2008).

Samuel Berridge (2008) a foreign policy officer at the St. Kitts/Nevis Ministry of Foreign Affairs and International Trade, and one of the CARIFORUM negotiators of the EPA noted that there was, a "sigh of relief when all major issues of the agreement had been agreed to by all parties in the wee hours of the morning."[34] Berridge's observation however raises many questions about the CARIFORUM negotiators who undoubtedly were tired and needed rest. Did the negotiations process tire them out forcing them to sign on to a deal as quickly as possible in Barbados, on December 16, 2007?

---

[34] Berridge, Samuel. 2008. "The Economic Partnership Agreements: Opportunity or Threat," *The Democrat Newspapers*, St. Kitts and Nevis, January.

Berridge (2008) made a number of points about the EPA, the relationship between Europe and the ACP, and the Lomé Conventions. The first is that the "successful conclusion" of the EPA has ushered in a "new dispensation in the political and economic relations between the European Union and the Caribbean." Second, he noted that the EC in the course of its interest has "contributed significantly to regional integration initiatives," since "a single market space would be in the interest of their investors and exporters to the Caribbean." If the EC has a real interest in regional integration because a single market space is better for it to deal with, why did the EC fractured the ACP for EPA negotiation purposes rather than dealing with it as a single market space?

Third, the EPA is merely "an upgrade to the longstanding economic relationship between Europe and its former colonies in Africa, the Caribbean and the Pacific regions" in which in a thirty-year period, the ACP countries "benefited from preferential access to the European market for specific products – sugar, bananas, rice and rum." These products had duty free access to European markets and a guaranteed special price, "usually above the global market value."

Fourth, the Lomé Conventions applied "high tariffs and quotas to non-ACP producing countries" in an arrangement that "discriminated against other producers like Brazil, Australia and Thailand in the case of sugar, and Ecuador, Nicaragua and other banana producers in Latin America," as well as in rice and rum. This is the same position as that of the opponents to the Lomé Conventions, spearheaded by US-led globalization, which forced the EU into speeding up its EPAs with the ACP states.

Fifth, the establishment of the WTO in 1995 characterized the "major turning point in the nature of the trade and economic relations between Europe and the ACP countries." Recognition that "the preferential access granted to the ACP countries" violated "multilateral trade rules" necessitated reform "to comply with the rules of the WTO." Furthermore, not only did the EU-WTO waivers kept "limited preferential trade agreement in place for a period of five years," but the arrangement "came at a very high price as countries negatively affected by the scheme had to be compensated for their restricted access to the EU market."

These views coming from one of the CARIFORUM negotiators of the EPA shows that they embraced the neoliberal criticisms that the Lomé Conventions were discriminatory and therefore harmful to free trade. They bought in to the neoliberal free trade theoretical framework of US-led globalization, and EU bloc imperialism. With such a mind-set there was no way that the CARIFORUM negotiators would have completed a deal other than the one they did. It would seem that the CARIFORUM negotiators were more sympathetic to the interest of the EU than they were to those of the long-term interests of the Caribbean states.

While the CARIFORUM negotiators embraced the position of the critics of the Lomé Conventions, they were well aware of the fact that as Berridge (2008) observed, "preferential trading agreements, where countries are allowed to discriminate against non-members are allowed in the WTO." According to Berridge (2008), "There is an abundance of such agreements; close to 200 have been notified to the WTO. Caricom, Mercosur and NAFTA are examples of such arrangements." Despite this fact, however, according to Berridge (2008) the EPA had to "pass the GATT Article 24 test," meaning, "It must cover 'substantially all trade' between the Members of the preferential trade agreement."

According to Berridge (2008) "Although there is no exact definition as to what constitutes 'substantially all trade,' the practice has been that at least 90 per cent of trade in goods must be liberalized," and in the case of the CARIFORUM states the EPA "liberalizes 92 per cent of the trade over a 25-year period." Based on Berridge's view, the Caribbean is therefore in the forefront in its obedience to WTO regulation liberalizing in excess of 90 percent of its trade in goods.

The level of liberalization schedule (Table 8.2) excludes 13.1 percent of the CARIFORUM imports from the EU, from tariff liberalization, placing them in an "exclusion basket." The "exclusion basket" is the same as a "sensitive list based on their value in generating revenue and the need to promote industrial development. The remaining 86.9 per cent of tariff lines will be liberalized over a twenty five year period, in five year increments" Berridge (2008).

Sixth, there is a number of "opportunities" that the EPA brings to the Caribbean. In the first instance there is "market access opportunities through the removal, or reduction of tariffs and non-tariff barriers" that would allow Caricom and the Dominican Republic producers "to export their goods free of duty to the European Union," selling them "at a more competitive price in the EU market." Also, small producers can consider "Europe as a niche market for their specialty products and build brand recognition and competitiveness beyond the free trade area." St Maarten and St Martin, and Guadeloupe and Martinique,

Table 8.2 Level of Liberalization Schedule in CARIFORUM-EU EPA

	% Imports from EU	% Total Trade
Zero Basket	52.8%	70.0%
Liberalize within 5 yrs	56.0%	72.0%
Liberalize within 10 yrs	61.1%	75.3%
Liberalize within 15 yrs	82.7%	89.3%
Liberalize within 20 yrs	84.6%	90.5%
Liberalize within EPA	86.9%	92.0%

Source: Samuel Berridge, "The Economic Partnership Agreements: Opportunity or Threat," *The Democrat Newspapers*, St. Kitts and Nevis, January 2008.

which are "politically and economically" part of the EU, could serve as "a natural gateway to mainland Europe" due to their closeness to the OECS states. Furthermore, most products from Europe will arrive in the Caribbean free of import duty and so will be generally cheaper, and will increase trade between the EU and the Caribbean.

Also, Berridge (2008) identified "opportunities" in the area of services for Caribbean service providers, whom he argues, "will also have temporary access to the EU market to provide services." Noting that the terms of access for Caribbean service providers, is more favorable than granted to non-members of the EPA, his view is that this offers opportunities to "professionals and service providers as they can now access the European market under easier terms." However, because of reciprocity, "European service providers will have access" to the Caribbean market, which will stimulate competition and serve as a strong incentive for regional service providers to improve their quality. In this connection, therefore, it would be a wise investment for Caribbean service providers "to attain certification from international standards setting bodies and professional associations," in order to make themselves more competitive.

Seventh, there are two major threats posed by the EPA – loss of revenue from import duties, and competition from European firms and service providers. Since the Caricom depends "heavily on import duties as a main source for government revenue," the EPA will have a direct impact on revenue loss due to the "cut in tariff rates in five-year intervals over a twenty-five year period." In order to address the problem of revenue loss, "Strident efforts were made to minimize the negative impacts on the revenue generation by placing the most sensitive items in the exclusion basket and by phasing out the less sensitive items in five year intervals" Berridge (2008).

According to the level of liberalization schedule above (Table 8.2), the CARIFORUM countries have "until 2013 to remove tariffs on 56 per cent of imports from Europe. By 2023, this figure should increase to 82.7 per cent before the ultimate level of 86.1 per cent." The Caribbean countries could use the transitional period for tariff reduction as an opportunity "to find other creative ways to generate government revenue, as well as strengthen" their "capacity to collect outstanding revenues." Berridge's shortsighted view means however that the Caricom states must give up revenue from import duties to the EU, and tax the people more, to fill in the loss-in-revenue gap. Furthermore, lacking any sense of time he believes that 25 years is a long time!

Eight, competition "is a doubled-edged sword" that could spur domestic and regional producers "to improve their products and services," but could enable "European entrants into the market to engage in predatory practices which kill domestic producers and abuse their dominant position in the market" (Berridge 2008). Nonetheless, the chapter on Competition Policy in the EPA, "forces business enterprises to comply with rules of competition and consumer protection." Furthermore, the "OECS Competition Authority and the Caribbean Competition Commission will play an active role in enforcing the rules of competition in the implementation of the CSME and EPA" (Berridge 2008).

The view about the enforcement of competition policy is more easily expressed that achieved, especially in the areas of Internet gambling, agriculture, manufactured goods, geographic indicators (GI), and services. For example, although Antigua won its gambling case against the US at the WTO, it still cannot get the US to comply with the WTO's ruling. Furthermore, the EU, the US and other rich countries like Japan subsidize their agriculture at the same time that they force the developing countries to trade their agricultural products on the free market. The EU and the US promise not to eliminate their agricultural subsidies but merely to cut them. The US announced that it would cap its farm subsidy at $15 billion – roughly a third of the limit now but double current spending, while the EU and Japan protect their "sensitive" farm products – beef, dairy, poultry and rice in the case of Japan – from the impact of tariff cuts.[35]

The West African countries nonetheless have demanded that the US implements deeper cuts in its subsidy payments to its cotton producers. The subsidy has not only depressed world cotton prices, but also damaged West African cotton exports. The US agreed that it would cut its subsidy to cotton deeper than those it pays to wheat and corn, but linked its actions to tariff cuts made by China and other major developing cotton importers. The US argues that a reduction in "those tariffs would open new markets for West African cotton growers as well as its own farmers."[36]

Also, the difficulty for the CARIFORUM states to impose competition policy is evident from the issues in the manufactured goods sectors at the Doha negotiations. The rich countries are forcing the emerging economies such as Brazil and China "to open up their fast-growing markets for more imports of high-value goods such as cars, chemicals or machine tools." The manufacturers in the EU and the US fear that their home countries "will cut their tariffs to very low levels but they will not be able to export to the likes of Brazil or India where new competitors are gathering strength." Furthermore, the US takes the position that there should be "separate agreements where a critical mass of countries would voluntarily agree to cut tariffs in certain industrial sectors sharply, perhaps to zero," but several developing countries oppose that idea.[37]

Geographic indicators (GI), is another source of conflict that would make it very difficult for the CARIFORUM states to enforce competition policy. GI is the means by which the EU and other countries want "to protect the names of some farm products," such as "Parma ham from Italy or basmati rice from India," from being "copied and used by producers not in those same regions." Also, GI seeks to "tighten up existing protection for wine and spirit names." The developing countries in turn "have linked the GI plan to their calls for more disclosure

[35] "FACTBOX-Issues on the table at troubled WTO talks," Forbes.com, July 25, 2008.

[36] "FACTBOX-Issues on the table at troubled WTO talks," Forbes.com, July 25, 2008.

[37] "FACTBOX-Issues on the table at troubled WTO talks," Forbes.com, July 25, 2008.

by pharmaceutical firms." They want these companies to disclose the "origin of products derived from indigenous plants or animals such as drugs based on an Amazon herb or folk wisdom."[38] While, in the area of services, the US, the EU, and other developed countries want to open new markets in developing countries for their banks, telecommunications, express delivery, insurance, distribution and computer-related services companies.

Critique by Prominent Caribbean Academics

The Caribbean region has a rich intellectual history on both the left and right of the ideological spectrum. On the right, Arthur Lewis (1950) challenged the prevailing colonial paradigm that the West Indies was best suited only for agriculture, and he outlined his alternative theory about how the region could become industrialized. Clive Thomas (1974) outlined an alternative theory based on the economics of the transition to socialism. Labor unions in the West Indies for example, the British Guiana Labor Union (BGLU) also ingrained itself in leftist theory in its early beginnings and wanted to establish a socialist state in Guyana. West Indian political parties and politicians and Prime Ministers such as Cheddi Jagan, Michel Manley, and Maurice Bishop among others espoused Marxist/socialist ideologies.

It is therefore surprising that despite such a strong history of defiance and search for independent anti-colonial development alternatives in the Caribbean that the opposition to the EPA is so feeble and basically of a reformist nature. The neoliberal counter-revolution has done an almost perfect job on the Caribbean of expunging independent thought in the region. The combination of structural adjustment, the US invasion of Grenada in 1983, and the collapse of the former Soviet Union in 1989 have wrought the eventual retreat and almost decimation of the Caribbean left. EU bloc imperialism in the region provides a good opportunity nonetheless for the rekindling of whatever leftist sentiments that remain in the Caribbean, in a search for alternatives. The failure of the structural adjustment market liberalization model, and the EU bloc imperialist re-colonization of the

[38] "FACTBOX-Issues on the table at troubled WTO talks," Forbes.com, July 25, 2008.

Caribbean are sufficient to generate a new impetus for alternative development models in the region.

Caribbean intellectuals have actively analyzed the implications of the EPA for the region. The views covered here are those presented by four leading Caribbean scholars and policy makers – Havelock Brewster, Norman Girvan, Vaughn Lewis,[39] and Clive Thomas.[40] Brewster, Girvan and Lewis (2008) produced a memorandum entitled "Renegotiate the EPA" in which they outlined their opposition to the agreement with regard to its process and content, options, and have identified a possible course of reform action for the Caricom.

In the first instance, they pointed out that the EPA is a legally binding treaty of indefinite duration that would be difficult to amend once it takes effect. They noted that the EPA covers subject areas that were previously dealt with by domestic or regional policy, and that there were only a few people in the Caribbean who really knew about or understood the subject area despite the fact that there were so-called stakeholder dialogue and consultations on the EPA.

Second, they identified a list *albeit* not exhaustive of specific issues for concerns with regard the content of the EPA, noting that the development component, "has taken a back seat" to the emphasis on "trade and investment liberalization," although sustainable development is a stated objective of the EPA. They noted that the high unequal level of development between the EU and the CARIFORUM states requires that any reciprocal trade agreement between the two areas involve the adequate transfer of resources from the EU to the CARIFORUM countries "to build up their productive capabilities in infrastructure, human capital, and enterprise plant, equipment, and technology" (Brewster, Girvan and Lewis 2008).

[39] Havelock Brewster, Norman Girvan and Vaughan Lewis, Renegotiate the CARIFORUM EPA, A memorandum submitted to the Reflections Group of the Caricom Council for Trade and Economic Development (COTED) on February 27, 2008. Also, see Norman Girvan, "Implications of the Economic Partnership Agreements," South Bulletin, Issue 8, February 1, 2008; Norman Girvan, Caribbean Integration and Global Europe: Implications of the EPA for the CSME, 18/08/2008, http://normangirvan.info

[40] Clive Y. Thomas, Caricom Perspectives on the CARIFORUM-EC Economic Partnership Agreement, (part of a larger work entitled A First Look at the Political Economy of North-South Partnership Agreements: The CARIFORUM-EC EPA forthcoming), Institute of Development Studies, University of Guyana, Revised Draft, May 2008.

The EPA's failure to guarantee the transfer of such appropriate resources will cause trade liberalization to worsen the inequalities between the EU and the CARIFORUM states since the EU is in a better position to take advantage of the opportunities. The EU has structural and social cohesion funds to facilitate resource transfers among its member states, but "resource transfers are not part of the legally binding obligations of the EPA." Although the European Development Bank (EDB) provides resources to the ACP countries under the ACP-EU Cotonou Agreement, they are "woefully inadequate," amounting "to €165mn under the 10th EDF, which when shared between 15 countries over the five year period, amounts to €2.2mn per country per year" (Brewster, Girvan and Lewis 2008).

Third, they called for a careful evaluation of "the effect or potential effect of tariff elimination on items representing 82.7 percent of imports from the EC." The evaluation must be carried out "with respect to government revenue, income, production and employment; and country by country" to determine the net effects. A net negative effect would contradict "the stated objective of the EPA to reduce poverty," and would necessitate "a longer transition period or compensatory resource transfers" from the EU to the CARIFORUM states to cushion the harmful effects.

Fourth, they noted that although the Caribbean had duty free quota free access to European markets for the majority of its exports since 1975 under the Lomé conventions, "growth of non-traditional exports to EU markets has been insignificant," which confirms the fact that "market access" does not by design translates into "market presence." Indeed, the UN Conference on Trade and Development (UNCTAD) has established as a fact that "the utilization of market access preferences by LDCs has been relatively low."[41]

The major constraints faced by the Caribbean private sector in connection with market access, which the EPA does not address properly, are "restrictive Rules of Origin and onerous Technical Barriers to Trade (TBT), including Sanitary and Phytosanitary Standards (SPS)." The EPA is silent on the specific needs of CARIFORUM firms especially, small and medium size enterprises (SMEs), which require "targeted

[41] UNCTAD, Main Recent Initiatives in favour of Least Developed Countries in the Area of Preferential Market Access: Preliminary Impact Assessment, Geneva, 6–17 October, 2003.

product-specific and firm-specific assistance to raise their supply capabilities and competitiveness to enable them to meet competition from duty-free imports from Europe and to take advantage of new export opportunities" (Brewster, Girvan and Lewis 2008).

Fifth, the concept "development cooperation" regularly stated in the CARIFORUM-EU EPA is not "quantified and time-bound" thus, it leaves "the way open for the EU to decide what to support, when and by how much without any legal recourse available to CARIFORUM countries." For example, the EPA opens up 29 services sectors and 11 professional services in the EU to CARIFORUM service providers. However, there are significant barriers that CARIFORUM service providers must overcome before they can operate in the EU. This has the effect of the EU "giving with one hand and taking with the other." CARIFORUM entertainers that already had access to the EU for performances must now register locally. However, "registration systems are at best embryonic in the region and, when established, will be required to meet EC approval" (Brewster, Girvan and Lewis 2008).

Also, there are no EU commitments "in respect of visa, immigration, work permit and residency regulations relating to service providers," but the CARIFORUM side is very lax on these issues due to tourism. The EPA does not help CARIFORUM peoples to travel to the EU a necessary condition to promote business activities, which is no real "development cooperation" to talk about. Meanwhile, the CARIFORUM has "committed to opening 75% of its service sectors to EU service providers for MDCs and 65% for LDCs in respect of commercial presence," which clears the way for "larger and better-endowed EU firms" to displace and/or acquire domestic firms (Brewster, Girvan and Lewis 2008).

This fosters a need for an understanding of "the strategic implications" for the "vulnerability to foreign decision-making and for the potential development of Caribbean-owned regional firms that are capable of going global." The EPA includes " 'WTO-plus'[42] commitment

[42] "The concept of WTO Plus is not totally new. In the past, it was sometimes called 'Multilateral Plus' or 'GATT (General Agreement on Tariffs and Trade) Plus.' " It usually refers to the idea that "liberalization should go deeper and broader than those of the WTO, while at the same time, complementing WTO… The concept of WTO Plus was first initiated in narrow discussion topics in APEC, but through various advanced liberalization discussions it has gradually become a strongly binding decision-making norm." See Soh Changrok and Jo Chang-Yong, "The Influence of the United States on

in services, intellectual property, competition, public procurement, investment and e-commerce." This is unnecessary however "to secure approval of the EPA under WTO rules, which require only WTO compatibility." The "WTO-plus" commitments "will require CARIFORUM states to adopt legislation, regulations, practices, and policies that will be onerous in terms of money and scare technical manpower." In addition, there is need to quantify "the costs of compliance" that has not yet been done, and there is no rationale for CARIFORUM conformity to these commitments (Brewster, Girvan and Lewis 2008).

Furthermore, "the WTO-plus commitments pre-empt and proscribe CARIFORUM governments' policies in key areas of development policy," as well as "the pending CSME (Caribbean Single Market Economy) regimes in these areas." In this connection, it would have been better and "more desirable to craft CSME regimes that reflect Caricom's own circumstances, priorities and development objectives before making commitments to the EU." Also, there is need for the "National treatment" requirements in the EPA to be carefully inventoried and evaluated. These requirements "forbid governments from discriminating in favor of local and regional firms," but "they may prejudice the ability of governments to foster the development of local and regional firms capable of competing globally" (Brewster, Girvan and Lewis 2008).

The EPA sidelines the CSME but emphasizes "integration with the EU economy (and the Dominican Republic) in goods, services, capital and economic policies." Given the reasons for creating the CSME such as it being a "platform for more efficient production and exporting to the world economy and for pooled bargaining power" the EPA has ruled out CSME as a "path for dealing with globalization" (Brewster, Girvan and Lewis 2008).

Sixth, the implementation of the EPA will place a strain on the scarce resources of the CARIFORUM states. The EU will "hold the upper hand because of the leverage of market access and development 'assistance.'" This is true despite the fact "that CARIFORUM states have veto power over legally binding decisions made by the Joint Committees set up between the EU and the Dominican Republic with powers that "may supersede Caricom's own organs of governance."

'WTO Plus' in the Asia-Pacific Economic Cooperation (APEC)." Available at http://www.koreagsis.ac.kr/research/journal/vol3/3-03-Soh%20Changrok,%20Jo%20Chang-Yong.pdf

The Caricom is not a party to the EPA, which is an agreement between the EU and 15 CARIFORUM states acting collectively. It is not discernable that the Caricom, "under its present governance arrangements, has the legal power to act collectively like the EC does," under the EPA. This could lead ultimately to the "widening of intra-regional inequalities" and "regional disintegration rather than integration" (Brewster, Girvan and Lewis 2008).

The CARIFORUM and Caricom would be better served if they "negotiated an EPA limited to what was necessary for 'WTO compatibility,' with carefully calibrated import liberalization attuned to the development of local production capabilities." There should be "specific commitments for assistance targeted at key infrastructure inputs, firm-level technical support and establishing market presence in EU markets." Instead, the EPA includes "WTO-plus areas in services, competition, public procurement, and investment" that "could be deferred pending WTO agreement in these areas, or at least pending completion of the relevant CSME regimes" (Brewster, Girvan and Lewis 2008).

Assessing the EPA, Thomas (2008)[43] "contrasts key forecasted long-run benefits with front-loaded implementation costs that are already occurring." With respect to the long-term benefits, Thomas (2008) argues that the negotiators of the CARIFORUM-EU EPA did not even had the "limited assurance of supporting long-term quantitative economic and trade assessments, or the customary computable general equilibrium multi-sector multi-country model projections of the likely effects of trade policy changes" but yet they asserted or speculated with confidence that the EPA will bring about substantial benefits to the region. These benefits posited, include significant trade creation, development reform, sustainable regional integration and development, the enhancement of capacity from within the region to eradicate poverty and other social and economic problems, the placing of trade at the service of development, and the region becoming a "net capital importer and recipient of official resource inflows" (Thomas 2008).

---

[43] Clive Y. Thomas, Caricom Perspectives on the CARIFORUM-EC Economic Partnership Agreement, (part of a larger work entitled A First Look at the Political Economy of North-South Partnership Agreements: The CARIFORUM-EC EPA forthcoming), Institute of Development Studies, University of Guyana, Revised Draft, May 2008.

The negotiators give the assurance that the CARIFORUM-EPA contains ample protection from economic disaster due to its provisions on rules-of-origin for CARIFORUM exports, the phase-in periods for CARIFORUM obligations, "safeguard mechanisms, such as the designation of sensitive industries/sectors, and 'zero for zero treatment' of agricultural subsidies," and the delinking of "market access opportunities for the EU to agreements seeking to build institutional capacity of the region in trade-related areas (Singapore issues) for example government procurement" (Thomas 2008). These assurances are given however, although there is an absence of a CARIFORUM Customs Union, substantial liberalization of trade in goods and services,[44] the removal of export and other duties and charges, the existence of trade-related issues in the EPA, and the EU's 'denunciation' of the Sugar Protocol, a substantial foreign exchange earner (Thomas 2008).

The front-loaded costs are those associated with the reduced Sugar Protocol a major source of foreign exchange, employment and rural livelihoods in several Caricom countries. More such costs include the erosion of the Special Preferential Sugar (SPS); the reduction in the political, economic, and geo-strategic weight of the ACP; setbacks for the activities of the Small Island Developing States (SIDS); the sacrificing of multilateralism for expedient bilateralism; the prejudicing of Caricom integration in both trade and development; the undermining of developing countries coalitions at the WTO; and the sacrificing of the search for a Cotonou plus agreement (Thomas 2008).

Thomas (2008) identified eight causalities of, and fourteen unresolved WTO issues in the CARIFORUM-EU EPA (Schedule 8.1). The causalities have three sources – the first being that the theoretical propositions in the EPA are not supported by "empirical evidence." Second, there is the glaring disagreement and a lack of consensus among scholars and analysts over several of the "evaluations, assessments and interpretations" that underlie the EPA. Third, the design and architecture of the EPA, and its negotiating modalities are fundamentally flawed (Thomas 2008).

[44] For trade-in-goods "61 percent of EU imports in 5 years and 83 percent in 15 years," and for trade-in-services "based on W120 list of services immediate sectoral coverage of 50–62 percent and tariff-line coverage of 75 percent for Caricom developed countries and 65 percent for lesser developed countries, with 80 percent for the Dominican Republic" (Thomas 2008).

Schedule 8.1 Causalities of the EPA and Unresolved WTO Issues in EPA

No	*Causalities of the EPA*
1	Africa-Caribbean Pacific (ACP) Group of Countries established 1975
2	The Sugar Protocol established 1975
3	Special Preferential Sugar established 1995/1996
4	Small Islands Developing States
5	Original Cotonou plus Goal
6	Coalition around unresolved WTO issues
7	Multilateralism
8	Caricom as an autonomous development-oriented open integrated process creating the basis for effective integration into the global market
	Unresolved WTO Issues in the WTO
9	Trade in Services (GATS, Article 5)
10	Investment (Trade-related)
11	Intellectual Property Rights
12	E-Commerce
13	Competition Policy
14	Technical Barriers to Trade (TBT)
15	Sanitary and Phytosanitary Measures (SPS)
16	Current and Capital Payment
17	Environment
18	Social Factors (Trade conditionalities, e.g. crime control, financing terrorism, money laundering)
19	Government Procurement
20	Special and Differential Treatment (and Preferences) (mainly SIDS)
21	Safeguard Mechanisms (including sensitive products)
22	Subsidies (Agriculture)

Source: Clive Y. Thomas, Caricom Perspectives on the CARIFORUM-EC Economic Partnership Agreement, (part of a larger work entitled A First Look at the Political Economy of North-South Partnership Agreements: The CARIFORUM-EC EPA forthcoming), Institute of Development Studies, University of Guyana, Revised Draft, May 2008.

Conclusion: Critique of the Critics

The first two groups of critics of the CARIFORUM-EU EPA are basically in the same category as the "opponents" of "free trade" such as Ha-Joon Chang (2007 and 2008) and Erik Reinert (2007), who do not aspire to transform the "free trade" model but merely to reform it, to make it better to deepen capitalist exploitation. Chang (2007 and 2008) and Reinert (2007) both oppose the current approach to globalization calling instead for protectionist measures to develop the manufacturing sector in the poor countries. However, the development of the manufacturing sector through protectionism has nothing to do with finding an alternative to neoliberal "free trade" capitalism. It is merely a tactic in the same "free trade" capitalist development strategy.

Protectionism is used to develop a particular manufacturing industry, which after it becomes well fortified, is removed from behind protective walls at which time it is allowed to engage in "free-trade." This approach could be called "free trade" through protectionism. The problem however is with the notion of "free trade" itself, and not with how it might be achieved. The issue is whether "free trade" is possible, since when the well-fortified industry engages in "free trade," it does so in the self-interest of its owners. In its self-interest it will squeeze-out similar industries that are in a weaker position.

Chang (2007 and 2008) and Reinert (2007) also argue that important as agriculture is, it does not possess the capacity by itself to bring about the development of a country. In their view, manufacturing is the key to economic, social and political development. This is a mistaken view that has taken hold among some policymakers in the Caribbean, who argue that the region should play down its agricultural sector and promote tourism as an alternative avenue to generate economic growth.[45]

The EPA nonetheless does not guarantee the economic diversification of the Caribbean into manufacturing. Indeed, neoliberal globalization because of its emphasis on "free trade" has led to de-industrialization in the poor countries a point well made by Reinert (2007). The closure of the bauxite and aluminium industries in Guyana due to neoliberal policies is evidence of the de-industrialization that

[45] This issue is addressed below in the Chapter 9 on the food crisis where it is argued economic liberalization policies that encouraged ACP countries to play down their agricultural sectors are the main cause of the food crises.

has taken place in the Caribbean. However, the argument by Chang (2007 and 2008) and Reinert (2007) is problematic in that they oppose neoliberal globalization on the grounds that "free trade" leads to de-industrialization in the poor countries. Nonetheless, they argue a case for the protection of the infant industries in these countries, until they are fully developed and are able to cope with competition, before they engage in "free trade." Thus, on the one-hand, they point out the evils of "free trade" but on the other, they are arguing for more "free trade," and not for an alternative economic system.

These critics of the CARIFORUM-EU EPA however are not as forthright as Chang (2007 and 2008) and Reinert (2007) in that they do not advocate protection as a necessary condition to develop the manufacturing sector in the Caribbean. Instead, their opposition to the CARIFORUM-EU EPA has led them to repeat old calls for economic diversification in the Caribbean and to increase the region's competitiveness, which in the current period of neoliberal globalization and EU bloc imperialism, means in essence lowering production costs that translates into unemployment, lower wages and diminished worker benefits. Their critique of the EPA has led them to repeat old demands for support for traditional agriculture such as sugar production in the Caribbean.

CHAPTER NINE

CARIBBEAN EPA NEGOTIATORS IN THE BOSOM OF EU BLOC IMPERIALISM

Introduction

Kwame Nkrumah's theses on neo-colonialism[1] that deconstructed the power relations in the early post-independent former European colonies broke new grounds on the theory of imperialism. In essence the neo-colonials were the domestic political and economic elites who took over the reigns of power in the former colonies as the colonial system collapsed. The neo-colonials collaborated with the European colonial powers to be installed as the new rulers of the politically independent states in Africa and the Caribbean, and then went on to govern in the interest of the former colonial masters. Neo-colonialism represented that new configuration of power relations between the newly independent states and their former colonial masters.

Neo-colonialism is regarded as a situation in which a state is independent in theory but in reality its economic system and political policy is directed from foreign powers. The method of neo-colonialism takes various shapes and forms including military occupation and state control, economic or monetary means, mercantilist trade arrangements, a consortium of financial interests, the breaking-up of large territories into small unviable states that must depend on the former colonial power for defence and internal security, the collaboration of a subservient neo-colonialist government, etc. Power over the neo-colonial state is in the hands of the former colonial masters. That power may be transferred such as in the Caribbean after World War II when the US took over the reigns of control from Britain. Foreign capital is used to exploit rather than to develop the newly independent state, and to widen the gap between the rich and poor countries. Thus, neocolonialism means power without responsibility.

[1] Nkrumah, Kwame. 1965. *Neo-Colonialism: The Last Stage of Imperialism*. New York, International Publishers.

The Caribbean portrays all and many more of these features of neo-colonialism, since the countries became politically independent from the 1950s. Politically, however, Caribbean states have experimented with various forms of nationalism within the neo-colonial system. Also, there were experiments with democratic socialism in Jamaica, a populist band of socialism in Grenada, and the state-capitalist, mortgage-finance "cooperative socialism" in Guyana. The socialist experiments in Jamaica and Grenada were attempts at genuine political and economic change, whereas US capital buttressed "cooperative socialism."

The neo-colonial ruling elites in the Caribbean consolidated their domestic power by political patronage and their use of the state apparatus they controlled to accumulate wealth for themselves. This was done in a failed attempt to break out from neo-colonial strangulation, although they did succeed in securing a reasonable amount of power, domestically, which they wielded within the parameters of neo-colonialism.

Undoubtedly, European bloc imperialism also needs the collaboration of the domestic ruling elites in order to be fully operational and effective in the ACP countries. The concept neo-colonialism however does not aptly capture the phenomenon of cooperation between the domestic elites in the ACP regions with EU bloc imperialism. Neo-colonialism describes a phenomenon that took place with the sham transfer of power from the imperial powers to locals in the newly independent states. The negotiators of the EPA however are involved with EU bloc imperialism in two different but related sets of power relations at the international and domestic levels.

First, internationally, they are participating in the struggle between US-led globalization and EU bloc imperialism for global hegemony, but on the side of the latter. Their role is crucial in helping the EU to compete with the US for markets in the Caribbean, for example, a region that the US regards as being in its "front yard" and off-limits to European powers since the Monroe Doctrine that emphasised separate spheres of influence for Europe and the Americas, non-colonisation, and non-intervention.

Second, by cooperating with EU bloc imperialism the EPA negotiators are playing a major role domestically in the transfer back to Europe, of whatever little power the neo-colonials have mustered and consolidated through nationalistic policies and the use of the state apparatus to accumulate wealth. They are engaged in the dismantling of the neo-colonial power relations in Caribbean society, depleting the independent neo-colonial states of power rather than enhancing their power. The EPA negotiators are worse than the neo-colonials in that by their actions power is being taken out of the hands of the neo-colonial economic and political elites in the ACP regions, and transferred back to the Europe, as a bloc. This phenomenon where local elites are negotiating with Europe to transfer power from the neo-colonials back to Europe is yet to be fully explored and labelled in domestic or international political economy.

The EPA dismantles existing neo-colonial power relations in the Caribbean by establishing regional structures with authority over the Caribbean. Power is being handed back to Europe via the governance structure of the EPA that excludes the traditional neo-colonial elites and regional power structures. The neo-colonial state is under attack by the governance structure of the EPA, since an overarching regional authority, in the control of the EU bloc imperialists, will make decisions for it.

This chapter presents the arguments of the negotiators of the EPA and their allies in support of the EU bloc imperialist CARIFORUM-EU EPA. Its main purpose is to outline the facts in support of the thesis that the CRNM is involved in the transfer of power from the neo-colonials in the Caribbean, back to the Europe as a bloc.

The Caribbean Regional Negotiating Machinery[2]

The restructuring of global capitalism in the 1980s presented the Caribbean with many challenges. The region became involved in a multiplicity of negotiations, but it had a limited amount of human and financial resources to face those challenges. The Caribbean governments responded by creating the CRNM in 1997 in an effort to streamline its negotiating structures. The CRNM was given the responsibility to coordinate the external negotiations of the Caricom. The CRNM's areas of focus are negotiations for the Free Trade Area of the Americas (FTAA); the Economic Partnership Agreement (EPA) with the European Union as part of the Group of African Caribbean and Pacific States (ACP); and the World Trade Organisation (WTO).

The Caricom established a governance structure for the CRNM such that the latter reports to the Caricom Council for Trade and Economic Development (COTED). The COTED provides the CRNM

[2] See CRNM and the Caricom Websites that supplied the information for this section for more on the creation of the CRNM.

with guidance and its negotiation mandate. The Director General of the CRNM is also responsible to the Caribbean Heads of government through the Prime Ministerial Committee on External Negotiations. The CRNM's finance committee is responsible for the financial governance of the CRNM. The finance committee comprises representatives from some member states, a representative of the Caricom Secretariat, and the CRNM Director General and Directors.

The CRNM engages in negotiations on four general levels – the multilateral level that includes negotiations within the World Trade Organization (WTO); the inter-regional level involving the negotiations of the Economic Partnership Agreement (EPA) with the European Union; the hemispheric level involving the negotiations of the Free Trade Area of the Americas (FTAA) that have been dormant since 2003; and the bilateral level involving the negotiating of agreements between Caricom and other countries such as Canada, Costa Rica and the Dominican Republic.

Richard Bernal, the Director General of the CRNM was appointed as the EPA's Principal Negotiator to conduct the negotiations on behalf of CARIFORUM, assisted by the Caricom and OECS secretariats. The Regional Preparatory Task Force (RPTF), which completes the negotiating structure of the CRNM, supposedly establishes the link between trade, aid, and the developmental needs arising from the EPA.[3]

Given such a structure it would seem that there would have been more oversight by the Caricom Secretariat of the activities of the CRNM. The negative responses by Caribbean governments, civil society and the private sector to the EPA point to a rupture in the relationship between the CRNM and the regional public, civil and private bodies. It would seem that the CRNM abrogated to itself the power to negotiate the EPA without properly ensuring that the different regional constituencies understood what it was doing.

The CRNM's Strategy against Its Critics

It would seem that a central part of the CRNM's strategy in carrying out its role in support of EU bloc imperialism at the international and domestic levels, is in private conversations to push its critics in a

[3] South Commission. 2008. EPA Negotiations in the Caribbean Region: Some Issues of Concern. *Analytical Note* SC/AN/TDP/EPA/12, January.

corner as individuals and groups that are out of touch with reality – leftists hankering after Marx, socialism and communism. The characterization of its opponents as socialists or communists is a worn-out tactic of the right. It seems that the CRNM has taken a position quite similar to the forces of imperialism in the Caribbean during the cold war that labelled their opponents as communists in order to win favours from the rich anti-communist, capitalist countries.

The strategy to defend the EPA takes on a particular character such that privately its supporters paint their critics as looking back to Karl Marx, while the EPA proposers looked towards Adam Smith, David Ricardo, Alfred Marshall and other stalwarts of the capitalist theoretical framework. This tactic is an attempt to raise the "communist bogey" regarding certain critics of the EPA. The tactic still has certain effectiveness in the Caribbean because of events in the 1970s namely the US invasion of Granada. That gruesome act effectively intimidated the Caribbean left to the extent that reportedly some scholars burnt their "subversive" books, and converted to Christianity. Kari Levitt (2006) laments the dearth in critical thought in Caribbean scholarship since the 1970s, and made a bold call for the resurgence of such thinking. The Sir Arthur Lewis Institute of Social and Economic Studies (SALISES), at the University of the West Indies, selected for its theme at its ninth annual conference in 2008, "Reinventing the Political Economy Tradition in the Caribbean," in an attempt to counter the neoliberal approach that has taken hold of Caribbean academia.

However, branding the critics of the EPA communist shows that the defenders of the EPA are out of touch with what is really taking place globally. The defeat of Eastern European communism, the rise of the US neoconservatives, and the 911 attacks on the US, shifted the focus of the global hegemon to the "terrorist threat." Nowadays, the US forces countries to implement anti-terrorist measures, "democracy" and "free trade". The US now defines the Caribbean as its "front yard" in its "war on terror," as it speaks of Venezuela its nemesis in the region in terrorist terms, whereas during the cold war anti-communist propaganda it regarded the Caribbean as being in its "backyard."

By accusing its critics of looking back to Marx, the CRNM is not only lumping them with the old communists, but also identifying them as the new anti-establishment forces in the region. The CRNM is fingering its critics to the EU bloc imperialists, as the forces with whom EU bloc imperialism must contend in the struggle for dominance in the Caribbean in the twenty-first century. The CRNM does not even bother to consider the fact that as argued in the previous chapter, its critics are merely reformers, who would like to make the CARIFORUM-EU EPA work better for the Caribbean. Furthermore, the anti-EPA forces in the Caribbean are weak and do not represent a real alternative to EU bloc imperialism. The true opponents to EU bloc imperialism are those forces that reject the EPA model outright and argue instead for alternative trade and development approaches such as the ALBA.

The negotiators of the EPA are educated elites who were products of the neo-colonial system; were never in power in terms of exercising control over the state as elected officials; and were mere employees who were co-opted and given a considerable amount of authority to act on behalf of the state in negotiating the EPA. However, the CRNM negotiators usurped state power in their self-interest and on behalf of those of their supporters in the state bureaucracies. Furthermore, due to their shared ideological position, they have also been drafted in to work in the interest of EU bloc imperialism. The ideological interests of the CRNM's chief negotiator can be gleaned from his academic publications,[4] which fit squarely within the neoliberal theoretical framework. These works are pro-neoliberal globalization calling among other things for the "strategic global repositioning" of the Caribbean or in other words the surrender of the Caribbean to the current form of neoliberal global capitalism.[5]

The CRNM in Denial of EU Pressure and Defends the EPA

Amidst reports that the EU pressured the CARIFORUM into agreeing to the EPA Bernal (2007a) denied in an article he wrote in the

---

[4] Bernal, Richard. 2000. "The Caribbean in the International System: Outlook for the First 20 Years of the 21st Century", in Kenneth Hall and Denis Benn, eds., *Contending with Destiny: The Caribbean in the 21st Century*. Kingston: Ian Randle, pp. 295–325; Bernal, Richard. 1996. Strategic Global Repositioning, and Future Economic Development in Jamaica. *The North-South Agenda* (18). Florida: University of Miami North-South Center; and Bernal, Richard. 2007. The Globalization of the Health-care Industry: Opportunities for the Caribbean. *CEPAL Review* 92: 83–99.

[5] See Canterbury, Dennis. 2005. Globalization, Inequality and Growth in the Caribbean. *Canadian Journal of Development Studies* (26) 4: 847–866 for a critique of Bernal's idea about "strategic global repositioning."

Jamaica Gleaner as a guest writer on October 21, 2007 that there was no such pressure.[6] Bernal (2007a) argued that the EPA was "in the best interest of the region" that "failure is not an option," and that "resolving the outstanding issues in time is not only desirable but attainable." Furthermore, Bernal (2007a) said "the prospect of completing the negotiations is enhanced by the current political will on both sides to achieve an EPA of mutual interest." Why did Bernal saw negotiations beyond the December 31, 2007 deadline set by the EU as a failure that was not an option? Why Bernal defends the EPA as the best deal the Caribbean could enter into at this historical conjuncture?

First, it seems that Bernal personalized the negotiations to the extent that he believed that if the talks failed then he too was a failure. There seems to be a certain kind of desperation in the stance – "failure is not an option." It seems that Bernal placed his personal ambition for success over the economic and political interests of the Caribbean people. To him, it was better to conclude a deal that was bad for the Caribbean than to go down in history as a failure. But, which is worse for Bernal, in terms of his historical legacy, a bad deal that destroys the economy and lives of millions of Caribbean people and benefits him and his EU bloc imperialist allies, or a deal that secures a strong future for Caribbean peoples. Undoubtedly, the real issue was that a failure to conclude the EPA negotiations within the deadline set by the EU would have placed Bernal at odds with EU bloc imperialism.

Second, there is the view that the CARIFORUM was driven by pragmatic reasons, which did "not emanate from pressure from the EU," to arrive at the EU deadline to conclude an EPA (Caribbean Media Corporation 2007).

A third view is that the EPA was not only "a good deal" but the only "sensible deal" for the region.[7] The CRNM's argument is that given the current context, objectives and circumstances the EPA is a good deal. Claiming that "in any negotiations you don't get everything,"

[6] Bernal, Richard. 2007. Finalizing EPA Trade Pact 'Pragmatic' for CARIFORUM. *Jamaica Gleaner*, October 21; *Caribbean Media Corporation*. 2007. Regional Trade Negotiators Dismiss Charges of EU Pressure. *Caribbean Media Corporation*. October 19.

[7] Caribbean Broadcasting Corporation. 2008. CRNM Head Defends EPA. February 15.

(Bernal 2008), the expressed view is that neither the EU nor the Caribbean got everything they wanted from the negotiations. Accordingly, while the region was not able to hold on to its preferential arrangements for sugar and bananas, the CRNM is satisfied that the Caribbean would be getting development assistance, "and more than ample time, in some cases as much as 25 years, to open up markets to competition" (Bernal 2008).

The above view equates the Caribbean with the EU and conveys the impression that the EU and CARIFORUM will be affected in the same way by each side giving-up something. It is obvious from the historical relations between the two regions that they cannot be equated, especially in trade negotiations. The giving-up of preferential arrangement for sugar and bananas is of greater import in the CARIFORUM compared with whatever the EU gave up. Sugar and bananas is the lifeline of several Caribbean states and to give up preferential treatment for those items would be almost like a death sentence to those countries that depend on them for their survival.

The CRNM's neoliberal position is that "permanent one-way preferential trade" is "not possible in today's world" and that "If you can't get your preferred option you have to do the next best thing and that's what we tried to do in the EPA" (Bernal 2008). The conclusion is drawn that "all those people who are talking about preferential trade indefinitely are living in the past, it's a fantasy" (Bernal 2008).

Fourth is the outright rejection of the argument that "no agreement is better than a bad agreement," which is described as an option that is "simply incorrect," and would do "a disservice to the negotiating structure" that had a mandate "to finish the negotiations on the schedule mutually designed and agreed" (Caribbean Broadcasting Corporation 2008). In the CRNM's view "the rationale of these instructions is that the region would be worse off without an EPA in place on January 1st 2008, and that completion at a later date would put the region in a disadvantageous position." There is no evidence however to support these claims made by the CRNM. The CRNM seems to have embraced the view – if you do not sign the EPA then you will suffer or perish in hell – as religious gospel.

Fifth, there is the refutation of the suggestions that the region could have negotiated a better alternative to a full EPA. The CRNM claims that the Caribbean would have been worse off had it opted for any of the two alternatives including an interim "goods only" agreement or for the Generalised System of Preferences (GSP) under which some items would have been subjected to higher duty (Caribbean Broadcasting Corporation 2008). Its position is that the "goods only" option would be difficult given the liberalization of goods and services, and the GSP would make the region worse-off since the GSP "involved some products paying duty and some products paying more duty and tariff than they did before" (Caribbean Broadcasting Corporation 2008).

However, EU member states expressed concerns over the impact of the imposition of GSP duties on non-LDC ACP exporters if, no EPA agreements were concluded by the end of 2007. But, the EC observed "it was no longer possible to conclude complete agreements with the six ACP regions by the end" of that year, and proposed "partial interim agreements covering trade in goods and any other areas where a consensus exists." In spite of all this evidence the CRNM chose to take the position to conclude a comprehensive EPA by December 31, 2007.

Sixth, the CRNM sees the EPA as an opportunity that the CARIFORUM must seized upon. While speaking at the American Chamber of Commerce of Jamaica, the CRNM's Director General called on the CARIFORUM states to "seize the opportunities that are currently available under the" EPA.[8] The Director General claimed that the EU market has 50 million consumers and that the EU is one of the region's main trading partners representing some 15 percent of Caribbean imports, and some of the critical exports from the region such as sugar and bananas. Furthermore, he urged the Caribbean to embrace the benefits, which the global market offers small states, arguing that if the region does not "react positively, proactively and strategically" to the EPA, it will be a loser, "marginalized," and its economic future jeopardized (Jamaica Information Service 2008).

Terms like "losers" "marginalized," etc. are typical jargons in the neoliberal globalization literature. These are the usual threats from the rich countries to the poor in the present period – you must either join in your exploitation from the unfair trade deals with the powerful capitalists states and blocs, or run the risk of marginalization or of becoming losers. No one likes to be a "loser," so countries sign-on to economic neoliberal arrangements that exploit them.

---

[8] Jamaica Information Service. 2008. *E-Newsletter*, Vol. 8, No. 9, February 29, 2008.

Table 9.1 Services contribution as a percentage of GDP and total exports Caricom countries, 2002

Country	Percentage	Services as % of exports	Country	Percentage	Services as % of exports
Antigua	92.9	91.4	Jamaica	71.1	56.6
St. Kitts	87.1	81.9	Trinidad	12.5	67.9
St. Lucia	84.2	68.2	Belize	44.8	62.4
Barbadoa	84.1	n.a	Haiti	37.6	61.8
Grenada	83.9	72.1	Suriname	18.6	61.5
St. Vincent	83.3	66.9	Guyana	21.1	46.5
Dominica	76.4	n.a	Barbados	79.6	
The Bahamas	n.a.	78.6			

Source: IDB (2005) Institute for the Integration of Latin America and the Caribbean, Caricom Report No. 2, Buenos Aires, quoted in South Center, Analytical Note, SC/AN/TDP/EPA/17, April 2008.

Seventh, a central neoliberal idea peddled in the Caribbean, which the CRNM advocates is that the region should promote services as the engine of its economic development (Table 9.1). Noting that in excess of 60 percent of Caribbean GDP comes from mostly tourism, the CRNM urges the region to diversify its service base by exploring "unexploited opportunities like higher education" (Jamaica Information Service 2008).

The services sector however is no basis on which to build sustainable economic development in the Caribbean. Already, the foreign-based TNCs control the Caribbean's tourist industry – hotels, imported foods, water, etc. By switching to services, the region will lose whatever grip it had on its economy and deepens its domination by foreign powers. Also, the jobs created in tourism are low skilled and cannot by themselves, take the region to higher heights. In addition, there are major barriers to entry of a variety of Caribbean services into US, Canadian and European markets that the EPA does not adequately address (Watson 2003).

The CRNM opposes the argument by the leading institutions at the university level in the Caribbean that the region should exclude foreign universities from providing services to the region. The basis for the CRNM's argument is that the Caribbean universities "have a comparative advantage" and should not fear competition.[9] However, the pitfalls in this position are many. First, there are many known problems with the offshore education sector in the Caribbean. Besides problems with curriculum standards, etc., the US has already conducted a military invasion of Grenada under the pretext of rescuing US students there. Second, the comparative advantage idea has major problems and is seriously criticized in many quarters. For example, while British colonialism treated the Caribbean as having a comparative advantage in agriculture in which it should specialize, Sir Arthur Lewis laid the theoretical foundation for the industrialization of the region, which was in opposition to the colonial comparative advantage argument. Also, Chang (2006 and 2008) and Reinert (2007) have excellent critiques of the comparative advantage misnomer, but for the wrong reasons. Their real mission is a gradualist approach to free trade and the deepening of capitalism rather than contributing towards the building of an alternative system.

Eight, the CRNM explained the rationale for the EPA in the following manner. The WTO rulings had struck down the preferential arrangements for sugar and bananas. In the light of this, "We wanted to salvage as much of the preferential arrangement as we could and therefore we wanted to move quickly to replace the existing trade arrangements with a new arrangement which would lock in the remnants of that preferential arrangement."[10]

Ninth, critics of the EPA urged that the CARIFORUM needed to take action in consort with the African countries, but the CRNM countered that the "African countries have a fundamentally different situation" to the Caribbean. In its view the African countries are largely LDCs with duty-free, quota-free access under the Everything But Arms (EBA) initiative. The Caribbean in contrast had "no cushion … other than a replacement trade agreement," which would then deliver similar duty-free, quota-free access for Caribbean exports to the EU, particularly important for the banana, sugar and rice sectors. The CRNM believes that without an EPA the region "would have put at risk the remnants of the preferential arrangements with sugar and bananas"

[9] Jamaica Information Service. 2008. *E-Newsletter*, Vol. 8, No. 9, February 29, 2008.

[10] Jamaica Information Service. 2008. *E-Newsletter*, Vol. 8, No. 9, February 29, 2008.

and would have left itself "open to challenge from other developing countries in the WTO."[11] Despite this the view is that the "CRNM was not pressured to conclude negotiations for an EPA."[12] Furthermore, the CRNM's position is that the negative effects of reciprocity were manageable because 15 percent of imports from the EU are excluded from tariff elimination commitments, 75 percent of which are agricultural goods.

Despite this prognosis on agriculture, however the data showed that since 2000 "the value of Caribbean agricultural exports to the EU has fallen by 18.1 percent" and the value of the region's "total exports to the EU has risen by 19.6 percent." Undoubtedly, "the importance of agricultural exports" has been reduced "from 34.9 percent of total Caribbean exports to the EU in 2000 to 23.9 percent in 2007 having fallen as low as 20.3 percent in 2006."[13]

Tenth, the CRNM says that a comprehensive EPA gives to the region's banana exports the security they need because it "will insulate all aspects of market-access arrangements for Caribbean banana from further challenge in the WTO." It suggested that the conclusion of the EPA "means that the recent ruling by the WTO's dispute settlement panel against preferential EU market access and prices to ACP banana exporters will not apply to Caricom/Dominican Republic producers."[14] This is not the case however, as gleaned from the failed WTO ministerial negotiations in July 2008. The Banana dispute continued at that meeting and the EU without consultations with the Caribbean made an offer to the Latin American banana producers to "make annual cuts to its tariff of 176 Euros ($280) per tonne of bananas to reach 116 Euros by 2015."[15] In return the EU wanted the Latin American banana growers to sign a "peace clause" to drop their lawsuits against the EU. Of course the EU proposal angered the

[11] Myers Jr., John. 2008. Bernal Defends Economic Partnership Agreement. *Jamaica Gleaner*, May 13.

[12] Myers Jr., John. 2008. Bernal Defends Economic Partnership Agreement. *Jamaica Gleaner*, May 13; *Caribbean Media Corporation*. 2007. Regional Trade Negotiators Dismiss Charges of EU Pressure. *Caribbean Media Corporation*. October 19.

[13] Agritrade, http://agritrade.cta.int/en/content/view/full/857

[14] Agritrade, Responses to the Signing of the Comprehensive EPA. http://agritrade.cta.int/en/content/view/full/3704

[15] Reuters. 2008. EU, Latin 'Banana Wars' in Focus at WTO Talks. Reuters, July 16; African Agriculture. 2008. ACP Countries Under Pressure to Reach Banana Deal at WTO Talks. Africa News Network, July 29.

Caribbean banana exporters who saw it as undermining their economic livelihoods.

The CRNM merely repeated a number of the talking points of the EC, in its rebuttal of its critics. However, the decision of the ministerial meeting in Guyana in November 2007 and the CRNM's position highlighted the glaring division between the CRNM and Caribbean governments. According to the ECDPM weekly update on November 22nd, the Caribbean ministers at the ministerial meeting in Guyana on November 15th stated that "neither the signature of a trade in goods agreement with a built-in agenda for other disciplines nor an interim agreement as defined by the EU were tenable options." The ministers declared, "if a complete and satisfactory agreement could not be concluded by the end of 2007 CARIFORUM would continue the negotiations with the aim of concluding early in 2008." Caribbean negotiators reportedly received a new negotiating mandate after the November 15th ministerial meeting in Guyana and the November 17th heads of government meeting in Barbados." The CRNM therefore chose to place itself at odds with the Caribbean states by declaring that the EU December 31 deadline was a must.

The CRNM published a pamphlet in which it outlined what it considers its critics points as fictions as against the facts about the EPA.

The CRNM's 'Facts' versus Its Critics 'Fiction' on the EPA[16]

The CRNM launched its rebuttals against the critics of the ERP in a series entitled "The EPA: Fact vs. Fiction" that appeared in three issues. The CRNM describes the points made by its critics as fictions versus the "facts" it presents as guides to address the misconceptions and clarify facts about the EPA. The first group of what the CRNM identifies as 'fictions' raised by its opponents is, the EPA replaces the Cotonou Agreement, has not honoured the commitment to the principle of asymmetry, and its market liberalisation will be too fast for CARIFORUM and will disrupt production and employment. The 'fictions' identified in the second issue of the series are, since the developing

[16] This section is based on data taken from CRNM publications entitled "The EPA: Fact vs. Fiction" in three issues.

countries rejected the inclusion of the Singapore Issues[17] in the Doha Round of negotiations, these issues should not have been included in the EPA; the Chapter on Government Procurement in the EPA includes provisions on market access; and the EPA negotiation process was undertaken without the benefit of stakeholder consultation and guidance from regional officials.

The third set of 'fictions' according to the CRNM is, the EPA commitment to 'national treatment' requires the CARIFORUM states to remove domestic subsidies; the EPA has usurped the rights of the CARIFORUM states to determine the direction and pace of Caribbean integration; and the EPA creates a supranational governance structure. The final two 'fictions' the CRNM identifies are first, in the negotiations of the EPA that was intended to replace the trade provisions of the Cotonou Agreement, reciprocity was forced upon the Region quite unexpectedly; and second, the EPA makes no distinction between the Caricom MDCs and LDCs. The CRNM made a point-by-point refutation of these so-called 'fictions.' The responses however do not address the fundamental flaws of the EPA outlined by its critics.

According to the CRNM the first fiction is the belief that the EPA replaces the Cotonou agreement. It claims that the fact is that the EPA does not replace the Cotonou agreement, but only the section of it that deals with trade. This is merely a, play on words because the EPA does replace the non-reciprocal trade arrangements in the CPA. That is precisely the idea of neoliberal globalization to replace Lomé and the stopgap CPA with trade arrangements that are reciprocal. The WTO waiver that allowed non-reciprocal relations in the CPA expired in 2007, and that is the reason why the EU felt pressurized to complete the EPA by December 31, 2007. The CRNM mentioned this fact without placing proper emphasis on it, choosing to emphasise instead the 2020 expiration date of the CPA.

The second "fiction" the CRNM chose to explain is the criticism that the EPA has not honoured the commitment to the principle of asymmetry. It claims that the EPA obligations are highly asymmetrical with the EU obligations being more extensive and adjustment periods shorter than those for the Caribbean. It notes that the asymmetry is most evident in the area of market access in goods where the EU is liberalizing all eligible imports from CARIFORUM from 1 January 2008 (apart

[17] The "Singapore issues" refer to investment, competition, transparency in government procurement and trade facilitation.

from rice and sugar after a brief transition), whereas CRIFORUM is liberalizing most of its imports from the EC over a 15-year transition with a number of sensitive imports liberalized over periods up to 25 years (CRNM 2008). Furthermore, the CRNM points out that CARIFORUM does not have to begin to liberalise imports before 1 January 2011 and will permanently exclude some highly sensitive products from liberalisation (CRNM 2008).

In the area of services the CRNM argues that the EU has made liberalisation commitments in 94 percent of the sectors whereas the corresponding figures for the CARIFORUM LDCs and MDCs are 65 percent and 75 percent, respectively. The CARIFORUM countries have thus been able to exclude a larger number of service sectors, including sensitive ones, than the EU (CRNM 2008). Finally, the CRNM argues that the EU has also committed to providing development support to buttress regional integration, facilitate the implementation of EPA commitments, assist adjustment and boost competitiveness and supply capacity in accordance with priorities identified by CARIFORUM, across the broad spectrum of sectors negotiated (CRNM 2008). In CRNM's view this approach is consistent with the differing economic and adjustment capacities of the two partners.

The Caribbean and the EU however, cannot be true equal partners because of the historic unequal economic relations between the two sides. What makes the CRNM thinks that it could negotiate an equal trade agreement with its colonizers, while simultaneously adopting the same positions of the colonizers? In the first instance for there to be a more equal economic relationship between Europe and the Caribbean, the latter's position in the international division of labor must change radically from being a mere supplier of raw materials and agricultural goods to embrace manufacturing as well.

Second, despite its sustainable development objective, the EPA is a trade arrangement, and therefore cannot deliver the goods with respect to the industrialization of the Caribbean. Third, 2011 is just around the corner and 25 years is a might short time in which to sell the Caribbean "forever," since the EPA is legally binding for an indefinite period and it is unclear how the region might get out of it. In addition, by the CRNM's logic the asymmetry will only last for 25 years and thereafter the EU regains the upper hand. Fourth, the promises of development support are not new, they have been on the books for decades but the Caribbean still remains poor.

The fourth "fiction" according to the CRNM is the criticism that EPA market liberalization will be too fast for CARIFORUM and will disrupt production and employment. The CRNM argues that the "EPA reflects the objective of minimizing negative liberalization impacts, which consumed a major share of CARIFORUM's coordination effort. However, since the origins of the idea in the current period of neoliberal globalization about minimizing the negative impact of liberalization on poor and vulnerable countries and communities, inequalities within and between countries increased considerably.

Social inequality in the Caribbean is reflected for example by the percentage of the population that lives in poverty,[18] and the adult literacy. Guyana had the highest incidence of poverty, 43% of the population in 1998, compared with 5%, in The Bahamas, and 8%, in Barbados. Trinidad and Tobago and Jamaica had 21% and 16%, respectively, of their population in poverty in the same year.

Income inequality within the more developed countries (MDCs), least developed countries (LDCs,) and Organization of Eastern Caribbean States (OECS) can be gleaned from Table 9.2 that shows their respective Gini coefficients. Despite their limitations, the available data showed that income inequality was the highest in Trinidad and Tobago. Belize had the highest income inequality for the LDCs, while in the OECS income inequality was highest in St Vincent and the Grenadines. Overall income inequality was the lowest in the British Virgin Islands, and highest in St Vincent and the Grenadines. Comparing the three areas within the Caribbean income inequality is the highest in the OECS.

The CRNM argues that it is a "fiction" that the EPA has usurped the rights of CARIFORUM States to determine the direction and pace of Caribbean Integration. It states that the fact is that regional integration initiatives are understood by CARIFORUM states as important to enabling their effective participation in the global environment (CRNM 2008). It argues that the Preamble of the Treaty of Chaguaramas acknowledges the significance of regional integration in the sustained economic development of Caricom.

It notes that integration is also enshrined in the Fundamental Principles of the CPA, and that the EPA is based on the Fundamental Principles of the CPA. None of these stated facts however discounts the

[18] The poverty statistics were obtained from Caribbean Group for Cooperation in Economic Development. 2000. Caribbean Economic Overview 2000. Report No. 20460-LAC, The World Bank, June.

Table 9.2 Gini Coefficients by Country

Country	Gini Coefficient
More Developed Countries (MDCs)	
Guyana	Not Available
Barbados	0.39 (1997)
Jamaica	0.38 (2001)
Trinidad and Tobago	0.42 (1992)
Least Developed Countries (LDCs)	
Anguilla	0.31 (2002)
Belize	0.51 (1996)
British Virgin Islands	0.23 (2002)
Turks and Caicos Islands	0.37 (1999)
Organization of Eastern Caribbean States (OECS)	
Commonwealth of Dominica	0.35 (2002)
Grenada	0.45 (1999)
St Kitts	0.40 (2000)
Nevis	0.37 (2000)
St Lucia	0.50 (1995)
St Vincent and the Grenadines	0.56 (1995)

Source: Mc Donald Thomas and Eleanor Wint, "Inequality and Poverty in the Eastern Caribbean," Prepared for Eastern Caribbean Central Bank (ECCB) Seventh Annual Development Conference, Basseterre, St Kitts November 21–22, 2002.

criticism of the divisiveness of the EPAs. It is difficult to fathom how integration is going to take place amidst the divisions in the Caribbean caused by the EPA.

Another "fiction" that the CRNM accuses its critics of is that the EPA creates a supranational governance structure. The CRNM argues that the fact is that supra-nationality, understood conceptually as governance structures that transcend established borders or spheres of influence held by nation states, is not established through the EPA (CRNM 2008). According to the CRNM there are certain bodies created through the EPA namely the Joint CARIFORUM-EC Council, the CARIFORUM-EC Trade and Development Committee, the CARIFORUM-EC Parliamentary Committee, and the CARIFORUM-EC Consultative Committee to help the EPA fulfil its development dimension. These institutional structures will supervise "the implementation of the Agreement," facilitate "dialogue and cooperation between the Parties," and enable "the open participation of CARIFORUM and EC stakeholders in the process of implementing the EPA" (CRNM 2008). But, although the CRNM tries to convince the public that the EPA does not create a supranational governance structure in the region, it is a fact the EPA ties in Caribbean states to trade arrangements with Europe, and that the Caribbean states do not have national control over the governance institutions of the EPA.

Singing in the CRNM's Chorus

The CRNM's spokespersons in different parts of the world also made their contributions to the debate on the EPA, strengthening the argument about the CRNM's embrace of EU bloc imperialism. Lodge (2008) identified three notable ways in which the EPA constitutes "new territory," six rationales for the comprehensive CARIFORUM-EU EPA, and thirteen key elements and their treatment within the CARIFORUM-EU EPA.

It is argued that the EPA constitutes "new territory" in three notable respects (Lodge 2008). The first is that it is "a GATT Article XXIV-consistent Free Trade Agreement and thereby represents a radical departure from the Lomé/Cotonou paradigm of non-reciprocal market access" (Lodge 2008). Secondly, "the range of technical disciplines on which commitments are assumed is comprehensive and not confined to tariff liberalization" (Lodge 2008). Finally," the EPA recognizes regional integration as a pro-development tool and therefore applies CARIFORUM-wide commitments (Lodge 2008).

Six rationales were identified for the comprehensive CARIFORUM-EU EPA, which were considered as "the region's motivation for agreeing to this modern trade and development compact" (Lodge 2008). The first is that the CARIFORUM "needed to bind current levels of EU preferences and immunize such preferences from WTO litigation" (Lodge 2008). The idea was that the "spate of challenges to the EU's preferential regimes for sugar and bananas under the Dispute Settlement Understanding strengthened the need to secure the existing EU preferences to ACP countries" (Lodge 2008).

The second motivation, according to Lodge (2008) was that the CARIFORUM states are trade dependent economies and "need to improve their access to the EU market – the world's largest regional bloc and a longstanding trading partner." This is considered important because, with the exception of Guyana and Suriname, the CARIFORUM States "have a service sector that is the most significant contributor to GDP," making preferential access to the EU services market "a prime requirement to drive increased growth of Caribbean economies" (Lodge 2008).

Third, the region was compelled to enter into the EPA because of "the combination of preference erosion and secular decline in agricultural prices" (Lodge 2008). This position is justified on the grounds that the CARIFORUM is characterized by small economies that exhibit high production costs, undiversified export base, constrained production volumes, and high transportation costs – all of which challenges the region to enhance its competitiveness, and to "graduate into branded and high-value products and develop innovation systems as a strategic tool." The Caricom has six major exports to the EU – alumina comprising 15.6 percent of export share; rum, 11.3 percent; petroleum, 11.1 percent; sugar, 9.5 percent and natural gas 4.7 percent, while the Dominican Republic had a similar export pattern to the EU comprising primarily ferro-alloys, bananas and rum (Lodge 2008).

Fourth, the Caribbean entered into the EPA because "implementation of Caribbean regional integration has been sub-optimal." Although the CSME was promulgated since 1989, "a number of regional rules and regulatory framework are yet to emerge," and "the Common External Tariff (CET) remains uncommon in terms of the rates applied by each of the 12 CSME members." Furthermore, the Caricom signed an FTA with the Dominican Republic in 1998, but implementation has been limited to goods, while progress on services, government procurement, intellectual property and trade facilitation awaits the completion of CSME regimes. Nonetheless, the timetable to fully implement the CSME by 2015 was renewed by the Caricom Heads of Government in 2006.

The slowness on the part of the CARIFORUM to integrate will be corrected by the "EPA's thrust on regional integration," which "should engender the injection of greater dynamism into the CARIFORUM-designed" integration effort. Furthermore, the EPA will stimulate Caribbean integration because "the EPA includes CARIFORUM development priorities," which would "facilitate the delivery of European Commission development assistance to support CARIFORUM regional integration."

The first problem with the line of reasoning that blames the Caricom and the lack of Caribbean integration for the CRNM's decision to complete a comprehensive EPA with the EU is that the CRNM is an organ of the Caricom usurped by private individuals. If the Caricom states take their time to evolve regional rules and regulations concerning Caribbean integration, it shows that states do not rush these matters, as the CRNM did with the EPA. These relationships must evolve and not be forced down the throats of the weak by the powerful. The second problem with that argument is that is implies that the Caribbean needs EU bloc imperialism to stimulate its integration process. Since the Caribbean states are moving too slowly on the matter of regional integration they need outside forces to intervene to help to bring the region together.

EU bloc imperialism nonetheless will only foster regional integration in the Caribbean in a manner that benefits the EU. This would not be the first time that Europe recognizes the need for regional integration in the Caribbean as a strategy of economic and political control to facilitate wealth extraction from the region. Historically, different European imperial powers attempted to promote regional integration in their colonies that now comprise the ACP states. The difference today is that the Europe as a bloc, and not individual European states, as in the past, is seeking to forge regional integration in the ACP regions in its self-interest.

For example, the European powers divided-up Africa amongst them and then almost immediately sought to integrate their respective colonies. The French were the first to seek to integrate their colonies in Africa to further French colonial interests on the continent. The British did the same thing with the formation of the Organization of African Unity (OAU), in the 1960s when British colonialism was about to make its final exit from the continent. In the Caribbean, the British also proposed to integrate its colonies as a cost saving device in the 1800s. In every case, regional integration promoted by the colonial powers in the colonies has failed to bring about real development in the ACP countries.

Fifth, the CARIFORUM was motivated to sign the EPA because although the Caribbean firms had preferential market access in the EU through the Lomé Conventions and the Cotonou Agreement, their ability to contest in those markets "required the assessment of regulatory issues and productive capacity" (Lodge 2008). This requires the mastery of the rules of the "modern and competitive trading environment" concerning Technical Barriers to Trade, Sanitary and Phytosanitary Measures, Services, Investment, Government Procurement, Competition Policy, Trade Facilitation, Trade Defense

Measures and Intellectual Property Rights. The EPA will support the promotion of a regional policy framework concerning these rules.

Sixth, the EPA is a "forceful signal to both investors and development partners of the earnestness of a Caribbean's program of economic reform" (Lodge 2008). The CARIFORUM states are net capital importing countries that "can use an EPA to lever increased investment and heighten the region's appeal as a premier investment destination." The EPA does not only present "CARIFORUM development partners" with "an advanced trade and development framework that requires long-term funding," it is also "a vehicle aimed at reversing the declining share of development assistance extended to the Caribbean" (Lodge 2008).

This argument is untenable in the light of the global financial and economic crises, a product of the so-called economic reform to liberalize factor, goods and services including the financial markets. Rather than seeing its declining share of development assistance reversed, the Caribbean is bracing itself for even further declines in direct foreign investments, remittances, economic growth, etc., due to the current global financial and economic crises.

The thirteen key elements and their treatment within the CARIFORUM-EU EPA are as follows. The first key element is liberalization. CARIFORUM will liberalize 86.9% of the value of its imports with 82.7% within the first 15 years. The Agreement will result in the liberalization of 92% of bilateral CARIFORUM-EU trade. The second is a moratorium on tariff liberalization. CARIFORUM will apply a general moratorium on its tariff liberalization commitments on all products for the first three years of the Agreement. For revenue sensitive items such as gasoline, motor vehicles and parts, the moratorium is extended to 10 years. The third is other duty charges (ODS). These are to be maintained during the first seven years and then phased out during the subsequent three years.

The fourth is the Sugar Protocol (SP). The SP quotas will remain on a transitional basis until September 2009 when Duty-Free Quota-Free will be introduced. During the transitional period, a Tariff Rate Quota of 60,000 tones split evenly between CARIFORUM SP members and the Dominican Republic will complement the SP quotas. In addition, a joint declaration commits both Parties to ensure, within the structures of the SP rules that shortfalls of any CARIFORUM SP member will be reallocated to another CARIFORUM SP member.

The fifth is the treatment of agriculture. There is a chapter in the EPA on agricultural, which establishes rules consistent with the objectives of pursuing sustainable development, poverty eradication, enhanced competitiveness, and food security. Most notable in the provisions on agriculture is the zero for zero treatment of EU export subsidies. That is, the EU eliminates export subsidies on all agricultural products that CARIFORUM liberalizes.

Sixth is multilateral safeguard measure in which the EU shall exclude the CARIFORUM exports from any contemplated use of a multilateral safeguard measure and consider the use of constructive remedies before imposing anti-dumping or countervailing duties in respect of products imported from the CARIFORUM States. Seventh, is the Most Favored Nation (MFN) provision through, which both the CARIFORUM and the EU automatically confer on each other any better treatment, granted by one Party, to a major trading partner. Such entities are defined as countries or regional blocs garnering 1%, or 1.5% and above, of world merchandise exports. This MFN provision covers both goods and services.

Eight is the area of services in which, the EU liberalizes 94 percent of W120 list[19] of sectors while the respective figures for CARIFORUM LDCs and MDCs are 65 percent and 75 percent, respectively. The Bahamas and Haiti have six months within which to submit their respective liberalization schedules. The commitments also include a standstill clause and provisions for future liberalization.

Ninth is the temporary movement of natural persons. In the case of the temporary movement of natural persons (Mode 4) the EC has granted market access for Caribbean professionals in 29 sectors for Caribbean Contractual Service Suppliers (CSS) to enter the EU to supply services once a contract has been secured. This includes entertainment services for all EU Member States – except Belgium and Italy. The EU has liberalized 11 sectors for temporary entry by the CARIFORUM Independent Professionals (IPs) or self-employed persons.

Tenth is access to the EU entertainment market. The CARIFORUM access to the EU entertainment market is complemented by a Protocol on Cultural Cooperation that provides for greater collaboration on all cultural fronts and with special provisions on audiovisual activities. In particular, co-produced audiovisual products involving European and Caribbean creative teams will qualify as European works and thereby satisfy cultural content rules in all EU member states.

[19] The name of the official WTO document, which provides a list of all sectors for possible negotiations under the GATS.

Eleventh is Rules on investment. The rules on investment confer predictability and transparency on market access in agriculture and forestry, manufacturing, mining and service sectors in both EU and CARIFORUM. Both regions have liberalized most areas of manufacturing except for some sensitive areas in CARIFORUM and the EU. However, public services and utilities and other sensitive sectors have not been liberalized to EU investors. CARIFORUM has also maintained special reservations for small and medium enterprises in some sectors.

Twelfth is investors safeguard obligations. The EPA also contains obligations that will ensure that investors safeguard the environment and maintain high labor, occupational health and safety standards. Furthermore, the Agreement proscribes the Parties from lowering environmental and social standards in order to attract investment, and forbids investors from engaging in corruption to secure special concessions from public officials. Finally, regional preference (whatever concession is granted by one CARIFORUM state to the EU should automatically be conferred on all other CARIFORUM states) will be implemented in one, two and five years respectively in CARIFORUM MDCs, LDCs and Haiti.[20]

In Further Defence of the EPA

The CRNM is not defending the EPA all by itself there are other voices in the region that support the EPA. In some cases, the defenders of the EPA enter into a blame game accusing the Caribbean governments and not the CRNM for the failures of the EPA. Elaine Campbell, a legal researcher in The Netherlands, argues that the EPA is not called Economic Partnership Agreement for nothing pointing out that "it is not a Development Aid package but rather a trade agreement, one of many, such as its predecessor the Cotonou Agreement."[21] She noted that EPA merely seeks to realign the preferential business/trade relationships between Europe and the ACP countries. Campbell (2008) argues that

[20] The source for each of these thirteen key elements and their treatment in the EPA is Lodge, Junior. 2008. CARIFORUM-EPA Negotiations: An Initial Reflection. *Trade Negotiations Insights* 7:1.

[21] Campbell, Elaine. 2008. Renegotiate the EPA: A Very Optimistic Approach. *Jamaica Observer*. March 15.

> The concerns voiced by the academics are typical of a "reactive approach" taken by peoples of our region. The academics claimed that representatives have made the deal of EPA with their eyes wide shut. The truth is it is not for the representatives to make deals. They are channels of information. It is for the elected Caribbean leaders to make sensible decisions on our behalf. At this point, leaders are aware, or at least should have been aware, of the consequences of the UK's membership of the EU. There was time enough, more than 30 years, in which our leaders should have created a strategic plan in which Jamaica, after almost 46 years of independence, would have been able to step up to the challenges of playing ball on an unlevelled international field.[22]

While not calling the demand to renegotiate the EPA "useless" Campbell (2008) stated "I do think that this would cause our representatives in Brussels to become beggars without a cause," since "Our region has no cohesive plan of getting us out of a peripheral position of merely surviving as 'Third World countries.'" The view is that the efforts by the CRNM negotiators are "ineffective at changing the underlying economical intensions of the EU."

Campbell (2008) noted that the EPA would make it easier for professionals from the Caribbean to enter the EU, so governments in the region "ought to be aware of the next great brain drain from the region." Campbell (2008) observed, "Most of our teachers, doctors, and much-needed personnel have already migrated to the UK, US and Canada. The EU needs workers and is seeking a way of finding people to shore up its economy so as to keep its stronghold on the international stage." Campbell (2008) called on the Caribbean people to "wake up from their colonial slumber and take a 'proactive approach' in building" the Caribbean. A concrete way to do this she believes is to provide more adequate staff to the CRNM. She claims that it is "highly unprofessional to see the few good civil servants being ostracised when they do what they can when attending meetings on our behalf." She thinks it is optimistic to think that the Caribbean can renegotiate the EPA, "We are simply not prepared."

The CRNM's Approach to the EPA Negotiations

It is a well-established fact that the EU member-states are involved in training the negotiators from the ACP countries for the EPA

[22] Campbell, Elaine. 2008. Renegotiate the EPA: A Very Optimistic Approach. *Jamaica Observer*. March 15.

negotiations.[23] It is no accident therefore that the ACP negotiators are so verse in the neoliberal positions for which they strongly argue.

It is pointed out that the EPA negotiators "carefully calibrated" their provisions to comply with four approaches. The first approach is with regards to "special and differential treatment,' particularly asymmetry. The second had to do with consideration for "CARIFORUM regional integration." The third involved the development of "a modulated tariff liberalization schedule" in order to "facilitate the reform of national tax regimes while safeguarding trade-generated fiscal revenue and domestic production." Finally, the negotiators had to develop "a holistic approach that combined the articulation of rules with the definition of CARIFORUM priorities to benefit from EU development assistance" (Lodge 2008).

The view with respect to "development cooperation" was resoluteness by the Caribbean governments about the infusion of this subject in all provisions of the EPA. The CRNM adopted the approach that the region's "development ambitions should not be conflated with development cooperation" (Lodge 2008). The two generic approaches on development cooperation agreed to by the principal negotiators were first "there would be a prominently placed "Development Chapter" that would reflect the pro-development logic of an EPA" (Lodge 2008). The "Development Chapter" monitors the EPA "to ensure its continued relevance and ability to meet stated objectives," and focuses on "cooperation in international forums (most notably in the WTO)," the "promotion of CARIFORUM regional integration," the "pursuit of the principle of sustainable development," and on "development cooperation instruments" (Lodge 2008).

Second, the principal negotiators agreed that "CARIFORUM development priorities" should be articulated in "subject-specific chapters" to "complement the specific rules" (Lodge 2008). Thus, the section on agriculture, for example charts a number of "cooperation priorities to be supported by EU development assistance," such as the enhancement of "the competitiveness of potentially viable production," the development of "export marketing capabilities," and the "CARIFORUM capacity to comply with and adopt quality standards relating to food production and marketing – including standards relating to

[23] South Africa Development Community. 2005. Training On Trade Negotiation Skills, Trade Data & Policy Analysis For Negotiators From SADC Member States In Preparations For EPA Negotiations. http://www.sadc.int/archives/read/news/386

environmentally and socially sound agricultural practices and organic and non-genetically modified foods" (Lodge 2008).

Message of Appreciation from the CRNM Principal Negotiator

In a New Year message of appreciation to the CARIFORUM stakeholders on the completion of the EPA, the CRNM Principal Negotiator stated:

> The conclusion of the CARIFORUM – EU EPA negotiations is poignant moment of distinction in the history of this Region. Through this achievement, we have, once again, collectively attested our maturation as a people and our capacity to command our course of development for the benefit of our generation and for generations to come.[24]

The CRNM Principal Negotiator was satisfied with what he had done on behalf of the Caribbean clique and the EU bloc imperialist he represented. Further, he declared:

> The Caribbean Group of countries is the first to engage and complete an EPA with Europe. As such, we are pioneers in redefining our relationships with an important historical trading partner. We have through this agreement shifted the alignment of our economic history with Europe and have mapped a new course towards prosperity and the development of the Caribbean people.

The CRNM Principal Negotiator did not want to be second or third, he wanted to have the distinction of being the first to fashion a new albeit colonial agreement with the emerging EU bloc imperialism. The CRNM Principal Negotiator wanted to make history, regardless of whether he emerges as a notorious or glorious negotiator. Indeed, he has made history, but for the wrong reasons – the first to negotiate a colonial agreement with the EU bloc imperialism, and moreover behind the backs of the Caribbean people despite the inadequate consultations undertaken by the CRNM. The public outcry against the CARIFORUM-EU EPA would not have been that great if the Caribbean "stakeholders" had appropriate knowledge of its contents, and had been a part of its negotiation. The CRNM failed to communicate effectively with the Caribbean people on a colonial deal the EU bloc imperialism forced it to sign.

---

[24] Caribbean Regional Negotiating Machinery. 2008. Message of Appreciation from the CARIFORUM Principal Negotiator to CARIFORUM Stakeholders, Message_of _Appreciation_EPA_Conclusion.pdf, crnmadmin, 09/01/2008

But, the CRNM Principal Negotiator Bernal was not finished there was more that he had to say as he gloated in his New Year message:

> The task has not been simple. Indeed, few meaningful endeavors are easy to dispatch. I therefore wish to commend the herculean efforts of all regional stakeholders across all spheres of government and civil society who participated in this process since its advent. Special accolades must be afforded to the technical experts, academics, professionals, the members of the private sector, and the leadership of the NGO community. In particular, your participation in the technical and public discourse, and extensive, erudite contributions during the Meetings of the Technical Working Group have sealed a civil ownership of this negotiation process, which is unparalleled in many other corners of the world. As we, not immodestly, celebrate our achievement, I wish, at this time, to also extend warmest Season's Greetings to all. May the confidence we feel collectively serve us well in the New Year.

This gloating by the CRNM's Principal Negotiator also appeared in the text of its Update 0716 on December 17, 2007, after the completion of the EPA negotiation.[25]

---

[25] The CARIFORUM EPA Negotiations have been completed. The text was initialled in the wee morning hours on December 16, 2007. While the culmination of this negotiation process has come later than previously scheduled, CARIFORUM countries, by completing the EPA before the end of the year, have ensured that their product exports to the EU will not have to face GSP treatment or face MFN duties in 2008. Effective January 1, 2008, with a temporary exception for rice and sugar, all CARIFORUM goods will be entitled to duty-free and quota-free access to the European Union. Importantly, CARIFORUM is the first group within the ACP to secure a comprehensive agreement that covers not just goods but services, investment, and trade related issues such as innovation and intellectual property.

Principal Negotiator, CRNM's Director General Ambassador Dr. Richard Bernal, after completing the negotiations said,

> This is a momentous and proud achievement for the Region. Our success in completing this agreement, though hard won, has secured opportunity for trade expansion, economic development and the improvement of the welfare of the CARIFORUM people. What we have attained within this agreement is unprecedented within the Region. Certainly, the CARIFORUM region is the only of the six negotiating ACP groups to successfully complete a comprehensive EPA with Europe. The stewardship of the Heads and the active, robust participation of our Region's stakeholders, including the technicians, the private sector, the officials and civil society have made this possible.

In the recent past, it was uncertain whether CARIFORUM–EU negotiations would have resulted in the requisite compromise to seal an Agreement in time. The priority of CARIFORUM countries has always been to ensure that the details of the Agreement met core standards to make it 'a good deal.' As the Principal Negotiator continued to explain "This is a sound agreement and strong on the key areas necessary to cultivate development within the Region."

Conclusion: Requiem for the CRNM[26] *or Reigning in the Putsch*

In the end, the neo-colonial ruling elites reigned-in the CRNM, which had seized the decision-making power of the state in the EPA negotiating

---

He highlighted, with respect to market access in goods, that

> It is a commonly accepted interpretation of international rules that in Regional Free Trade Agreements like the EPAs, the requirement to liberalize 'substantially all trade' suggests liberalization at a level of 90% within 10 years. The CARIFORUM EU EPA has transcended that understanding. Instead, given our development peculiarities, we have reached an agreement, which has reduced the burden of liberalization for CARIFORUM but in a manner that would still allow us to meet WTO requirements. Furthermore, we have secured flexibilities that in some cases provide an unprecedented grace period of 25 years before liberalization may be fully implemented, which will give CARIFORUM countries the time to adjust to the brunt of liberalization.
>
> In services we placed emphasis on the inclusion of market access, and financial as well as non-financial development assistance for the subsectors of tourism and entertainment in particular. This we insisted was important to bring almost immediate dividends to a number of CARIFORUM people. In this regard, CARIFORUM was triumphant in securing the commitment of the European Commission. The EC should also find satisfaction in this triumph as Europe, despite its own domestic reservations and sensitivities was able to give meaningful concessions in such areas so critical and vital to our Region's development.
>
> We were also able to protect the interests of our vulnerable small and medium enterprises in a manner that is consistent with their development needs. This was evident for example in our negotiations in transparency in government procurement. By not negotiating market access commitments, small and medium enterprises will not be in danger of being pushed out of the market for government contracts by European firms. Member States determined that this was not to our detriment but on the contrary, was very much to our benefit. Securing transparency for government contracts helps reduce the likelihood of corruption. Additionally, it signals to investors and the rest of the business world that this Region is open to business and follows international best practice. Furthermore, transparency in the process of government procurement provides opportunities for regional firms to aspire to the standards necessary to attain large government contracts. These examples are but a few. This agreement has been well crafted and I am confident that it is indicative of the best possible deal.

The DG was also clear to conclude that notwithstanding the strength of the Agreement it was necessary that the EPA be used appropriately as a tool for development. He said,

> While the Region's stakeholders have worked earnestly to complete this Agreement appropriately, the Region has only just begun to embark on the task at hand. The focus in the New Year for all stakeholders must shift to the implementation of the Agreement to help chart the repositioning of our Region's economies. Caribbean Regional Negotiating Machinery. 2007. The EPA Negotiations Completed. RNM Update 0716, December 19.

[26] Requiem for the CRNM. 2009. Jamaica Observer Editorial, July 15.

process. The Principal Negotiator of the CRNM resigned under pressure, and his deputy took over the reigns. The Caricom Heads of Government then disbanded the CRNM converting it into the Office of Trade Negotiators a department of the Caricom Secretariat. But, the damage had already been done the CRNM had by then handed back power to the EU bloc imperialist through the elaborate institutional structure of governance[27] agreed to in the EPA.

The Caribbean governments allowed the CRNM to rest power from their hands in a classic case of intra-elite class struggle. The CRNM utilised its power in the interest of the EU bloc imperialism, or put the other way the EU used the CRNM as its "fifth column" in the struggle to re-colonize the Caribbean. The European Centre for Development Policy Management (ECDPM) reported on the division between the CRNM and some Caribbean governments over the scope of the EPA.[28] The levels of trade liberalization that the EPA places on the table were not agreed to by the Caribbean states.

The Joint CARIFORUM-EC Council, at the top of the EPA governance structure, is a ministerial body with the power to "take decisions on all matters related to the agreement." Its decisions are "binding on the parties," with "automatic legal force over member states, buttressed by an enforcement machinery that provides for the resort to trade sanctions in certain instances."[29] Although on paper the Caribbean will have veto power, the EU will have the upper hand in the power relationship due to its leverage over market access and development assistance. The EU has already used that leverage in its negotiations of the EPA.

The CRNM Principal Negotiator resigned as Director-General of CRNM with effect from June 30, 2008 to assume the post of Alternate Executive Director for the Caribbean at the Inter-American Development Bank (IDB) in Washington. The Principal Negotiator was not

---

[27] Girvan, Norman. 2008. Implications of the EPA: Supra-national - CARIFORUM-EC Joint Council consensus decisions supreme. *Jamaica Gleaner*, February 15.

[28] European Centre for Development Policy Management (ECDPM). 2007. EPA Negotiations: Where Do We Stand. Weekly Updates. November 15. http://www.acp-eu-trade.org/library/files/ECDPM_15-11-07_EPA%20Negotiations%20-%20Where%20do%20we%20stand.pdf; European Centre for Development Policy Management (ECDPM). 2007. EPA Negotiations: Where Do We Stand. Weekly Updates. November 22. http://www.acp-eu-trade.org/library/files/ECDPM_22-11-07_EPA%20Negotiations%20-%20Where%20do%20we%20stand_final.pdf

[29] Girvan, Norman. 2008. Implications of the EPA: Supra-national - CARIFORUM-EC Joint Council consensus decisions supreme. *Jamaica Gleaner*, February 15.

gloating as he went out the door, as he did in his message of appreciation to stakeholders. The Principal Negotiator merely said: "It has been my honor and privilege to serve this region and I remain committed to continuing to do so in my future endeavors."[30]

The Deputy Director-General of the CRNM became the new Principal Negotiator and DG of the CRNM. However, at the Twentieth Inter-sessional Meeting in Belize City, Belize, in March 2009, the Caricom Heads of Government decided that the CRNM would report to the Caricom Secretariat and through the Secretariat to the Councils of the Community. The new Principal Negotiator of the CRNM tendered his resignation with effect from June 30, 2009, following the decisions taken by the Conference of the Heads of Government of the Caricom to incorporate the CRNM into the Caricom Secretariat as a Specialized Department. The Principal Director said: "I believe that the new dispensation for the functioning of the CRNM that the Conference mandated at its Twentieth Inter-Sessional Meeting could best be given effect under new leadership."[31]

The 30th Meeting of the Conference of Heads of Government of the Caricom on July 4, 2009, took the decision to rename the CRNM the Office of Trade Negotiations (OTN) recognizing and providing for the special nature of its role and functions, in an attempt to reform the governance of the CRNM. The OTN will report only to the Caricom Council for Trade and Economic Development (COTED) and, by extension, to the Heads of Government through the Secretary General of the Caricom Secretariat. Until now, the CRNM reported directly to the Prime Ministerial Sub-Committee (PMSC) on External Negotiations, which was chaired by the Prime Minister of Jamaica.[32] The Caricom Heads of Government extended the mandate of the OTN to include all external trade negotiations on behalf of the Community, and to place priority on negotiations with Canada, to be followed by a focus the Southern Common Market (MERCOSUR) comprising Argentina, Brazil, Paraguay and Uruguay.[33]

---

[30] Caribbean Regional Negotiating Machinery. 2008. Bernal Resigns as Director General of the CRNM. CRNM Press/News Release, April 29.

[31] Caribbean Regional Negotiating Machinery. 2008. CRNM DG Resigns. CRNM Press/News Release, May 11.

[32] Caribbean Regional Negotiating Machinery. 2008. From CRNM to OTN. CRNM Press/News Release, July 8.

[33] Caribbean Regional Negotiating Machinery. 2008. From CRNM to OTN. CRNM Press/News Release, July 8.

The friends of the CRNM celebrated a requiem for its demise. The view was expressed that the "rebranding" of the CRNM "is a triumph of form over performance."[34] The achievements of the CRNM were stated as its completion of the Cuba-Caricom trade agreement, the Caricom-Dominican Republic trade agreement and the CARIFORUM-EU Economic Partnership Agreement. It was stated that among other achievements the CRNM "provided the technical work to inform the negotiating positions of the region and led the negotiations at the technical level, earning international encomiums from the World Trade Organization, the World Bank and bilateral development organizations. It thus became a model for developing country co-operation."[35]

Five reasons were advanced for the Caricom governments' decision to transfer the functions of the CRNM to a specialized department of the Caricom Secretariat. First, the governments "allowed themselves to be bullied by a fit of peak of one of their colleagues who retroactively repudiated mandates based on consensus in which he was in full and formal agreement." Second, "rampant institutional rivalry and professional jealousy by institutions that felt the CRNM was executing a function which had and should belong to them." Third, "the accusation that the CRNM was not properly supervised and hence the abolition of the Prime Ministerial Sub-committee on External Negotiations - ironically headed by recent Caricom honoree, Mr. P J Patterson. Since he was honored for his role in external negotiations his conduct is not being questioned. The new arrangements, however, represent less political supervision." Fourth, "we understand that there was a problem of "personalities" and insufficient deference." Fifth, "the CRNM was accused of not reporting as fully as desired, although no instances of failing to report have been documented. The real problem was that it had different perspectives on issues, which in our book, is not necessarily a bad thing."[36]

---

[34] Requiem for the CRNM. 2009. Jamaica Observer Editorial, July 15.

[35] Requiem for the CRNM. 2009. Jamaica Observer Editorial, July 15.

[36] Requiem for the CRNM. 2009. Jamaica Observer Editorial, July 15.

CHAPTER TEN

THE EPA AND THE FOOD AND FUEL CRISES

Introduction

The US badgered the EU to liberalize its trade relations with the former European colonies that now comprise the ACP Group of countries. The EU and the ACP countries resisted US pressure until they EU finally caved-in and sacrificed the ACP countries at the altar of US-led market liberalization. The liberalization of the EU trade relations with the ACP countries takes the form of EU-inspired economic partnership agreements (EPAs). The EPAs tie the ACP countries to indefinite mercantilist trade arrangements with the EU giving rise to the phenomenon identified as EU bloc imperialism.

The EPA will continue to operate on neoliberal policy measures that have stimulated the fuel and food crises, and therefore it only harbors more of those kinds of problems for the ACP countries in the future. The food crisis resulted from rising prices for food due to neoliberal policies that led to the folding of agriculture in the developing countries and increasing their dependence on agricultural imports supplied by the European and US agricultural transnationals. Also, fuel price increases resulted from neoliberal policies – marketization and democratization – that led to the invasion of Afghanistan and Iraq, and the expansion in demand for fuel due to neoliberal globalization. The food and fuel crises are connected because the increase in fuel prices bring about a rise in the price for food creating a food crisis, which in turn reduces food security or increases food insecurity that negatively reverberates throughout the economy.

As the ACP countries liberalize their economies due to pressure from US-led globalization in the form of structural adjustment, and EU bloc imperialism through the EPAs, the US is at the tail end of its globalization experiment. It has made a turn to open state-interventionist and protectionist policies that it forced the EU to dismantle in its trade relations with the ACP countries. The US is currently promoting a "buy America" and not a market liberalization strategy to dig itself out of its current recession. The ACP countries are in a state of confusion as they liberalize their economies at the dictates of the

US-led globalization and EU-led EPAs, while the US and EU engages in state-interventionist and protectionist measures, nationalizing banks and other companies in the major industries.

The purpose of this chapter is to explore the link between the EPA and the food, and fuel crises now impacting the ACP countries. It takes the position that neoliberal policy prescriptions are the main link between them. Neoliberal policies, the very measures that are the foundation for the EPA, are the main causes of the food and fuel crises. It explores this issue in the light of the CARIFORUM-EU EPA, focusing first on the problems in the Caribbean's agricultural sector that bolster the food crisis and food insecurity in the region. It analyzes neoliberal views to downplay Caribbean agriculture, the food crisis, food security, and policies to combat these issues in the region. The second part focuses on the fuel crisis in the Caribbean region and the possible role of Petrocaribe as a solution to the problem.

The food and fuel crises are a result of neoliberal market liberalization policies to deregulate the agricultural, energy and financial sectors. The solution to these problems would require the ACP states to step back from those policies and to re-evaluate the role of the developmental state in the process of economic development. This needs to be the case especially because the developed countries have never really fully embraced market liberalization in agriculture and currently are stepping back from market liberalization in the financial sector and in some manufacturing industries.

Food price increases have resulted in millions of additional malnourished people worldwide, but there are inadequate policies to address the problem. In general, governments have adopted fiscal, policies, monetary and exchange rate policies, and trade and other policies to deal with the food crisis. Fiscal measures include "reductions in fuel and food taxes and tariffs, increases in universal subsidies, expansions in transfer programs, and public-sector wage increases."[1] Monetary and exchange rate policies are implemented to stave off headline and generalized inflation, while trade and other policies include export restrictions and export taxes focused on key food items such as rice and cereals.[2]

---

[1] International Monetary Fund. 2008a. Food and Fuel Prices—Recent Developments, Macroeconomic Impact, and Policy Responses. Washington, DC., June 30.

[2] International Monetary Fund. 2008a. Food and Fuel Prices—Recent Developments, Macroeconomic Impact, and Policy Responses. Washington, DC., June 30.

In Africa, for example, the "African government have only put in place a number of temporary measures to help deal with the impact on the poor of last year's high food prices" (Burke 2009). These measures "involve reducing import tariff rates on important food commodities and making sure that prices remain stable for those commodities" (Burke 2009).

What the neoliberal theorist do not say however is that the cause of the food crisis is the structural adjustment policies implemented in the poor countries from the 1970s (Bello 2008). These policies removed needed government support for the agricultural sector that drove up the price for farm inputs, which pushed many farmers off the land, reduced food output and increase food prices due to the disconnect between food supply and demand. The neoliberal structural adjustment policies forced governments to privatize the state-run Marketing Boards that helped to stabilize food prices and farm income through buffer-stock measures in which they bought and stored agricultural surplus in gluts and sold them in times of shortages due to bad weather and other factors.

Neoliberal policies are also the source of the problem of high fuel prices that have a significant impact on the poor countries. Again, the neoliberal theorists do not identify their policies as the real sources for the global fuel crisis. They blame the crisis on the increase in demand for fuel by China and India, but do not source it at the neoliberal market liberalization and democratization policies, reflected for example in the wars in Iraq and Afghanistan that reduce food supply and push-up prices.

The food and fuel crises have thrown the Millennium Development Goals (MDGs) in the ACP countries off-course. Although, the MDGs are ideals to support the flawed neoliberal theoretical social policy framework spawned them. The MDGs "rest upon completely new principles with long-term effects that are neither well thought through nor well understood" (Reinert 2007). The "MDGs do not represent good social policy in the long run" because they are based on "foreign financing of domestic social and social redistribution policies, rather than on domestic financing by the developing countries themselves" (Reinert 2007). The financing of the MDGs threatens to place "a large number of nations permanently 'on the dole' – a system similar to 'welfare colonialism'" (Reinert 2007).

This critique of the MNG is also problematic nonetheless, because it does not consider the fact that the rich countries have plundered the

ACP countries to obtain their riches, and in a globe characterized by the high levels of inequalities as it does the transfer of wealth from rich to poor states is absolutely necessary. Since the rich states can only maintain their wealth through continuous pillage of the poor countries, it therefore behooves the former to assist the latter by engaging them in economic activity and deliberate arrangements that would allow more of the wealth produced in the poor states to remain their.

The first general area of analysis is, the central issues in Caribbean agricultural and neoliberal views. Second, the focus is on the food security crisis in the Caribbean, followed thirdly by agricultural trade concerns of small states. Fourth, there is an analysis of the policies to reverse the food security crisis in the Caribbean. Finally, the focus shifts to the fuel crisis and Petrocaribe as its possible solution for the Caribbean states.

Caribbean Agriculture: Central Issues and Neoliberal Views

The food crisis and food security problems in the Caribbean are directly related to the failures of the agriculture sector in the region. These failures are associated with the lack of appropriate land reform, agricultural diversification, and neoliberal globalization that liberalized the agricultural sector removing the safeguards against fluctuating farm incomes and commodity prices.

Central Issues in Caribbean Agriculture

The first set of issues is that two dominant ideas have emerged from the first generation of English-speaking Caribbean scholars as to what constituted the essential problems in the region's agriculture. These ideas formed the hub of the criticism against colonial agricultural policy and attempts at nationalist counter-policies. The first problem that occupied the attention of these scholars and policy-makers in the nationalist and post-independence periods is the asymmetric structure of the agricultural sector. The standard observation is that a small number of large-scale privately owned farms occupy the most fertile lands, and a large number of small-scale peasants or semi-peons inhabit the least productive lands. Large-scale agriculture was traditionally the domain of foreign-owned transnational corporations until post-independence nationalizations created large state-owned farms, especially in Guyana. Policies in marketing, technology, finance, transport, infrastructure, training, education, etc. favored large farms while small farmers faced perennial problems in those areas. The second problem highlighted by first generation Caribbean scholars is the over-dependence on one staple export crop that dominates regional agriculture, whether it is sugar or bananas. This crop structure was essentially the outcome of colonial agricultural policy formulated primarily by the planter class that dominated the state.

The solution to these two basic problems required a reorientation in agricultural policy to close the gap between large and small farms, and promote mixed rather than mono-crop farming. The planter-dominated colonial state would not take the lead to reform agriculture along the lines of genuine land redistribution, and crop diversification. Instead, it focused on failed land settlement schemes that distributed small plots of land, and on the rehabilitation of the large-scale, plantation agriculture sector. Land settlement schemes aimed at restructuring the peasantry, in order to create a new social order for the rural areas under colonial domination.[3] These colonial policies failed because land distribution was too small-scaled to transform inequalities in landholdings and plantation control over rural resources, or to be economical for cultivation.

The nationalist view was that Caribbean people needed to control the state in order to implement substantial agricultural reform. When the nationalists secured power however they failed to take the necessary steps to bring about radical transformation in the agricultural sector. They neglected to develop a real alternative agricultural strategy to that of the colonials. Instead, they merely sought to redouble the effort at implementing the colonial formulated land-settlement schemes, and rehabilitate large-scale plantation agriculture.

Colonial and nationalist policies nonetheless did combine to bring about some improvements in Caribbean agricultural. These benefits involved land settlement schemes, rehabilitation of export crops, diversification of export cash crops, incentives to agro-processors, and some institutional reform and development.[4]

---

[3] Thomas, Clive Y. 1988. *The Poor and the Powerless, Economic Policy and Change in the Caribbean*. New York: Monthly Review Press, pp. 122–126.

[4] Canterbury, Dennis C. 2007. Caribbean Agriculture under Three Regimes: Colonialism, Nationalism and Neoliberalism in Guyana. *The Journal of Peasant Studies* (34) 1: 1–28.

Caribbean nationalism combined with the revolutionary fervor that Cuba spawned in the region during the 1960s and 1970s, led to an increase in the number of state farms through nationalization, and government intervention. Besides land-settlement schemes, nationalization of foreign agricultural assets was the main radical option to redress the lopsided land distribution structure in the region. Not all Caribbean countries took the path of nationalization of foreign owned assets. Guyana and Jamaica were in the forefront in this regard, although Trinidad and Tobago had the largest state sector through state investments in the economy rather than by nationalization.

Although the problems that result from internal asymmetries and over-dependence on a single export crop are real, the greatest challenge to Caribbean agriculture has historically come from external sources. External factors usually threaten to destroy the entire agriculture sector, while domestic asymmetries and over-dependence on a single export crop do not. However, external factors, domestic asymmetries, and mono-crop dependence reinforce each other to perpetuate the status quo in agriculture in the Caribbean.

Caribbean agriculture nonetheless has always survived externally determined turmoil, while reinforcing its asymmetric and mono-crop structure. This was the region's experience in the tumultuous processes characterized by the break-up of the colonial slave mode of production, and the great depression. None of these really threatened food security in the region because at the time of economic crisis and transformation Caribbean people have always resorted successfully to farming to feed themselves. The Caribbean will therefore survive the current danger to agriculture posed by neoliberal globalization that has spawned a global food crisis, which threatens the food security of the region.

The biggest challenge to Caribbean agriculture in the immediate future is whether its reorganization that results from neoliberal globalization and the EPA bring about radical land reform to bridge the gap between large and small farmers, and genuinely diversify the sector. It is unlikely that agricultural liberalization and the EPA in the Caribbean would achieve those results. If anything, agricultural liberalization and the EPA seem set to squeeze out domestic farmers, and reinforce the domination of Caribbean agriculture by the EU and US agricultural transnational corporations. Agricultural liberalization and the EPA will increase food imports, heighten the food crisis and reduce food security. They will lead to a change in tastes for agricultural produce thereby squeezing-out domestic farmers, reinforcing old and new asymmetries in land distribution, and increasing mono-crop dependence.

Regional scholars and policymakers therefore correctly insist on preferential treatment for small states in global trade. It is unlikely, however, that their insistence on preferential treatment will bear fruit unless within the neoliberal framework of the WTO. The policymakers in the ACP countries need to demonstrate the political will to develop and embrace alternative trade arrangements to those of the WTO. The ALBA is an example of such an alternative trade arrangement. Hopefully, the first summit of BRIC (Brazil, Russia, India and China) in Yekaterinburg, Russia in June 2009[5] is a step towards the formulation of alternative financial architecture and a multi-polar world order that breaks out from neoliberal WTO domination and accommodates alternative regional trade arrangements such as the ALBA.

The second set of issues in Caribbean agriculture is that since the incorporation of the Caribbean into the global capitalist system of commodity production for market exchange, periodic reform in global capitalism has produced turmoil in the region's agricultural sector that threatens to dislodge it. There are three distinct periods of crisis in Caribbean agriculture, driven by reform activities in global capitalism – the collapse of the colonial slave mode of production[6] seriously threatened plantation agriculture; the great depression, World War II and the accompanying reform in global capitalism; and the end of the cold war and the new global order characterized by US led globalization and the emergence of EU bloc imperialism.

The break-up of the colonial slave mode of production with the end of the system of slavery and indentured labor in the Caribbean represented a major reform in the organization of global capitalist commodity production. The plantation was the main means of global capitalist commodity production in the Caribbean.[7] At the time, it was the most

[5] Faulconbridge, Guy. 2009. Developing World Leaders Show New Power at Summits. *Reuters*, June 16; Filger, Sheldon. 2009. BRIC Summit Sees End of Dominance of U.S. Dollar. *The Huffington Post*, June 16.

[6] Also, see Williams 1964 on 'slavery-cum-capitalism' and Beckford and Witter 1980 'slave mode of production' which are alternative characterization of the region's political economy, to Thomas 1984a 'colonial slave mode of production.'

[7] Thomas (1984a) defines the plantation as a means of production, unlike the plantation dependence school that equates the plantation with the society as a whole. See Hettne (1995) for an in-depth discussion on the plantation school.

efficient way to organize, effectively the capitalist labor process in the region. It provided the capitalist with a hierarchy of power that enabled a few individuals to maintain control over a large number of slave and bound laborers. This involved large-scale farming and the manufacture of the farm produce, for example sugarcane into sugar, for domestic, international and industrial consumption.

Market liberalization was embedded in the strategy to dismantle the colonial slave mode of production. The policy prescriptions at the time involved the liberalization of the labor market in the Caribbean. Initially spearheaded by the agricultural capitalist, globalization (the spread of capitalism from Europe to the rest of the globe) resulted in the accumulation of the wealth invested to develop industrial societies in Europe. The class of capitalist that had an interest in industrial development, however, challenged in theory and practice, the inefficient plantation production methods of the agricultural capitalist. The industrial capitalists therefore led the movement to reform the plantation production system erected by mercantile globalization, and to liberalize the labor market. Slave and indenture labor and the method of remuneration wasted scarce economic resources, and held back the full potential for capital accumulation. For capitalism to achieve its full potential, as a global system of commodity production, there was need for labor market liberalization.

Labor market liberalization was gradual in that indentured labor replaced slave labor. The labor reform did not go all the way it stopped short at fashioning a truly liberalized labor market. The direct producers that produced the economic surplus were no longer slave laborers but neither were they totally, free. The indenture labor system was a compromise to allay the fears of the agricultural capitalists, who saw an end to plantation farming and indeed to the entire plantation sector. The scrapping of the indentured system brought to a close the reform period in the production sphere. Global capitalism had now come of age where it no longer depended on any form of un-free labor to accumulate wealth. This development stimulated by the activities of the slaves and indentured laborers, and by the external forces of globalization accelerated major social change, regionally.

Labor market liberalization in plantation agriculture transformed not only the workers and management but also the entire society. It brought about social, political, and economic transformations. Workers were able to organize politically, to bring about an improvement in their social and economic conditions. The problem remained however that labor market liberalization did not bring about social and economic equality it indeed had the opposite effect. Furthermore, the workers bore the cost of labor market liberalization by paying taxes and user fees for improved social services. Thus, "The survival of the plantation economy during the century after Emancipation was at the expense of those who worked in it ..."[8]

The later period characterized by the great depression and the World War II was also stressful for Caribbean agriculture. As it is today in the current phase of neoliberal globalization and the EPA, the Caribbean region could not insulate itself from, crisis and reform in global capitalism. The region became embroiled in rebellious turmoil in the 1930s and 1940s that forced open political, economic, and social spaces in society for the common people to become upwardly mobile. Thus, by the time the depression and war were over Jamaica achieved self-rule and the doors of Caribbean nationalist politics were flung wide open. The challenge to Caribbean agriculture during the great depression and World War II was due to depressed prices and the severe disruption in export trade.[9]

The up side of the war however, was that it "shifted the focus of domestic production towards servicing the local market," and led to the establishment of "a wide range of local industries and a number of import-substituting activities" that produced "for the domestic market and exporting regionally."[10] The lime and limestone, matches, and industrial gases industries are cases in point. Also, there emerged "some secondary industries serving the local market (food, drink, tobacco, clothing, household items, etc.), as well as some local handicraft and artisan output."[11]

The disruption of Caribbean-European trade during the war stimulated intra-regional trade, industrial diversification, and domestic and regional markets in the Caribbean. This is evidence that given the space Caribbean agro-industry could advance to generate the region's

---

[8] Bolland, Nigel. 2001. *The Politics of Labor in the British Caribbean.* Kingston: Ian Randle, p. 126.

[9] For details on the decline in prices and disruption in export trade see Nigel Bolland, *The Politics of Labor in the British Caribbean*, Kingston, Ian Randle publishers, 2001.

[10] Thomas, Clive Y. 1988. *The Poor and the Powerless, Economic Policy and Change in the Caribbean.* New York: Monthly Review Press.

[11] Thomas, Clive Y. 1988. *The Poor and the Powerless, Economic Policy and Change in the Caribbean.* New York: Monthly Review Press.

independent development and on its own terms. Trade under conditions of colonialism, imperialism, US-led globalization or EU-bloc imperialism hampers rather than stimulate Caribbean independent development by restricting the region's freedom to formulate economic policies in its self-interest. Mercantilism restricted Caribbean trade to specific metropolis states. US-led globalization hampers Caribbean trade through liberalization policies that place the region's farmers at a tremendous disadvantage. EU bloc imperialism ties Caribbean trade to the EU indefinitely without any clear legal means out from the CARIFORUM-EU EPA.

The down side of the war was that it heightened US influence in the Caribbean. The US from as early as 1832 however had made a power play to control the region through the Monroe Doctrine that interpreted interference in the Western Hemisphere by any European power as 'unfriendly'. However, because of the war the UK allowed the US military forces legal entry in the British West Indies. The war forced the British government to engage the US in 'lend-lease arrangements' in which the US supplied Britain with war materials in exchange for the erection of US military bases in the British West Indies. Thereafter, the US assumed to itself the right to 'protect' the Caribbean from foreign and local threats. Consequently, to promote its hemispheric interests, the US government engaged in several military invasions, threats, forced treaties, and economic and political destabilization in the region.[12]

It is in this context that Caribbean agricultural trade pattern began to shift from the UK to the US. Indeed, the US came to the rescue of the Caribbean affected by the war by becoming the main supplier of imports to the region and providing it with a sizable market for its exports. This came at a high cost to the Caribbean however because it gave the US greater economic and political sway over the region. The new trade relations developed with the US did not address the fundamental asymmetries and mono-crop structure of the region's agricultural sector. The war ended without enough time for alternative crops to take root as major exports. In the aftermath of the war, the British rehabilitated the sugar industry, while alternative crops suffered. The British restored the agricultural status quo, although the US now had a stronger presence in regional trade.

[12] Thomas, Clive Y. 1988. *The Poor and the Powerless, Economic Policy and Change in the Caribbean*. New York: Monthly Review Press.

The current threat to Caribbean agriculture comes from neoliberal economic liberalization policies formulated by the US and EU and imposed on the ACP regions. Caribbean agricultural sectoral policies under the IMF/World Bank structural adjustment programs focus for example on price incentives, rehabilitation of infrastructure, foreign private investment, privatization of state farms, and cost recovery to relieve budgetary constraints, and maintain drainage, irrigation, and road infrastructure. However, the new US-EU hegemony over the ACP agriculture was struck a serious blow with the collapse of the Doha talks in July 2008.[13]

Agricultural policies practiced in the US however are tantamount to dumping in the form of food aid. The EU and US protect their agricultural and manufacturing industries and their markets in labor services. They protect their farmers by fending off competition from imported agricultural commodities, and protect their agricultural labor market by curtailing the free movement in farm workers into their countries through visa restrictions, etc.[14] Also, their trade policies restrict ACP farmers and industries from gaining full access in US and EU markets.[15]

The argument by Bhagwati (2005) that it is unfair to criticize the protectionist policies of the rich states while failing to do so for the poor countries does not provide any defense of globalization, but really exposes the liberalization myth. The implication of his analysis is that protection by both rich and poor countries renders liberalization the biggest myth perpetuated by neoliberal globalization. Bhagwati's (2005) argument is groundless because the Euro-American imperial powers forcefully impose liberalization on the poor countries while at the same time protecting US and European industries in numerous ways as identified by Oxfam.[16]

To offset the threat to Caribbean agriculture the region joined forces with the ACP countries, the G-90 comprising, Africa Union (AU), and

[13] Common Dreams Progressive Network. 2008. Collapse of WTO Doha Negotiations: A Blow to the US – EU Hegemony – The Collapse Paves a New Way Forward for Developing Countries. July 29.

[14] Anderson, Sarah. 2005. U.S. Immigration Policy on the Table at the WTO. *Foreign Policy in Focus* Silver City, NM & Washington, DC:, November 30.

[15] For further discussion on this issue see Green, Duncan. 2005. What Happened in Hong Kong? Initial Analysis of the WTO Ministerial. *Oxfam Briefing Paper* 85.

[16] For further discussion on these issues see Green, Duncan. 2005. What Happened in Hong Kong? Initial Analysis of the WTO Ministerial. *Oxfam Briefing Paper* 85.

the Least Developed Countries (LDCs), to push their development needs and interests at the Fourth WTO Ministerial Conference in Doha, Qatar in November 2001. The development priorities of these countries are market access for products of export interest to members, the obligations undertaken by these countries should be proportional and commensurate with their level of development, and increased financial assistance for countries that will experience adjustment costs, and technical assistance for trade capacity building and for improving the competitiveness of the countries.[17] Thus, the three major pillars of agricultural negotiations at the WTO are domestic support, market access, and export competition.

The EU and US need to reform their agricultural policies to create a fairer trading system that would allow the ACP and developing countries in general to achieve their developmental goals. The ACP countries, the EU and the US, have different positions on WTO agricultural trade negotiations to allow for 'fair trade.' The EU's general approach to agricultural negotiations is rooted in the on-going process of Common Agricultural Policy (CAP) reform to cut the link between subsidy and production. The single farm payment scheme is proposed as the main means to achieve this reform in the EU. This payment scheme does not link support to current production but to the 'historical subsidy receipts and current land area.'[18]

The US employs a two-stage approach to agricultural reform, favoring an initial stage of significant reductions in trade distortions, phased over five years. An interlude of five years follows to review the effects of the first stage of reforms. The second stage of reductions will take place, unless members agree to change course, culminating in the total elimination of remaining measures after five years, including safeguard measures.

Although developing countries operate as a bloc, the most recent being G-110 formed in Hong Kong at the sixth WTO Ministerial, expectedly, there is division among them on some issues and unity on others. The relative size, economic strength, factor endowment, etc. of the developing countries cause their concerns to differ to some extent.

---

[17] For elaboration on these issues see Africa, Caribbean and Pacific Group. 2005. ACP Declaration on the Sixth WTO Ministerial Conference. ACP/61/047/05, Brussels, November 29; Africa, Caribbean and Pacific Group. 2005. G-90 Declaration. ACP/61/057/05 Rev.2, Brussels, December 5.

[18] Technical Center for Agricultural and Rural Cooperation (CTA). 2005. In the Run-up to Hong Kong. *Agritrade* Special Edition, November.

However, they need support in their effort to arrive at a common strategy in dealing with the EU and US. Preference erosion is a thorny issue that divides developing countries, especially between the ACP states that favor preferential treatment, and those that oppose because they want to expand their market access. The developing countries unite on the issue of domestic support in OECD countries. They want trade arrangements that substantially and effectively reduce trade-distorting support in the rich countries.

Caribbean agriculture stands to benefit immensely if the Caribbean countries along with their partners in the ACP, retain appropriate policy space to pursue agricultural policies that support their developmental goals, food security, and livelihoods. The benefits would multiply, as was the case during World War II, if there is increased market access in both primary and processed agricultural goods. The broad goal of the Caribbean nations is to contribute to the realization of an equitable and fair multilateral trading regime that will ensure their continued economic survival and development.

It is no secret however that Caribbean agriculture has loss ground[19] in the pecking order of Caribbean governments due to neoliberal market liberalization policy a fact that regional officials acknowledge. The region's ability to respond to the challenge of growing more food domestically is hindered by a lack of resources for meaningful agricultural research and development work. The evidence of this problem is not hard to find given the suspension of the agricultural research program at the University of the West Indies (UWI), and the severe lack of funding for the Caribbean Agricultural Research and Development Institute (CARDI). The research and development units within the Agricultural Ministries in the Caribbean are also severely hamstrung due to a lack of necessary resources and manpower. There has been a continuous decline in government budgetary allocation to agriculture compared with other sectors. Official figures for nine Caribbean countries including Barbados, Guyana and Trinidad and Tobago showed that funding for agriculture has either remained constant or declined. The agricultural sector has loss ground to hotel, entertainment and housing construction, and expanding urbanization and its attendant social and recreational facilities.[20]

---

[19] Richards, Peter. 2008. Caribbean: Agriculture Literally Losing Ground. *Inter-Press Service*, October 9.

[20] Richards, Peter. 2008. Caribbean: Agriculture Literally Losing Ground. *Inter-Press Service*, October 9.

These problems are compounded by other setbacks such as the loss of preferential treatment in global markets, low productivity, commercial banks not recognizing agriculture as viable business, disasters, insurance companies taking less risk, rising input prices beyond reach of many farmers, and climate change that affect seasonal production. The sugar industry in St. Kitts-Nevis was abandoned completely, and the authorities are now concentrating on developing the services sector. Barbados and Trinidad and Tobago have drastically reduced their sugar industries. The banana or "green gold" industry in Dominica, Grenada, St. Lucia and St. Vincent and the Grenadines, which in its heyday netted US$137M annually to the economies of these islands, is fighting for survival, now generating just under US$37M.[21]

There is an acknowledged disjuncture between agriculture policy and implementation in the Caribbean. The countries have had little choice but to import more and produce less food, since farmers are not empowered under the neoliberal agenda pushed on the region. The annual food import bill in the Caribbean stands at US$3.5 billion and increasing given the current increases in inputs due to higher energy cost.[22]

Neoliberal Views on Caribbean Agricultural

The current neoliberal thinking is that the nationalist agricultural policies in the Caribbean are to be blamed for the problems in the agricultural sector because they shielded the Region's export agriculture from international competition, leaving it unprepared for the new trading regime based on competitiveness. The Caribbean scholars who hold this view have bought into the idea that export trade is the engine of economic growth and as a consequence they criticize the failure of agriculture exports to stimulate consistent regional growth. Evidence of this is that non-agricultural exports have performed better than agricultural exports as the mainstay of the regional economy under liberalization, indicating that regional economies have undergone a fundamental transformation from being agricultural-based to non-agricultural-based economies.

---

[21] Richards, Peter. 2008. Caribbean: Agriculture Literally Losing Ground. *Inter-Press Service*, October 9.

[22] Richards, Peter. 2008. Caribbean: Agriculture Literally Losing Ground. *Inter-Press Service*, October 9.

The neoliberals have failed however to explore the cause for the current march towards the liberalization of agricultural trade in the Caribbean. The failed colonial and nationalist policies are not the cause of economic liberalization policies. These policies are the product of US-led globalization and EU bloc imperialism the current approaches to capital accumulation on a global scale. Preferential agricultural market stands in the way of capital accumulation of the giant transnational corporations in agriculture and food production.

As Caribbean agricultural exports decline, agricultural imports increase completing the cycle of wealth transfer out of the region to the shareholders of the transnational corporations in the rich countries. Agricultural liberalization increases the accumulation of capital of the TNCs in agriculture by destroying the regional agricultural sector, reducing its agricultural exports, and increasing its agricultural imports, thereby transferring the region's agricultural wealth to external locations. The food crisis in the ACP countries is a product of the process of their conversion from being net producers and exporters of agricultural commodities, to net importers of these items. This situation represents the new imperialism spearheaded by US-led globalization and the EU's economic partnership agreements, compared with the old European imperialism that had the exact stagnating effect on Caribbean agriculture simultaneously that agricultural wealth extracted from the region accumulated in Europe.

The challenge faced by anyone studying the agricultural sector is to unravel the nature of US-Led globalization and EU bloc imperialism in order to foster a better understanding of Caribbean agriculture in its current global context. We cannot separate Caribbean agriculture from the process of global capital accumulation, since the region is a product of that process and continues to be an integral part of it, operating at its very center rather than its margins. If the Caribbean is marginal then why the US, the most powerful country on earth finds it necessary to invade Caribbean countries, destabilize Caribbean government, and declared the region as its frontier in its so-called "war on terror." In the eyes of the US-led globalization and EU bloc imperialism no country or geographic region is marginal because they are potential markets and sources of raw materials. This is why the EU is bent on forcing the EPA on the Caribbean and other ACP regions. The modern imperialisms call for policies that de-emphasize agriculture and to reinforce the problematic theory of comparative advantage arguing that countries need to find "their new demonstrated areas of comparative advantage in non-agricultural exports."[23]

The present-day neoliberal scholars and policy makers fail to explore deeper the real reasons why agriculture dominated the Caribbean economy, and to criticize the Ricardian trade theory, the basis of colonial policy in the region. They do not even bother to explore the relevance of Raul Prebisch's convincing arguments against comparative advantage in Latin America, as justification for import substitution, or the strong case built by Sir Arthur Lewis for the industrialization of the British West Indies, as a major refutation of the colonial policy that condemned the Caribbean to agricultural production. Neoliberal ideologues throw out those views as being irrelevant to the goal of market liberalization.

However, several important indicators such as the regional agricultural terms of trade, and the regional ratio of export agriculture earnings to regional GDP, have declined consistently under agricultural liberalization. The decline in regional agricultural exports is a major cause for the decline in regional ratio of foreign exchange earnings relative to earnings by the regional export sector as a whole. As the neoliberal adherents attempt to formulate policy without understanding the causes for the transformation in the agricultural sector, they focus on long-term trends failing to realize that possibly in the next fifty years under a different world order conditions then will require another approach to agriculture.

The neoliberal recommendation is that the Caribbean countries should "de-emphasize agriculture production and exports and to reorient resources towards export services." The neoliberal argument is that the food security strategy of these countries lies "in developing food reserves rather than in the development of agriculture per se."[24] The recommendation is for the establishment of food reserves on a national, sub regional, or regional basis. It is suggested that the countries with a relatively strong agricultural sector "can be used as depositories or as suppliers of food stocks for the region as a whole."[25]

[23] Patrick Kendall and Marco Petracco. 2003. The Current State and Future of Caribbean Agriculture, Economics Department, Caribbean Development Bank, January.

[24] Kendall, Patrick and Marco Petracco. 2003. The Current State and Future of Caribbean Agriculture. Economics Department: Caribbean Development Bank, January.

[25] Kendall, Patrick and Marco Petracco. 2003. The Current State and Future of Caribbean Agriculture. Economics Department: Caribbean Development Bank, January.

However, instead of pursuing this kind of neoliberal policy, an alternative approach could be the mechanization of the region's agricultural sector to make it more competitive, by producing manufactured or canned products.

Guyana, Belize and Jamaica the largest Caricom countries and also Dominica and Suriname are seen to possess the appropriate resource endowment that allows them to focus on "agricultural exports and competitive import replacement...strategies for the foreseeable future." Export diversification as a policy option in the nationalist and liberalization periods in these countries however have failed to bring about the requisite transformation in their agricultural sector. The neoliberals reinforce the failed IMF/World Bank policy recommendations, namely to rationalize traditional agriculture, meaning the "closing down of some industries or firms in certain industries" such as in the sugar and banana sub-sectors, as the desired change in agricultural strategy to achieve export stimulation and competitive import replacement.

The neoliberals recommend the exploration of "other export commodities, which have proved their competitiveness, being currently exported outside preferential arrangements." However, this is the old policy option to stimulate the "other crops" or "non-traditional" agricultural sector comprising fruits, vegetables, and ground provisions, a strategy that had greater success in the nationalist period compared with the current liberalization policies. The neoliberal strategy to promote non-traditional agriculture will contribute to the food crisis and food insecurity in that the region will export these "other crops" thereby depleting the amount available for consumption on the domestic market. Their focus is on production for export and not for domestic consumption.

The neoliberals fell right back on the old recommendations for Caribbean agriculture such as stimulating the non-traditional sector, and agro-processing, but in all of this, they fail to identify the real cause for the failure of these policies in the past. They identified the old causes for the failure of this strategy in the past, including the lack of extension services, training, effective marketing, transportation difficulties, skewed distribution of land resources, trade barriers, etc., and recommend regional co-operation as a possible solution to the barriers of growth in non-traditional agriculture, and the promotion of agro-processing in both traditional and non-traditional crops. This is a good point but an old one that Fidel Castro, William Demas, Clive Thomas and Havelock Brewster, and others have recommended a long time ago. Regional economic integration is already a development approach in the Caribbean. The neoliberals however do not establish the connection between agricultural policy and output in the Caribbean and the global accumulation of capital. Also, the CARIFORUM-EU EPA poses a very serious threat to regional economic integration in the Caribbean, by rendering the Caricom and the Caribbean Single Market Economy (CSME), useless.

The neoliberals divided the Caribbean into two broad areas for the purposes of agricultural policy options – countries whose resource endowment allow them to specialize in agriculture and those that should de-emphasize agriculture and move into non-agricultural alternative niche areas. They fell back on the neoclassical marginal utility equilibrium model to justify their argument for competitive import replacement, adjusting it "to move the consumer towards the point where marginal utility is equated with marginal social cost and benefit so that consumption can be more socially efficient." In that perspective social efficient food production and consumption is "where marginal private benefit equals price equals marginal cost equals marginal social benefit/utility."[26]

They argue that the Caribbean needs to regard international competitiveness in terms of social cost rather than private cost because due to diseconomies of scale regional economies will not be as cost competitive as foreign exporters. According to them, this is changing the rules to suit yourself, in that if you cannot be competitive based on private cost then measure your competitiveness in terms of social cost where you will fare better. In essence, therefore this proposal is no real solution but an avoidance of the problem that agricultural production in the Caribbean is high cost. The region will become competitive in social cost but remains uncompetitive in private cost.

The neoliberals claim that their proposal "implies a completely new approach to production and marketing in the Region." It requires the revision of "Current modes…and significant training undertaken in order to ensure that production takes place with the objective of ensuring a healthy, environmentally friendly and sustainable food supply at the cheapest possible social cost." In their view, "This may very well imply reorienting agricultural production towards a more organic

[26] Kendall, Patrick and Marco Petracco. 2003. The Current State and Future of Caribbean Agriculture. Economics Department: Caribbean Development Bank, January.

approach." They argue that their approach has an additional advantage in "that world market in various commodities, including a wide range of fruits and vegetables, are already moving in this direction and unless the Caribbean adapts, it will not be able to participate in those markets."[27]

A major problem with the promotion of organic food production is its class nature. Consumption of organic foods is a class symbol because those foods fetch a higher price than non-organic foods, and only certain middle class elements consume them in the US and European markets. These foods will always play a secondary role to non-organic foods given the level of investments in the latter by the giant TNCs. The neoliberals are pushing the Caribbean into areas that depend on the sustenance of middle class incomes in the EU, US and Caribbean, and which have no real chances to attract large scale investments. Because of the scarcity of investment funds, Caribbean organic farmers will always remain small.

Furthermore, they overlook the fact that the giant TNCs in agribusiness control seeds and bioengineering, processes over which Caribbean farmers have no control. We need to understand the processes by which Caribbean agriculture evolved into its current state, before we can provide solutions to its current problems. The agricultural sector does not exist outside of the imperial relations between the Caribbean the US and Europe, but is at its center, and therefore requires analysis in that context. Caribbean agriculture was at the very center of the process of the industrialization of the capitalist productive system spearheaded by British imperialism, and the region remains center stage in the new imperialisms headed by the US-led globalization and the EU-EPAs.

The neoliberal views identified above are mere justification for US-led globalization and EU bloc imperialism currently dismantling Caribbean agriculture through market liberalization. The EU and the US are both forcing Caribbean countries to reorient their agricultural sectors towards globalization the code word for the new imperialism. This reorientation includes some countries de-emphasizing agriculture and finding ways out of banana and sugar production.

---

[27] Kendall, Patrick and Marco Petracco. 2003. The Current State and Future of Caribbean Agriculture. Economics Department: Caribbean Development Bank, January.

Food Security Crisis and the Caribbean

Undoubtedly, neoliberal globalization has exacerbated poverty and inequalities in the developing countries. The "free trade" dimension of globalization that focuses on export expansion through trade liberalization, also the goal of the CARIFORUM-EU EPA, has had a negative impact on poverty and food security in the developing countries. The limited resources of the small farmers effectively constrain their participation in expansion and new markets and negatively affect their incomes level and livelihoods. Trade liberalization transforms the status quo in agriculture by increasing the presence of agricultural transnationals in the Caribbean. At the same time it reinforces the divisions in the sector that concentrates a large proportion of the fertile lands in the hands of a few large farmers both domestic and TNCs. This places a squeeze on small farmers and adversely compromises their livelihoods. Furthermore, export production displaces traditional crops and has a negative impact on food security.

The neoliberal theoretical argument however is that there are three principal causes for the food crisis. The first is that increased bio-fuels production in the US and EU resulted in the consumption of about a half of the major food crops in 2007. It is argued that the drive for alternative liquid fuels from food crops is a major factor to the current world food crisis (Magdoff 2008). This diverts food from the kitchen to the factory. Second is the growth in per capita income in newly emerging states that stimulates and increases their demand for food that put pressure on food supply. Third, the increase in prices in agricultural commodities is due to higher costs associated with energy and fertilizer. These are considered long-term structural price increases that are permanent. The neoliberal ideologues point to temporary factors that caused the food crisis in Africa. These are natural factors such as droughts in wheat producing countries south of the equator in 2007, and post-election violence in Kenya that pushed up food prices in neighboring countries.

Because of the new situation concerning the food crisis, there has been a paradigm shift on the issue of food security.[28] It is argued that the "paradigm of 'food security' has suddenly shifted back to the

[28] Khor, Martin. 2008. Food Crisis, Climate Change, and the Importance of Sustainable Agriculture. Third World Network (TWN), June.

traditional concept of greater self-sufficiency, instead of prioritizing the option of relying on cheaper imports" (Khor 2008). There seems to be a recognition that in the "immediate period, there is need for emergency food supplies to affected countries, but that a long-term solution must include increased local food production in developing countries" (Khor 2008). The issue therefore is for the ACP countries to recognize the "barriers to local production" and to find ways to remove them.

The causal factors identified for the food crisis include climatic conditions such as drought, high input prices of oil-based products, and the increased use of lands to produce biofuels instead of food (Khor 2008). A longer-term reason for "the decline in agriculture in many developing countries," which is at the center of the food crisis, is in most cases "the structural adjustment policies of the IMF and World Bank." The developing countries were asked or advised by the IMF and World Bank "to (1) dismantle marketing boards and guaranteed prices for farmers' products; (2) phase out or eliminate subsidies and support such as fertilizer, machines, agricultural infrastructure; (3) reduce tariffs of food products to low levels."[29]

The character of neoliberal globalization is such nonetheless that the rich states subsidize their agriculture while the developing countries are forced remove subsidies and to open their markets. Subsidized agricultural exports from the rich states negatively impact Caribbean economies.[30] There are many studies since the 1970s, which "have consistently reported that agricultural surpluses generated under protective and subsidized regimes in the US, the EU and other OECD countries and dumped onto world markets have proved detrimental to developing countries" (Ballayram 2004). The estimated loss to the developing countries from these subsidies is "US$20 billion in net agricultural export per annum" and a reduction in "income in these countries by about US$30 billion per year" (Ballayram 2004). Neoliberal policies converted several developing countries from net exporters to net importers of agricultural commodities.

The enduring legacy of European colonial, imperialist and nationalist post-independence agricultural policies in the Caribbean are the perpetuation of export dependence on a single crop referred to as

---

[29] Khor, Martin. 2008. Food Crisis, Climate Change, and the Importance of Sustainable Agriculture. Third World Network (TWN), June.

[30] Ballayram, Poverty, "Food Security and Globalization: Challenges for Regional Development," Caribbean Food and Nutrition Institute, 2004.

traditional agriculture (sugar, bananas, and citrus). In the nationalist period, the new dimension of agricultural policy in the region was its gearing towards European preferential markets, a form of development assistance to the Caribbean. In the new global order spearheaded by US-led globalization and EU bloc imperialism, agricultural policies in the Caribbean have made a radical shift towards the removal of preferential trade arrangements in favor of agricultural liberalization. Bad as they were in terms of their failure to achieve stated objectives, agricultural policies under the old system of preferential markets contributed more to regional economic growth "in terms of real income growth, employment and foreign exchange earnings"[31] than liberalization policies.

The food crisis must be appreciated in terms of the inability of common people to secure food for their families. The understanding of food security that emerged in the early post-World War II period was in terms of food production and availability. However, economic accessibility to foods became an important part of the definition of food security by the 1970s. Furthermore, situating food security "at the household level, with particular attention to women, children and other vulnerable groups" became a concern in the 1980s. Nowadays, "Given the nutritional and epidemiological transitions that developing countries are currently experiencing" food security "must embody health and nutritional issues."[32] In the Caribbean, "Nutritional related chronic diseases such as obesity, diabetes, high blood pressure, stroke, heart diseases, and cancer have replaced malnutrition and infectious diseases as the major public health problems." Food security, therefore, "is an integral part of the process of nutrition and health development and embodies several major components – food availability, household access, nutritional adequacy, sustainability and vulnerability."[33]

This understanding of food security means that it involves multiple overlapping socio-economic sectors such as health, agriculture,

[31] Patrick Kendall and Marco Petracco. 2003. The Current State and Future of Caribbean Agriculture, Economics Department, Caribbean development Bank, January.

[32] Ballayram, Beverly Lawrence and Fitzroy Henry. 2002. Food Security and Health in the Caribbean: Imperatives for a New Policy. Paper presented at the Sir Arthur Lewis Institute of Social and Economic Studies (SALISES) and Mona School of Business Conference, University of the West Indies, Kingston, Jamaica, April 2–4.

[33] Ballayram, Beverly Lawrence and Fitzroy Henry. 2002. Food Security and Health in the Caribbean: Imperatives for a New Policy. Paper presented at the Sir Arthur Lewis Institute of Social and Economic Studies (SALISES) and Mona School of Business Conference, University of the West Indies, Kingston, Jamaica, April 2–4.

environment, marketing, and trade. A major foreseeable difficulty concerning food security in the Caribbean is that the trade regime associated with the EPA "is pushing for fundamental changes in the legal, institutional and economic infrastructure of developing countries," and is "impacting both the inter-sectoral and intra-sectoral linkages in Caricom economies."[34] The linkages of the sectors necessary to positively impact food security are distorted by the neoliberal trade regime fostered by the EPA.

It is argued, "Food security exists when the household has access to food needed for a healthy life for all its members and is not at risk of losing such access."[35] Defining food security in this way focuses on the broader dimension of the problem that considers the socio-economic and nutritional aspects of food rather than concentrating narrowly on food sufficiency. Thus, food security and poverty overlap, with the former being an integral part of a process of nutrition and health development and embodies food availability, household access, and biological utilization of food.[36]

The food crisis refers to the rising prices of food that enriches the producers and punishes the consumers. In the Caribbean, Guyanese farmers may make a windfall from increasing food prices, but the Guyanese and other consumers in the region will face food insecurity. The connection between food security and the food crisis in the Caribbean is that the latter reduce food security or increases food insecurity. The Caribbean Food and Nutrition Institute (CFNI) also takes the position that there is an overlap between food security and insecurity, nutrition, health, trade, agriculture environment, marketing, and culture.

Liberalization affects all sectors of the economy including the elimination of trade barriers, free trade (non-discrimination, fiscal and

---

[34] Wedderburn, Judith. 2007. Hunger Anywhere is a Threat to Peace Everywhere Food Sovereignty, Nutrition Security and Poverty Alleviation: An NGO Perspective. In Poverty Alleviation and Food Security Strategies in the Caribbean: A Policy Dialogue, Kingston: Caribbean Food and Nutrition Institute. Macroeconomic Impact, and Policy Responses An Update. September 19.

[35] Ballayram. 2007. Conceptual Framework for Food and Nutrition Security within Poverty Alleviation Strategies, in Poverty Alleviation and Food Security Strategies in the Caribbean: A Policy Dialogue. Kingston: Caribbean Food and Nutrition Institute, pp. 5–9.

[36] Ballayram. 2007. Conceptual Framework for Food and Nutrition Security within Poverty Alleviation Strategies, in Poverty Alleviation and Food Security Strategies in the Caribbean: A Policy Dialogue. Kingston: Caribbean Food and Nutrition Institute, pp. 5–9.

regulatory independence of the state), service provision, intellectual property, education, health and safety standards, etc.[37] Furthermore, "The WTO Agreement on Agriculture exacerbates the existing inequalities in world agricultural trade" and "does less to promote agricultural trade between countries and more to foster accumulation and profit-taking for a handful of large agribusinesses."[38] In addition, "Agribusiness corporations, primarily from the North, supported by massive subsidies, promote global market distortions, which threaten the survival of small farmers, turning many rural people into landless agricultural workers who must sell their labor in order to buy food."[39] The conclusion, therefore, is that "As a result of their socially-defined roles, women who head more than 40 percent of households in many Caribbean countries become "default providers" of food with responsibility for the nutrition of families and other demands of social reproduction as market-driven reforms take place."[40]

Addressing the Caricom Heads of Government 29th Conference, Luis Alberto Moreno, President of the Inter-American Development Bank observed, "Rising food and oil prices are hitting the Caribbean more than any other region in the Western Hemisphere."[41] According to IDB estimates, "the average negative net impact of high oil and food prices on the trade balance for Caribbean countries (except Guyana and Trinidad and Tobago) is 5.4 percent of GDP, compared to 4 percent

[37] Wedderburn, Judith. 2007. Hunger Anywhere is a Threat to Peace Everywhere Food Sovereignty, Nutrition Security and Poverty Alleviation: An NGO Perspective. In Poverty Alleviation and Food Security Strategies in the Caribbean: A Policy Dialogue, Kingston: Caribbean Food and Nutrition Institute. Macroeconomic Impact, and Policy Responses An Update. September 19.

[38] Wedderburn, Judith. 2007. Hunger Anywhere is a Threat to Peace Everywhere Food Sovereignty, Nutrition Security and Poverty Alleviation: An NGO Perspective. In Poverty Alleviation and Food Security Strategies in the Caribbean: A Policy Dialogue, Kingston: Caribbean Food and Nutrition Institute. Macroeconomic Impact, and Policy Responses An Update. September 19.

[39] Wedderburn, Judith. 2007. Hunger Anywhere is a Threat to Peace Everywhere Food Sovereignty, Nutrition Security and Poverty Alleviation: An NGO Perspective. In Poverty Alleviation and Food Security Strategies in the Caribbean: A Policy Dialogue, Kingston: Caribbean Food and Nutrition Institute. Macroeconomic Impact, and Policy Responses An Update. September 19.

[40] Wedderburn, Judith. 2007. Hunger Anywhere is a Threat to Peace Everywhere Food Sovereignty, Nutrition Security and Poverty Alleviation: An NGO Perspective. In Poverty Alleviation and Food Security Strategies in the Caribbean: A Policy Dialogue, Kingston: Caribbean Food and Nutrition Institute. Macroeconomic Impact, and Policy Responses An Update. September 19.

[41] Inter-American Develkopment Bank. 2008. Caribbean Hardest Hit by Food and Energy Price Shocks. Caribbean Press Releases.com, July 4.

of GDP in the Central American countries."[42] Moreno noted, "Oil- and gas-exporting Trinidad and Tobago is benefiting from higher fossil fuel prices, while in Guyana the negative impact of high oil prices is partially offset by higher export prices for commodities such as rice, bauxite and gold." In its analysis the IDB established "that the effects of high oil prices exceed those related to food in most of the Caribbean."[43]

Agricultural Trade Concerns of Small States[44]

The food crisis and food security situation in the Caribbean is exacerbated first by the fact that Caribbean states are small, and second by the current global agricultural trade arrangements imposed on them by structural adjustment, the World Trade Organization, and the CARIFORUM-EU EPA. The agriculture sector is significant to the small states in the ACP regions because of its importance in the determination of the quality of life in these countries in which a majority of poor people live in rural areas.

Thomas (2007) identified a number of concerns of the small islands developing states (SIDS) in the ACP regions with the current global agricultural trading arrangements. First, the agricultural sector in these states perform " 'multifunctional roles,' as the term is recognized in the WTO," as well as "food security, food sovereignty, and broader development roles aimed at making trade in food compatible with sustained human development."[45]

The small island developing states have a second concern concerning the global processes of vertical and horizontal integration in agriculture. There concern is that

> the global process of increasing vertical integration and consolidation of agricultural functions (e.g., supply inputs, trading, processing, and retailing), along with the horizontal integration and consolidation of

[42] Inter-American Develkopment Bank. 2008. Caribbean Hardest Hit by Food and Energy Price Shocks. Caribbean Press Releases.com, July 4.

[43] Inter-American Develkopment Bank. 2008. Caribbean Hardest Hit by Food and Energy Price Shocks. Caribbean Press Releases.com, July 4.

[44] The data in this section is taken from Thomas, Clive Y. 2007. Making Global Trade Work for People: The Concerns of Small States in the Global Trade Regime. *RESILIENCE Series* 6 UNDP/BDP/CDG.

[45] Thomas, Clive Y. 2007. Making Global Trade Work for People: The Concerns of Small States in the Global Trade Regime. *RESILIENCE Series* 6 UNDP/BDP/CDG.

> one or two dominant firms at each function, create special difficulties for small states not only because they are small but also because small farmers often account for much of their agricultural output (Thomas 2007).

As a consequence of the present situation, it is illusionary to believe that "market forces are truly guiding global agriculture resource allocation, production and consumption decisions when, in fact, the exercise of monopoly power and rent taking are the dominant features" (Thomas 2007).

Third, the developed countries are the worse offenders in terms of the practice of market-distortion policies "both in absolute and proportionate terms." Consequently, "The net effect is that OECD countries overproduce (because of high domestic prices), under-import (because of protection), and over-export at low prices (because of subsidies)," thus undermining small farmers in small states, "since the OECD countries account for two-thirds of world agricultural trade" (Thomas 2007).

Fourth, small states in the ACP regions experience a "higher-than average output volatility" requiring measures "to bring the volatility of agricultural commodity prices under control and/or to put in place some global compensatory mechanism."

Fifth, macroeconomic management in small states is severely constrained by "price volatility and declining terms of trade" in these countries. The data reveal the high volatility in agricultural commodity prices. Also the data confirm that the terms of trade of the SIDS, which are highly dependent on agricultural commodity exports negatively impact critical macroeconomic variables such as "the price level, exchange rates, interest rates, the availability of credit, the balance of payments, public finance, internal and external debt, employment, consumption, investment, and foreign exchange earnings" (Thomas 2007).

A sixth concern is the WTOs termination of "international commodity agreements," which "sought to provide buffer stocks, practice supply management, and introduce price support schemes," and the dismantling by structural adjustment programs of "domestic supports (in addition to trade barriers and subsidies), which sought to shield domestic markets from volatile prices and, in some instances, to keep prices low." These have combined to make more vulnerable "small states reliant on commodity exports and food importation, particularly in light of the consolidation of global agricultural trade."

At present, "three to six transnational corporations" control "more than 80 - 90 percent of global trade in the 10 most important commodities," and "increasingly, supermarket chains are rapidly growing in influence over the global food trade." A re-evaluation of international commodity agreements and domestic support mechanisms in agriculture is necessary to help overcome the problems associated with the food crisis and food security.

A seventh concern of the small states in the ACP regions has to do with the pressure exerted on them to remove their subsidies to the fisheries sector. In the SIDS, poor households depend on domestic fishing as a major source of their protein consumption, employment, and foreign exchange earnings from fish export. Subsidies to this sector "seek to integrate the in-shore and artisanal fisheries with other sectors of the domestic economy, and to improve the benefits to be derived from offshore fishing for export." The argument by the SIDS is that "subsidies are typically aimed at compensating investors for the disadvantages of small size, location, and environmental risk, a situation that does not apply to large countries" (Thomas 2007).

Policies to Reverse Food Security Crisis

The Revised Treaty of Chaguaramas forms the basis of Caricom's agricultural policy. The goals of the Caricom Agricultural Policy are:

> a. the fundamental transformation of the agricultural sector towards market oriented, internationally competitive and environmentally sound production of agricultural products; b. improved income and employment opportunities, food and nutrition security, and poverty alleviation in the Community; c. the efficient cultivation and production of traditional and non-traditional primary agricultural products; d. increased production and diversification of processed agricultural products; e. an enlarged share of world markets for primary and processed agricultural products; and f. the efficient management and sustainable exploitation of the Region's natural resources, including its forests and the living resources of the exclusive economic zone, bearing in mind the differences in resource endowment and economic development of the Member States.[46]

[46] Caribbean Community Secretariat. 2001. Revised Treaty of Chaguaramas Establishing the Caribbean Community Including The Caricom Single Market and Economy, Georgetown.

These policies outlined by the Caricom embrace the neoliberal view on agriculture. Caribbean states need to pursue nonetheless a multi-pronged approach to address the problems associated with the food crisis and food security. It is argued that "these states should pursue diversification, improve their competitiveness, and be afforded the opportunity for new products and increased value added to existing products to emerge" (Thomas 2007). On the other hand, these countries "should be provided with compensatory financing" for the removal of subsidies.

There is an "urgent need" for the small farmers to gain "secured entitlements to land, access to technology, markets and microfinance"[47] as a means to counter the food crisis and insecurity. Furthermore, the Caribbean countries must urgently establish "food and nutritional goals so that the region's agriculture and food systems can deliver adequate and nutritionally appropriate quantities of food, especially to low-income and vulnerable groups."[48] Caribbean policy makers continue to focus instead on increasing agricultural production and productivity to meet food security goals.

The policy makers must "reassess the role of agriculture and its relationship with other sectors in the economy." This is a serious problem because "Nutrition-related chronic non-communicable diseases," which "cut across socio-economic, spatial and demographic lines," and are "associated with a sedentary life style, and changes in diets which can be linked to domestic and imported food policies," have "emerged as the major causes of death in the region." It is evident that "These nutritional and epidemiological transitions" require that policy makers re-conceptualize "food security that combines food access, availability, and nutritional and health considerations, and for forging links among agriculture, health and nutrition."[49]

Although regional experts have been advising the Caribbean governments on the need to refocus food security policies, the Heads of

---

[47] Caribbean Food and Nutrition Institute (CNFI) and Inter-American Institute for Cooperation on Agriculture (IICA). 2007. Reducing Poverty and Food Insecurity in the Caribbean. Kingston Jamaica.

[48] Ballayram, Beverly Lawrence and Fitzroy Henry. 2002. Food Security and Health in the Caribbean: Imperatives for a New Policy. Paper presented at the Sir Arthur Lewis Institute of Social and Economic Studies (SALISES) and Mona School of Business Conference, University of the West Indies, Kingston, Jamaica, April 2–4.

[49] Ballayram, Beverly Lawrence and Fitzroy Henry. 2002. Food Security and Health in the Caribbean: Imperatives for a New Policy. Paper presented at the Sir Arthur Lewis Institute of Social and Economic Studies (SALISES) and Mona School of Business Conference, University of the West Indies, Kingston, Jamaica, April 2–4.

Government continue to see the solution to the problem merely in terms of increasing agricultural output. In reviewing the impact and regional response to rising prices globally and the developments in energy and climate change and the implications for the region's food and nutrition security, the Heads of Government at their 29th Conference in July 2008, issued a communiqué that addressed the problem of food security and energy cost. The communiqué emphasized the need for governments to provide the necessary budgetary support and incentives for investment in agriculture.[50]

Furthermore, in keeping in line with the focus on increasing food production in the Caribbean there was a call on the FAO to assist Member Countries with seeds, fertilizer and other inputs to assist the farmers to carry out a rapid production of agricultural products. The call made at the World Food Summit in Rome, also championed the view that food production increases in the region is necessary to help to provide a cushion for small farmers. These farmers buy part of their food from markets with rising food prices. Increased food production would hopefully lead to a surplus that could be sold to increase their income and enhance the rural and urban populations access to food.[51]

This emphasis on increasing food production stems from the fact that food prices soared unprecedentedly by 52 percent between 2007 and 2008. This has had severe economic, social and political consequences in the poor countries. Also, higher prices for agricultural inputs have become a major obstacle to the efforts by the developing countries to increase their agricultural production.[52]

The United Nations World Food Program (WFP) response to the food crisis is to increase food aid through "a new four-year strategic plan to tackle soaring levels of hunger caused by the global food crisis." According to the WFP, its food aid "strategic plan marks a revolution in food aid that supports local markets in breaking the cycle of hunger."[53]

---

[50] Caribbean Community. 2008. Communiqué Issued at the Conclusion of the 29th Meeting of the Conference of Heads of Government of the Caribbean Community (Caricom). Bolans, Antigua and Barbuda, 1–4 July.

[51] Caribbean Press Release. 2008. St. Kitts and Nevis to Get Assistance From the FAO. Caribbean PressReleases.com, July 11.

[52] Caribbean Press Release. 2008. St. Kitts and Nevis to Get Assistance From the FAO. Caribbean PressReleases.com, July 11.

[53] Caribbean Press Release. 2008a. UN Food Agency Launches 4 Year Plan for Global Food Crisis. Caribbean PressReleases.com, June 13.

World leaders gathered in Rome at the WEP conference on World Food Security among other things to talk about hunger and agriculture development issues in the light of high global food and fuel prices. The tools they laid out in the plan to tackle the food crisis include early warning systems, vulnerability analysis, preparedness and disaster reduction and mitigation, and effective emergency response in life-saving situations. The plan also includes spending to strengthen smallholder farming, augment local transport and communication networks, reinforce school meals and buttress mother-and-child health and nutrition programs.[54]

The imperatives for new policies include a paradigm shift in agriculture and forging synergies in food and health. The view is that the new paradigm in agriculture must augment the existing production/sustainability orientation, and incorporate items related to diets, health and nutrition. The idea is to make health issues a substantive part of agricultural and other sectors, and not merely an appendage to them.[55] The starting point for finding new initiatives to forge synergies in food and health must be the recognition that each sector must find "common grounds in order to maximize mutual benefits." This requires policy coherence "directed at seeking synergies between policies of different sectors that support their common goals." To achieve this coherence it is suggested that there is need for "frequent dialogues, constructive engagement and coordinated action among policy makers from all sectors" to bring about "the right balance among the various objectives and goals of the sectors."[56]

There are major obstacles however to the development of agriculture in the Caribbean, which threaten, to prevent the region from achieving food security. These obstacles include inadequate financing and insufficient levels of new investments. The agricultural health and food safety systems (AHFS) in the region are inefficient and outdated, while agricultural research and development are inadequate. Land and

[54] Caribbean Press Release. 2008a. UN Food Agency Launches 4 Year Plan for Global Food Crisis. Caribbean PressReleases.com, June 13.

[55] Ballayram, Beverly Lawrence and Fitzroy Henry. 2002. Food Security and Health in the Caribbean: Imperatives for a New Policy. Paper presented at the Sir Arthur Lewis Institute of Social and Economic Studies (SALISES) and Mona School of Business Conference, University of the West Indies, Kingston, Jamaica, April 2–4.

[56] Ballayram, Beverly Lawrence and Fitzroy Henry. 2002. Food Security and Health in the Caribbean: Imperatives for a New Policy. Paper presented at the Sir Arthur Lewis Institute of Social and Economic Studies (SALISES) and Mona School of Business Conference, University of the West Indies, Kingston, Jamaica, April 2–4.

water distribution systems are pathetic, and risk management measures are deficient and uncoordinated. Besides the inadequacy of transportation for farmers, the weak and un-integrated information and intelligence systems compound the problem. Finally, marketing arrangements are deficient, and there is a lack of skilled and quality human resources in the agricultural sector.[57]

The Fuel Crisis and Petrocaribe

Undoubtedly, the rising fuel prices pose major challenges for GDP growth, stimulate inflation, and pressurize external balances. The higher prices are passed on to the consumers requiring policies to protect the poor and the most vulnerable sections of society. These policies nonetheless could take the radical option such as Petrocaribe, or the reformist positions that emanate from the global institutions. The neoliberal theorists do not identify their market liberalization and democratization policies as the real sources for the global fuel crisis. They blame the crisis on the increase in demand for fuel by China and India.

The Fuel Crisis

The increase in fuel prices peaked in early summer 2008, intensifying effects of higher prices on the balance of payments, budgets, and domestic prices. The high fuel prices caused a weakening of the balance of payments and stimulated inflation in a large group of low- and middle-income countries.[58] Not only did the low- and middle-income countries experienced these effects, the IMF asserted that high commodity price volatility cloud outlook and slow global growth that could increase vulnerabilities, globally.

In sub-Saharan Africa for example, the rising fuel prices pose major challenges for GDP growth, stimulate inflation, and pressurize external balances. The higher prices are passed on to the consumers requiring policies to protect the poor. The oil importing countries in Africa

[57] Pilgrim, Calrence E. 2008. Caribbean Food Security and US $3 Billion Imports. *Caribbean New News*, October 20.

[58] International Monetary Fund. 2008a. Food and Fuel Prices—Recent Developments, Macroeconomic Impact, and Policy Responses. Washington, DC., June 30.

for example experienced an average increase in the oil import bill of 2 percent of GDP due partly to corresponding increases in export prices for non-oil commodities.[59] The IMF (2008) estimates that the impact of higher oil prices on Sub-Saharan African countries will be a slowing down of the growth in their GDP by about 0.2–1 percent, and that the behavior of other non-oil commodity prices will also have an important effect on growth for countries in the region.[60]

Some scholars argue however that although fuel prices rose "to US140 per barrel" there were no "dire worldwide economic consequences" (Williams 2008). According to Williams (2008), "the global economy saw the price of a barrel of oil rise from just under US$25 at the start of this decade to almost US$100 as at the end of 2007, and in this same period developing countries registered the highest growth rates in decades."[61] It was pointed out that the growth rate in Latin America averaged at 6 per cent in the period 2002–2006, the highest for any five-year period since the 1970s. In the same period, Williams (2008) noted that growth in the Caribbean averaged around 5 per cent.[62]

Also, it is suggested that although there was a rapid increase in international oil prices and the US economy slowed down tourist arrivals continued to be strong, up 10 percent from the previous year in Barbados. Jamaica had a similar trend in tourism, while the expectation was that Trinidad and Tobago would continue to record robust growth due to its economic structure that depends heavily on energy. The projections for 2008, however, were only for modest slowdown in the rest of the region.[63]

The rise in fuel prices however stimulated increases in commodity prices leading a return to a "high inflation environment." The environment is reflected in the Caribbean where inflation has moved from an average of around 5 per cent in 2002–2006, to 6.8 per cent in 2007, and was expected to reach close to double digits in 2008. Inflation in the

[59] International Monetary Fund. 2008. Fifty Countries Still Hurt by Food, Fuel Crisis. *IMF Survey Magazine*, September 24.

[60] Mc Donald, Calvin and Drummond, Paulo. 2008. Africa Growing Rapidly, But Faces Risks. *IMF Survey Magazine*, February 28.

[61] Williams, Ewart S. 2008. The Impact of Global Events on the Caribbean Economies. Address, at the ICATT 26th Annual Caribbean Conference, June 27.

[62] Williams, Ewart S. 2008. The Impact of Global Events on the Caribbean Economies. Address, at the ICATT 26th Annual Caribbean Conference, June 27.

[63] Williams, Ewart S. 2008. The Impact of Global Events on the Caribbean Economies. Address, at the ICATT 26th Annual Caribbean Conference, June 27.

Caribbean is not distributed evenly among the countries. In Jamaica, for example "headline inflation for the 12-month period ended March 2008 was 20 per cent." In Trinidad and Tobago, the "latest data show headline inflation at 10 per cent," and in Barbados the projection was that inflation would rise to 9 per cent from 4 per cent in 2007. In the Eastern Caribbean Currency Union (ECCU) countries, inflation "hovered at around 2-3 percent" but "is now around 6.1 per cent."[64]

Petrocaribe to the Rescue

The Petrocaribe is an Energy Cooperation Agreement between Venezuela and Caribbean countries in which member states seek to fight against poverty, unemployment, and illiteracy while simultaneously addressing other matters such as inadequate medical services in their countries.[65] The Petrocaribe Energy Cooperation Agreement has the objectives to

> minimize the risk associated with the security of energy supply; defend the sovereign right of countries to administer the rate of development of renewable and non-renewable natural resources; minimize the costs of energy transactions among member countries; make proper use of energy resources to close the gap among member countries within the framework of regional integration; create mechanisms to guarantee that resources generated by energy bill savings, within the framework of Petrocaribe, are used for social and economic development, promotion of employment, and to increase production and services, public health, educational, cultural and sports activities.[66]

Under Petrocaribe for example, Jamaica will be supplied with 21,000 barrels a day of crude oil, and the financial arrangements will allow 40 percent of the purchase price of petroleum products to be provided as concessionary loans for 25 years. Interest will be charges at a rate of one percent per annum when prices equal US$50 a barrel. The loan amounts will be calculated on the basis of price prevailing at the date of purchase. Petrocaribe allows Caribbean countries to purchase up to 185,000 barrels of oil per day on financial terms that see only a few countries buying oil at market value but only a certain amount is

---

[64] Williams, Ewart S. 2008. The Impact of Global Events on the Caribbean Economies. Address, at the ICATT 26th Annual Caribbean Conference, June 27.

[65] Petrocaribe. 2005. Communiqué on Second Petrocaribe Summit. Montego Bay, Jamaica, September 6.

[66] Petrocaribe. 2005. Communiqué on Second Petrocaribe Summit. Montego Bay, Jamaica, September 6.

needed up front, while the remainder can be paid in 25 years at one percent interest. Petrocaribe also allows for countries to pay a part of the cost for the oil with other products provided to Venezuela such as bananas, rice, and sugar.

Through Petrocaribe, Venezuela is making its presence felt in the Caribbean in a very strong way much to the chagrin of the US. Petrocaribe has played a significant role in keeping oil prices relatively lower in the Caribbean. Indeed, since its implementation the price of fuel going into the region is comparatively low. In St Vincent for example, fuel going to the new plant in Lowmans Bay was up to $1.50 cheaper than that at Cane Hall and Bequia. But despite this the St. Vincent government instituted a surcharge on fuel and pointed out that "the fuel surcharge could have been as high as 67 cents, had it not been for" Petrocaribe.[67] The consumers of electricity in St. Vincent however have experienced increases in their electric bills due to the surcharge. In June 2008, the fuel surcharge increased from 55 cents per unit in April and May to 63 cents, due to increasing world oil prices. However, the St. Vincent government decided to institute a 6 cents subsidy for persons who consume 100 units and less each month.

Indeed, Petrocaribe is building an "anti-crisis, anti-hunger shield" among seventeen countries in Central America and the Caribbean.[68] Through Petrocaribe the seventeen countries "are to make down payments of only 40 percent on Venezuelan oil, while cooperating to expand their food supply, and calling on the North to take measures to curb speculation on futures markets, which is resulting in surging crude prices."[69] President Hugo Chávez of Venezuela noted at the Fifth Summit of the South-South alliance that, "Petrocaribe must become an anti-crisis shield to protect" the region "from hunger." The summit proposed to create "a bloc of the 57 poorest nations in the South who are net oil importers to lobby for a global cooperation agreement with oil producers, and to demand changes in the rules for futures markets."[70]

---

[67] Caribbean Press Release. 2008b. Fuel Surcharge Increase Expected in St Vincent Soon. Caribbean PressReleases.com, June 29.

[68] Márquez, Humberto. 2008. Petrocaribe Building 'Anti-Crisis, Anti-Hunger Shield'. Inter-Press Service July 14.

[69] Márquez, Humberto. 2008. Petrocaribe Building 'Anti-Crisis, Anti-Hunger Shield'. Inter-Press Service July 14.

[70] Márquez, Humberto. 2008. Petrocaribe Building 'Anti-Crisis, Anti-Hunger Shield'. Inter-Press Service July 14.

In addition, it proposed that, "Petrocaribe address the issue of fertilizers, which have tripled in price in the last three years, threatening food production on Caribbean islands." Fertilizers "cost an average of 268 dollars a tonne in 2005, 405 dollars in 2007, 875 in 2008, and is being quoted at 998 dollars a tonne for 2009." Caribbean farmers cannot produce at those prices and if they do the prices for domestic produce will be higher than that for imported food, increasing the region's food dependency. The summit created a new structure – the Council of Agriculture Ministers to address the food crisis and agriculture, similarly to that of the Energy Ministers, which addresses energy matters.

The beneficiaries of Petrocaribe are Antigua and Barbuda, Bahamas, Belize, Cuba, Dominica, Dominican Republic, Grenada, Guatemala, Guyana, Haiti, Honduras, Jamaica, Nicaragua, St. Kitts and Nevis, St. Vincent and the Grenadines, and Suriname. Costa Rica was present as an observer at the summit in 2008.[71] Costa Rican President Oscar Arias, "came to Petrocaribe after his country spent 838 million dollars on oil imports between January and April" 2008, "an amount 88 percent higher than for the same period in 2007." President Álvaro Colom of Guatemala, which became a full member of Petrocaribe at the summit, "announced that his country would produce food for export to Venezuela, which imports more than 60 percent of its food." In the first quarter of 2008, "Guatemala paid 749 million dollars for fuel, 63 percent more than it spent in the same quarter of 2007."

According to Venezuelan Energy Minister Rafael Ramírez, "Under the Petrocaribe agreement, Venezuela has been sending 92,000 barrels per day (bpd) to Cuba and has made available up to 135,000 bpd for the other countries, although the effective demand has been 86,000 bpd."[72] Márquez (2008) points out that "In three years, Venezuela has supplied 59 million barrels of crude to its Petrocaribe partners, for which they paid 50 percent of its value within 90 days and the rest on credit over 25 years, with a two-year grace period and an interest rate of one percent a year, saving them 921 million dollars."[73] Márquez (2008) noted, "Venezuela is also developing joint venture companies to provide infrastructure for storage and distribution costing 550 million

[71] Márquez, Humberto. 2008. Petrocaribe Building 'Anti-Crisis, Anti-Hunger Shield'. Inter-Press Service July 14.

[72] Márquez, Humberto. 2008. Petrocaribe Building 'Anti-Crisis, Anti-Hunger Shield'. Inter-Press Service July 14.

[73] Márquez, Humberto. 2008. Petrocaribe Building 'Anti-Crisis, Anti-Hunger Shield'. Inter-Press Service July 14.

dollars, and has invested another 100 million dollars for social purposes in these countries."[74]

According to Márquez (2008) "Beneficiaries will be paying only 40 percent of their oil bill within 90 days, with the rest on the same terms as before. Chávez announced that if the price of oil reaches 200 dollars a barrel, only 30 percent would have to be paid in 90 days." Furthermore, President Chávez encouraged the Central American and Caribbean countries to make their down payments for oil "with cattle, beans or tourism services." Also, "Venezuela, which produces two million tonnes of urea a year, offered to sell 100,000 tonnes a year to its Petrocaribe partners at a 40 percent discount, half to be paid on receipt of the product and half when the crop is harvested."

According to Márquez (2008) "The outcome document of the Fifth Petrocaribe Summit urges the regulatory authorities of the futures markets in the New York and London stock markets to take the necessary measures to eliminate speculation as a factor in the international prices of oil and other commodities." In addition, "Venezuela, for its part, made a commitment, to set aside 50 cents of each dollar for every barrel of oil exported outside Petrocaribe at a price over 100 dollars, in order to create a sub-regional fund for food security initiatives." It is expected that such a fund would accumulate around one million dollars a day.

The advent of the global financial and economic crises has led to calls to adjust the Petrocaribe agreement to meet the new conditions.[75] Also, there have been reports that due to the crises Venezuela would alter Petrocaribe to allow members to pay up front for oil. The Venezuelan government nonetheless said that it had no plans to do so.

---

[74] Márquez, Humberto. 2008. Petrocaribe Building 'Anti-Crisis, Anti-Hunger Shield'. Inter-Press Service July 14.

[75] Caribbean360.com. 2009. Call for "tweaking" of Petrocaribe Deal. Caribbean360.com. June 15.

CHAPTER ELEVEN

THE GLOBAL FINANCIAL AND ECONOMIC CRISES AND THE EU-EPAS

Introduction

The European Union-Economic Partnership Agreements (EU-EPAs) with the Africa, Caribbean and Pacific (ACP) regions have generated considerable debate on their merits and demerits. This chapter focuses on the point of intersection of the EU-EPAs and the global financial and economic crises with the aim to provide a better understanding of the magnitude of the problem facing the ACP regions entering into EPAs with EU bloc imperialism. In the light of the current global financial and economic crises, the debate on the EU-EPAs must be expanded to consider how the crises will impact on these trade arrangements and the implications of this for the ACP-EPA regions. This chapter is intended as a contribution towards that debate.

It outlines some basic propositions concerning the EPAs in the light of the current global financial and economic crises. It identifies the problematic concerning the contradiction whereby the EU and the powerful capitalist states that comprise it engage in state protectionist and government interventionist measures to correct the global financial and economic crises while at the same time forcing the ACP regions characterized by poor countries to enter into "free market" economic partnership agreements, which restrict them from pursuing state interventionist and protectionist measures. It argues that the global financial and economic crises symbolize the failures of the neoliberal free market system. Evidence is provided of the rapid spread of the financial and economic crises in Europe and the state interventionist solutions by the European states. The crises are discussed in terms of the layoffs of hundreds of thousands of workers and social unrest, and the neoliberal about turn evidenced by the state-led policy recommendations of the G-20 and IMF.

State Protection for the Powerful, Free Market for the Poor

This section presents some basic and pertinent propositions to the global financial and economic crises. The EPA is the current means by which the EU intends to continue to accumulate wealth at the expense of the ACP countries but the current global financial and economic crises will constrain the EU's ability to aggressively pursue its EPA commitments. The crises will also limit the ACP regions in the pursuit of their EPA commitments, and deplete wealth in both the ACP countries and the EU creating an even greater urge for wealth accumulation. Because of its financial, political and economic leverage over the ACP countries however the EU will gain more from the necessary adjustments to alleviate the crises. While the EU is experiencing problems associated with the crises and showing signs of disunity, judging from the different positions taken by the leading European political leaders on how to fix the problem, the ACP states could use the situation as an opportunity to realign themselves with the emerging economies, and work themselves out of the EPA trap.

The financial crisis has disrupted the EU's economy more so than it has that of the CARIFORUM countries. The CARIFORUM states need to be emboldened to challenge the EU to discontinue the CARIFORUM-EU EPA in the light of the failure of free market fundamentalism reflected in the crash in the global financial system and the current economic crisis now gripping the EU and the rest of the globe. The CARIFORUM states need to maximize their benefits from the crises and take measures to insulate themselves, with the anticipation that because of their close ties to the US and EU economies the crises would eventually spread to them. The CARIFORUM states must not only seek to realign themselves with the emerging economies, the latter need to step-up their activities to help to bring about a permanent transformation of economic and political power globally in which the ACP states could break-out from the stranglehold of EU bloc imperialism, and US imperialism disguised as globalization. The ACP states need to deepen trade relations with Russia, China, India, Brazil, South Africa, and within regional unions such as the Bolivarian Alternative for Latin America and Petrocaribe. The first BRIC (Brazil, Russia, India and China) summit in Yekaterinburg, Russia in June 2009[1] seems to be

[1] Faulconbridge, Guy. 2009. Developing World Leaders Show New Power at Summits. *Reuters*, June 16; Filger, Sheldon. 2009. BRIC Summit Sees End of Dominance of U.S. Dollar. *The Huffington Post*, June 16.

a step in that direction. These are concrete ways to bring about a permanent realignment and dispensation of global political and economic power.

The EU would like to aggressively re-colonize the ACP countries through the EPAs under the pretext of sustainable development and good governance as a means of transferring more wealth into its coffers. The financial crisis and its accompanying economic downturn however have placed constraints on the EU that would negatively affect it in its bid to re-colonize the ACP states. The global financial crisis has to be understood in terms of its impact on both the EU and the ACP countries, and the ways in which it will force alterations in the strategies of EU bloc imperialism to re-colonize the ACP regions through the EPAs, and working people resistance to the EPAs. The crises are therefore causing the EU to lose wealth from the economic collapse, and the non-implementation of the EPAs. Furthermore, the fact that the ACP regions will definitely be emboldened due to the crises to resist the EPAs will not be of much help to the EU. The effects of this could be prolonged crises in the EU that weakens EU bloc imperialism and strengthens the hands of the ACP regions. The EU is currently caught in a situation where it is fighting to preserve the life of the capitalist system through massive government interventions and state regulation of its economy. However, the EU-EPAs are founded on the theoretical foundation that the ACP states must deregulate their economies.

The problem is that the promoters of neoliberal globalization have acknowledged that the current global financial and economic crises are the evidence that their market capitalist model has failed, and they now openly advocate state regulations as the only solution to the crises, but the EU-ACP EPAs are founded on the very failed model. This contradiction between the EPA and the policy prescriptions to solve the global financial and economic crises is not under consideration in EU or in the ACP states. There is no attempt to understand how this contradictory situation will impact on the socio-economic wellbeing of working people in the ACP-EPA regions.

The daunting task is to assess the EU bloc imperialist economic partnership agreements with the ACP countries in the context of the global financial crisis. The units of analyses therefore are the underlying class forces associated with EU bloc imperialism, economic partnership agreements, the global financial crisis and the ACP countries. Undoubtedly, EU bloc imperialism is a class project manifested through the EU's economic partnership agreements with the ACP regions. It is the mechanism through which the EU will re-colonize the ACP states. Within the ACP regions there are domestic class forces that in collaboration with EU bloc imperialism support the economic partnership agreements and those that oppose the EPAs. The class nature of the global financial crisis is clear in terms of the Wall Street billionaires and the US ruling elites in their control who created the crises, working and middle class people who are most affected by the crises in terms of job-layoffs etc., and the financial bailout of the banks the chief culprits in the crises.[2]

In this situation, the goal of the ACP countries must be to secure their independent socio-economic development with the help of the rich states, but depending on their own strengths and acumen and not on handouts or aid. What is the impact of the financial crisis on the EU? In what ways will the financial crisis force the EU and the ACP regions to alter their economic outlooks and how would this affect their relationships in the economic partnership agreements? In the light of the financial crisis what is the nature of the class struggle against the EPAs and the policy prescriptions advocated by the rich countries?

The EU is a state-driven entity designed to bring the greatest support to EU multinational corporations and businesses. The financial crisis is forcing the EU to resort to even greater state interventions to correct its current economic and financial problems both at the levels of the EU and the individual states that comprise that bloc. The financial crisis teaches us that the EU may be a powerful imperialist bloc, but in times of economic crisis individual countries resort to economic nationalism to protect their national interest, while undermining the collective imperialist interests of Europe as a bloc.

The EPAs call on the ACP countries to do exactly the opposite to what the EU is doing (state intervention) to maintain and improve the living standards of citizens of the EU. The EPAs want the ACP countries to downplay the role of their states in the trade arrangements with the EU, and allow free market forces to take over. The EU, and the international financial institutions such as the IMF and World Bank all recommend government intervention, to halt the economic decline.

---

[2] For an excellent discussion on the class dimensions of the crises see Petras, James. 2009. *Global Depression and Regional Wars.* Atlanta, Ga.: Clarity Press.

This contradiction, should force ACP countries to walk-away from the EPAs, in recognition of the decisive role of the state in the capitalist development process.[3]

Since the global financial crisis came to the fore in earnest from around mid-2007, there have been many serious developments that have shaken the capitalist system to its core. The world stock markets are in turmoil declining steeply, several large financial institutions have buckled or were taken over, and in the rich capitalist countries rescue packages were implemented to bail out their financial systems. Several leading capitalist investors and academics have even reasoned that the current economic upheaval signals the end of a free-market model ushered in by the financial deregulations of the 1980s that has since dominated the capitalist countries.[4] Financial deregulation that began with the Regan administration in the 1980s has produced a series of crises that forced governments to intervene to rectify the situation. While the regulators have abrogated their responsibilities, free-market fundamentalism has proved to be a miserable failure.

Financial Crisis Detonates

The current global financial crisis epitomizes the collapse of neoliberal free market policies that took hold of the global economy since the 1970s. The deregulation of financial markets paved the way for fraud and plunder of unsuspecting victims by market sharks. The US banks classified loans as prime and subprime according to the borrowers'

[3] See for example Kategekwa, Joy. 2008. The Financial Crisis: Lessons for the EPA Trade Negotiations. *South Bulletin: Reflections and Foresights* 25, October 16; Amin, Samir. 2008. Financial Collapse, Systemic Crisis? Illusory Answers and Necessary Answers. Paper introducing the World Forum of Alternatives, in Caracas, October; Tandon, Yash. 2008. Collapse of an Ideology. *Development and Cooperation* (49) 11: 430–4; Hudson, Michael and Jeffrey Sommers. 2008. The End of the Washington Consensus. *Counterpunch*, December 12/14; Wade, Robert. 2008. Financial Regime Change? *New Left Review* 53: 5–21; Khor, Martin. 2008a. Financial Crisis Calls into Question GATS Finance Negotiations. *South-North Development Monitor* 6556, September 26; Chang, Ha-Joon. 2008a. The Economics of Hypocrisy: After Implementing the Largest Government Bail-out in History, the US Continues to tell other Nations, 'do as I say, not as I do,'" Guardian.co.uk, October 20; Khor, Martin. 2008b. Double Standard in the West's Crisis Policies. *South-North Development Monitor* 65.

[4] el-Gabry, Walid. 2009. Soros Says Economic Crisis Signals End of a Free-Market Model. Bloomberg.com, February 23.

credit, with the interest rate of subprime mortgages being higher than that of prime mortgages, since the former has a much higher rate of default. The US banks pooled the high-risk subprime mortgages with low-risk ones in what they call Collateralized Bond Obligation (CBO) thereby reclassifying the high-risk mortgages as low-risk ones, giving them a higher rating and then selling them to unsuspecting victims, knowing full well that the CBOs were not worth their stated value. While the CBOs represent different levels of credit risk, the Collateralized Mortgage Obligation (CMO) is similar to the CBO but different in that it collects together different levels of maturities. The CMO is a mortgage-backed security that creates separate pools of pass-through rates for different classes of bondholders with varying maturities, called tranches.

For many years, the US Federal Reserve Bank pursued an expansionary currency policy as a means of staving off a recession in the US.[5] The cheap money due to low Federal Reserve interest rates fuelled indebtedness, low saving, encouraging Americans to borrow to consume excessively. The Federal Reserve Bank lowered its interest rates 13 consecutive times from 6.5 percent to a historic low of 1 percent, between January 2001 and June 2003. These policies combined to encourage excessive borrowing and investment in housing, referred to as the housing bubble. The optimistic estimations of a continuous rise in housing prices encouraged banks, eager to earn higher interest, to extend housing credit to more consumers with very low credit. The subprime mortgage market developed rapidly under these conditions causing the housing bubble to expand (Hongjiang 2009).

The US housing bubble began to burst in 2006, and within two years the Federal Reserve Bank increased its interest rate 17 times, from 1 percent to 5.25 percent, placing great pressure on borrowers (Hongjiang 2009). The housing market began to cool down from the second quarter of 2006, with prices starting to fall in many parts of the US. Borrowers began to find it difficult to sell their houses or to refinance through mortgages. The result was that large numbers of subprime mortgage clients were unable to repay their loans in time and foreclosures accelerated in the US in late 2006, triggering a global financial crisis through 2007 and 2008 (Hongjiang 2009).

---

[5] Hongjiang, Wang. 2009. "Backgrounder: Subprime Mortgage Crisis," www.chinaview.cn, November 15.

The second largest subprime mortgage lender in the US, New Century Financial Corporation, filed petitions for bankruptcy protection on April 2, 2007. Several other financial institutions providing subprime credit were also facing financial difficulties. The subprime mortgage crisis emerged, leading to violent turbulence in the US stock market. In addition, several lending institutions began to transform substantial amounts of "subprime mortgage credit to securities and sold them to investment institutions," which promptly "developed the securities into various derivatives and sold them to hedge funds or insurance companies" (Hongjiang 2009).

The National Bureau of Economic Research reported that "US subprime mortgages had reached 1.5 trillion dollars and some 2 trillion securities were issued on the basis of the mortgage, leading to over 1 trillion Collateralized Debt Obligation (CBO) and billions of dollars of credit default swaps" (Hongjiang 2009). The problem nonetheless, is that "in the so-called innovation of financial products, the US government has failed to strengthen supervision and financial operations increasingly lack transparency" (Hongjiang 2009). Due to the size and interconnectedness of its economy with the rest of the world, "The subprime mortgage crisis in the United States finally became a financial crisis affecting the whole world, posing great danger to the global economy" (Hongjiang 2009).

Europe in Crisis the State to the Rescue

The financial and economic crises spread rapidly in the 27-member EU forcing the European leaders to take major state interventionist corrective actions, between September and December 2008. In Britain for example, the government announced plans in September 2008, to nationalize mortgage lender Bradford & Bingley Plc. Banking. British Prime Minister Gordon Brown claimed that the IFIs needed some $500 billion and called for the adoption of a "global New Deal" to save the world economy.[6]

In October the British government announced a 50-billion-pound bailout scheme for the financial system to help its biggest retail banks survive. Subsequently it publicized plans to invest up to 37 billion

[6] McGroarty, Patrick. 2009. European Leaders Back Sweeping Financial Regulations. *Huffington Post*, February 22.

pounds in three British banks – Royal Bank of Scotland, HBOS (Halifax Bank of Scotland), and Lloyds TSB (Trustee Savings Bank). Then in November, the Bank of England announced it would slash its interest rate by 1.5 percentage points to 3 percent, following pressure from industry for a major cut in the face of a looming recession. Britain's Chancellor Alistair Darling also unveiled a series of measures, including a VAT cut from 17.5 percent to 15 percent for 13 months in his pre-budget report, to boost the ailing British economy.

The governments of Belgium, the Netherlands and Luxembourg agreed to invest a total of 11.2 billion euros (about 14.48 billion U.S. dollars) in Dutch-Belgian banking and insurance group Fortis in return for a minority stake in the group. The Dutch government also announced it bought all the Dutch operations of Fortis for16.8 billion euros. The Netherlands government also agreed to provide state guarantee to inter-bank loans of up to 200 billion euros in a bid to increase market liquidity by restarting capital flows among banks. Also, Belgium, France and Luxembourg provided nearly 6.4 billion euros to save Franco-Belgian bank Dexia, another victim of the global credit crunch in Europe. These governments also took measures to guarantee all new borrowings and bond financings of the troubled lender Dexia until November 2009.

The EC President Jose Manuel Barroso called on EU member-states to have a joint response to the financial crisis. The European leaders from the eurozone countries at their summit in Paris came up with a joint action plan to fight the financial crisis. French President Nicolas Sarkozy urged EU countries to set up their sovereign wealth funds to buy stakes of troubled banks falling prey to the financial crisis. In November, a special EU summit coordinated the bloc's positions ahead of the G-20 summit on financial crisis scheduled for Washington on November 15. The European Commission unveiled a significant economic stimulus package worth 200 billion euros in a bid to steer the EU economy from a deep recession.

The EU took measures to take care of its own by raising the ceiling for assistance to each member state in financial difficulty from the current 12 billion euros to 25 billion euros. Also, the European Central Bank lowered its benchmark rate by 0.75 percent in order to revitalize the slumping European economy. Furthermore, Gordon Brown, Nicolas Sarkozy and Jose Manuel Barroso met in London, and called for more cooperation among EU leaders to respond to the economic crisis.

The German government took the political steps to restore public confidence in the banking system. It pledged to guarantee private deposits, to inject 70 billion euros into the banking system as a part of a rescue package for the financial sector worth up to 500 billion euros. The Irish parliamentarians voted to enact radical legislation guaranteeing Irish bank deposits and debts up to a total of 400 billion euros. The governments of the four biggest EU economies – Germany, Britain, France and Italy – vowed to work in a coordinated way in tackling the financial crisis, as Nicolas Sarkozy and German Chancellor Angela Merkel called for joint actions from Europe or even the world to fight the financial crisis. The Norwegian government and the country's central bank announced that they would issue up to 350 billion kroner in new government bonds which can be used as collateral in Norwegian banks' funding operations, to boost confidence in the financial market in the country.

The EU leaders reached agreement on several proposals for presentation to US President Obama in April 2009. The agreement called for doubling the resources of the IMF to $500 billon and for an "international early-warning system and a boost in bank-capital requirements to create a cushion that increases in good times and that banks can access in bad spells ."[7] These proposals are in possible anticipation that not only additional cash would come from China, which "has almost $2 trillion in foreign-exchange reserves," but that in exchange, "China will rightly demand increased voting rights at the IMF that would come at the expense of Europe's quota (Sesit 2009). The Europeans also proposed to "regulate hedge funds," and wanted *inter alia* to put a halt to "tax havens" by creating a new system that would place "sanctions" on "uncooperative jurisdictions" (Sesit 2009).

Also, the EC approved emergency efforts by the Latvian government to facilitate financing for the JSC Parex Bank. The Commission also approved an Austrian financial bailout plan of billions of euros in guarantees, capital injections and loans to banks (1 U.S. dollar = 0.77369 euro).

As the EU put in place measures to prop up the banks and big businesses working people were being laid-off and being told to wait until an economic turn-around before they could get a piece of the pie.

---

[7] Sesit, Michael R. 2009. Fighting Global Crisis Isn't Meant to Be Easy. Bloomberg .com, March 2.

Worker-Layoffs and Social Unrest

The layoffs of hundreds of thousands of workers in major corporations around the world and social unrest are also important indicators of the global financial and economic crises. The EPAs have also generated mass protests in Africa and other regions.[8] Undoubtedly, working and middle-class people, farmers, small-businesses and the poor in general are severely affected by the current crises. Between November 20, 2008 and February 11, 2009 there were reports of job cuts of thousands of workers by leading corporations in different industries and countries around the world. For example, the British Rolls Royce Company announced it would cut 2,000 jobs, while South Korea promised to trim its public sector, the Indian IT sector planned to eliminate 50,000 jobs, the British financial sector 15,000, and companies in Indonesia's electronics and manufacturing sectors planned to layoff 40,000 by the end of 2008. Also, Credit Suisse, Switzerland's second largest bank announced plans to layoff 5,300 workers, Sweden's Volvo automakers 3,400, France's fashion company Chanel 200, and French second biggest auto parts maker Valero 5,000, and Japan's Sony 8,000.[9]

Sweden's wireless equipment maker Ericsson announced it would cut 5,000 jobs, Warner Brothers entrainment giant 800, following layoffs at other media companies General Electric's NBC Universal and Viacom, owner of Paramount that already had job cuts. Caterpillar in the US announced it would eliminate 20,000 jobs, and Intel Corp., the world's biggest chipmaker 6,000, closing text facilities in Malaysia and Philippines, its water fabrication facility in Oregon, and some operations in Santa Clara, California. Also, the German company SAP the world's leader in professional software announced it planned to layoff 3,000 workers, Starbucks coffee retailer 6,700 at 300 stores, Japan's Panasonic electronics 15,000, and Wal-Mart between 700–800 at its northeastern Arkansas headquarters. The Detroit based General Motors indicated that it too would eliminate 10,000 jobs worldwide (China View Factbox 2009).

The crises sparked social unrest that caused much disruption across many countries in Europe.[10] For example, thousands of Greeks were

[8] Schnatterer, Tinette. 2008. Mass Protests against Economic Partnership Agreement with EU. www.socialistworld.net, 6 February.

[9] China View Factbox. 2009. Global Job Cuts, www.chinaview.cn, accessed March.

[10] The data on the social unrest in Europe were taken from Cutler, David. 2009. Financial Crisis Sparks Unrest in Europe. *Reuters*, April 2.

involved in a nationwide strike on April 1, 2009. The Greek workers were aggrieved over low salaries and job cuts. Public and private unions that represent about half of Greece's 5 million workforce called the one-day-strike that disrupted the transport system and closed down services in the country. Unions in Greece argued that the measures to alleviate the financial crisis place a heavier share of the burden on the poor. The social unrest in the context of the global crises coincided with the worst riots in Greece in decades after the police fatally shot a fifteen-year old in December 2008. The riots were stimulated by the economic hardships and youth unemployment in Greece.

An estimated 35,000 protesters including trade unions, aid agencies, religious groups and environmentalists participated in a march in London on March 28 under the slogan "Put People First" to demand world economic reform. During a day of protest against the G-20 meeting in London, police clashed with approximately 4,000 demonstrators in front of the Bank of England. Also, British workers at power plants protested against the employment of foreign contractors at critical energy cites. The British workers only ended their strikes after French oil group Total agreed to hire more British workers at its Lindsey oil refinery.

The demands by farmers in the Czech Republic, Germany, Austria, Slovakia, Slovenia and Poland for higher milk prices, and subsidies to boost their declining incomes due to the economic crisis, led thousands of them to march through the streets of Prague on March 12. Also, France had its share of protests when approximately 3 million demonstrators marched through its streets in a second wave of strikes on March 19 in opposition the manner in which the Sarkozy administration handled the economic crisis. Protesters in Paris demonstrated under the slogan "We will not pay for their crisis."

The French government also had to deal that a six-week general strike that crippled its Caribbean island of Guadeloupe. The Guadeloupian strikers demanded an increase in their wages to cope with the high prices that resulted from the fuel and food crises. The French police murdered one of the strike leaders, and people burnt and looted shops in retaliation. The Guadeloupian unions and the French government signed a deal on March 5 to end the strike. Then, in Reunion, the Indian Ocean territory of France, thousands of workers took to the streets on March 5 and 10 in a campaign of strikes and protests to push for wage increases.

In Berlin, approximately 15,000 workers took to the streets in protest against the financial crisis. Some of the protesters who were clad in black threw rocks and bottles at police who made several arrests during the demonstration. Then about 14,000 of the protesters assembled in the German financial capital, Frankfurt. Also, there was a rally by about 15,000 Opel workers from Germany at the company's headquarters to demand that General Motors, the parent company of Opel, drops its plans to close plants in Europe.

Ireland was hit by protests by taxi drivers and airport workers over their job prospects. This was an escalation of protest activities when nearly 100,000 people marched through the streets of Dublin in protest against government cutbacks. Primarily arms industry workers in Poland joined in a 10,000 worker-strong demonstration against layoffs after the Polish government announced its cuts in the defense budget. Also, the power producer Energa in Gdansk, Poland faced a protest by 3,000 workers who opposed the company's job cut plans.

The socialist government of Portugal also faced street demonstrations when thousands of protestors marched through the streets of Lisbon on March 13. The unions argued that the policies of the government at a time of crises increase unemployment and favor the rich. Also, a small group of demonstrators numbering about 1,000 in a peaceful march in Vladivostok on March 15 called on the Russian government to resign. Approximately 800,000 Russian workers lost their jobs between December and January, which increased the unemployment level in Russia to over 6 million people, or 8.1 percent of the workforce. Sixteen steelworkers at ESTAR's Zlatoust went on a hunger strike over the economic hardship faced by workers. They ended the strike on March 14 only after the management had agreed to some of their demands.

The Efficient State and Inefficient Market: A False Debate

The theoretical debate on the state versus the market serves as a major distraction from the real issue of finding alternatives to capitalism. The debate is so intense that many scholars on the left end up taking the side of the state overlooking the need for replacement of the capitalist state. There seems to be amnesia on the part of some of these scholars concerning Marx's theory about the smashing of the capitalist state, and about Lenin's ideas about the socialist state. The neoliberal onslaught on state-led development strategies has pushed these scholars to settle on countering neoliberalism by merely defending the state, the very mechanism for class control and oppression.

Thus, the view about overthrowing the capitalist state is hardly visible in the current literature. Instead there is comparison between the state-developmental approaches and the neoliberal free market approach to establish empirically that in the poor countries the former brought more economic prosperity than the latter. The dilemma faced by these scholars is that they do not theorize about the overthrow of the capitalist state, but rather hanker after it due to the so-called prosperity it has brought to poor countries in the "golden age of capitalism" in the post-World War II period up until around the late 1960s, early 1970s. Neoliberalism has not only had debilitating economic effects on the poor countries, it has also destabilized the debate on finding alternatives to the capitalist state. Neoliberalism has shifted the debate from exploration of ideas about how to overthrow the capitalist state, to finding reformist means to restore the developmental capitalist state dismantled by the neoliberal policy.

Now, these left scholars and the neoliberals are on the same side in a particular sense. Having argued for decades that the state was inefficient and that the market was the most efficient allocator of resources the neoliberal theorist now regard the state as the only agency that could resolve the global financial and economic crises. The neoliberals whose only solution to the global financial and economic crises is state-intervention now join the left scholars, who promote the state as the more efficient allocator of resources than the market in opposition to neoliberal free market fundamentalism.

This shameless about turn by the neoliberals nonetheless, regardless of whether it considers the state as only temporally the most efficient allocator of resources in times of crises, should not cloud the true class nature of the crises. The state is an instrument of the ruling class in the direct control of the rich and powerful. The laws it makes are to protect the private property of the rich and to subjugate working people to the social relations of the capitalist labor process. This fact must not be overlooked in the critical analysis of the global financial and economic crises and the state-led solutions advocated by the ruling classes in the capitalist societies.

The state-led solutions advanced by the G-20 and IMF must be understood in the context of the state as an instrument of the ruling class. State-led solution to economic crises in a working class state is different to a situation of state-led solutions to economic crises in a capitalist society where the state is in the control of the capitalists. The difference is that the former favors working people, while the latter strengthens capitalist class rule. Thus, rather than merely applauding the neoliberal about turn and engaging in left triumphalism, which is meaningless so long as the state remains in the control of the capitalist, consorted efforts must be made to use the current crises in global capitalism to further the establishment of working class states. Left triumphalism is no better than right triumphalism such as was experienced after the collapse of the former Soviet Union, and which Francis Fukuyama's "The End of History and the Last Man" is probably the most notorious embodiment.[11] The capitalist state cannot solve the problems of working class people.

Another myth to dispel is the impression given by Left triumphalism that the espousal of state-led solutions by the neoliberals is a turn to the left. This causes confusion and leads to the incorrect celebration of the proposed so-called state-interventionist solution to the global financial and economic crises, as a turn to left strategies. But, while the proponents of neoliberalism argue that their approach is based on the free market that reduces the role of the state in the economic affairs of countries, their critics have long-observed that the neoliberal model is based on the state because it is the state that has all of the responsibility to formulate and implement market liberalization. Thus, the state-led solution to the current global financial and economic crises should not be heralded as a swing from free market fundamentalism to state-interventionism meaning a turn from the right to the left. The free market fundamentalist approach was always based on state-interventionist measures to guarantee the "free" operations of the market.

The G-20 and IMF State Interventionist Prescriptions

The G-20 summit in November 2009 on financial markets and the global economy agreed to an action plan of immediate and medium-term measures to cope with the financial and economic woes now gripping both developed and developing world. It emphasized strong and significant actions to stimulate national economies, "provide liquidity, strengthen the capital of financial institutions, protect savings and deposits, address regulatory deficiencies, unfreeze credit markets," and ensuring "that international financial institutions (IFIs) can provide

[11] Fukuyama, Francis. 1993. *The End of History and the Last Man*. New York: Harper.

critical support for the global economy."[12] The G-20 leaders urged more actions "to stabilize financial markets and support economic growth," in the light of the substantially slowing economic momentum in major economies, weakened global outlook, and the increasing adverse impact of the financial crisis on the emerging market economies that have helped to sustain the world economy this decade, although these economies are still experiencing good growth.

The G-20 agreed that against the background of deteriorating economic conditions worldwide, "a broader policy response is needed, based on closer macroeconomic cooperation, to restore growth, avoid negative spillovers and support emerging market economies and developing countries." The immediate steps recommended to achieve these objectives and to address longer-term challenges aim to

> continue the vigorous efforts and take whatever further actions are necessary to stabilize the financial system; recognize the importance of monetary policy support, as deemed appropriate to domestic conditions; use fiscal measures to stimulate domestic demand to rapid effect, as appropriate, while maintaining a policy framework conducive to fiscal sustainability; help emerging and developing economies gain access to finance in current difficult financial conditions, including through liquidity facilities and program support; encourage the World Bank and other multilateral development banks (MDBs) to use their full capacity in support of their development agenda, and [embrace] the recent introduction of new facilities by the World Bank in the areas of infrastructure and trade finance; ensure that the IMF, World Bank and other MDBs have sufficient resources to continue playing their role in overcoming the crisis.[13]

The G-20 stressed the importance for the IMF's crisis response, welcomed its new short-term liquidity facility, and urge the ongoing review of its instruments and facilities to ensure flexibility.

The agreed common principles for reform of financial markets include the strengthening of "financial markets and regulatory regimes so as to avoid future crises," with "national regulators who constitute the first line of defense against market instability" having the first and foremost responsibility for regulation. The G-20 believe that due to the global scope of financial markets "intensified international cooperation among regulators and strengthening of international standards,

[12] G-20 Summit Communiques. 2008. November 16.

[13] G-20 Summit Communiques. 2008. November 16.

where necessary, and their consistent implementation is necessary to protect against adverse cross-border, regional and global developments affecting international financial stability." Another common principle for reform of financial markets proposed by the G-20 is that "Regulators must ensure that their actions support market discipline, avoid potentially adverse impacts on other countries, including regulatory arbitrage, and support competition, dynamism and innovation in the marketplace." Finally, the G-20 believe that "Financial institutions must also bear their responsibility for the turmoil and should do their part to overcome it including by recognizing losses, improving disclosure and strengthening their governance and risk management practices."

The IMF recommended four lines of action to tackle the global financial crisis based on international cooperation.[14] The first recommendation is for there to be a temporary government guarantee of liabilities due to the fragile public confidence in the financial system. The view is that the government should guarantee retail bank deposits as well as interbank and money market deposits to stimulate activity in them. The second line of action recommended by the IMF is that of the recognition of losses. The view is that the government needs to purchase troubled assets and force the recognition of losses. The third recommendation is for the government to provide capital because of the scarcity of private money. The IMF believes that there should be a matching of new private capital subscriptions with government capital. The fourth recommendation is for the promotion of a cooperation approach. In the view of the IMF a high degree of international cooperation is urgent since the collapse in confidence in the markets has been matched by a collapse in confidence between countries, which is forcing countries to take unilateral actions in their national interests.

Civil society organizations have also put forward their views on the issue in their background document to the UN development conference on the world financial and economic crisis and its impact on development. The call was made for a more long-term inclusive process to fundamentally transform the economic and financial system, and "to make social and gender justice and the fulfillment of human and environmental rights the key objectives of all crisis-related measures."[15]

[14] International Monetary Fund. 2008b. IMF Presses Four-Step Plan to Halt Financial Spiral. *IMF Survey Magazine* October 10.

[15] International Trade Union Confederation. 2009. Civil Society Background Document to UN Development Conference. New York: ITUC.

It called for a global stimulus plan for all countries "to stimulate their economies in a sustainable manner, and implement counter-cyclical policies, without, however, reverting to the same export-led growth model based on unsustainable over-production and over-consumption" (ITUC 2009).

The first set of recommendations by civil society for the UN conference has to do with international stimulus packages for development. The view is that the stimulus packages in the rich countries must not distort the economic playing field or create a new form of financial protectionism. In this connection, the rich countries should help to finance rescue packages in the poor countries as proposed by the Stiglitz Commission. The rich countries must provide this support in addition to existing aid commitments. The poor countries must benefit through special grant arrangements and ODA and not through debt-creating loans. The rich countries must deliver on their aid promises, which should become legally binding. The developed countries should not renege on their G-8 promise to increase aid to by US$50bn, half of which would go to Africa, by 2010.

It is estimated that a compensatory and development financing plan in the tune of $1 trillion for 2009–2010 is needed for the poor countries. Furthermore, the introduction of an internationally coordinated Transaction Tax is necessary to mobilize additional funds for a short-term Global Stimulus Fund and the implementation of internationally agreed development goals in the long-term. The international stimulus packages must serve the goals of economic recovery, social justice, environmental protection and sustainable use of natural resources. Also, there must be unconditional debt cancellation and repudiation of illegitimate debt, and fiscal stimulus focus on social protection of the vulnerable such as women and minorities, and building equitable and sustainable growth. There should be unemployment benefit schemes supplemented by direct job creation schemes.

The second set of recommendation focus on systemic reform to provide global financial and economic regulation. Among the several recommendations the basic view is that there is need for a Global Panel on Systemic Risks in the World Economy, which brings together academics, civil society and policy makers. Also, there is a call to reform the governance structure of the International Financial Institutions based on democratic principles that are transparent, consultative and inclusive, involving all stakeholders and not just shareholders. The regulatory tools for finance, trade and investment negotiations should be revamped and strengthened at all levels, especially within the WTO and regional and bilateral Free Trade Agreement negotiations on financial services, should be put on hold.

Also, the view is that a new agreement of cooperation is necessary between the UN and the Breton Woods Institutions to enhance coordination and policy coherence. There should be an end to the practice of policy conditionality, since these are harmful and undemocratic. Countries should have the right to pursue their own policies, and the IMF and World Bank should cease to intervene in the development and implementation of national trade and investment policies. There should also be the creation of a, Global Economic Council to address areas of concern in the functioning of the global economic system, and a, Global Reserve System to support the development needs of the poor countries and serve to stabilize the global financial system.

The rich capitalist countries boycotted the UN conference on the financial and economic crisis. Nonetheless, the conference was only able to come up with a draft outcomes document, which has many proposals for prompt and decisive action. The four areas in which the UN conference suggested that prompt action be takes are as follows. First, the idea is that global stimulus must work for all countries. Second, the view is that measures must be implemented to contain the effects of the crisis and improve resilience for the future. Third, there should be improved regulation and monitoring, and finally there is need for international financial and economic governance reform.[16]

The magnitude of the financial crisis as revealed in policy recommendations by the EU, the G-20, the IMF, and civil society speak directly to the difficulties that the ACP countries face in light of both the financial and economic crises and the EU EPAs. The financial crisis is severe in the EU and will negatively affect its financial and economic performances, and its ability to keep its EPA commitments to the ACP countries. Furthermore, the drastic reversal in policy recommendations by the IMF from market to state-led solutions to resolve the financial crisis and stimulate economic growth, and the state-led actions by the EU to tackle the crisis, contradicts the market-led EPAs that the EU is pushing on the ACP countries.

British Prime Minister Gordon Brown has declared that the Washington Consensus is dead and is no longer the basis for economic

[16] European Network on Debt and Development. 2009. UN Conference on the Financial Crisis and Development. May 27.

policy. In his view the G-20 meeting had to come up with a new set of rules for global economic policy. However, the Washington Consensus constitutes the market-led policy basis for the EPAs. In the light of these developments, the ACP regions must halt all negotiations on the EPA, not only to await the newly designed World Order but also to simultaneously take the appropriate actions to realign themselves with the emerging economies that are helping to reshape the balance of power globally.

The G-20 meeting and recommendations nonetheless, could be seen as the "new Bretton Woods" that seek to resurrect the IMF and place the institutions that were a part of the problem as a central part of the solution (Bello 2009). The very IMF, which as the spearhead of neoliberal structural adjustment that ran havoc on the ACP countries, is now being asked to take charge of the process to alleviate the financial and economic crises! But, the double standard of the rich capitalist states to the ACP countries have been exposed as evidenced by how quickly the massive stimulus packages to rescue the Western corporate sector were put in place. The IMF is revived to continue its disruptive policies in the ACP countries, while the state in the leading capitalist countries is bailing out the corporate sector.

CHAPTER TWELVE

THE CARIBBEAN IN THE GLOBAL FINANCIAL AND ECONOMIC CRISES

Introduction

The EU economic partnership agreement represents a major turning point in the relationship between the Caribbean and Europe. It expands on the economic and political relationships that individual Caribbean countries have had with individual European countries to embrace new forms of economic and political relationships based on the Caribbean and Europe as two blocs. This chapter focuses on the general contradiction that the Caribbean now faces – pursuing the free trade based CARIFORUM-EU EPA while embroiled in the global financial and economic crises, which the EU, US, G-20 and IMF seek to resolve by implementing state-interventionist measures that contradict those of the CARIFORUM-EU EPA.

The underlying concern is that the Caribbean is simultaneously preoccupied with the CARIFORUM-EU EPA, and the global financial and economic crises. This is like a double jeopardy for the Caribbean that over-stretches its scarce resources. Caribbean peoples need to find an approach to both dangers that would bring about a unique solution that frees the region from the domination of EU bloc imperialism and US-led globalization. First, there is an assessment of the impact of the global financial and economic crises on the Caribbean. This is followed by a discussion of the fraud perpetuated on the region by the Stanford Financial Group, and the collapse of the CL Financial Group and the bailout by the Trinidad and Tobago government. Finally, there is discussion of the proposed policy options for the Caribbean region.

Assessing the Impacts of the Crises on the Caribbean

Hitherto assessments of the impact of the global financial crisis on the Caribbean seem to concentrate on whether the crisis actually has effects on the region, what the possible effects could be in the absence of immediate corrective policy action, or the possible policy initiatives the region could implement to deal with the crisis. There is little or no attempt in the Caribbean literature to assess the intersection of the crises and the CARIFORUM-EU EPA. The globe is about to be reorganized possibly on the basis of the G-20, in which a larger number of countries with greater sway compared with those that organized the global order established at the Bretton Woods conference, will have a say on its reshaping. The G-20 is less inclusive that Bretton Woods, since more countries were involved in the latter.[1] But, the G-20 comprises more countries with greater economic strength compared with Bretton Woods. Furthermore, the G-20 is merely recycling failed Bretton Woods institutions, such as the IMF.[2]

The US and powerful European countries dominate the Bretton Woods world order. Today, however, there is a larger number of countries with greater economic power that will have a role in reshaping the global economic order. This new situation presented by the global financial and economic crisis comes on the heels of the singing of the CARIFORUM-EU EPA, which demands an understanding of the intersection of the three processes – EU bloc imperialism, the CARIFORUM-EU EPA, and the global financial and economic crises, at the present historical juncture. Undoubtedly, the global financial and economic crises, the fraud at the Stanford Financial Group, and the collapse of CL Financing, will negatively impact the Caribbean's commitments to the CARIFORUM-EU EPA.

The decline in economic growth associated with the crises will increase the need for funds in the region at a time when the region is set to lose money due to the trade liberalization measures of the EPA. This will increase poverty in the Caribbean because the region will be hemorrhaging from two sources – the EPA and the financial and economic crises. At the political level, the EPA transfers power from the Caribbean state to the EU through a supra-national governance structure, while the global financial and economic crises requires the Caribbean state to take defensive protectionist actions. The future contradictions here at both the economic and political levels are quite obvious.

---

[1] Bello, Walden. 2009. G-20: Will the Global Economy Resurface? *Foreign Policy In Focus*, Washington, DC: March 30.

[2] Bello, Walden. 2009. G-20: Will the Global Economy Resurface? *Foreign Policy In Focus*, Washington, DC: March 30.

In assessing the impacts of the crises on the Caribbean at these points of intersection with the CARIFORUM-EU EPA, it is important to provide a detailed account of some of the main viewpoints that have emerged concerning the crises and the Caribbean. In the first instance, it is believed that there are three reasons why the current global economic conditions would not place a damper on the economic performance of the Caribbean (Williams 2008).[3] These reasons are said to be first, that the shift to a multi-polar world is reducing the reliance on the US as the engine of the global economy. The view is that the US economy would be worse off had it not been the resilience of some emerging market economies and developing countries. Furthermore, it is argued that the momentum in the US economy is only being maintained by that country's export sector and the depreciation of its currency.

The presence of China in the Caribbean and Latin America is identified as an example of the claim about multi-polarity. Indeed, it is argued that the current five-year boom in Latin America is due to a rise in commodity prices triggered by increased Chinese and Indian demand, which "has made it possible for many governments in the region to pay their debts."[4] The Chinese presence has been identified as becoming even more extensive in the Caribbean in the past decade. China has become a member of the Caribbean Development Bank (CDB) since 1998, established diplomatic relations with Dominica and Grenada, and participated in the UN Stabilization Mission in Haiti.

China has also increased its trade and investment with Cuba and the Caribbean region in general, with trade growing at an average of 32 percent a year from 2001 to 2006, to US$4.4 billion (Heine 2008). Several Caribbean countries – Cuba, Bahamas, Dominica, Grenada, Guyana, Jamaica, and Suriname now have permanent embassies in Beijing. China has permanent missions in all the Caribbean countries, with which it has diplomatic relations giving it, arguably, a greater diplomatic presence in the Eastern Caribbean than the US. The US has downsized its embassies in the region consolidating all of them into one located in Bridgetown, Barbados, in an effort to cut cost (Heine 2008).

---

[3] Williams, Ewart S. 2008. The Impact of Global Events on the Caribbean Economies. Address, at the ICATT 26th Annual Caribbean Conference, June 27.

[4] Heine, Jorge. 2008. The Dragon in the Archipelago. *Jamaica Gleaner Online*, Sunday, August 17.

This multi-polar world is said to be responsible for the resilience of the Caribbean economy in three respects. The first is the "geographical diversification in the source of tourist arrivals – with the US share declining and that of Europe increasing, due in part to the strengthening of the British pound and the Euro" (Williams 2008). There is also available statistical evidence that suggests "tourism from Trinidad and Tobago to the rest of the region has increased markedly, helping to offset any global slowdown." The second is that the slowdown or recession in the US is less costly in terms of employment because of the strength of the export sector in the US. Thirdly, the low cost in employment is the cause that remittances to the region from the US, an important source of domestic demand and foreign exchange earnings for many Caribbean countries, did not decline sharply as was previously expected. However, others have argued that the expected decline in remittances due to the crises will definitely have a negative impact on Caribbean economies, as historically, an increase in living costs and decline in employment in North America and Europe decrease remittances to Caribbean people from their family and friends in those countries (Jessop 2008, Odle 2008).

Williams' (2008) view on employment however is out of sink with the current realities of increasing layoffs in the US and Europe and the widespread social unrest especially on the latter continent. Also, it is contrary to the views of Jessop (2008), Odle (2008), and the World Bank (2008) that in the current period of crises remittances to the developing countries, and in particular Africa, will definitely be negatively affected.[5] The decline in remittances is identified by several other Caribbean authors however as one of the possible impact of the current global financial and economic crises on the region.

The relative strength of the Caribbean's financial sector is the second overall reason advanced as to why the global economic conditions are not putting a greater damper on the Caribbean region (Williams 2008). The view is that Caribbean banks "have not been directly affected by the subprime crisis, because they have not held any of these assets and because their lending operations have been based on the growth of deposits rather than on borrowing from foreign banks" (Williams 2008). The Caribbean region took steps to consolidate and strengthen

[5] World Bank Group. 2008. World Bank to Help Mitigate Impact of Global Financial Crisis on Africa's Development. November 19.

its banking system in the light of the financial crisis in Jamaica in the late 1990s. This consolidation and strengthening is reflected in the fact that the Caribbean banks are "in a position to continue lending and supporting domestic activity even in an environment of tight global liquidity," because they have succeeded in increasing their capital and reducing sharply their non-performing loans. Furthermore, increasingly Caribbean businesses and governments find it difficult to raise capital in global markets, and have been turning to the capital market of Trinidad and Tobago for financing to maintain investment spending.

Improvements in the macro-economic management of the Caribbean in recent years are identified as the third general reason for the better resilience of Caribbean economies from the global economic conditions (Williams 2008). The view is that robust macro-economic management in the Caribbean is reflected in some of the main economic parameters. Fiscal deficits in the region have been reduced, the public debt is in decline, and the net international reserves have increased sharply (Williams 2008).

The IMF (2008) takes a different view however, arguing "the Caribbean has been buffeted by slower global growth and the sharp rise in international commodity prices since 2005."[6] GPD growth in the Caribbean was projected at 3¼ percent for 2008 below the 4 percent average annual growth in 2003-2007, while inflation was estimated at 8 percent the highest rate since the mid-1990s. The IMF argues that the slowdown in the advanced economies is dampening demand for tourism, a key regional export, which is being negatively affected by "more stringent travel requirements for U.S. citizens, the reopening of the Cancun market, as well as weaker economic conditions in the United States." However, although demand by Canadian and European tourists was buttressed by the weak US dollar, tourism demand is expected to decline due to the economic slowdown in these countries (IMF 2008).

The IMF (2008) noted that the increase in fuel cost has forced major airlines to cut back their routes and prices skyrocketed along with higher food and fuel costs. Food plays a major role in the consumer's basket in most Caribbean countries "reaching 54 percent in St. Vincent

[6] International Monetary Fund. 2008c. Economic and Financial Surveys, Regional Economic Outlook: Western Hemisphere, Grappling with the Global Financial Crisis. Washington, D.C.

and the Grenadines." In Jamaica, food price inflation increased up to 35 percent due to hurricane-related damages, while in several countries, higher international fuel prices passed-through fully to domestic prices, and the fall in value of the US dollar and strong domestic demand have pushed prices up even further. The higher price of imports increased the current account deficit in many countries, with the expectation that the rise in food and fuel prices will push the "current account deficits to as high as 35 percent of GDP in the Eastern Caribbean Currency Union." Foreign direct investment and external assistance mostly from Petrocaribe are expected to continue to finance the current account deficit in several of these countries (IMF 2008).

The IMF (2008) noted that the Caribbean region "has been relatively unaffected by the global financial crisis," although the "key near-term policy challenge is to weather the difficult period ahead." In the view of the IMF (2008) the Caribbean needs to "ensure adequate liquidity for the financial system and foreign exchange reserves to support external payments." Furthermore, the IMF (2008) believes that the region "should seek ways to establish precautionary credit lines," and that "fiscal discipline and a restrained credit policy would help safeguard net international reserves and signal continued commitment to ease high public debt burdens both of which would be key to support confidence among market participants." Countries such as Barbados, Belize, Jamaica, and St. Lucia among others now "are targeting lower fiscal deficits." To reduce the negative consequences of high food prices on the poor many countries have introduced measures such as "cuts to domestic tax rates and import tariffs" and "targeted subsidies" (IMF 2008).

In another section of the literature, the view is expressed that the consequences of the global financial crisis are likely to be severe both in the short- and medium-term in the Caribbean.[7] The prediction is that "market turmoil and a rapid decline in economic growth in the region's major markets will affect tourism, the industry that has become the driver of Caribbean growth" (Jessop 2008). The tourism sector will definitely "reflect within months the downturn in economic fortunes," and when combined with high fuel and food prices, higher airfares, and fluctuations in exchange rates will "make middle income earners vacation closer to home or not at all." Also, the tourism

[7] Jessop, David. 2008a. The Financial Crisis and the Caribbean. BBCCaribbean.com, October 3.

industry will find it "difficult to raise capital to finance its development" (Jessop 2008).

The crises are also said to be posing a serious threat to the construction boom the region experienced in the last decade due to enhanced tourist arrivals and increasing value of real estate. It is believed that most of the current construction projects will be completed but that it will become more difficult to finance new investments, as "banks and others look ever more closely at the viability of projects and more particularly at the credit profile of those who promote them" (Jessop 2008). It is argued that investment in other sectors that drive Caribbean economic activity will face a similar problem.

The expectation is that due to the crises some Caribbean governments will face problems financing their debt or covering the shortfalls in their recurrent expenditure. It is estimated that Trinidad and Tobago and Jamaica are well placed to endure the crisis by "making use of their reserves," but that the smaller Caribbean states "may have to choose between increasing taxation, turning to regional partners like Venezuela or cutting expenditure as they attempt to reduce their budget deficits" (Jessop 2008).

The Caribbean Development Bank (CDB) provided a summary list of possible impacts of the global financial crisis on the Caribbean and identified the potential ways in which the bank could respond.[8] Brunton (2008) list the impacts as a decline in GDP growth rates, actual contraction in GDP, increased fiscal pressures, increased pressure on reserves, rising levels of protection, rising current account deficits, declining credit and other financial flows, and declining asset quality. Brunton (2008) suggested that the CDB's response should be through mechanisms to support debt sustainability, support fiscal consolidation, help to support GDP growth to mitigate the impact on employment, and facilitate the social protection mechanisms.

Odle (2008) examined the impact of the financial crisis on the Caribbean's financial sector, foreign exchange reserves, cost of borrowing, flow of remittances, tourist arrivals, other export earnings, foreign direct investment, and economic growth rates.[9] The view is that the

---

[8] Brunton, P. Desmond. 2008. The Global Financial Crisis and the Caribbean: Impact & Response CDB Response. Bridgetown, Barbados: Caribbean Development Bank.

[9] Odle, Maurice A. 2008. Sub-Prime to Sublime Disaster: Implications for the Caribbean Region of the Current Financial Crisis in the USA. Caricom, Turkeyen, East Coast Demerara, Guyana, September 18.

intensity of the impact of the crisis would vary according to sector, and that the small size and underdeveloped nature of the Caribbean's financial sector is a reason why the US investment banks did not dump mortgage backed securities onto the Caribbean financial market. For those reasons it is believed that the Caribbean's financial sector is fairly insulated from the current global crises. There are several products and services in Jamaica and Trinidad and Tobago inter alia that have insurance or re-insurance coverage from AIG. Thus, despite the US government bailout of AIG, Caribbean customers may be asked to pay higher premiums.

According to Odle (2008) the region's concern with Merrill Lynch's problems has to do with the fact that the company manages certain Caribbean pension funds such as those of the Caricom Secretariat. Like Williams (2008), Odle (2008) observed that the financial crisis in Jamaica in the 1990s resulted in a fairly tightly regulated commercial banking sector in the Caribbean, and for this reason there was no alarm sounded thus far by the sector. This is partly due to the fact that US corresponding banks, which handle the daily dollar transactions of Caribbean banks, are themselves commercial banks, which are on the periphery of the financial crisis, rather than investment banks, which are at the center of the crisis.

It is believed that the region will lose foreign exchange since its Central Banks have investments of about US$20 billion abroad as foreign exchange reserves in government bonds and equity that constitute "sovereign wealth funds" whose earnings have fallen due to the crisis (Odle 2008). Trinidad and Tobago reserves are "managed by a subsidiary of Lehman Brothers" investment bank that has filed for bankruptcy. Recurring financial crises in the global capitalist system Odle (2008) believes, should prompt the Caribbean to review its foreign exchange reserve holding strategy in terms of weather a country should allow a single overseas investment bank to manage its foreign exchange reserves, hold its foreign exchange reserves in a single international currency, and the adequacy of the foreign exchange reserves. At the end of the financial crisis in South East Asia in 1997-98, Caribbean Central Banks consciously decided to increase their foreign exchange holdings above the traditional three months import cover figure and some now have over five months import cover. Trinidad and Tobago went even further and placed US$9 billion of its petroleum and gas earnings into a Heritage and Stabilization Fund (Odle 2008).

Although Caribbean public and private sector agencies might have an excellent credit rating, due to the credit crunch in the developed countries, they will experience some difficulty borrowing in international capital markets. Trinidad and Tobago, nonetheless, has emerged in recent years as a major creditor to Caribbean government and corporate entities and at a lower interest rate than that of international lenders.

Odle (2008) noted that the expected decline in the flow of remittances to the region is definitely an issue of concern in the Caribbean. Remittances from the US alone were estimated for Jamaica at US$1.9 billion, Haiti US$1.8 billion, Guyana US$424 million, Trinidad and Tobago US$125 million, Suriname US$115 million and Belize US$105 million (Odle 2008). Undoubtedly, remittances is a crucial source of income in some Caribbean countries estimated at 43 percent of Guyana's GNP, 35 percent in Haiti and 18 percent in Jamaica. The view is that the expected fall in remittances will negatively impact retail establishments and related consumption sectors, which will experience a decline in their activity (Odle 2008).

Remittance is presented as a development strategy in the Caribbean but the expected impact on it by the financial crisis is further evidence that it is an unsustainable development approach. Furthermore, there is no evidence that remittances to the Caribbean have stimulated the region's industrial development. Remittances seem to be more concentrated in consumption items, which really stimulate demand in the sending countries and consumption in the receiving countries. Also, it is highly likely that there is a negative net flow of resources from the Caribbean comparing the cost of out-migration of highly trained professionals and skilled workers from the region, with the inflow remittances.

There is widespread belief that the financial crisis will compound the negative effect on Caribbean tourism already under stress due to the energy crisis that stimulated airlift problems, caused the collapse of the certain airlines, the elimination of certain destinations, a reduction in the frequency of flights and an increase in airfares (Odle 2008). It is expected that fewer people will be able to take an overseas holiday due to the financial crisis, and when coupled with the adverse effect of the reduction in baggage allowance and natural disasters such as hurricanes, will make things difficult for the hotel and entertainment industry in the Caribbean (Odle 2008).

It is estimated that US demand for Caribbean manufactured goods through the Caribbean Basin Initiative (CBI) and the Caribbean Basin

Trade Partnership Act (CBTPA) will fall negatively affecting the, region's export earnings. Caribbean currencies are tied to the US dollar, which means that a fall in the value of the dollar will put a downward pressure on export earnings that accrue to the area. But, this decline is partially compensated for by sales to Europe where the Euro and Pound are stronger. Nonetheless, the tendency towards currency realignment will remove the gain from increased sales to Europe (Odle 2008).

Furthermore, the deepening of the financial crisis will suppress European demand for major Caribbean exports – bananas, rice and sugar, and Chinese and Russian demand for the region's bauxite resources. According to Odle (2008) Trinidad and Tobago will experience difficulties from the decline in petroleum and gas prices from the high reached at the highpoint of the fuel crisis, while Guyana and Suriname are set to gain more from gold exports, as speculators gravitate towards that commodity in times of financial crisis.

In Odle's (2008) view the adverse effect on Caribbean capital will result from "reverse remittances" or low intensity capital flight to mainly the USA, Canada and Britain. This activity has been going on for many decades due to the lack of confidence by businessmen and individuals in the regional economies stemming from perceived notions of socio-economic and political instability in the Caribbean. The drop in earnings from stocks, bonds and real estate could slow down capital flight from the region.

Foreign direct investment (FDI) in the Caribbean area is expected to decline in the light of the fact that the US accounts for a substantial share of it. US investors hard hit by the financial crisis will lack the capital and business confidence necessary to undertake big investments in natural resource extraction, construction, and infrastructure in the Caribbean, with the possible exception of exploration and drilling activity in the area of petroleum and natural gas. FDI in the Caribbean was US$3.8 billion in 2006, an estimated US$4.5 billion for 2007, with the figure for 2008 expected to be less than that for 2007. Odle (2008) recommends that the region redoubles its "investment promotion efforts" and promotes "greater geographical diversification of the sources of investment inflows," in addition to encouraging "intra-Caribbean investment."

Finally, it is predicted that the global financial crisis will suppress the growth rate in the Caribbean in 2008 below the 2007 level. The

Caribbean Development Bank estimated that economic growth slowed in nine countries in the region while increasing in only four. With respect to the entire region, however, there was a decline in economic growth from 6.9% in 2006 to 3.9% in 2007. This decline was "as a result of rising oil and commodity prices, slower growth by major trading partners, depreciation of the USA dollar and the high cost of intra-regional travel." In the light of the global financial crisis the growth rate in 2008 will likely show a 1-2% fall (Odle 2008).

The ECLAC has estimated that the Caribbean MDCs GDP will experience 1.8% growth in 2009, down from the already meager 2.4% growth in 2008, based on preliminary data (Table 12:1). The Eastern

Table 12.1 GDP Growth Rate, 2008–2009f (%)

	2008p	2009f
MDCca	**2.4**	**1.8**
Bahamas	1.5	0.5
Barbados	0.7	−1.0
Belize	3.8	2.0
Guyana	3.1	2.0
Jamaica	−0.5	−2.0
Suriname	5.0	3.5
Trinidad and Tobago	3.5	1.5
ECCUa	**3.2**	**1.4**
Anguilla	2.7	1.0
Antigua and Barbuda	5.0	1.5
Dominica	2.1	1.0
Grenada	1.6	1.5
Montserrat	4.7	2.5
At. Kitts and Nevis	4.3	1.0
St. Lucia	2.9	1.5
St. Vincent and the Grenadines	2.2	1.0

Source: Economic Commission for Latin America and the Caribbean. 2009a. Preliminary Overview of the Caribbean 2008–2009. Port of Spain, Trinidad and Tobago: Subregional Headquarters for the Caribbean, March 9.

a = Simple average
b = preliminary
c = forecast

Caribbean Currency Union (ECCU) countries will have a similar experience with their GDP declining from the preliminary figure of 3.1% for 2008 to 1.4% in 2009. Also, the ECLAC estimated that "with the exception of Suriname and Trinidad and Tobago – countries abundant in minerals and/or hydrocarbons whose prices have been high in recent years – all other countries have experienced twin deficits" – fiscal and current account deficits, during last year.[10]

The Stanford Financial and CL Financial Groups

The Stanford Financial Group's fiasco, and the collapse of CL Financial (CLF) Group comprising the Colonial Life Insurance Company Limited (CLICO) and CLICO Investment Bank (CIB) resulting in a Trinidad and Tobago government bailout of CLF have caused much concern in the Caribbean due to the anticipated financial and economic fallout. The situation at both Stanford Financial Group and CL Financial came in the midst of the global financial crisis and economic slowdown, and as the region entered into the CARIFORUM-EU EPA. Their effects are therefore to be understood in the context of those of the global financial and economic crises, and the CARIFORUM-EU EPA.

The Stanford Group was a casualty of the global financial crises in the sense that regulatory authorities have stepped up their oversight of the financial sector in the US, and in that process the alleged Stanford scam became exposed. Possibly, if the Wall Street meltdown had not taken place the alleged Stanford scam would remain, for the time being, uncovered. The collapse of CL Financial had to do more with two factors first the fact that the global financial crisis created much anxiety around the world that could have helped to fuel the rush on the bank creating its liquidity problems, and second with the poor banking practices by CL Financial.

The Stanford Financial Group

The US Securities and Exchange Commission (SEC) brought charges against Mr. Stanford and two of his colleagues for defrauding scores of

[10] Economic Commission for Latin America and the Caribbean. 2009. Preliminary Overview of the Caribbean 2008–2009. Port of Spain, Trinidad and Tobago: Subregional Headquarters for the Caribbean, March 9.

investors around the world. Described as a massive and ongoing fraud that stretched from the Caribbean to Texas, and around the world, the Stanford scam involved approximately $8 billion in high-yielding certificates of deposit held in the firm's bank in Antigua. The US Securities and Exchange Commission in a civil suit accused Mr. Stanford and two of his colleagues of fraudulently peddling the $8 billion in high-yielding certificates of deposit to scores of investors.[11] Mr. Stanford promised his investors that they would receive lucrative returns on relatively safe certificates of deposit that were often more than twice the going rate offered by mainstream banks.[12]

The reality was however that the bulk of the bank's portfolio was in very illiquid real estate and private investments portfolios monitored only by Mr. Stanford and Mr. James Davis, a director and chief financial officer of the Stanford Group. The Antiguan government auditor did not audit the bank's portfolio or verified its assets. According to the SEC Stanford advertised giving investors the belief that they were investing in liquid securities by purchasing certificates of deposits (CDs) from the bank, and that the CDs paid higher rates because the bank makes consistently high returns on investor assets. Stanford also claimed that investments in his company were safe because a team of more than 20 analysts monitored them and that the Antiguan regulators carried out yearly audits of the investments. The SEC pointed out that none of Stanford's claims were true.[13]

It is envisaged that Caribbean regional economies will suffer undue distress from the Stanford fraud because the company invested heavily in infrastructure in Antigua and Barbuda, and participated in the Caribbean regional airline industry, the financial services sector, and West Indies cricket. Stanford is the second largest employer in Antigua and Barbuda, after the government and hundreds of his employees will be out of work. It is estimated that about 1,000 workers are in Stanford's employ in Antigua. Stanford also provided his workers with benefits such as health care that were unheard of on the island. Furthermore,

---

[11] Krauss, Clifford, Zweig, Phillip L. and Creswell, Julie. 2009. Texas Firm Accused of $8 Billion Fraud. *New York Times*, February 18.

[12] Krauss, Clifford, Zweig, Phillip L. and Creswell, Julie. 2009. Texas Firm Accused of $8 Billion Fraud. *New York Times*, February 18; Economist Magazine. 2009. Financial Fraud: Howzat! Economist.com, February 18.

[13] Krauss, Clifford, Zweig, Phillip L. and Creswell, Julie. 2009. Texas Firm Accused of $8 Billion Fraud. *New York Times*, February 18; Economist Magazine. 2009. Financial Fraud: Howzat! Economist.com, February 18.

it is unlikely that the company will be operational to sponsor future regional cricket competitions.[14]

The Stanford fraud will also affect the Caribbean in other ways. For example, it will hinder the efforts by those Caribbean countries currently engaged in formulating legislation to make themselves centers of international financial and banking institutions. Another possible effect of the Stanford affair is that it could bring additional pressure on regional governments to give up their aspirations to become centers of global and /or offshore financial services and similar industries.[15]

Stanford did not appear on the Caribbean scene overnight, he moved to Antigua and Barbuda in the late 1980s, after it is alleged that he encountered problems with the authorities in the British Caribbean colony of Montserrat. The regimes of Vere and Lester Bird in Antigua and Barbuda helped to create the Stanford financial empire in the Caribbean. Lester Bird who became the Prime Minister of the country after his father Vere Bird died in 1994 continued his predecessor's policies to make Antigua and Barbuda one of the Caribbean's most attractive destinations for offshore money. Their policies included the removal of business taxes and the granting of citizenship to prominent foreign businessmen. Thus, for example, Stanford who belongs to Texas in the US was not only granted citizenship of Antigua and Barbuda, but Knighted by the government of Antigua and Barbuda as "Sir Allen Stanford."

The governments of both Vere and Lester Bird were accused of corruption and an investigation was launched in 2002 to investigate the disappearance of $230 million in state health insurance money. The labor government was allegedly implicated in utilizing the state insurance money as a personal slush fund to pay for parties and kickbacks to government allies. Then, there was the case of the Swiss banker and alleged money launderer Bruce Rappaport that an investigation found guilty of robbing the island of millions of dollars with the help of Lester Bird. Rappaport agreed to pay back $12 million to the government of Antigua and Barbuda.[16]

---

[14] Barbados Advocate. 2009. Crisis Coming Closer to Home. Barbados Advocate, February 23.

[15] Barbados Advocate. 2009. Crisis Coming Closer to Home. Barbados Advocate, February 23.

[16] The Voice. 2009. Stanford Crisis Leaves Caribbean Shaken. *The Voice*, Issue: 1361, March 2.

Undoubtedly, corruption in Antigua and Barbuda helped to perpetuate the Stanford fraud. The Bank of Antigua, Stanford International Bank and the Stanford Development Company, covered the corporate side of Stanford's business in Antigua and Barbuda. When the scam became clear the government of Antigua and Barbuda seized Stanford's assets. Stanford also owned the Sticky Wicket and Pavilion restaurants in St John's, the Antiguan capital. The Venezuelan government also seized Stanford's assets in that country. It is estimated that 28,000 victims of the alleged fraud are Venezuelans, who have lost an estimated $2bn. The US court closed Stanford's offices in the Caribbean island of St. Croix in which Stanford owns deeds to about $34.7 million in property. Officials also went after Stanford's personal assets including a home and a 120-foot yacht. Also, several local businesses including a property surveyor, two architecture firms, and providers of asphalt and solar panels, filed $1.2 million in claims against Stanford's properties. Also, in Christiansted, St. Croix's largest city, five claims totaling about US$1 million have been filed against Stanford.[17]

Several critics accused Stanford of attempting to re-colonize Antigua and Barbuda and of behaving like a colonial master. The United Progressive Party (UPP) of Antigua and Barbuda campaigned on Bird's corruption and defeated his government in the national elections in the 2004. Stanford made donations to the candidates of the Bird's Labor Party in the elections, only to find his plans in Antigua and Barbuda cramped by the new UPP government. Stanford's arrest is regarded by many Antiguans as just part of a pattern of corruption of the Bird government.[18]

The CL Financial Group

The CL Financial Group (CLF) is a holding company headquartered in Port of Spain, Trinidad and Tobago. The company had more than 70 subsidiaries and affiliated companies and operates in over 32 countries, mainly in the Caribbean, Central and Latin America, North America, Europe and the Middle East – Oman, Saudi Arabia and Qatar. It focused on methanol plants in the Middle East and had plans to expand

---

[17] The Voice. 2009. Stanford Crisis Leaves Caribbean Shaken. *The Voice*, Issue: 1361, March 2.

[18] The Voice. 2009. Stanford Crisis Leaves Caribbean Shaken. *The Voice*, Issue: 1361, March 2.

these plants in that region. With an estimated asset base of US$15 billion, the company has a wide range of financial operations concentrated in banking, brokerage and insurance. It has investments in energy and related products, real estate in various countries in the Caribbean and US, the manufacturing of beverages, forestry and agriculture, and a host of services. The largest of its subsidiaries in the Caribbean estimated at US$500 million, is located in Barbados.[19]

The collapse of CLF and its bailout by the government of Trinidad and Tobago is blamed on the activities of the group and insufficient government regulation. CL Financial had identified for sale three of its valued assets – the Caribbean Money Market Brokers (CMMB), the Republic Bank, and Methanol Holdings to offset funding provided by the government of Trinidad and Tobago to CLF subsidiaries Colonial Life Insurance Company Limited (CLICO) and CLICO Investment Bank Limited (CIB). First Citizens Bank of Trinidad and Tobago will acquire 100% of the shares of CMMB, which will continue to conduct business as a separate operating company and operate as normal in Trinidad, Barbados and St Lucia.

The CIB and CLICO faced liquidity problems that became obvious when there was an "unusually high level of withdrawal request" that placed a strain on available liquid resources forcing CLICO to seek financial assistance from the Trinidad and Tobago Central Bank in January 2009. As at end-January 2009, CLICO had policy surrender requests on maturing obligations of $650 million, and the monthly payment for pensions and annuities is $40 million. CLICO at the time of writing had a bank balance of $15 million, in addition to a sizable bank overdraft.[20]

The audited accounts of CLICO revealed surpluses in the Statutory Fund in 2004, 2005 and 2006, but these surpluses shifted to a deficit of about $600 million in 2007. The un-audited accounts for 2008 showed that the Statutory Fund deficit, measured on the same basis as in the period 2004-2007, has escalated to $5.1 billion. CLICO's Statutory Fund, in recent years, has included several inter-group assets, such as deposits in CIB and securities issued by the parent CL Financial. These instruments are now of little value, which if excluded from the Statutory

[19] Thomas, Clive Y. 2009. CL Financial Group: Meltdown and Bailout. *Sunday Stabroek*, April 12.

[20] Williams, Ewart S. 2009. Update on CIB/CLICO/CMMB. Central Bank of Trinidad and Tobago, Port-of-Spain, February 13.

Fund calculation for 2008, the notional deficit rises to $10 billion, on a policyholder liability base of $16.7 billion. CLICO was a major source of cash, in the CL Financial business model, much of which was used to finance investments held in the name of other entities in the Group. CLICO, the money-tree ended up as guarantor for many of the CL Financial Group's assets most of which are heavily pledged.[21]

Arguably, the run on CIB had to do with the concern of depositors about the impact of the sharp decline in the prices of methanol and real estate on the overall financial situation at CL Financial. The Governor of the Trinidad and Tobago Central Bank believe however that the financial problems at CIB and CLICO have more to do with the behavior of the companies, and other structural problems. It is believed that the first apparent cause of the financial problem had to do with the "excessive related-party transactions, which carry significant contagion risks." The second problem had to do with the "aggressive high interest rate resource mobilization strategy to finance equally high risk investments, much of which are in illiquid assets (including real estate both in Trinidad and Tobago and abroad)." The third problem concerned "a very high leveraging of the Group's assets, which constrains the potential amount of cash that could be raised from asset sales." The fourth issue involved the inadequate legislative framework to give the Central Bank the authority to demand that CIB redress those deficiencies.[22]

The CL Financial group account for about 10 percent of Trinidad and Tobago's GDP and has substantial impact elsewhere in Caricom. The Trinidad and Tobago government has bailed out CL Financial and took over the company's shares in some of its other entities. It is believed that the CL Financial issue will exacerbate the effects of the worldwide recession on the Caribbean. The crisis will become more acute given the deepening integration of Caribbean economies due to the Caribbean Single Market Economy (CSME), and the overall regional integration project. For example, CL Financial owns 40 per cent of a Jamaican investment bank and other regional firms are heavily invested in CLF.

[21] Williams, Ewart S. 2009. Update on CIB/CLICO/CMMB. Central Bank of Trinidad and Tobago, Port-of-Spain, February 13.

[22] Williams, Ewart S. 2009. Update on CIB/CLICO/CMMB. Central Bank of Trinidad and Tobago, Port-of-Spain, February 13.

The situation at CL Financing demonstrates the callous manner in which both the Trinidad and Tobago government and banking institutions treat workers. The Banking, Insurance and General Workers Union (BIGWU) of Trinidad and Tobago exposed the inappropriate manner in which the government and banking institutions have treated the workers concerning the problem at CIB and CLICO. The workers only learnt about the situation from the media like the general public. Thus, the CIB workers turned up for work but found the doors closed with a notice informing them that they were locked-out. After making enquires at the Trinidad and Tobago Central Bank, the workers "were told that they would be paid the sum of one month's notice ... were not entitled to severance pay and that they would be required to effect some final activity associated with the closure of CIB."[23] Many workers in the finance sector, are now de-motivated and unsure of what the future holds for them despite the appeals to them that they should not be worried.[24]

Policy Options for the Caribbean Region

What policies the Caribbean should implement at this historical juncture characterized by the CARIFORUM-EU EPA, the current global financial and economic crises, the collapse of Stanford Financial and CL Financial groups and the government bailout of the latter, and the state-interventionist policies by the IMF, EU, US, G-20? This question remains unanswered in the current recommended policy options for the Caribbean. Instead, in the Caribbean the question formulated and answered is as follows: What are the policy options for the Caribbean in the light of the global financial crisis, the CL Financial failure and bailout, and the collapse of the Stanford Financial Group on fraud charges? This question has stimulated many ideas about possible policy options for the Caribbean region to address the problems.

Brunton (2008) recommended the instruments that the CDB could use in its response to the global financial crisis. These should include, policy-based loans, policy-based guarantees, interest subsidization

[23] Cabrera, Vincent. 2009. President BIGWU, Media Conference Remarks February 4.

[24] Cabrera, Vincent. 2009. President BIGWU, Media Conference Remarks February 4.

fund, investment loans for infrastructure, credit lines to financial institutions, and direct poverty reducing investments. In addition it is suggested that there is need to investigate the use of innovative financing instruments – securitization of future-flow receivables, and Diaspora bonds.

Strengthening the regulatory framework in the Caribbean nonetheless is the principal idea that is supported by the region's academics and policymakers. Odle (2008) suggested that the Caribbean government regulators should follow the example of Jamaica and Trinidad and Tobago and "decree that commercial banks hold deposit insurance, moral hazard notwithstanding." There were other suggestions that the crises provide the Caribbean community with an opportunity to signal, from the highest level, a wish to synchronize its regulatory framework. The view is that the scam at Stanford Financial group is an indication of the lax regulatory framework in the Caribbean, which needs to be fixed. There is a strong view in the Caribbean that the financial crisis points to "the need for governments to have strong regulatory agencies," which must be "independent of their central governments." These regulatory agencies should report to parliament and not to a government minister or permanent secretary in a process, which is "opened to coverage by the news media."[25] The idea is that the large privately held companies in the Caribbean should also have to report to the regulatory agencies, and that the report must be "opened to scrutiny other than by a private auditor."[26]

The crises therefore reinforced the significance of the role of the state in the economic affairs of the economy. Thus, for example, the view is expressed that "Only decisive action by governments, especially in countries at the heart of the crisis, will be able to control the disorder that has spread through the world's financial sector, with perverse impacts on the daily lives of millions of people."[27] This requires "the Caribbean to engage in a perhaps painful debate about its thinking on 'development.' "[28]

---

[25] Powlett, Angela. 2008. Caribbean Powers must Watch over Private Businesses. *Nation News*, Barbados, October 6.

[26] Powlett, Angela. 2008. Caribbean Powers must Watch over Private Businesses. *Nation News*, Barbados, October 6.

[27] Jessop, David. 2008a. The Financial Crisis and the Caribbean. BBCCaribbean .com, October 3.

[28] Jessop, David. 2008a. The Financial Crisis and the Caribbean. BBCCaribbean .com, October 3.

The Caribbean leaders held a special one-day summit in Barbados to discuss the crises on Wednesday March 4. At the end of the meeting the leaders announced new mechanisms to deal with some of the problems plaguing the region's financial sectors, occasioned not only by the ongoing global crisis, but by several homegrown scandals as well. The Caribbean governments have given assurances that there will be more contact between Caribbean regulators so that they can verify the accuracy of information, share information about the adequacy of statutory funds or assets owned by insurance companies to ensure compliance with the appropriate legislation and to ensure that there is an arms length relationship between the trustees that are holding the assets in trust for the insurance company.[29] The Caribbean governments hope to boost the stability of the regional financial system in the light of the alleged fraud at Stanford Financial Group, the meltdown and bailout of CL Financial Group, and the global financial crisis.

Alternatives to Proffered Policy Options

The policy prescriptions identified above merely seek to plaster over the sore rather to bring about a long-lasting solution to the problem. From a historical perspective, crises such as the current global financial and economic crises, and the state-led solutions put in place perpetuate the class framework that has dominated the Caribbean for centuries. The solutions do not offer a genuine alternative to the socioeconomic system that has created the crises. State-intervention cannot erase the fact that the capitalist system is in a state of perpetual oscillation from crisis to crisis. The so-called state-interventionist solutions within the framework of global capitalism will not work. They cannot insulate the Caribbean from future crises in the global capitalist system.

Furthermore, the proffered state-led solution does not adequately address the question of power. At the end of the crises which classes will be in power? In view of the fact that power will remain in the hands of the very classes that created the crises, the solutions do not mean much for working people. The urgent need is for there to be a dismantling of the power structure of the global capitalist system that

[29] Richards, Peter. 2009. Caribbean: Bank Scandals Add to Region's Economic Woes. *Inter Press News Agency*, March 5.

condemns the ACP states to the poor conditions that they currently experience, while enriching the already rich capitalist states.

What then should the Caribbean contemplate to do in the light of the current crises and the CARIFORUM-EU EPA? First, the Caribbean needs to reject the theoretical foundation on which the CARIFORUM-EU EPA is founded. This is the very framework that is the cause of the current crises. Second, the Caribbean states must reject the current CARIFORUM-EU EPA on the basis that it contradicts the very solutions that the EU proposes for itself to resolve the current crises. Third, the Caribbean needs embrace alternative regional trade arrangements such as the ALBA and Petrocaribe. Fourth, the policy focus in the Caribbean should be on realigning the regional economies with the emerging countries among the developing states. It is quite likely that the Caribbean will find more favorable conditions from these economies, as the region continues to press its European colonizers to contribute more by way of more equitable trade deals, to the development of the region.

CHAPTER THIRTEEN

EU BLOC IMPERIALISM, GOVERNANCE AND SUSTAINABLE DEVELOPMENT

Introduction

The lofty ideal of EU bloc imperialism is to promote good governance and sustainable development in the ACP countries, the stated goals of EU-ACP economic partnership agreements. The historical practice of imperialist economic relations between Europe and the ACP countries despite their stated goals has been however basically the generation of poverty in the ACP states and the accumulation of wealth in Europe. The idea about good governance originated in the neoliberal counter-revolution to development theory,[1] while that of sustainable development emerged from environmental concerns in the 1970s that the neoliberals have taken over and marketized. This chapter undertakes a critical analysis of these two hallmark concepts of EU bloc imperialism in the context of the EU-ACP economic partnership agreements. Its basic arguments are first that the EU bloc imperialist goal of 'good governance' in the ACP countries is really to institutionalize a political framework that would provide the political protection for the smooth and uninterrupted transfer of wealth from the ACP regions to Europe. Second, the EU bloc imperialist goal of 'sustainable development' is to secure and maintain the supply of raw materials to Europe, and open-up markets in the ACP regions for EU corporations to operate freely to sell their products.

The EU-ACP EPAs therefore have two fundamental goals one political – good governance, and the other economic – sustainable development that was a part of the agenda of US-led globalization, but which the EU adopted for its own use to fill the European coffers. Good governance is founded on the liberal democratic tradition, while

[1] The neo-liberal counter-revolution refers to the reversal of the idea that there was a need to have separate theories of development to bring about development in the poor countries, and its replacement with the idea that all countries, developed, under-developed, or developing are subject to the same economic principles of free trade in a free market.

sustainable development is based on the free-trade model. The ascent of neoliberal theory from the 1970s deepened the application of these political and economic objectives in the ACP countries. The Bretton Woods institutions[2] and the nation states at their helm cultivated and pushed good governance policy prescriptions on the ACP countries. Being tied to the Bretton Woods system of financing for their development and the associated political conditionality of democratization in the neoliberal period as a means of obtaining loans and aid, the ACP countries were forced to embrace the notion of good governance as their principal political objective.

EU bloc imperialism does not depend on the Bretton Woods institutions for its success but it does make use of some of their policy goals for the ACP countries, objectives that the leading EU states helped to formulate under the hegemony of US-led globalization. The EU is well placed through its EPAs to enforce the idea of good governance in the ACP states, in its self-interest. The EU has created its own institutional frameworks through the EPAs for the implementation and evaluation of good governance in the ACP regions.

The first part of this chapter provides an outline of "governance" as an imperialist concept. It offers a critique of governance and good governance. It presents the development vision of the European bloc imperialists, and identifies major problems with that vision. The second part examines the EU's sustainable development strategy; sustainable development as alternative development theory; and provides various critiques of the neoliberal sustainable development theory. It questions whether the EPA represents sustainable development or European bloc imperialism. It concludes by establishing some linkages between good governance and sustainable development.

Governance – Outline of An Imperialist Concept

The term "governance" has many definitions in different social sciences disciplines such as political science and economics. The neoliberal

[2] The Bretton Woods institutions are the complex of organizations established at the conference in Bretton Woods, New Hampshire, in the United States of America after World War II to regulate the global economy. These institutions include the United Nations and its organs, the International Monetary Fund (IMF), the International Bank for Reconstruction and Development (World Bank), etc.

literature claims that the origins of the concept had to do with the absence of an appropriate term in economics and political science that transmitted sundry meanings not covered by the traditional word "government." It is believed that economics lacked a concept that adequately captured the phenomenon now described as "corporate governance," while the same problem obtained in political science concerning the phenomenon now called "state governance." In this context, therefore, both corporate and state governance involves the actions taken by executive and judicial bodies and assemblies. Governance is therefore a concept that is identified with "the so-called post-modern form of economic and political organization." The term governance is said to have six different meanings as used in contemporary social sciences – the minimal state, corporate governance, new public management, good governance, social-cybernetic systems and self-organized networks.[3]

The White Paper on European Governance[4] adopted by the European Commission in 2001 poses the governance problem, as "acknowledged by national parliaments and governments alike" in the EU, in terms of a paradox – the European people want their political leaders "to find solutions to the major problems confronting" their societies, while increasingly they "distrust institutions and politics or are simply not interested in them" (Commission of the European Communities 2001). This problem is seen to be "particularly acute at the level of the European Union," as it is argued "Many people are losing confidence in a poorly understood and complex system to deliver the policies that they want" (Commission of the European Communities 2001). The EU "is often seen as remote and at times too intrusive."

The White Paper pointed out that Europeans expect the EU "to take the lead in seizing the opportunities of globalization for economic and human development" (Commission of the European Communities 2001). It is also believed that Europeans require the EU to be in the forefront in "responding to environmental challenges, unemployment, concerns over food safety, crime and regional conflicts" (Commission of the European Communities 2001). Furthermore, according to the

---

[3] Rhodes, Roderick A.W. 1996. The New Governance: Governing without Government. *Political Studies* (44) 4: 652–667.

[4] Commission of the European Communities. 2001. European Governance: A White Paper. Brussels.

White Paper "They expect the Union to act as visibly as national governments," and that "Democratic institutions and the representatives of the people, at both national and European levels, can and must try to connect Europe with its citizens" (Commission of the European Communities 2001). The view is that the EU must use these expectations as the starting condition for more effective and relevant policies (Commission of the European Communities 2001).

But, according to the White Paper the disconnect between the people and the ruling elites is not the only governance problem that required reform in terms of the adapting of EU institutions and the establishment of more coherence in its policies, it is about strengthening the EU so that it could "better lead in the world." Thus, the EU governance problem "concerns the way in which the Union uses the powers given by its citizens," and "requires effort from all the other Institutions, central government, regions, cities, and civil society in the current and future Member States" (Commission of the European Communities 2001).

The White Paper establishes the EC's five principles of European governance as "the rules, processes and behavior that affect the way in which powers are exercised at European level, particularly as regards *openness, participation, accountability, effectiveness and coherence*" (Commission of the European Communities 2001). The EU takes its governance problem beyond Europe to the realm of global governance, and proposes, "to apply the principles of good governance to its global responsibilities." It aims "to boost the effectiveness and enforcement powers of international institutions." In order to promote good governance globally, the EU seeks to "Improve the dialogue with governmental and non-governmental actors of third countries when developing policy proposals with an international dimension," and proposes "a review of the Union's international representation in order to allow it to speak more often with a single voice." This really mean that the EU will tie its supposedly development activities in the ACP regions to the issue of good governance.

The EU formulated the governance problem for the ACP countries in the context of applying "the principles of good governance to its global responsibilities." Thus, the ACP states must connect with EU governance policies, which link the EU and ACP ruling elites in a common cause to subject the ACP masses to EU-style liberal democracy and free trade. The governance and free trade stranglehold of EU bloc imperialism over the ACP states is visible most in the area of development theory and practice. For historical reasons the ACP countries look towards Europe for development assistance, but now, EU bloc imperialism links governance conditionality to development assistance. The EC's document on governance and development[5] best outlines the position of EU bloc imperialism on the subject.

The EC formulated nine points concerning the link between governance and development the first being that "The structures and the quality of governance are critical determinants of social cohesion or social conflict, the success or failure of economic development, the preservation or deterioration of the natural environment as well as the respect or violation of human rights and fundamental freedoms" (Commission of the European Communities 2003). The second point is in sink with the statement in the UN Millennium Declaration to the effect that the creation of "an environment that is conducive to development and to the elimination of poverty depends, *inter alia*, on good governance within each country, on good governance at the international level and on transparency in the financial, monetary and trading systems" (Commission of the European Communities 2003). The EU therefore equally links "Governance, democratization and development" in its "general objectives" in the ACP countries. The third link between governance and development identified by EU bloc imperialism is that "Governance is a key component of policies and reforms for poverty reduction, democratization and global security" (Commission of the European Communities 2003).

The fourth point is that although there is "no internationally agreed definition of governance, the concept has gained importance and over the last ten years all development partners have expanded their work in that field." In this connection governance is defined in terms of "the state's ability to serve the citizens," a sufficiently broad definition that allows the EU "conceptually to disaggregate governance and other topics such as human rights, democracy or corruption." It also sees governance in terms of "the rules, processes, and behavior by which interests are articulated, resources are managed, and power is exercised in society." To this effect, the "real value of the concept of governance is that it provides a terminology that is more pragmatic than democracy, human rights, etc." Governance is said to be "a meaningful and practical

[5] Commission of the European Communities. 2003. Governance and Development. Brussels.

concept relating to the very basic aspects of the functioning of any society and political and social systems," and could "be described as a basic measure of stability and performance of a society." The EU bloc imperialist view is further asserted as follows:

> As the concepts of human rights, democratization and democracy, the rule of law, civil society, decentralized power sharing, and sound public administration gain importance and relevance as a society develops into a more sophisticated political system, governance evolves into good governance. Today governance is generally used as a basic measure of quality and performance of any political/administrative system (Commission of the European Communities 2003).

The fifth point is that in accordance with Article 9.3 of the Cotonou Partnership Agreement, "good governance is the transparent and accountable management of human, natural, economic and financial resources for the purpose of equitable and sustainable development." In the view of the EU, this represents "a political and institutional environment that upholds human rights, democratic principles and the rule of law," and "entails clear decision-making procedures at the level of public authorities, transparent and accountable institutions, the primacy of the rule of law in the management of resources and capacity building for elaborating and implementing measures aiming in particular to preventing and combating corruption" (Commission of the European Communities 2003).

The sixth point is that "Good governance is first and foremost a domestic issue," which according to the EU requires adequate domestic policies to bridge the widening gap "between the poor and the rich, both within and between countries and regions." To this effect the EU believes that "good governance at all levels of the international system – national, regional, multilateral levels – is crucial to a legitimate, effective and coherent global governance system," which involves the continued improvement in "policy coherence in all relevant areas, such as for example, environment, trade or agriculture."

The seventh point by the EU bloc imperialists in their linking of governance and development is stated as follows:

> Good governance is key to the effectiveness of development assistance, and towards the achievement of objectives towards which we should strive. However, achieving good governance is a process. Therefore, as long as good governance has not been achieved, pragmatic approaches must be pursued to support progress. Indicators should not in this context be considered as a simple list of issues to be included in a scoreboard

> aimed at setting up a purely governance based selectivity, but rather as a tool to mainstreaming governance in all EC financed interventions and strategies (Commission of the European Communities 2003).

According to the eight point identified by the EU bloc imperialist there is the need for "capacity building and dialogue on governance in different types of situations." Finally, the EC's objectives concerning governance and development aims at identifying practical ways

> to build capacity for governance and increase partner countries' ownership of the formulation of the relevant reform programs; to ensure synergies and coherence between the different EC and EU policies and instruments; to reinforce the partnerships for development on a country or regional basis, in order to achieve co-ordination between donors' priorities and partner countries' agendas through the policy dialogue as well as complementarity between donors; to contribute to the protection of human rights and to the spreading of democracy, good governance and the rule of law (Commission of the European Communities 2003).

Also, the EU bloc imperialists discussed their position on democracy, good governance, human rights, and the rights of children and indigenous peoples in a statement entitled the European Consensus on Development.[6] They pledged to promote "democracy, good governance, human rights and the rights of children" in "partnership with all countries receiving" development assistance from the EU, and to systematically incorporate these issues into the EU's "development instruments through all country and regional strategy papers." They argue, "The key principle for safeguarding indigenous peoples rights in development cooperation is to ensure their full participation and the free and prior informed consent of the communities concerned."

Critique of Governance and Good Governance

US-led globalization as imperialism insisted on democratization in the ACP countries as a political conditionality for IMF and World Bank assistance. EU bloc imperialism however, insists on good governance as political conditionality in the ACP countries for EU assistance.

---

[6] Commission of the European Communities. 2005. Joint Statement by the Council and the Representative of the Governments of the Member States Meeting within the Council, the European Parliament and the Commission 'The European Consensus on Development' Part I: The EU Vision of Development 14820/05 ATR/kl 1 ANNEX I DG E II.

Democratization and good governance however, are to pacify the people in the ACP regions to cause them to fit in to a routine of national elections in every four years and assuming the semblance of people's participation in power whereas the reality is that a small class of overlords wield political and economic power as is evident in the leading democracies on the planet.

The experience with democracy in the so-called free world is such that change takes place within a cocoon comprising the richest and most powerful individuals within the society. Working people are incited into frenzy at elections time to vote in support of the class agendas of these powerful individuals – and that is called good governance. Good governance is therefore the process by which one group of class oppressors replaces another group of class oppressors by the ballot and is characterized by the processes, which maintain political stability until the next round of elections. Good governance is about soothing the masses, lulling them to accept the liberal democratic tradition. It is about the curtailment of revolutionary activity among the masses that could overturn the *status quo* and establish alternative socio-economic and political systems. It is the current trajectory of a tradition supposedly founded on the 'rule of law' – laws made by the ruling elites – meaning the freedom of the dominant class forces to make and enforce laws to protect their property and constrain mass political action for revolutionary change.

The problem with the push for good governance is that it is not coming from the masses but from the elites in the EU and global institutions that are not themselves accountable to the ACP constituencies. Good governance conceived along the lines of EU bloc imperialist political ideology is more about external political control of ACP states than it is about the creation of popular democracy in the ACP countries. In essence, good governance revolves around the neoliberal view that liberal democracy is the best form of political arrangement to facilitate capitalist economic growth and development. However, research has established that there is no correlation between economic growth and type of political system (Przeworski, 2003).

Between 1951 and 1999, total GDP grew at an annual rate of 4.40 percent under so-called dictatorships and at a rate of 3.69 percent under so-called democracies (Przeworski, 2003). This is not an argument in favour of dictatorships but a critique of EU bloc imperialism, which identifies good governance as a political condition for economic prosperity and development. Rather than bringing about popular democracy, good governance merely promotes liberal democracy a type of political system in which the rich dominates the poor – a condition in which the latter willingly participates through manipulation by the former.

US-led globalization as imperialism for example needs a new form of authoritarianism called "democratization" to guarantee the smooth operations of its mega-corporations in their extraction of the economic surplus from the ACP countries. The US regards good governance, which USAID operatives define as a concept that encompasses the capacity of the state to deliver public services, the commitment to the public good, the rule of law, and the degree of transparency and accountability (Franco, 2005), as an integral component of its national security strategy. USAID spends millions of dollars on "democracy promotion," which in essence is the Americanization of political processes in developing countries. For example, USAID budget for democracy promotion efforts for fiscal year 2004 was $685 million, with an additional $500 million for democratization efforts in Afghanistan and Iraq (McConnell, 2005). USAID increased its financing on building democracy, strengthening governance, promoting human rights and addressing conflict in Latin America and the Caribbean region from approximately $106 million to about $271 million between 2001 and 2005 (Franco, 2005).

The US efforts to Americanize the political system in Latin America and the Caribbean is undeniable. USAID is involved with "creating and strengthening the justice-sector institutions, including independent prosecutors, constitutional courts, judicial councils, and human rights ombudsmen" in the region (Franco, 2005). Furthermore, the US has "trained thousands of judges, prosecutors, litigators, law professors, and community activists to ensure the smooth transition to modern judicial systems" in the region (Franco, 2005). In this way, the US seizes control of the judicial system in the region. US imperialism therefore takes over the economic system through economic adjustment, and the political and judicial systems through good governance. While economic adjustment strips ACP countries of their economic resources and wealth, democratization and good governance take away their political freedom. Similarly, the EU economic partnership agreements will strip the ACP countries of their economic resources, while good governance takes away their political freedom.

ACP politicians and civil society organizations however have embraced the neoliberal rhetoric about "good governance," as an integral component of the democratization process sponsored by EU economic partnership agreements. In essence however "good governance" is really about providing the appropriate political environment for EU multinational corporations to operate smoothly in their extraction of the economic surplus produced in the ACP states, and to facilitate capital flight. For example, in Ghana since the emphasis on good governance with the advent of structural adjustment in 1983 and the country initialling an interim EU-EPA, the flow of gold out of the country has increased tremendously.[7] There is a definitely positive correlation between good governance and the extraction of gold from Ghana by foreign transnationals.

The criticisms of "good governance" presented here are not in opposition to democracy, but for more democracy, premised on the fact that neoliberal democratization has produced various forms of new authoritarian states in the developing countries and in the former communist states.[8] Neoliberal democratization has not produced democracy for the masses in these countries; it merely reproduces the conditions for wealth extraction by the TNCs and their local political elite clientele and for the protection of their property. These states are described as semi-authoritarian, representing a mixture of liberal democratic principles such as periodic national elections, simultaneously that there exist authoritarian state structures in them (Ottaway 2003).

Despite the chatter about good governance in the Caribbean, for example, the political economy of Guyana is under the domination of a new phenomenon dubbed the "criminalized state."[9] The characteristics of the criminalized state include an absence of government support for the public's right to share economic information and to participate in decision-making. The "criminalized state" has emerged with the full protection of the forces of globalization, namely the international financial institutions (IFIs) that do not uphold in poor countries such as Guyana the same standards of democracy they identified for themselves.

---

[7] Agbesinyale, Patrick K. 2003. Ghana's Gold Rush and Regional Development: The Case of Wassa West District. Dortmund, SPRING Centre.

[8] Canterbury, Dennis C. 2005. *Neoliberal Democratization and New Authoritarianism*. Aldershot, Hampshire: Ashgate; Ottaway, Marina. 2003. *Democracy Challenged: The Rise of Semi-Authoritarianism*. Washington: Carnegie Endowment for International Peace.

[9] Thomas, Clive. 2003. Guyana and the Wider World. *Stabroek News*, Georgetown, Guyana.

European Bloc Imperialist Development Vision

EU bloc imperialism stipulated its development vision in a statement in 2005 entitled the European Consensus on Development. The EU claims that development is at the heart of its external actions, along with its foreign, security and trade policies, and that poverty eradication in the context of sustainable development and the achievement of the Millennium Development Goals is the primary and overarching objective of its development policy. The EU's position is that its partnerships and dialogue with the ACP states promote respect for human rights, fundamental freedoms, peace, democracy, good governance, gender equality, the rule of law, solidarity and justice.

The EU pointed out that it is the largest donor of official development assistance, and that it has also improved its aid assistance to the ACP states. Its consensus on development outlines the common principles and objectives for development cooperation and "reaffirms EU commitment to poverty eradication, ownership, partnership, delivering more and better aid and promoting policy coherence for development." It claims that the consensus on development will guide its development cooperation activities and its member states "in all developing countries." What are the common objectives of the EU consensus on development?

First is the primary and overarching objective to eradicate "poverty in the context of sustainable development," which includes the "pursuit of the Millennium Development Goals (MDGs)." The eight MDGs are the eradication of extreme poverty and hunger; achievement of universal primary education; promotion of gender equality and empowerment of women; reduction in the mortality rate of children; improvement in maternal health; combating HIV/AIDS, malaria and other diseases; ensuring environmental sustainability and development of a global partnership for development. The development cooperation activities of the EU are defined as ODA as agreed on by the OECD/DAC.

Second, the EU reaffirms "that development is a central goal by itself; and that sustainable development includes good governance, human rights and political, economic, social and environmental aspects." Third, the EU claims to be "determined to work to assist the achievement of these goals and the development objectives agreed at the major UN conferences and summits." Fourth, the EU reaffirms that it is committed "to promoting policy coherence for development, based upon ensuring that the EU shall take account of the objectives of development cooperation in all policies that it implements which are likely to affect developing countries, and that these policies support development objectives."

Finally, the EU claims its "Development aid will continue to support poor people in all developing countries, including both low-income and middle-income countries (MICs)." The EU pledges to continue to prioritize its support to the least-developed and other low-income countries (LICs) "to achieve more balanced global development, while recognizing the value of concentrating the aid activities of each Member State in areas and regions where they have comparative advantages and can add most value to the fight against poverty."

Problems with EU Development Vision

These objectives are problematic for a number of reasons. The first problem is the false fundamental theoretical premise of the EU development vision. In this vision, development assistance takes place in the context of free trade. The historical evidence demonstrates however that the ACP countries are victims of free trade. The economic relations between the former colonies (ACP) and their colonizers (EU) are the main cause of the perpetuation of poverty in the former regions. There is no guarantee that EPAs and the associated assistance through development cooperation will change that historical fact. In this connection the EU consensus on development is a front to allow the EU to continue to transfer wealth from the ACP regions to Europe, while it simultaneously reinforces poverty in the ACP countries.

The second problem is that the Millennium Development Goals emphasizes the "foreign finance of domestic social goals rather than developing/industrializing countries so they themselves, internally, can solve their own problems of redistribution."[10] The MDGs approach raises, the question concerning the extent to which it "will put a large group of nations permanently 'on the dole,'" in a system similar to the 'welfare colonialism.'[11]

---

[10] Reinert, Erik S. 2005. Development and Social Goals: Balancing Aid and Development to Prevent 'Welfare Colonialism'. *Post-Autistic Economics Review*, (30) 21: 1.

[11] Reinert, Erik S. 2005. Development and Social Goals: Balancing Aid and Development to Prevent 'Welfare Colonialism'. *Post-Autistic Economics Review*, (30) 21: 1.

The third problem has to do with international cooperation in the form of aid as imperialism that was addressed since the 1970s.[12] The theory of economic development as does the EU's vision of development has identified "overseas development assistance" (ODA) or "foreign aid," as a major mechanism to transfer wealth to the ACP countries as a principal means of their development. The real significance of foreign aid in the development of the ACP countries has been the subject for "academic and policy debate among liberals and structuralists, neoliberals and neostructuralists."[13] The real issue however, is not whether aid contributes to development in the ACP states buy whether it is used as a mechanism in the furtherance of the political and economic agendas of EU bloc imperialism by opening-up these countries to domination by EU multinationals. The conclusion may be drawn based on the historical evidence that if foreign aid "is a catalyst of anything it is not development but regression."[14]

The fourth point concerns the weakness associated with the notion of good governance discussed above and that of sustainable development addressed in the following section. The general conclusion can be drawn that the common objectives of the EU consensus on development will enhance the economic domination of the ACP countries by EU bloc imperialism.

The EU's Sustainable Development Strategy

The EU's first sustainable development strategy entitled "A Sustainable Europe for a Better World: A European Union Strategy for Sustainable Development" in 2001 stated, "Sustainable development is a global objective. The European Union has a key role in bringing about sustainable development, within Europe and also on the wider global stage, where widespread international action is required."[15] The EU sustainable development strategy seeks to add an environmental

---

[12] Hayter, Teresa. 1971. *Aid as Imperialism*. Harmondsmouth: Penguin Books.

[13] Petras, James and Henry Veltmeyer. 2004. "Aid and Adjustment: Policy Reform and Regression", in Henry Veltmeyer, ed., *Globalization and Anti-Globalization: Dynamics of Change in the New World Order*. Aldershot: Ashgate, pp. 24–53.

[14] Petras, James and Henry Veltmeyer. 2004. "Aid and Adjustment: Policy Reform and Regression", in Henry Veltmeyer, ed., *Globalization and Anti-Globalization: Dynamics of Change in the New World Order*. Aldershot: Ashgate, pp. 24–53.

[15] Commission of the European Communities. 2001a. A Sustainable Europe for a Better World: A European Union Strategy for Sustainable Development. Brussels.

dimension that builds on and complete on the EU's political commitment "to become the most competitive and dynamic knowledge-based economy in the world capable of sustainable economic growth with more and better jobs and greater social cohesion." It "recognizes that in the long term, economic growth, social cohesion and environmental protection must go hand in hand" (Commission of the European Communities 2001).

The EU's long-term vision of sustainable development is outlined as embracing a set of commendable ideals, although the practice of sustainable development discussed below, is quite different. The EU's sustainable development strategy states:

> Sustainable development offers the European Union a positive long-term vision of a society that is more prosperous and more just, and which promises a cleaner, safer, healthier environment – a society which delivers a better quality of life for us, for our children, and for our grandchildren. Achieving this in practice requires that economic growth supports social progress and respects the environment, that social policy underpins economic performance, and that environmental policy is cost-effective. Decoupling environmental degradation and resource consumption from economic and social development requires a major reorientation of public and private investment towards new, environmentally friendly technologies. The sustainable development strategy should be a catalyst for policy-makers and public opinion ... and become a driving force for institutional reform, and for changes in corporate and consumer behavior. Clear, stable, long-term objectives will shape expectations and create the conditions in which businesses have the confidence to invest in innovative solutions, and to create new, high-quality jobs (Commission of the European Communities 2001).

These are the values, which the EU proposes will govern its external economic relations with the ACP countries. These values are developed further in an EC document entitled "Towards a global partnership for sustainable development," in 2002.[16] The document developed on the external dimension of the EU sustainable development strategy and the EU's contribution to global sustainable development and the strategic components for a "Global Deal" on sustainable development. The EU outlined the case of a global partnership on sustainable development by arguing that for development to be sustainable it "must strike a balance between the economic, social and environmental

[16] Commission of the European Communities. 2002. Towards a Global Partnership for Sustainable Development. Brussels.

objectives of society, in order to maximize well-being in the present, without compromising the ability of future generations to meet their needs" (Commission of the European Communities 2002).

The objective of the EU's sustainable development strategy is to maximize the benefits of globalization while minimizing the costs. In this regard, the priority objectives of the EU are to "ensure that globalization contributes to sustainable development." To bring this about the EU proposes to:

> Ensure that the developing countries are integrated equitably into the world economy and help them to reap the benefits of trade and investment liberalization through complementary policies; Provide incentives for environmentally and socially sustainable production and trade; and Strengthen the international financial and monetary architecture and promote better and more transparent forms of financial market regulation to reduce global financial volatility and abuses of the system (Commission of the European Communities 2002).

The EU believes that because it is "the world's largest donor of aid, the world's biggest trading partner, and a major source of direct private investments," and given the fact that it has "developed and promoted a great number of clean technologies," it is "well placed to assume a leading role in the pursuit of global sustainable development" (Commission of the European Communities. 2002).

The EU adopted a Declaration on the Guiding Principles for Sustainable Development in 2005.[17] The declaration reaffirmed that sustainable development is a key objective of the EU and that it aims at the continuous improvement of the quality of life on earth of both current and future generations, and "safeguarding the earth's capacity to support life in all its diversity." The declaration states that sustainable development "is based on the principles of democracy and the rule of law and respect for fundamental rights including freedom and equal opportunities for all" (Council of the European Union 2005). In the EU's view sustainable development "brings about solidarity within and between generations," and promotes "a dynamic economy with full employment and a high level of education, health protection, social and territorial cohesion and environmental protection in a peaceful and secure world, respecting cultural diversity" (Council of the European Union 2005).

---

[17] Council of the European Union. 2005. Declaration on Guiding Principles for Sustainable Development. Brussels.

To attain these aims the EU is committed to pursue and respect the following objectives and principles. The first objective is environmental protection to safeguard the earth's capacity "to support life in all its diversity," while respecting the planet's limited natural resources, ensuring "a high level of protection and improvement of the quality of the environment," preventing and reducing environmental pollution and promoting "sustainable production and consumption to break the link between economic growth and environmental degradation" (Council of the European Union 2005).

The second objective is social equity and protection, which involves the promotion of "a democratic, socially inclusive, cohesive, healthy, safe and just society with respect for fundamental rights and cultural diversity that creates equal opportunities and combats discrimination in all its forms" (Council of the European Union 2005). The third objective is economic prosperity, based on the promotion of "a prosperous, innovative, knowledge-rich, competitive and eco-efficient economy which provides high living standards and full and high-quality employment throughout the European Union" (Council of the European Union 2005).

The fourth objective is the meeting of its international responsibilities, namely to "Encourage the establishment and defend the stability of democratic institutions across the world, based on peace, security and freedom" (Council of the European Union 2005). This involves the active promotion of "sustainable development worldwide and ensure that the European Union's internal and external policies are consistent with global sustainable development and its international commitments" (Council of the European Union 2005).

The guiding principles of the EU's policy for sustainable development are first the promotion and protection of fundamental rights, which entails the centering of humans at the heart of the EU's policies, through the promotion of "fundamental rights, combating all forms of discrimination and contributing to the reduction of poverty and the elimination of social exclusion worldwide." The second principle has to do with solidarity with and between generations, to deal with the "needs of current generations without compromising the ability of future generations to meet their needs in the European Union and elsewhere." The third principle involves the promotion of open and democratic societies, to guarantee citizens' rights of access to information, ensure access to justice, and develop adequate consultation and participatory channels for all interested parties and associations. The fourth principle concerns the involvement of citizens, to enhance their participation in decision-making, 'promote education and public awareness of sustainable development, inform citizens about their impact on the environment and their options for making more sustainable choices."

The fifth and sixth principles are involvement of business and social partners, and policy coherence and governance, respectively. The involvement of business and social partners will "Enhance the social dialogue, corporate social responsibility and private-public partnerships to foster cooperation and common responsibilities to achieve sustainable production and consumption." Policy coherence and governance will "Promote coherence between all European Union policies and coherence between local, regional, national and global actions in order to enhance their contribution to sustainable development."

The seventh and eight principles are policy integration, and the use of the best available knowledge, respectively. Policy integration seeks to promote the "integration of economic, social and environmental considerations" to make them coherent and mutually reinforcing, using the "instruments for better regulation, such as balanced impact assessment and stakeholder consultations." The use of best available knowledge is to bring about the development, assessment and implementation of policies "on the basis of the best available knowledge and that they are economically sound and cost-effective."

Finally, there is a precautionary principle, which states that in cases where there is scientific uncertainty, evaluation procedures must be implemented, and appropriate preventive action taken to avoid damage to human health or to the environment. The last principle is to make polluters pay so that "prices reflect the real costs to society of production and consumption activities" and ensure that "polluters pay for the damage they cause to human health and the environment."

In appearance, the EU's sustainable development strategy is noble indeed, but in reality it is quite ignoble for the ACP countries for whom, it is intended. This argument is made in the next section, which examines sustainable development as an alternative development theory. Sustainable development does not transfer the social relations of production such that power changes hand from the capitalist to the working peoples.

Sustainable Development as Alternative Development Theory

Neoliberal Sustainable Development

The debate on sustainable development emerged from environmentalism or concerns about environmental conservation by scholars and policy makers (McMichael 2008), which could be classified under the general rubric of alternative development theory, or the rethinking of development that has gone on since the 1970s. Sustainable development surfaced as an attempt to maintain and expand the capitalist mode of production while simultaneously protecting the environment. Neoliberal sustainable development is the application of neoliberal free market and liberal democratic ideology to environmental conservation. It is the foundation of the EU's sustainable development strategy. Neoliberal sustainable development like good governance also had its origins in the Bretton Woods institutions that took the high ground to preserve the environment for the future of humanity, while simultaneously addressing the basic needs of impoverished individuals, classes, and nation-states, in all geographic regions on planet earth.

The story about neoliberal sustainable development originated as far back as the UN Conference on the Human Environment in Stockholm in 1972. Conservation and Development were also the themes of the International Union for the Conservation of Nature and Natural Resources (IUCN) General Assembly in Banff, Alberta Canada in 1972. The IUCN, World Wildlife Fund (WWF) and UN Environmental Programme (UNEP) prepared a World Conservation Strategy (WCS) throughout the 1970s that was published in 1980.

Seven years later, the World Commission on Environment and Development (WCED) Bruntland Report *Our Common Future*, (1987), echoing the WCS, gave a great fillip to environmental concerns in development studies. The WCS (1980), the Bruntland Report, the IUCN's *Caring for the Earth*, (1991), and Agenda 21, the product of the Earth Summit in 1992, form the core of what emerged as the neoliberal sustainable development strategy.

The Brandt Reports, *North-South: A Program for Survival*, (1980) and *Common Crisis North-South: Cooperation for World Recovery*, (1983), also had a role in the evolution of neoliberal sustainable development in that the Bruntland Report built on what Brandt said about the environment. Thus, in the twenty-year span between 1972 and

1992 sustainable development became a central tenet in the neoliberal agenda to promote free trade and good governance, and a struggle between the rich and poor countries, with the former pushing their environmental agenda on the latter.

The major theoretical challenge that environmentalism and sustainable development presented was to refocus social analysis on the problem of scarcity, by arguing that the ecological system does not have the capacity to sustain current levels of growth and consumption unless there is environmental conservation. Thus, ecology is a constraining factor on capitalist production for market exchange. Indeed, according to the "impossibility theorem" of former World Bank economists Herman E. Daly "a U.S.-style high resource consumption standard for a world of 4 billion people is impossible" (McMichael 2008), since there are natural ecological limits to growth. It requires that ecologically constrained development be regarded as a kind of natural law of progress in human society, in replacement of the neoclassical view of development as unlimited economic growth. The environmentalist school therefore promoted the idea of zero growth in the 1970s, but it came in for criticism by perpetrators of the economic theory of unlimited growth.

Sustainable development also recognizes scarcity as a constraining factor on economic growth, but the difference with environmentalism is that the physical environment is not the cause, but rather technology and social organization (Adams 1996). As determined by the Bruntland Report, sustainable development is for continuous growth, necessitating the revitalization and maintenance of the world economy. Two basic ideas of the Bruntland Report are first basic needs and the primacy of development action for the poor, and second, the idea of environmental limits set by technology and social organization.

The preoccupation with scarcity was the reason that the classical political economists foresaw a crash in the capitalist economic system caused by the Ricardian relativist notion of diminishing returns and the Malthusian absolutist idea about population pressure (Hettne, 1995). Marxism also regards scarcity as a constraining factor of productive forces under capitalism, and presents socialism as a socio-economic alternative to eradicate resource conflict theories of bourgeois economics founded on social activities of humans in an environment of scarcity (Hettne 1995). Neoclassical economics shifted the focus from scarcity to economic growth. Its proponents believe in indefinite growth, meaning that it is possible for an economy to grow *ad infinitum*, regardless of the scarcity of productive factors.

While the Brandt report returned to Keynesian organized management of the world economy, the principal idea about neoliberal sustainable development is that environmental protection must not limit economic growth. The Bruntland Report actually countered neo-Malthusian ideas about overpopulation pressures on the environment as constraints on economic growth. Sustainable development became, entrapped in the age-old theoretical debate about the possibilities for limitless economic growth, a debate that the neo-classical growth theorist claimed to have resolved in the affirmative.

The Earth Summit in Rio, Brazil, in 1992 reviewed the progress of the Bruntland report and produced a document called Agenda 21 that details a global sustainable development program for the twenty-first century. In Agenda 21, developing countries committed themselves to a fundamental change in the pattern of development, and the interlinked problems of pollution, global warming and sea-level rise; soil erosion and desertification; and population growth and poverty (Hettne 1995). The developing countries embraced the developed states concerns to reduce carbon dioxide emissions, and preserve biodiversity and the rain forests to "save" planet earth (Escobar 1995).

While joining in the call for sustainable development, the developing countries demanded in return the financial assistance of the rich states, with the understanding that "poverty is the greatest polluter." To counteract poverty and thereby "save" planet earth from poverty driven environmental destruction, the poor countries insisted that the developed states invest in them substantially in sustainable development including in health, sanitation, education, technical assistance, and conservation (Escobar 1995). This demand placed the question of global inequalities on the table in the negotiations concerning environmental protection and sustainable development.

If poverty reflects inequality and it is the cause of environmental degradation, and the rich states are so concerned with protecting the environment and sustainable development, then it follows that they must share their wealth with the poor to help "save" the planet. The UNCED sidestepped the issue of global inequalities and stressed instead the need to protect the environment as a development priority, while simultaneously ensuring the free international movement of goods and capital (Escobar 1995). In other words, although the poor countries must make environmental protection and sustainable development a top priority in their development strategy, they must do so in a manner that would not disrupt international trade and foreign direct investments by the TNCs. This major contradiction reveals that although the rich and poor countries chatter about sustainable development, it takes second place to capital accumulation through trade and foreign investment. This is the major problem with the EU vision of development and strategy for sustainable development outlined above.

In two important senses, Agenda 21 replaced the focus of the Bruntland report by placing "global management of the environment over local/national concerns," and maintaining the viability of the global economy rather than addressing deteriorating economic conditions in the South (Escobar 1995). Neoliberalism brought sustainable development in line with the free market imperative. Another significance of the Rio Summit nonetheless was the politicization of sustainable development (Hettne 1995).

For example, it is standard practice nowadays for the mining transnational corporation (TNCs) to undertake an environmental impact assessment (EIA) before they begin or continue their operations in the poor countries. Several countries now have an Environmental Protection Agency as part of the institutional arrangement for sustainable development that undertakes these EIAs according to internationally determined standards. Consequently, sustainable development became a new strategy of the TNCs operating in the poor countries to demonstrate that they are good corporate citizens who are conscious of the environment and the need for sustainable development. National and international regulations subject the mining TNCs to an EIA as an environmental conditionality for their operations.

However, the Environmental Protection Agencies are creatures of neoliberal sustainable development that must not hinder international trade and foreign direct investment, so TNCs are usually, given permission to proceed to carry out their operations, having scored positively on their EIAs. The hypocrisy of all this is that the rich states have exported their "dirty industries" that is, those that pollute the environment the most, to the poor countries. Furthermore, mining TNCs continue their destruction of the environment in poor countries despite the existence of Environmental Protection Agencies and EIAs, and the concerns about sustainable development.

Further Critique of Neoliberal Sustainable Development

At the outset, we must state that neoliberal sustainable development represents a usurpation of radical and mainstream attempts in development studies to find genuine development alternatives. The appropriation of sustainable development by neoliberalism manifests itself in the admonitions by the World Bank that sustainable development must embrace an undistorted, competitive, and well-functioning market (Meier and Stiglitz 2001). This is also the case with the EU's vision of development and sustainable development strategy. The marketization of sustainable development strips the concept of its originality as a formidable challenge to mainstream development theory that is in pursuit of endless economic growth. It converts sustainable development into just another theory in the service of imperialism, formulated by elite scholars in prestigious universities and supported by the IMF and World Bank.

Agenda 21 is another indicator of the usurpation of sustainable development in the service of neoliberalism. Its emphasis on global management of the economy takes the power over their environment out of the hands of local communities and places it in the hands of global environmental police in the control of global capital, forcing poor countries to become signatories to numerous regional and global agreements to protect the environment. These agreements in many cases are conditions for financial support, so the poor countries must join in the hypocritical game of environmental protection and sustainable development. The EU and international environmental agencies can therefore dictate environmental policies to poor countries depriving them of their political independence to determine their own destiny. Moreover, Agenda 21 concerns itself with the furtherance of globalization the new imperialism at the expense of the poor countries.

Furthermore, neoliberal sustainable development merely repackages mainstream economic development theories, by focusing on basic needs, population studies, natural and human resources, resource allocation, technology, institutional co-operation, food security, and industrialization (Escobar 1995). The result of the neoliberal turn in sustainable development is that in the extractive industries for example, TNCs continue to destroy the environment in both the rich and poor countries with impunity. The environmental destruction problem now appears to result from the activities of poor farmers and miners, when in reality the big TNCs in both the agricultural and mining sectors are the real culprits. In addition, the poor countries must embrace sustainable development, for fear of being ostracised, or left out of the club of "clean" countries.

The debate is unresolved over whether poverty or affluence is the root cause of environmental destruction. Nonetheless, framing the debate in that way fits in nicely with the neoliberal sustainable development theory because the poverty argument that poor people place a great stress on resources, resorts to Malthusian population control, and economic growth as the solution to the problem. The affluence argument is that global inequality and resource consumption in support of wealthy lifestyles pressurises scarce resources requiring income redistribution as the solution to close the inequality gap. The folly of that argument is that if all people in the world were wealthy in the capitalist sense of the term then the "impossibility theorem" will apply.

The problem with the "impossibility theorem" however is that it tends to contribute to a form of "environmental racism" and takes a hegemonic position in that the poor countries will never be able to achieve the level of consumption that the rich countries enjoy today. It speaks to a hegemonic hierarchical process whereby some geographic regions will persistently enjoy high levels of consumption and others low levels of consumption. It does not tell us what will maintain such a structure of unequal global consumption. Nonetheless, we conclude that neoliberal globalization will continue to perpetuate high levels of inequality between the rich and poor countries.

The elites that compiled the Bruntland report took the high ground of demonstrating concern with the common future of humans, without even finding out from the mass of humanity if it ever wanted to be a part of the envisaged common future. To adopt the position that humans have a common future, ties humanity to the mercantile/classical political economy system of progress through the accumulation of wealth, and to the structure of nation-states it created in which some are wealthy and others are poor. The subjection of all humanity to a common future means economic, political and social globalization. It is a new form of tyranny and presumption by the states with the economic and military power to subject all humanity to their assumptions about a common future, shaped in their likeness as the dominant powers.

EPA: Sustainable Development or European Bloc Imperialism

Sustainable development appears to be the backbone of the CARIFORUM-EU EPA, but in reality the concept has become a code phase for the promotion of neoliberal globalization and EU bloc imperialism. What is the theoretical basis of sustainable development contained in the EPA? We have already noted that the EPA is founded on Ricardian trade theory that reinforces a particular pattern of international division of labor based on the idea that the factor endowment of a country should determine the commodities in which it specializes in production for market exchange. By so doing, according to this theory, the country will derive the greatest benefits, because it will produce and sell the commodities that it is good at producing, and then uses the money it generates from such sales to buy commodities that it does not produce.

According to this logic, the Caribbean islands should specialize in tourism services because of their sunshine and beaches and import the manufactured goods they consume, and countries like Guyana and Belize should specialize in agriculture because of they have the land for that purpose. The economic system based on this notion of specialization will work well only if the Caribbean countries are able to freely sell their products to, and buy their imports from, any country they choose based on market principles. Nowadays, scholars present this same idea along the lines that the Caribbean needs to develop *niche* markets in which it will specialize to its greatest advantage. Now, where do we fit sustainable development into this picture?

The idea of sustainable development emerged several decades ago over concerns with human destruction of the environment. The simple notion that humans are destroying the environment in order to produce commodities for consumption, requiring measures to protect the environment has taken many twists and turns over the years. Sustainable development is one on the ideas to result from the concern with environmental protection. Like environmental protection the term sustainable development too has taken on a life of its own traversing a spectrum that ranges from advocates of anti-growth to neoliberal globalization. While the pursuit of limitless economic growth is seen as a cause of environmental destruction on the one hand, on the other the neoliberal view is to bring endless economic growth in line with the idea of sustainable development. In the latter instance, the claim is that it is possible for economic growth and environmental protection to proceed simultaneously. Furthermore, environmental protection must not serve as a constraint on the operation of the free market. The fact of the matter is that this view aligns sustainable development with the globalization of the capitalist market system, because sustainable development must uphold market freedom.

The EPA is a "trade partnership for sustainable development," it is not a partnership for sustainable production. It wants to eradicate poverty "through the establishment of a trade partnership consistent with the objective of sustainable development." The explicit focus on trade instructs us to regard the EPA as an instrument to promote the sustainable development of capitalist globalization through free markets. This is because neoliberal globalization is the process of capital accumulation through free trade, and the EPA serves that purpose rather than seeking to reform or change it.

According to the CARIFORUM countries and the EU, the objective of sustainable development will take into account "the human, cultural, economic, social, health and environmental best interests of their respective population and of future generations," and "decision-taking methods" will "embrace the fundamental principles of ownership, participation and dialogue." According to the agreement, the CARIFORUM countries and the EU support a "realization of a sustainable development centered on the human, who is the main beneficiary of development." The problem here is that "best interest" has no fixed definition. Poor countries may argue that it is in their best interest to attract Europe's "dirty industries" in order for them to become industrialized.

The CARIFORUM-EU EPA at the heart of which is neoliberal free trade theory therefore embraces a notion of sustainable development that we call neoliberal sustainable development. Sustainable development as gleaned from the EPA promotes market principles to the extent that it must not hinder free trade. Thus, the CARIFORUM countries could not easily place limitations on the importation of a commodity from the EU whose production destroys the environment, because that would be tantamount to interfering with free trade. It is more likely, however, that the EU could place limitations on the export of CARIFORUM commodities to the EU, deemed to be environmentally unfriendly, because of the leverage the EU has over the region in terms of development assistance, etc.

Conclusion: Linking Good Governance and Sustainable Development

In conclusion, a number of propositions are presented concerning the link between good governance and sustainable development arguing that the neoliberal debate on these development concepts represents a mere surface manifestation of a larger problem of imperialism in the twenty-first century. The debate fails to identify the real cause of a lack of good governance and sustainable development in poor countries. It does not make proper use of the historical method to analyse the political economy in the poor countries that would establish the real and strongest links between governance and sustainable development.

The main cause of this failure is the inability to recognize that capitalist commodity production is the principal source of the current problems with governance and sustainable development. The mere identification and formulation of the problem of good governance and sustainable development is a capitalist formulation. The problem is a derivative, a product of the actually existing system of capitalist commodity production. To understand the link between the concepts it is imperative that we unravel the intricacies of capitalist commodity production, its origins and persistence in the existing poor countries.

The introduction of capitalist commodity production in the ACP states produced authoritarian political and state arrangements simultaneously, in these countries, and disrupted their traditional forms of production and politics. In Ghana and Guyana, for example, the authoritarian state evolved into the current problems with good governance. Politics and the state in these countries are an extension of the colonial authoritarian political arrangements. Similarly, capitalist commodity production itself is the cause of problems with sustainable development because of its commoditization of all objects of nature, even human body parts. Nowadays, it is possible to buy a new lung, heart, kidneys, nose, and other human body parts.

The main purpose of the colonial authoritarian state was to preside over the maximum extraction of wealth by capitalist companies from the ACP countries and to transport it for storage or accumulation in Europe. This was to satisfy the mercantile/classical political economic theory that for a country to develop or progress it must continuously enlarge its stock of accumulated capital in the form of precious metals, and money. The pursuit of that development goal by the European states, which led them to colonize the ACP countries, marked the genesis of the governance and sustainability problem associated with capitalist commodity production in these regions.

The colonial authoritarian state pillaged ACP countries' wealth and cared less about good governance and sustainable development. However, the nationalist struggle against colonial rule was the true purveyor of good governance and sustainable development. The nationalist struggle was essentially democratic, that is, it brought more of the local people into the political process, and sustainable development can only take place when the ACP countries have full control over their natural resources.

The neoliberal IMF/World Bank and EU approaches to sustainable development represent the new authoritarianism under US and EU domination, just as the colonial system was the old authoritarianism under the hegemony of the European imperialist states that colonized the ACP countries. The new authoritarianism also encourages capitalist commodity production for market exchange that could care less about sustainable development or good governance. The neoliberal IMF/World Bank and EU approaches, force their political and economic policies such as good governance and sustainable development on the ACP countries in a fashion similar to the colonial economic and political policies forced on those regions.

The link between good governance and sustainable development has several components that need further exploration. The first general proposition is that the neoliberal component uses the concepts in furtherance of its globalization project, while the EU uses them to promote its vision of "global Europe," both aiming to subject the globe to free market forces and liberal democracy.

The second proposition is that the most important enduring link between good governance and sustainable development is that they are integral components of the neoliberal globalization agenda. They are both conditionalities for financial assistance by the rich to the poor countries. In this way, the globe comes under the complete domination of the new imperialisms.

The third proposition is that the link between good governance and sustainable development is that they are merely tools employed by the imperialist countries to secure natural resources and markets. The two go hand-in-hand because politics ultimately operates as both a constraint and stimulus to economic activity. In Bonapartist state conditions, politics dictates to the economic system in ways that can hinder the movement of capital. Good governance frees up the movement of capital to engage in productive activity that is destructive of the environment.

The fourth proposition is that the neoliberal debate on good governance and sustainable development does not recognize that the problematic posed by the two concepts are surface manifestations of a larger problem of the new imperialism in the twenty-first century, which the poor countries must counteract. What are the characteristics of the new imperialism with respect to linking good governance and sustainable development?

First, the new imperialism takes the high ground on good governance and sustainable development, seeking to lord it over the poor countries considered as having a deficit in those two connections. Thus, for example although foreign mining TNCs engage in environmental destruction in ACP countries, the view is that rich states have good governance and sustainable development under control, but the poor countries are the culprits. A second feature is the perceived benevolence of the new imperialism. For example, in the case of the US, the political platform of President Bush in 2000 was "compassionate conservatism," whose reality turns out to be the wanton slaughter of Iraqis in a "war on terror," purposely to free that country's oil fields to exploitation by US TNCs.

A third characteristic of the new imperialism is its recourse to sabotage, coercion, political destabilization, economic sanctions, etc. in the name of good governance and sustainable development. In the US, for example, the Bush administration adopted the dangerous policy that if any other country is "un-free" that country is a threat to US national interest (Bush, 2004), meaning that the US will invade that country and impose democracy and good governance on it. The Iraqis and Afghans are having a taste of the realities of neoliberal good governance and sustainable development imposed by the US.

Fourth, the classes in control of the imperialist forces in the rich countries have their allies among the elites in the poor countries that carry out their wishes to institute neoliberal good governance and sustainable development. Fifth, the primary purpose of the new imperialism is to open new markets, rule over old and new ones, and control raw materials, both strategic and non-strategic natural resources. Finally, the new imperialism forces poor countries through good governance and sustainable development to open their markets to imports from the rich countries, while simultaneously, the rich countries engage in mercantilist protective policies.

BIBLIOGRAPHY

Adams, William, M. 1996. "Sustainable Development and the Greening of Development Theory", in Frans J Schuurmam ed., *Beyond the Development Impasse: New Directions in Development Theory*. London: Zed Books, pp. 207–222.

African Agriculture. 2008. ACP Countries Under Pressure to Reach Banana Deal at WTO Talks. Africa News Network, July 29.

Africa, Caribbean and Pacific Group. 2005. ACP Declaration on the Sixth WTO Ministerial Conference. ACP/61/047/05, Brussels, November 29.

——. 2005. G-90 Declaration. ACP/61/057/05 Rev.2, Brussels, December 5.

Africa, Caribbean and Pacific Group and European Commission. 2003. ACP-EC EPA Negotiations Joint Report on the all-ACP-EC phase of EPA Negotiations. Brussels: ACP/00/118/03 Rev.1. European Commission Directorate General for Trade, 2006. Global Europe: Competing in the World. Brussels: Ref. 318/06

Agbesinyale, Patrick K. 2003. *Ghana's Gold Rush and Regional Development: The Case of Wassa West District*. Dortmund, SPRING Centre.

Ameyibor, Francis. 2008. EPA Divides AU. Amsterdam, The Netherlands: African News. February 2.

Amin, Samir. 2008. Financial Collapse, Systemic Crisis? Illusory Answers and Necessary Answers. Paper introducing the World Forum of Alternatives, in Caracas, October.

Anderson, Sarah. 2005. U.S. Immigration Policy on the Table at the WTO. *Foreign Policy in Focus* Silver City, NM & Washington, DC:, November 30.

Archibald, George. 1997. *Banana Baron Peeled off Half a Mil; White House Paid Back in WTO Fight*, Wash. Times, Aug. 25.

Arthur, Owen. 2000. Economic Policy Options in the Twenty-First Century. In *Contending with Destiny: The Caribbean in the 21st Century*, edited by Kenneth Hall and Denis Benn 12–25. Kingston: Ian Randle.

Atkins, Vincent J. 2002. The US Farm Bill of 2002: Implications for Caricom's Agricultural Export Trade. Caribbean Regional Negotiating Machinery, Staff Papers.

Ballayram. 2004. Poverty, Food Security and Globalization: Challenges for Regional Development. Kingston: Caribbean Food and Nutrition Institute.

Ballayram, Beverly Lawrence and Fitzroy Henry. 2002. Food Security and Health in the Caribbean: Imperatives for a New Policy. Paper presented at the Sir Arthur Lewis Institute of Social and Economic Studies (SALISES) and Mona School of Business Conference, University of the West Indies, Kingston, Jamaica, April 2–4.

Ballayram. 2007. Conceptual Framework for Food and Nutrition Security within Poverty Alleviation Strategies, in Poverty Alleviation and Food Security Strategies in the Caribbean: A Policy Dialogue. Kingston: Caribbean Food and Nutrition Institute, pp. 5–9.

Banana Link, http://www.bananalink.org.uk/content/view/72/32/lang,en/

Barbados Advocate. 2009. Crisis Coming Closer to Home. Barbados Advocate, February 23.

Barrett, Christopher B. and Daniel G. Maxwell. 2004. PL480 Food Aid: We Can Do Better, *Choices (The Magazine of Food, Farm, and Resource Issues)*, 19: 3.

Bauer, Peter Thomas. 1976. *Dissent on Development Revised Edition*. Cambridge, Massachusetts: Harvard University Press.

——. 1984. *Reality and Rhetoric: Studies in the Economics of Development*. Cambridge, Massachusetts: Harvard University Press.

Beckford, George. 1984. *Persistent Poverty*. London: Zed Press.

——. 1971. Plantation Society: Toward a General Theory of Caribbean Society. *Savacou* 5: 7–22.

Beer, Max. 1966. *An Inquiry into Physiocracy*. New York: Russell and Russell Inc.

Bello, Walden. 2009. G-20: Will the Global Economy Resurface? *Foreign Policy In Focus*, Washington, DC: March 30.

——. 2008. Globalization, Development, and Democracy: A Reflection on the Global Food Crisis. CASID 2008 Keynote Address: University of British Colombia, Vancouver BC, Canada.

Benhabib, Seyla, ed., 1996. *Democracy and Difference: Contesting the Boundaries of the Political*. New Jersey: Princeton University Press.

Benn, Denis and Kenneth Hall, eds., 2000. *Contending with Destiny: The Caribbean in the 21st Century*. Kingston: Ian Randle.

Benn, Denis. 1987. *The Growth and Development of Political Ideas in the Caribbean, 1994–1983*. Kingston: Institute of Social and Economic Research, University of the West Indies.

Benn, Denis M. 2004. *The Caribbean an Intellectual History 1774–2003*. Kingston: Ian Randal.

Bennett, Karl. 1995. "Capital Flight and Caribbean Economic Policy", in Ramesh F. Ramsaran, ed., *The Savings/Investment Environment in the Caribbean: Emerging Imperatives*, St. Augustine, Trinidad: Caribbean Centre for Monetary Studies, The University of The West Indies, pp. 43–59.

——. 1991. Capital Flight and Its Implications for Caribbean Development. In *Financing Development in the Commonwealth Caribbean*, edited by Compton Bourne and Dinesh Dodhia 289–310. London: Macmillan.

Berisha-Krasniqi, Valdete, Antoine Bouët and Simon Mevel. 2008. Economic Partnership Agreements between the European Union and African, Caribbean, and Pacific Countries: What Is at Stake for Senegal? *International Food Policy Research, (IFPRI)* Discussion Paper No. 00765, April.

Bernal, Richard. 2000. The Caribbean in the International System: Outlook for the First 20 Years of the 21st Century. In *Contending with Destiny: The Caribbean in the 21st Century*, edited by Kenneth Hall and Denis Benn 295–325. Kingston: Ian Randle.

——. 1996. Strategic Global Repositioning, and Future Economic Development in Jamaica. *The North-South Agenda* (18). Florida: University of Miami North-South Center.

——. 2007. The Globalization of the Health-care Industry: Opportunities for the Caribbean. *CEPAL Review* 92: 83–99.

——. 2007a. Finalizing EPA Trade Pact 'Pragmatic' for CARIFORUM. *Jamaica Gleaner*, October 21.

Berridge, Samuel. 2008. "The Economic Partnership Agreements: Opportunity or Threat," *The Democrat Newspapers*, St. Kitts and Nevis, January.

Best, L. 1968. Outline of a Model of Pure Plantation Economy. *Social and Economic Studies* (17) 3: 283–326.

Bilal, Sanoussi and Aurélie Walker. 2008. Economic Partnership Agreements and the Future of the ACP Group. Maastricht, The Netherlands. European Center for Development Policy Management, September 22.

Bogues, A. 1998. Investigating the Radical Caribbean Intellectual Tradition. *Small Axe* 4: 29–45.

Bohman, James and William Rehg, eds., 1997. *Deliberative Democracy: Essays on Reason and Politics*, Cambridge: Massachusetts Institute of Technology Press.

Bolland, O. Nigel 2001. *The Politics of Labor in the British Caribbean*. Kingston: Ian Randle.

Bolland, O. Nigel. 2004. *The Birth of Caribbean Civilization: A Century of Ideas about Culture and Identity, Nation and Society*. Oxford: James Currey Publishers.

Booker, Christopher and Richard North. 2005. *The Great Deception: The Secret History of the European Union*. London: Continuum.

Boron, Atilio A. 2005. *Empire and Imperialism: A Critical Reading of Michael Hardt and Antonio Negri*. London: Zed Press.

Bourne, Compton and Marlene Attzs. 2005. The Role of Economic Institutions in Caribbean Economic Growth: From Lewis to the Present. *Social and Economic Studies* (54) 3: 26–49.

Bourne, Compton. 2003. Small States in the Context of Global Change. Presented at 4th Annual Conference of Sir Arthur Lewis Institute of Social and Economic Studies (SALISES), University of the West Indies. Barbados: Sherbourne Conference Center.

Bowels, Paul. 2008. Globalization: A Taxonomy of Theoretical Approaches. In *Globalization and Anti Globalization: Prospects for a New World Order*, edited by Henry Veltmeyer 13–34. Aldershot, Hampshire: Ashgate.

Braithwaite, Edward. 1971. *The Development of Creole Society in Jamaica: 1770–1820*. Oxford: Oxford University Press.

Braverman, Harry. 1974. *Labor and Monopoly Capitalism: The Degradation of Work in the Twentieth Century*. New York: Monthly Review Press.

Brecher, Jeremy, Tim Costelo and Brendan Smith. 2000. *Globalization from Below: The Power of Solidarity*. Cambridge, Massachusetts: South End Press.

Brewer, Anthony. 1990. *Marxist Theories of Imperialism: A Critical Survey* (Second Edition). London: Routledge.

Brewster, Havelock, Norman Girvan and Vaughan Lewis. 2008. Renegotiate the CARIFORUM EPA: A memorandum submitted to the Reflections Group of the Caricom Council for Trade and Economic Development (COTED). February 27.

Brewster, Havelock. 2008. The Anti-Development Dimension of the European Community's Economic Partnership Agreement for the Caribbean. Paper presented at the Commonwealth Secretariat High Level Technical Meeting: EPAs: The Way Forward for the ACP. Cape Town, South Africa, 7–8 April.

Brewster, Havelock. 2007. Understanding Development Challenges in the Caribbean: Time to Take in the Begging Bowl. Available at http://www.normangirvan.info/understanding-developmentchallenges-in-the-caribbean/.

British Broadcasting Corporation. 2008. EPA: Caribbean Still Divided on Treaty. June 27.

Brown, Adlith and Havelock Brewester. 1974. A Review of the Study of Economics in the English-Speaking Caribbean. *Social and Economic Studies* (23) 1: 48–68.

Brown, William. 2002. *The European Union and Africa: The Restructuring of North-South Relations*. New York: IB Tauris and Co. Ltd.

Brunsden, Jim. 2008. EPAs Pose Threat to ACP Regional Integration. EuropeanVoice .com. March 19

Brunton, P. Desmond. 2008. The Global Financial Crisis and the Caribbean: Impact & Response CDB Response. Bridgetown, Barbados: Caribbean Development Bank.

Business Standard. 2008. WTO Director General says Doha Round not Dead. New Delhi, July 30.

Busse, M. and S. Lüehje. 2007. Should the Caribbean Countries Sign an Economic Partnership Agreement with the EU?: Challenges and Strategic Options. *Journal of Economic Integration* (22) 3: 598–618.

Cabrera, Vincent. 2009. President BIGWU, Media Conference Remarks February 4.

Callinicos, Alex. 2005. Imperialism and Global Political Economy. *International Socialism: A Quarterly Journal of Socialist Theory*. Issue 108. October 17.

Campbell, Elaine. 2008. Renegotiate the EPA: A Very Optimistic Approach. *Jamaica Observer*. March 15.

Canterbury, Dennis C. 2007. Market Liberalization: The Struggle between Foreign and Domestic/Regional Capital in the Caribbean. Paper presented at the Canadian Association for the Study of International Development (CASID) under the theme 'Bridging Communities: Making Public Knowledge-Making Knowledge Public' University of Saskatchewan, Saskatoon, Arts Building May 31-June 2.

——. 2007. Caribbean Agriculture under Three Regimes: Colonialism, Nationalism and Neoliberalism in Guyana. *The Journal of Peasant Studies* (34) 1: 1–28.
——. 2005. *Neoliberal Democratization and New Authoritarianism*. Aldershot, Hampshire: Ashgate.
——. 2005. Globalization, Inequality and Growth in the Caribbean. *Canadian Journal of Development Studies* (26) 4: 847–866.
——. 1991. Guyana's debt Crisis: Its Meaning and Effect. In *Problems of Development of the Guianas*, edited by Jack Menke and Henry Jeffrey 184–194. Paramaribo: Anton de Kom University of Suriname.
Caribbean360.com. 2009. Call for "tweaking" of Petrocaribe Deal. Caribbean360.com. June 15.
Caribbean Association of Industry and Commerce. 2008. Statement on the CARIFORUM-EU Economic Partnership Agreement. *CAIC Newsletter* 5: 2.
Caribbean Broadcasting Corporation. 2008. CRNM Head Defends EPA. February 15.
Caribbean Community Secretariat. 2008. Communiqué Issued at the Conclusion of the 29th Meeting of the Conference of Heads of Government of the Caribbean Community (Caricom). Bolans, Antigua and Barbuda, 1–4 July.
——. 2001. Revised Treaty of Chaguaramas Establishing the Caribbean Community Including The Caricom Single Market and Economy, Georgetown.
Caribbean Food and Nutrition Institute (CNFI) and Inter-American Institute for Cooperation on Agriculture (IICA). 2007. Reducing Poverty and Food Insecurity in the Caribbean. Kingston Jamaica.
Caribbean Forum and European Union. 2008. Economic Partnership Agreement between the CARIFORUM States, of the One Part, and the European Community and Its Member States, of the Other Part. http://www.crnm.org/documents/ACP _EU_ EPA/epa_agreement/EPA_Text%20_11june08_final.pdf.
——. 2008. Information Paper CARIFORUM-EU Economic Partnership Agreement: An Overview. *http://trade.ec.europa.eu/doclib/docs/2008/april/tradoc_138569.pdf.*
Caribbean Group for Cooperation in Economic Development (CGCED). 2000. Governance and Social Justice in Caribbean States. Development Research Group, The World Bank Report No. 20449-LAC.
——. 2000. Caribbean Economic Overview 2000. Report No. 20460-LAC, The World Bank, June.
Caribbean Media Corporation. 2007. Regional Trade Negotiators Dismiss Charges of EU Pressure. *Caribbean Media Corporation*. October 19.
Caribbean Press Release. 2008. St. Kitts and Nevis to Get Assistance From the FAO. Caribbean PressReleases.com, July 11.
——. 2008a. UN Food Agency Launches 4 Year Plan for Global Food Crisis. Caribbean PressReleases.com, June 13.
——. 2008b. Fuel Surcharge Increase Expected in St Vincent Soon. Caribbean PressReleases.com, June 29.
Caribbean Regional Negotiating Machinery. 2008. Bernal Resigns as Director General of the CRNM. CRNM Press/News Release, April 29.
Caribbean Regional Negotiating Machinery. 2008. Message of Appreciation from the CARIFORUM Principal Negotiator to CARIFORUM Stakeholders, Message_of _Appreciation_EPA_Conclusion.pdf, crnmadmin, 09/01/2008.
——. 2008. CRNM DG Resigns. CRNM Press/News Release, May 11.
——. 2008. Fact versus Fiction: Issues 1, 2 &3.
——. 2008. From CRNM to OTN. CRNM Press/News Release, July 8.
——. 2007. The EPA Negotiations Completed. RNM Update 0716, December 17.
——. 2007. "Response to the Memorandum entitled 'Problem Areas in the EPA and the case for Content Review' submitted for the consideration of the Reflections Group by Havelock Brewster, Norman Girvan and Vaughn Lewis." Kingston, Jamaica.
Carothers, Thomas. 2002. Democracy Promotion: A Key Focus in a New World Order. *Issues of Democracy* (5)1: 23–28.

Carter, Jimmy. 2005. *Our Endangered Values: America's Moral Crisis*. New York. Simon and Schuster.

Chang, Ha-Joon. 2008. *Bad Samaritans: The Myth of Free Trade and the Secret History of Capitalism*. New York: Bloomsbury Press.

——. 2008a. The Economics of Hypocrisy: After Implementing the Largest Government Bail-out in History, the US Continues to tell other Nations, 'do as I say, not as I do,'" Guardian.co.uk, October 20.

——. 2006. *Kicking Away The Ladder: Development Strategy in Historical Perspective*. London: Anthem Press.

Changrok, Soh and Jo Chang-Yong. The Influence of the United States on 'WTO Plus' in the Asia-Pacific Economic Cooperation (APEC). Available at http://www.koreagsis.ac.kr/research/journal/vol3/3-03-Soh%20Changrok,%20Jo%20Chang-Yong.pdf.

China View Factbox. 2009. Global Job Cuts, www.chinaview.cn, accessed March.

Chomsky, Noam. 2003. *Hegemony or Survival: America's Quest for Global Dominance*: New York: Henry Holt and Company.

——. 2006. Historical Perspectives on Latin American and East Asian Regional Development. *The Asia-Pacific Journal: Japan Focus*. December 20.

Chossudovsky, Michel. 2004. The Destabilization of Haiti. www.globalresearch.ca (accessed April 4, 2005).

Clegg, Peter. 2002. From Insiders to Outsiders: Caribbean Banana Interests in the New International Trading Framework. In The European Union and the Commonwealth Caribbean, edited by Stephen J.H. Dearden 72–113. Aldershot, Ashgate.

Clement, Christopher I. 2005. Confronting Hugh Chávez: United States "Democacy Promotion" in Latin America. Latin American Perspectives (32) 3: 60–78.

Clinton, Bill. 2001. Remarks as Delivered by Former President Clinton at the Yale University Tercentennial. Cross Campus, Yale University.

Commission of the European Communities. 2008. CARIFORUM-EU Economic Partnership Agreement Comments by Dr Lorand Bartels. Trinity Hall: University of Cambridge, 13 February.

——. (2007). *Growing Regions Growing Europe: Fourth Report on Economic and Social Cohesion*. Luxembourg: Office for Official Publications of the European Communities.

——. 2006. Global Europe: Competing in the World, A Contribution to the EU's Growth and Jobs Strategy. Brussels.

——. 2005. Joint Statement by the Council and the Representative of the Governments of the Member States Meeting within the Council, the European Parliament and the Commission 'The European Consensus on Development' Part I: The EU Vision of Development 14820/05 ATR/kl 1 ANNEX I DG E II.

——. 2003. Governance and Development. Brussels.

——. 2001. European Governance: A White Paper. Brussels.

——. 2001a. A Sustainable Europe for a Better World: A European Union Strategy for Sustainable Development. Brussels.

——. 2002. Towards a Global Partnership for Sustainable Development. Brussels.

——. 2002. The European Commission and Civil Society, General Principles and Minimum Standards for Consultation of Interested Parties by the Commission. Brussels: Commission of the European Communities.

Committee in Solidarity with the People of El Salvador (CISPES), North American Congress on Latin America (NECLA), and Upside Down World. 2009. The 2009 El Salvador Elections: Between Crisis and Change. A Joint Report, January.

Common Cause, Bush and Kerry fundraisers: What have they gotten, and what do they want? Washington DC: http://www.commoncause.org/site/pp.asp?c=dkLNK1MQIwG&b=196963

Common Cause and AARP. 2003. Brief of Common Cause and AARP as *Amici Curiae* in Support of the Constitutionality of the Bipartisan Campaign Reform Act of 2002, in the Supreme Court of the United States, No. 02–1674 & Consolidated Cases. Washington, DC: August 5.

Common Dreams Progressive Network. 2008. Collapse of WTO Doha Negotiations: A Blow to the US – EU Hegemony – The Collapse Paves a New Way Forward for Developing Countries. July 29.

Communique on Second Petrocaribe Summit. 2005. Montego Bay, Jamaica, September, 6.

Corden, W. Max. 1997. *Trade Policy and Economic Welfare*. Oxford: Clarendon Press.

Cornejo, Guillermo. 2008. Latin America and Europe: The Future Of EU-ACN Trade Negotiations. Council on Hemispheric Affairs, July 23.

Council of the European Union. 2005. Declaration on Guiding Principles for Sustainable Development. Brussels.

Cronin, David. 2007. EPAs Signed "Under Duress," Says South Africa. *Inter Press Service News Agency* December 21.

——. 2008. Africans Stuck with EU Deals. *Inter Press Service News Agency* January 29.

Cutler, David. 2009. Financial Crisis Sparks Unrest in Europe. *Reuters*, April 2.

Curtin, Philip. 1970. *Two-Jamaicas: The Role of Ideas in a Tropical Colony, 1830–1865*. New York: Athenum.

Daily Graphic. 2008. TWN To Mount Pressure On Government To withdraw From Signing EPA Pact. August 22.

Davenport, M., C. Kirton, N. Plaisier, and H. Poot. 2000. Caribbean Perspectives: Trade, Regional Integration and Strategic Global Repositioning Final Report. European Commission, ECORYS-NEI Macro and Sectoral Reform, Rotterdam.

Dearden, Stephen J.H. 1996. The EU Banana Regime and the Caribbean Island Economies. Manchester Metropolitan University, DSA European Development Policy Study Group Discussion Paper No. 1, December.

——. 2002. *The European Union and the Commonwealth Caribbean*. Aldershot: Ashgate.

Della Porta, Donatella, Massimillano Andretta, Lorenzo Mosca, and Herbert Reiter. 2006. *Globalization From Below: Transnational Activists And Protest Networks (Social Movements, Protest and Contention)*. Minneapolis: University of Minnesota Press.

Demas, William. 1965. *The Economics of Development in Small Countries, with Special Reference to the Caribbean*. Montreal: Mc Gill University Press.

Dent, Christopher M. 1997. *The European Economy: The Global Context*. London: Routledge.

Despres, Leo. 1967. *Cultural Pluralism and Nationalist Politics in British Guiana*. Chicago: Rand Mc Nally and Company.

Dickson, Anna K. 2003. The EU Banana Regime: History and Interests. *Banana Link*. January.

Dobb, Maurice. 1973. *Theories of Value and Distribution*. Cambridge: Cambridge University Press.

Dobriansky, Paula J. 2005. Strategies on Democracy Promotion, Remarks to the Hudson Institute. Washington, DC.

Downes, Andrew. 1992. The Search for a Sustainable Labor Market Response to Structural Adjustment Programs in the Caribbean. Paper presented at Regional Seminar for Senior Trade Unions Officials on "The Role of Trade Unions in Periods of Structural Adjustment Programs." Bridgetown, Barbados: Barbados Workers Union Labor College.

Eastern Caribbean Central Bank. 2007. *Economic Theory and Development Options for the Caribbean: The Sir Arthur Lewis Memorial Lectures 1996–2005*. Kingston: Ian Randal.

Economic Commission for Latin America and the Caribbean. 2009. Preliminary Overview of the Caribbean 2008–2009. Port of Spain, Trinidad and Tobago: Subregional Headquarters for the Caribbean, March 9.

Economic Commission for Latin America and the Caribbean (ECLAC). 2005. Long Term Growth in the Caribbean: A Balance of Payments Constraints Approach. Port of Spain, Trinidad and Tobago: Subregional Headquarters for the Caribbean.

Economist Magazine. 2009. Financial Fraud: Howzat! Economist.com, Febuary 18.

Ekelund Jr., Robert B. and Robert D. Tollison. 1997. *Politicized Economies: Monarchy, Monopoly, and Mercantilism*. College Station, Texas: Texas A & M University Press.

el-Gabry, Walid. 2009. Soros Says Economic Crisis Signals End of a Free-Market Model. Bloomberg.com, February 23.

Elster, Jon, ed., 1998. *Deliberative Democracy*. New York: Cambridge University Press.

Escobar, Arturo. 1995. *Encountering Development: The Making and Unmaking of the Developing*. Princeton, NJ: Princeton University Press.

Europa. The History of the European Union, http://europa.eu/abc/history/1945–1959/index_en.htm

European Centre for Development Policy Management (ECDPM). 2007. EPA Negotiations: Where Do We Stand. Weekly Updates. November 15. http://www.acp-eu-trade.org/library/files/ECDPM_15-11-07_EPA%20Negotiations%20-%20Where%20do%20we%20stand.pdf

——. 2007. EPA Negotiations: Where Do We Stand. Weekly Updates. November 22. http://www.acp-eu-trade.org/library/files/ECDPM_22-11-07_EPA%20Negotiations%20-%20Where%20do%20we%20stand_final.pdf

European Network on Debt and Development. 2009. UN Conference on the Financial Crisis and Development. May 27.

Faulconbridge, Guy. 2009. Developing World Leaders Show New Power at Summits. *Reuters*, June 16.

Federation of Independent Trade Unions and NGOS (FITUN). 2007. Letter to Prime Minister Patrick Manning. December 5.

Filger, Sheldon. 2009. BRIC Summit Sees End of Dominance of U.S. Dollar. *The Huffington Post*, June 16.

Forbes FACTBOX 2008. Issues on the Table at Troubled WTO Talks. 2008. Forbes.com, July 25.

Forero, Juan. US Considering Toughening Stance Towards Venezuela. *New York Times International*, April 26, 2005.

Foster, John Bellamy. 2001. Imperialism and 'Empire.' *Monthly Review*. (53) 7: 1–9.

Fukuyama, Francis. 1993. *The End of History and the Last Man*. New York: Harper.

Fuller, Max. 2005. Death-squad Style Massacres For Iraq, "The Salvador Option" Becomes Reality. Center for Research on Globalization. Montreal, June 2.

Furnivall, John S. 1939. *Netherlands India A Study of Plural Economy*. London: Cambridge University Press.

——. 1948. *Colonial Policy and Practice A Comparative Study of Burma and Netherlands India*. London: Cambridge University Press.

Franco, Adolfo. A. 2005. Transparency and Rule of Law in Latin America. Testimony of Assistant Administrator, Bureau for Latin America and the Caribbean, United States Agency for International Development before the Committee on International Relations, Subcommittee on the Western Hemisphere, U.S. House of Representatives, May 25.

Frey-Woutera, Adele Ellen. 1980. *The European Community and the Third World: The Lomé Convention and Its Impact*. New York: Praeger.

Gamarra, Eduardo A. 2007. Bolivia on the Brink. Washington. Council on Foreign Relations. CRS No. 24, February.

Girvan, Norman. 2008. Implications of the EPA: Supra-national – CARIFORUM-EC Joint Council consensus decisions supreme. Jamaica Gleaner, February 15.

——. 2008. Caribbean Integration and Global Europe: Implications of the EPA for the CSME. http://normangirvan.info 18/08/2008

——. 2008. Globalization and Counter-Globalization in the Caribbean. In *New Perspectives on Globalization and Anti-Globalization*, edited by Henry Veltmeyer 113–127. Aldershot, Hampshire.

——. 2008. Lewis and the New World Economists. *Guyana Review* May 28.

——. 2008. Implications of the Economic Partnership Agreements. *South Bulletin* Issue 8, February 1.

——. 2007. Reinterpreting Caribbean Development. In *Economic Theory and development Options for the Caribbean: The Sir Arthur Lewis Memorial Lectures 1996-2005*, The eastern Caribbean Central Bank 16-35. Kingston: Ian Randle.

——. 2006. Caribbean Development Thought Revisited. *Canadian Journal of Development Studies* (27) 3: 337–352.

Girvan, Norman, ed., 1997. *Poverty, Empowerment and Social Development in the Caribbean*. Mona, Jamaica: Canoe Press.

Girvan, Norman. 1976. *Corporate Imperialism, Conflict and Expropriation*. New York: Monthly Review Press.

Golinger. Eva. 2007. USAID in Bolivia and Venezuela: The Silent Subversion. Vnezuelananalysis.com, September 12.

——. 2006. *The* Chávez *Code: Cracking US Intervention in Venezuela*. Northampton: Olive Branch Press.

Gonzales, Anthony Peter. 2002. Globalization and Adjustment in the Caribbean: An Assessment. In *Caribbean Survival and the Global Challenge*, edited by Ramesh Ramsaran 299–336. Kingston: Ian Randle.

Gonzalez, Gabriel Espinosa. Disgracefully, For All of Its Talk about Democratization, the State Department's Ideologues Clamp Down on Open Dialogue. Washington: Council On Hemispheric Affairs, October 7.

Gotkine, Elliott. 2005. Bolivia Unions Intensify Protests. London. British Broadcasting Corporation News, March 10.

Goveia, Elsa. 1965. *Slave Society in the British Leeward Islands to the End of the 19th Century*. New Haven: Yale University Press.

Government of the United States of America, 2002. The National Security Strategy of the United States of America. Washington, DC.

Grant, Cedric. 2005. US-Caribbean Relations. *Foreign Policy in Focus* (5) 19: 1–3.

Green, Duncan. 2005. What Happened in Hong Kong? Initial Analysis of the WTO Ministerial. *Oxfam Briefing Paper* 85.

Green, W. John. 2004. Violence Remains a Viable Option Throughout 'Democratic' Latin America. Washington: Council On Hemispheric Affairs, March 29.

Hall, Kenneth and Benn, Denis, ed. 2000. *Contending With Destiny: The Caribbean in the 21st Century*. Kingston: Ian Randle.

Hamburger, Sarah. 2008. A Hidden Agenda: John McCain and the IRI. Council on Hemispheric Affairs. June 25.

——. 2008a. The "Bridge" in the Coup: The IRI in Venezuela. Council on Hemispheric Affairs. August 6.

Hanrahan, Charles E. 1999. The U.S.-European Union Banana Dispute, *CRS Report for Congress*. Washington DC. December.

Hansen-Kuhn, Karen. 2005. Central Americans Speak Out Against DR-CAFTA: Major Issues and Mobilizations. Alliance for Responsible Trade. Washington, DC., March.

Hardt, Michael and Antonio Negri. 2001. *Empire*. Cambridge: Harvard University Press.

Hattingh, Shawn. 2008. African Agriculture Uprooted by Economic Policies. *Inter Press Service*, June 19.

Hayes, Jack. 1996. Caricom Leaders Unlimber their Diplomatic Weaponry against White House Trade Onslaught. Council On Hemispheric Affairs. Washington: Memorandum to the Press 96.09, August.

Hayter, Teresa. 1971. *Aid as Imperialism*. Harmondsmouth: Penguin Books.
Heine, Jorge. 2008. The Dragon in the Archipelago. *Jamaica Gleaner Online*, Sunday August 17.
Henry, Padget. 1998. Philosophy and the Caribbean Intellectual Tradition. *Small Axe* 4: 3–28.
Hettne, Björn. 2003. Regionalism, Interregionalism and World Order: The European Challenge to Pax Americana. Washington. American University Council on Comparative Studies Working Paper Series, No. 3.
——. 1995. *Development Theory and the Three Worlds: Towards an International Political Economy of Development*, 2nd Edition. London: Longman.
Hewitt, Adrian. 1984. The Lomé Conventions: Entering a Second Decade. *Journal of Common Market Studies* (23) 2: 95–115.
Hilaire, Alvin D.L. 2000. Caribbean Approaches to Economic Stabilization, IMF Working Paper, WP/00/73.
Hilferding, Rudolf. 1981. *Finance Capital: A Study of the Latest Phase of Capitalist Development*. London: Routledge & Kegan Paul.
Higgs, Henry. 1963. *The Physiocrats*. Hamden, Conn.: Anchor Books.
Hirschman, Albert O. 1984. *Getting Ahead Collectively: Grassroots Experiences in Latin America*. Oxford: Pergamon Press.
Hongjiang, Wang. 2009. "Backgrounder: Subprime Mortgage Crisis," www.chinaview .cn, November 15.
Hongju Koh, Harold and Ronald Slye, eds., 1999. *Deliberative Democracy and Human Rights*. New Haven: Yale University Press.
Hosein, Roger and Clive Thomas. 2007. CSME and the Intra Regional Migration of Nurses: Some Proposed Opportunities. *Global Social Policy* (7) 3: 316–338.
Hudson, Michael. 2005. *Global Fracture: The New International Economic Order*, 2nd edition. London: Pluto Press.
Hudson, Michael and Jeffrey Sommers. 2008. The End of the Washington Consensus. *Counterpunch*, December 12/14.
Hurt, Stephen R. 2003. Co-operation and Coercion? The Cotonou Agreement between the European Union and ACP States and the End of the Lomé Convention. *Third World Quarterly*, (24) 1: 161–176.
Inter-American Develkopment Bank. 2008. Caribbean Hardest Hit by Food and Energy Price Shocks. Caribbean Press Releases.com, July 4.
International Monetary Fund. 2008a. Food and Fuel Prices—Recent Developments, Macroeconomic Impact, and Policy Responses. Washington, DC., June 30.
——. 2008. Fifty Countries Still Hurt by Food, Fuel Crisis. *IMF Survey Magazine*, September 24.
——. 2008b. IMF Presses Four-Step Plan to Halt Financial Spiral. *IMF Survey Magazine* October 10.
——. 2008c. Economic and Financial Surveys, Regional Economic Outlook: Western Hemisphere, Grappling with the Global Financial Crisis. Washington, D.C.
International Trade Union Confederation. 2009. Civil Society Background Document to UN Development Conference. New York: ITUC.
IUCN, UNEP and WWF. 1980. World Conservation Strategy: Living Resource Conservation for Sustainable Development. Gland: Switzerland.
Jacobs, Didier. 2007. *Global Democracy: The Struggle for Political and Civil Rights in the 21st Century*. Nashville: Vanderbilt University Press.
Jagdeo, Bharrat. 2008. The Caribbean Lost in the Negotiation with Europe. *South Bulletin* 8, February 1.
Jamaica Information Service. 2008. *E-Newsletter*, Vol 8, No. 9, February 29, 2008.
Jessop, David. 2008. Understanding the EPA – Institutional Arrangements Raise Concerns – Supranational Council Seen as Infringing Sovereignty. Jamaica Gleaner, March 7.

——. 2008a. The Financial Crisis and the Caribbean. BBCCaribbean.com, October 3.

Jianqing, Fan (2008). South Mercosur Summit Slams EU, U.S. While Spurring Internal Unity. *People's Daily* July 04.

Joint Statement of the BRIC Countries Leaders, June 16 2009, Yekaterinburg. 2009. http://msdfli.wordpress.com/2009/06/25/joint-statement-of-the-bric-countries-leaders-june-16-2009-yekaterinburg/. June 25.

Jones, Emily. 2007. Signing Away The Future: How Trade and Investment Agreements between Rich and Poor Countries Undermine Development. Oxford: Oxfam Briefing Paper No. 101, March 2007.

Joseph, Anita. Direct Intervention: A Call for Bush and Bolivia's Morales to Take a Leap of Faith and Change Presidential Issues into Personal Ones. Washington. Council On Hemispheric Affairs, June 8.

Josling, Timothy E. and Timothy G. Taylor, eds., 2003. *Banana Wars: The Anatomy of a Trade Dispute*. Cambridge, MA.: CABI Publishing.

Kagan, Robert. 2003. *Of Paradise and Power: America and Europe in the New World Order*, New York: Knopf.

Kagan, Robert and William Kristol, eds., 2000. *Present Dangers: Crisis and Opportunity in American Foreign and Defense Policy*. San Francisco, California: Encounter Books.

Kanth, D Ravi. 2008. US Blames India, China for Blocking Doha Talks. *Business Standard*. July 29.

Kategekwa, Joy. 2008. The Financial Crisis: Lessons for the EPA Trade Negotiations. *South Bulletin: Reflections and Foresights* 25, October 16.

Kendall, Patrick and Marco Petracco. 2003. The Current State and Future of Caribbean Agriculture. Economics Department: Caribbean Development Bank, January.

Kent, Calvin A., ed., 1987. *Entrepreneurship and the Privatizing of Government*, Westport, Connecticut: Quorum Books.

Kenety, Brian. 2001. Chiquita Blames EU Banana Regime for Its Bankruptcy Woes. Geneva, Switzerland. *Third World Network*, North-South Development Monitor (SUNS 4819).

Khor, Martin. 2008. Food Crisis, Climate Change, and the Importance of Sustainable Agriculture. Third World Network (TWN), June.

——. 2008a. Financial Crisis Calls into Question GATS Finance Negotiations. *South-North Development Monitor* 6556, September 26.

——. 2008b. Double Standard in the West's Crisis Policies. *South-North Development Monitor* 6573.

Kiely, Ray 2006. United States Hegemony and Globalization: What Role for Theories of Imperialism. *Cambridge Review of International Affairs*, (19) 2: 205–221.

Kirton, Claremont and Georgia McLeod. 2006. Remittances to Caricom Countries: Policy Issues and Options paper presented at the 38th Annual Conference of the Caribbean Centre for Monetary Studies (CCMS), Barbados, November 2006.

Köchler, Hans, ed., 1982. *The Principles of Non-alignment*. Vienna and London: International Progress Organization and Third World Centre.

Kozloff, Nikolas. 2008. John McCain: Mr. Big Stick in Latin America. *Counterpunch*, February 19.

Kramer, Kirstin. 2004. Caricom's Action on Haiti: Honor for a Few, Shame for Most. Washington: Council On Hemispheric Affairs, August 12.

Krauss, Clifford, Zweig, Phillip L. and Creswell, Julie. 2009. Texas Firm Accused of $8 Billion Fraud. *New York Times*, February 18.

Kristol, William and Christopher DeMuth. 1995. *The Neoconservative Imagination: Essays in Honor of Irvin Kristol*. Washington, DC: AEI Press.

Kwa, Aileen. 2008. Nigeria 'Threatens' Neighbors in Wake of Bilateral EPAs. *Inter Press Service News Agency* June 2.

Kwayana, Eusi. 1972. The Bauxite Strike and the Old Politics. Georgetown, Guyana: Bovell's Printery.

Lal, Deepak. 2003. Free Trade and Laissez Faire: Has the Wheel Come Full Circle? *The World Economy* (26) 4: 471–482.

——. 2000. Globalization, Imperialism and Regulation. *Cambridge Review of International Affairs*. (14) 1: 107–121.

——. 1983. *The Poverty of 'Development Economics'*. London: The Institute of Economic Affairs, Hobart Paperback 16.

Lande, Stephen. 2008. Caricom's Trade Relations with the European Union Undermining Its Relations with the United States. Manchester Trade Ltd. International Business Advisors, June 6.

Langenhove, Luk Van and Ana-Cristina Costea. 2005. The EU as a Global Actor and the Emergence of 'Third Generation' Regionalism. Tokyo: *UNU-CRIS Occasional Papers*, 0-2005/14.

Langley, Lester D. 1983. *The Banana Wars: United States Intervention in the Caribbean, 1898–1934*. Lexington, KY: University Press of Kentucky.

Lazare, Alick, Patrick Antoine, Wendell Samuel. 2001. Regional Negotiating Machinery/ Organization of Eastern Caribbean States Country Studies to Inform Trade Negotiations: Overview. March.

Leight, Jessica. 2004. The International Republican Institute: Promulgating Democracy of Another Variety. Council On Hemispheric Affairs, Washington: Memorandum to the Press 04.40, July 15.

Levitt, Kari. 2005. *Reclaiming Development: Independent Thought and Caribbean Community*. Kingston: Iran Randle Publishers.

Levitt, Kari and Best, Lloyd.1969. Export Propelled Growth and Industrialization in the Caribbean, 4 Volumes. Montreal: Mc Gill University.

Lewis, Rupert. 1998. *Walter Rodney's Intellectual and Political Thought*. Detroit: Wayne State University Press.

Lewis, Vaughn. 2000. "Looking from the Inside Outwards: The Caribbean in the International System after 2000", in Kenneth Hall and Denis Benn, eds., *Contending with Destiny: The Caribbean in the 21st Century*, Kingston: Ian Randle, pp. 326–346.

Lewis, W. Arthur. 1954. Economic Development with Unlimited Supplies of Labor. *The Manchester School* (22) 2: 139–91.

——. 1950. The Industrialization of the British West Indies. *Caribbean Economic Review* 2: 1–39.

Lodge, Junior. 2008. CARIFORUM-EPA Negotiations: An Initial Reflection. *Trade Negotiations Insights* 7: 1.

Luxemburg, Rosa. 1968. *The Accumulation of Capital*. New York: Monthly Review.

Magdoff, Harry. 2003. *Imperialism Without Colonies*, New York: Monthly Review Press.

Magnusson, Lars, ed., 1996. *Mercantilism: Critical Concepts in the History of Economics*. London: Routledge.

Maisano, Teresa and Tommaso Rondinella, eds., 2008. *Budgeting for the Future: Building another Europe European Economic Policies from a Civil Society Perspective*. Amsterdam, The Netherlands: Transnational Institute.

Mallaby, Sebastian. 2002. The Reluctant Imperialist: Terrorism, Failed States, and the Case for Empire Building. *Foreign Affairs* (81) 2: 2–7.

Mandelson, Peter. 2006. Global Europe Competing in the World. *Trade Issues*. http://ec.europa.eu/trade/issues/sectoral/competitiveness/global_europe_en.htm

——. 2006. Remarks to the Global Europe Conference. Brussels, 13 November.

Manning, Gareth. 2007. New Markets for Regional Farmers. Jamaica Gleaner, April 1.

Márquez, Humberto. 2008. Petrocaribe Building 'Anti-Crisis, Anti-Hunger Shield'. Inter-Press Service July 14.

Mars, Perry. 1998. *Ideology and Change: The Transformation of the Caribbean Left*, Detroit: Wayne State University Press.

——. 1989. "Competing Theories and Third World Political Practice", in Michael T. Martin and Terry R. Kandal, eds., *Studies of Development and Change in the Modern World*. Oxford. Oxford University Press, pp. 373–398.
Marshall, Alfred. 1910. *The Principles of Economics*. London: St. Martin's Press.
Marx, Karl. 1970. *Critique of Hegel's Philosophy of Right*. Cambridge: Cambridge University Press.
——. 1969. Class Struggles in France, 1848–1850, *Selected Works*, Volume 1, Moscow: Progress Publishers.
Mathis. William. 2009. US-Bolivian Relations: Halting an Avalanche. Washington. Council On Hemispheric Affairs, June 15.
McCollester, Charles. 2004. Haiti Matters! *Monthly Review* (56) 4: 26–46.
McConnell, K. 2005. Profound Shifts Toward Democracy Occurring, USAID Leader Says. USINFO.STATE.GOV, May 25.
McGroarty, Patrick. 2009. European Leaders Back Sweeping Financial Regulations. *Huffington Post*, February 22.
McManus, John F. 2009. EU Déjà Vu in the Caribbean. *New American Magazine*, January 23.
McMichael, Philip. 2008. *Development and Social Change: A Global Perspective*, 4th Edition. London: Sage.
——. 2006. Reframing Development: Global Peasant Movements and the New Agrarian Question. *Canadian Journal of Development Studies* (27) 4: 471–483.
Mead, Walter Russell. 2007. *God and Gold: Britain, America, and the Making of the Modern World*. New York: Knopf.
Meek, Ronald L. 1962. *The Economics of Physiocracy: Essays and Translations*. London: George Allen & Unwin.
Meier, Gerald, M. and Stiglitz, Joseph E., ed. 2001. *Frontiers of Development Economics: The Future in Perspective*. London: Oxford University Press.
Mhone, Guy. 1995. Dependency and Underdevelopment: The Limits of Structural Adjustment Programs and Towards a Proactive State-led Development Strategy. *African Development Review* 7: 51–85.
Miklaucic, Michael. 2008. Is Democratization Dead? *Harvard International Review* June 29.
Millar, David and Joseph Abazaam. 2008. African Indigenous Knowledge, Governance and Sustainable Development. In *Governance and Sustainable Development*, edited by Kendie, Steve and Pim Martens 58–68. Cape Coast, Ghana: Marcel Hughes Publicity Group.
Mills, Precious. 2008. Region has done quite well with regards to the negotiations of the EPA: Cort. *Sun* St. Kitts & Nevis, Tuesday February 12.
Montana, Ismael Musah. 2003. The Lomé Convention from Inception to the Dynamics of the Post-Cold War, 1957–1990s. African and Asian Studies (2) 1: 63–97.
Munroe, Trevor. 2000. Caribbean Thought and Political Process. In *Contending With Destiny: The Caribbean in the 21st Century*, edited by Kenneth Hall and Denis Benn 237–247. Kingston: Ian Randle.
Mustapha, Suleiman. 2008. Trade experts review EPA strategy. *The Statesman* 21/08: http://www.thestatesmanonline.com/
Mutume, Gumisai. 2008. EU Undermining African Economic Stability: New EU Trade Deals Divide Africa. Afrik.com. November 13.
Myers Jr., John. 2008. Bernal Defends Economic Partnership Agreement. *Jamaica Gleaner*, May 13.
Nabudere, D. Wadada. 1983. *The Political Economy of Imperialism: Its Theoretical and Polemical Treatment from Mercantilism to Multilateral Imperialism*. London: Zed Press.
——. 1979. *Essays on the Theory and Practice of Imperialism*. London: Onyx Press.
Network in Solidarity with the People of Guatemala. 2005. Popular Opposition to DR-CAFTA in Guatemala. NISGUA: Oakland, California.

Nichols, John, ed., 2005. *Against the Beast: A Documentary History of American Opposition to Empire*. New York: Nation Books.

Nkrumah, Kwame. 1965. *Neo-Colonialism: The Last Stage of Imperialism*. New York, International Publishers.

Nogueira, Uziel Batista. 1997. The Integration Movement in the Caribbean at Crossroads: Towards a New Approach of Integration. Working Paper Series 1, Buenos Aires, Argentina: Inter-American Development Bank, Integration and Regional Programs Department, Institute for the Integration of Latin America and the Caribbean.

Nolte, Stephan-Alfons. 2002. From Lomé IV to Cotonou and EBA – An Analysis of Trade Preferences and Redistribution of Economic Benefits. Abgabetermin: 20.11.

Odle, Maurice A. 2009. The Global Financial Crisis: How Did We Get Here and How Do We Move Forward? Paper prepared for presentation at the ILO Caribbean Tripartite Conference on Promoting Human Prosperity Beyond the Global Financial Crisis, Kingston, Jamaica, 1–2 April.

——. 2008. Sub-Prime to Sublime Disaster: Implications for the Caribbean Region of the Current Financial Crisis in the USA. Caricom, Turkeyen, East Coast Demerara, Guyana, September 18.

——. 1972. *The Significance of Non-Bank Financial Intermediaries in the Caribbean: An Analysis of Patterns of Financial Structure and Development*. Kingston, Jamaica: Institute of Social and Economic Research, University of the West Indies.

Ottaway, Marina. 2003. *Democracy Challenged: The Rise of Semi-Authoritarianism*. Washington: Carnegie Endowment for International Peace.

Oxfam America. 2005. Road Show of Central American Presidents Can't Prevent Growing Opposition to DR-CAFTA. Washington, DC., May 12.

Panich, Leo. 2000. The New Imperial State. *New Left Review*. 2: 5–20.

Panitch, Leo and Sam Gindin. 2004. *Global Capitalism and American Empire*. London: Merlin Press.

Panton, David. 2000. The Politics of Principles Proactive Pragmatism. In *Contending With Destiny: The Caribbean in the 21st Century*, edited by Kenneth Hall and Denis Benn 286–292. Kingston: Ian Randle.

Patterson, Orlando. 2000. Reflection on the Caribbean Diaspora and Its Policy Implications. In *Contending with Destiny: The Caribbean in the 21st Century*, edited by Kenneth Hall and Denis Benn 500–510. Kingston: Ian Randle.

Parfitt, Trevor W. and Sandy Bullock. 1990. The Prospects for a New Lomé Convention: Structural Adjustment or Structural Transformation? *Review of African Political Economy* (17) 47: 84–94.

Petras, James. 2009. *Global Depression and Regional Wars*. Atlanta, Ga.: Clarity Press.

Petras, James and Henry Veltmeyer. 2007. *Multinationals on Trial: Foreign Investment Matters*. Aldershot, Hampshire: Ashgate.

Petras, James. 2007a 'Who Rules America?' *Third World Traveller*. www.dissidentvoice .org, January 13.

Petras, James and Henry Veltmeyer, with Luciano Vasapollo and Mauro Casadio. 2005. *Empire with Imperialism: The Globalizing Dynamics of Neoliberal Capitalism*. London: Zed Press.

Petras, James and Henry Veltmeyer. 2004. "Aid and Adjustment: Policy Reform and Regression", in Henry Veltmeyer, ed., *Globalization and Anti-Globalization: Dynamics of Change in the New World Order*. Aldershot: Ashgate, pp. 24–53.

Petras, James. 2003. *The New Development Politics: The Age of Empire Building and New Social Movements*. Aldershot: Ashgate.

Petras, James and Henry Veltmeyer. 2003. *System in Crisis: The Dynamics of Free Market Capitalism*. London: Zed Books.

Petras, James. 2002. US Offensive in Latin America: Coups, Retreats, and Radicalization. *Monthly Review* (54) 1: 15–32.

Petras, James and Henry Veltmeyer. 2001. *Globalization Unmasked: Imperialism in the 21st Century*. London: Zed Press.

Petrocaribe. 2005. Communiqué on Second Petrocaribe Summit. Montego Bay, Jamaica, September 6.

Piening, Christopher. 1997. *Global Europe: The European Union in World Affairs*. Boulder, Colorado: Lynne Rienner.

Pilgrim, Calrence E. 2008. Caribbean Food Security and US $3 Billion Imports. *Caribbean New News*, October 20.

Powlett, Angela. 2008. Caribbean Powers must Watch over Private Businesses. *Nation News*, Barbados, October 6.

Prebisch, Raúl. 2008. Towards a Theory of Change. *CEPAL Review* 96: 27–74.

Prebisch, Raul. 1950. *The Economic Development of Latin America and Its Principal Problems*. New York: United Nations.

Premdas, Ralph. 2000. Diversity and Liberation in the Caribbean: The Decentralist Policy Challenge in the New Millennium. In Contending with Destiny: The Caribbean in the 21st Century, edited by Kenneth Hall and Denis Benn 161–178. Kingston: Ian Randle.

Przeworski, Adam. 2003. A Flawed Blueprint: The Covert Politicization of Development Economics. *Harvard International Review* (25) 1: 42–47.

Ravenhill, John. 1985. *Collective Clientelism: The Lomé Conventions and North-South Relations (The Political Economy of International Change)*. New York: Colombia University Press.

Reinert, Erik S. 2007. *How Rich Countries Got Rich … and Why Poor Countries Stay Poor*. London: Constable and Robinson.

——. 2005. Development and Social Goals: Balancing Aid and Development to Prevent 'Welfare Colonialism'. *Post-Autistic Economics Review*, (30) 21: 1.

Report of the Commission on Intellectual Property Rights, Integrating Intellectual Property Rights and Development Policy. 2002. London: September.

Requiem for the CRNM. 2009. Jamaica Observer Editorial, July 15.

Reuters. 2008. EU, Latin 'Banana Wars' in Focus at WTO Talks. Reuters, July 16.

Rhodes, Roderick A.W. 1996. The New Governance: Governing without Government. *Political Studies* (44) 4: 652–667.

Ribando, Clare. 2005. DR-CAFTA: Regional Issues. CRS Report for Congress. Washington.

Ricardo, David. 1996. *Principles of Political Economy and Taxation*. New York: Prometheus Books.

Richards, Peter. 2009. Caribbean: Bank Scandals Add to Region's Economic Woes. *Inter Press News Agency*, March 5.

——. 2008. Caribbean: Agriculture Literally Losing Ground. *Inter-Press Service*, October 9.

Rose, Dionne. 2008. CaribCan Negotiations Set for September. *Jamaica Gleaner*, July 4.

Rosenstein-Rodan, Paul N. 1943. Problems of Industrialization of Eastern and South-Eastern Europe. *Economic Journal* (53) 210/211: 202–211.

Rosenstein-Rodan, Paul. 1944. The International Development of Economically Backward Areas. *International Affairs* 20: 157–165.

Rostow, Walt W. 1960. *The Stages of Economic Growth: A Non-Communist Manifesto*. Cambridge: Cambridge University Press.

Rozo, Carlos A. 2001. Protectionism in the European Union: Implications for Latin America. *Intereconomics* (36) 3: 141–152.

Rubin, Joe. 2004. El Salvador: Pay Back. *Frontline*, October 12.

Rush, Rebecca. 2005. Banana Wars Continue – Chiquita Once Again Tries to Work Its Omnipotent Will, Now Under New Management: Likely Big Losers Will be Caricom's Windward Islands. Washington DC: Council on Hemispheric Affairs Memorandum to the Press, May 16.

Ryan, Selwyn. 2000. Caribbean Political Thought, from Westminster to Philadelphia. In *Contending with Destiny: The Caribbean in the 21st Century*, edited by Kenneth Hall and Denis Benn 248-273. Kingston: Ian Randle.

Savas, Emanuel S. 1987. *Privatization: The Key to Better Government*. London: Chatham House.

Sbragia, Alberta M., Mark A. Nordenberg, and Jean Monnet. 2008. The European Union and Trade Agreements: Development and Competition in a Post-WTO/Post-NAFTA World. Prepared for delivery at the conference "Europe and the Management of Globalization" Park City, Utah, May 24.

Schnatterer, Tinette. 2008. Mass Protests against Economic Partnership Agreement with EU. www.socialistworld.net, 6 February.

Seattle to Brussels Network. 2006. The New 'Global Europe' Strategy of the EU: Serving Corporations Worldwide and at Home. In *Budgeting for the Future: Building another Europe European Economic Policies from a Civil Society Perspective*, edited by Teresa Maisano and Tommaso Rondinella 173–179. Amsterdam, The Netherlands: Transnational Institute.

Sen, Amartya. 2001. Ten Theses on Globalization. *New Perspectives Quarterly* (18) 4: 9–15.

Sesit, Michael R. 2009. Fighting Global Crisis Isn't Meant to Be Easy. Bloomberg.com, March 2.

Shabalala, Dalindyebo, Marcos Orellana, Nathalie Bernasconi-Osterwalder and Sofia Plagakis. 2008. Intellectual Property in European Union Economic Partnership Agreements with the African, Caribbean and Pacific Countries: What way Forward after the CARIFORUM EPA and the Interim EPAs? Washington: Center for International Environmental Law, April.

Shorrock, Tim. 2002. Bush Shrugs Off Trade War Over Steel Decision. Penang, Malaysia: Third World Network No. 275, February.

Simes, Dimitri, K. 2003. America's Imperial Dilemma. *Foreign Affairs* (82) 6: 91–103.

Singer, Hans W. 1997. The Golden Age of the Keynesian Consensus: The Pendulum Swings Back. *World Development* (25) 3: 293–295.

Smith, Adam. 1991. *An Inquiry in to the Nature and Causes of the Wealth of Nations*. New York: Prometheus Books.

Smith, Michael. G. 1965. *The Plural Society in the British West Indies*. Los Angeles: University of California Press.

Smith, Raymond. 1962. *British Guiana*. London: Oxford University Press.

Smith, Sanya. 2008. EU's EPAs Can Spread Conditions for Finance Crisis to South Countries. *SUNS - South-North Development Monitor* #6559, October 2.

South Africa Development Community. 2005. Training On Trade Negotiation Skills, Trade Data & Policy Analysis For Negotiators From SADC Member States In Preparations For EPA Negotiations. http://www.sadc.int/archives/read/news/386

South Commission. 2008. EPA Negotiations in the Caribbean Region: Some Issues of Concern. *Analytical Note* SC/AN/TDP/EPA/12, January.

Spechler, Martin C. 1990. *Perspectives in Economic Thought*. New York: McGraw-Hill.

Srinivasan, T.N. 2004. China and India: Growth and Poverty, 1980–2000. Journal of Asian Economics, (15) 4: 613–636.

Statement by a Group of Concerned Caribbean Citizens Calling for Full and Public Review of the CARIFORUM-EC Economic Partnership Agreement (EPA), January 20, 2008.

Staritz, Cornelia, Ruben Atoyan, and Judith Gold. 2007. Guyana: Why Has Growth Stopped? An Empirical Study on the Stagnation of Economic Growth. IMF Working Paper, WP/07/86.

Stiglitz, Joseph E. 2003. *Globalization and Its Discontents*. New York: Norton and Company.

Striffler, Steve and Mark Moberg, eds., 2003. *Banana Wars: Power, Production and History in the Americas*. Durham, North Carolina: Duke University Press.

Strunk, Chris. The Bush Administration's Policy of Unilateral Interventions in Latin America. Council On Hemispheric Affairs, Washington, June 25.

Sutton, Paul. 1997. The Banana Regime of the European Union, the Caribbean, and Latin America. *Journal of Interamerican Studies and World Affairs* (39) 2: 5–36.

Tandon, Yash. 2008. Collapse of an Ideology. *Development and Cooperation* (49) 11: 430-431.

Technical Center for Agricultural and Rural Cooperation (CTA). 2008. A Comparison of the Experience of Agricultural Sector Trade and Production Adjustment Support in the French Overseas Territories of the Caribbean and the Caribbean Sugar Protocol Accompanying Measures Program Beneficiaries. Paper commissioned for the CTA-ECDPM dialogue meeting on 'Challenges of changing agricultural markets in the context of ACPEU trade: Identifying an Aid for Trade agenda for the agricultural sector' Brussels, 14–15 April.

——. 2005. In the Run-up to Hong Kong. *Agritrade* Special Edition, November.

The National Security Council. 2002. The National Security Strategy of the United States of America, 2002. Washington.

The Project for the New American Century. 2000. Rebuilding America's Defenses: Strategy, Forces and Resources For a New Century, A Report of The Project for the New American Century. Washington, DC.

The Secretariat of the African, Caribbean and Pacific Group of States. 2008. President Kufuor says EPAs Divide ACP. Brussels: ACP Press Statement 3. October 2

The Voice. 2009. Stanford Crisis Leaves Caribbean Shaken. *The Voice*, Issue: 1361, March 2.

Third World Network. 2009. EU EPAs: Economic and Social Development Implications: The Case of the CARIFORUM-EC Economic Partnership Agreement. Penang, Malaysia: Third World Network, February.

Thomas, Clive Y. 2009. CL Financial Group: Meltdown and Bailout. *Sunday Stabroek*, April 12.

——. 2008. Caricom Perspectives on the CARIFORUM-EC Economic Partnership Agreement. Institute of Development Studies: University of Guyana.

——. 2007. Making Global Trade Work for People: The Concerns of Small States in the Global Trade Regime. *RESILIENCE Series* 6 UNDP/BDP/CDG.

——. 2007. International Development Policy, Macroeconomic Management, Debt and Trade. In *Economic Theory and development Options for the Caribbean: The Sir Arthur Lewis Memorial Lectures 1996–2005*, The Eastern Caribbean Central Bank 165-190. Kingston: Ian Randle.

——. 2005. The Development Glass: Half Empty or Half Full: Perspectives on Caribbean Development. The Sixth William G. Demas Memorial Lecture, Caribbean Development Bank, Guyana, May 17.

——. 2003. Guyana and the Wider World. *Stabroek News*, Georgetown, Guyana.

——. 1996. Three Decades of Agriculture in the Commonwealth Caribbean. In *The Critical Tradition of Caribbean Political Economy: The Legacy of George Beckford*, edited by Kari Levitt and Michael Witter 243–280. Kingston: Ian Randle.

——. 1996. The Crisis of Development Theory and Practice: A Caribbean Perspective. In *The Critical Tradition of Caribbean Political Economy: The Legacy of George Beckford*, edited by Kari Levitt and Michael Witter 223–239. Kingston: Ian Randle.

——. 1988. *The Poor and the Powerless, Economic Policy and Change in the Caribbean*. New York: Monthly Review Press.

——. 1984. *Plantations, Peasants, and State: A Study of the Mode of Sugar Production in Guyana*. Los Angeles: University of California, Centre for Afro-American Studies.

——. 1983. State Capitalism in Guyana: An Assessment of Burnham's Cooperative Socialist Republic. In *Crisis in the Caribbean*, edited by Fitzroy Ambursley and Robin Cohen 27–48. New York: Monthly Review.
——. 1982. From Colony to State Capitalism: Alternative Paths of Development in the Caribbean. *Transition* 5: 1–20.
——. 1974. *Dependence and Transformation: The Economics of the Transition to Socialism*. New York: Monthly Review Press.
Toye, John. 1995. *Structural Adjustment and Employment Policy: Issues and Experiences*. Geneva. International Labor Office.
——. 1993. *Dilemmas of Development: Reflections on the Counter-revolution in Development Economics*. Oxford: Blackwell.
Tropical Products and Preference Erosion: Still No Deal. 2008. *Bridges Weekly Trade*.
United Nations Conference on Environment and Development. 1992. Agenda 21. Rio de Janerio, Brazil, June 3 to 14.
United Nations Conference on Trade and Development. 2007. Least Developed Countries Report 2007. United Nations: New York and Geneva.
——. 2006. World Investment Report 2006 FDI From Developing and Transition Economies: Implications for Development. New York and Geneva: United Nations.
——. 2006a. Top TNCs Present in 40 Host Countries on Average. *UNCTAD Investment Brief*, Number 5.
——. 2003. Main Recent Initiatives in favor of Least Developed Countries in the Area of Preferential Market Access: Preliminary Impact Assessment. Geneva October.
United Nations Industrial Development Organization (UNIDO). 2004. Industrialization, Environment and the Millennium Development Goals in Sub-Saharan Africa: The New Frontier in the Fight Against Poverty. Vienna, Austria: UNIDO Vienna International Center.
USATODAY. 2005. In South America, Democracy Stumbles in Second Act. Op/ED USATODAY.COM Monday April 25
US Department of Justice and Federal Trade Commission. 1995. Antitrust Enforcement Guidelines for International Operations. Washington DC., April.
US Department of State. 2004. *Patterns of Global Terrorism, 2003*. Washington.
Vaggi, Gianni and Peter Groenewegen. 2006. *A Concise History of Economic Thought: From Mercantilism to Monetarism*. New York: Palgrave Macmillan.
Veillette, Connie, Clare Ribando and Mark Sullivan. 2006. U.S. Foreign Assistance to Latin America and the Caribbean. Washington DC: Congress Research Service (CRS) Report for Congress.
Veltmeyer, Henry, ed., 2008. *New Perspectives on Globalization and Anti- Globalization: Prospects for a New World Order*. Aldershot, Hampshire: Ashgate.
Wade, Robert. 2008. Financial Regime Change? *New Left Review* 53: 5–21.
Watson, Noel. 2003. Study of Market Access Issues Re-The Export of Caricom Services to Canada and the USA: Report prepared for The Caribbean Regional Negotiating Machinery, April.
Watson, Hilbourne A. 2000. Global Neoliberalism, The Third Technological Revolution and Global 2000: A Perspective on Issues Affecting the Caribbean on the Eve of the 21st Century. In *Contending with Destiny: The Caribbean in the 21st Century*, edited by Kenneth Hall and Denis Benn 382–446. Kingston: Ian Randle.
Weber, Max. 1961. *General Economic History*. Translated, F.H. Knight. New York: Collier.
——. 1978. *Economy and Society: An Outline of Interpretative Sociology*, Vol. 2. Guenther Roth and Claus Wittich, eds., Berkeley: University of California Press.
Wedderburn, Judith. 2007. Hunger Anywhere is a Threat to Peace Everywhere Food Sovereignty, Nutrition Security and Poverty Alleviation: An NGO Perspective. In Poverty Alleviation and Food Security Strategies in the Caribbean: A Policy

Dialogue, Kingston: Caribbean Food and Nutrition Institute. Macroeconomic Impact, and Policy Responses An Update. September 19.

Weisskopf, Michael. 1997. *The Busy Back Door Men*, Time. March 31.

Williams, Ewart S. 2009. Update on CIB/CLICO/CMMB. Central Bank of Trinidad and Tobago, Port-of-Spain, February 13.

——. 2008. The Impact of Global Events on the Caribbean Economies. Address, at the ICATT 26th Annual Caribbean Conference, June 27.

Wolf, Eric R. and Sidney W. Mintz. 1957. Haciendas and Plantations in Middle America and the Antilles. *Social and Economic Studies* (6) 3: 380–412.

World Bank Group. 2008. World Bank to Help Mitigate Impact of Global Financial Crisis on Africa's Development. November 19.

——. 1997. World Development Report 1997. Oxford: Oxford University Press.

World Commission on Environment and Development. 1987. *Our Common Future*. Oxford: Oxford University Press.

Zunes, Stephen. 2009. The U.S. Invasion of Iraq: The Military Side of Globalization? *Globalizations* (6) 1: 99–105.

INDEX

www.ingramcontent.com/pod-product-compliance
Lightning Source LLC
Chambersburg PA
CBHW060021030426
42334CB00019B/2123

* 9 7 8 1 6 0 8 4 6 2 0 4 9 *